The Philippines:

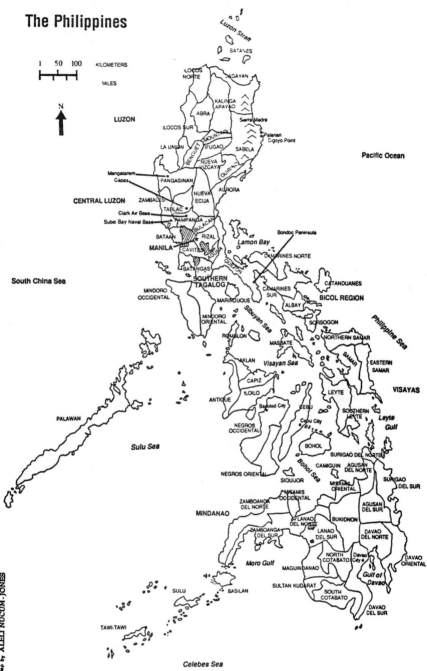

The Philippines

Reprinted from RED REVOLUTION: Inside the Philippine Guerrilla Movement, by Gregg R. Jones (1989), by permission of Westview Press, Boulder, Colorado.

The Philippines:

Colonialism,

Collaboration,

and Resistance!

WILLIAM J. POMEROY

International Publishers

New York

DEDICATION
To Celia
and to all our years
of Love and Comradeship

Library of Congress Cataloging-in-Publication Data

Pomeroy, William J., 1916–
    The Philippines : colonialism, collaboration, and resistance /
William Pomeroy.
        p.   cm.
    Includes bibliographical references and index.
    ISBN 0-7178-0692-8 : $9.95
    1. Philippines--History--1898-1946- 2. Philippines-
-History--1946-   I. Title.
DS685.P64 1992
959.9'03--dc20   92-35454
                                                           CIP

TABLE OF CONTENTS

Other books by William Pomeroy

MAPS, pp. ii and 75

Cover photo:
A 1990 demonstration by trade unions and
progressive organizations for the removal
of U.S. military bases in the Philippines.

The Philippines:

I

Suppressing a Nation—1

Nearly a century has elapsed since a U.S. fleet of nine warships, under the command of a Commodore George A. Dewey, steamed into Manila Bay in the Philippine Islands on the morning of May 1, 1898, and almost casually destroyed a Spanish fleet defending what was then a colony of Spain. By that act the United States emerged on the world scene as an imperialist power in the standard mold set by Britain, France, Spain, the Netherlands, Belgium, Portugal and other powers possessing colonies. The Philippines, with all its people, became a possession of the United States.

The holding of outright colonies, the possession of other peoples, has been a contentious issue in U.S. history. For one thing, the United States itself was born out of a revolutionary war of liberation to free the 13 colonies that became the original 13 states from the imperial rule of Britain. To swing full circle and become a colonial power, too, seemed to violate the traditions on which the U.S. was founded, and the episode in Manila Bay and the events that followed aroused a strong movement of opposition among the American people.

Furthermore, by that time virtually all areas of the world were divided as colonies among the other major capitalist powers. To acquire any territory of value meant seizing it from another power. To do so, the U.S. had to become a predator, to launch a war of aggression. The Spanish-American War of 1898 was such a war, the more indefensible because Spain by then was a weak and decadent nation, no match for the ascendent capitalist vigor of the U.S. Wresting the Philippines, Puerto Rico and Cuba from Spain was like mugging an elderly victim in the street, and progressive Americans regarded it with shame, heightened by the jingoistic slogans that rallied recruits to The Flag.

Worst of all to democratic Americans was the manner in which the Philippines was then converted into a U.S. colony. Shortly before the

1

war against Spain started, the Filipino people had begun a revolution for independence from Spanish rule. It was still in progress when the U.S. invasion forces arrived. Filipino leaders were led to believe that the U.S. would recognize their country's independence, especially since they cooperated with the U.S. in its war against Spain. The Filipino revolutionists did more to defeat and compel surrender from the Spanish garrison than the U.S. army did. Considering their independence won, they established their own Philippine Republic, with a democratic constitution, a fully functioning government, a national Congress, and local government throughout the country. U.S. recognition was expected.

The U.S. ignored this achievement of a freedom-loving people. Filipino representatives were excluded from the Peace Treaty negotiations with Spain, which awarded the Philippines to the U.S. in total disregard of the Philippine Republic and its proclaimed independence. The U.S. army then immediately embarked upon a war of conquest to suppress and destroy the Republic and to eliminate Filipino resistance to U.S. rule.

That war, which lasted on a large scale from 1899 to 1902 and in sporadic guerrilla form until 1912, was conducted in the most ruthless, savage fashion by U.S. forces. No mercy was shown to Filipinos who resisted, who began by attempting regular defensive warfare but, in the face of greatly superior military power, had to turn to guerrilla warfare to maintain their independence struggle. Hearings conducted by a U.S. Senate Committee on the Philippines in 1902 (Senate Document 331, 57th Congress, 1st Session, "Hearings in Relation to Affairs in the Philippine Islands") are a grim record of the use of torture (especially the "water cure"), indiscriminate killing, concentration camps for civilians, scorched earth tactics and other brutal methods to subjugate Filipinos. The Fil-American War was the forerunner of numerous imperialist wars that the U.S. has waged in the 20th century to impose its control upon smaller countries desiring self-determination and the chance to develop. Conservative estimates are that over 200,000 Filipinos died as a direct result of U.S. military conquest; other figures of direct and indirect deaths reach up to one million. By such holocaustic means the Philippine colony was pacified and made governable.

Such policies, regarded by a great many U.S. citizens as contrary to every democratic principle extolled in U.S. life, contributed to the growth and activity of an Anti-Imperialist League, which had very broad membership and support and strongly influenced the Democratic Party platform in the presidential election of 1900 and in varying degrees in future elections. A relinquishing of the colony and the granting of the right to independence to the Filipino people were called for by the League, which condemned the war of conquest. The anti-imperialists did not succeed. The pro-imperialist Republican Party won in 1900, electing its candidates William McKinley and Theodore Roosevelt as president and vice-president on an expansionist program. Soon after, McKinley was assassinated by an anarchist (an act that had nothing to do with the Philippine question). Roosevelt, who, as a secretary of the navy imbued with expansionist ardor, had sent Dewey and his fleet to East Asian waters to be ready to seize the Philippines, replaced him. President Teddy Roosevelt finished the war of conquest and installed a colonial administration in the Philippines.

However, the issue of imperialist expansion and the possession of colonies was not settled by suppression of Filipino resistance or by elections in the U.S. The drive of U.S. capitalism to expand its surpluses, its trade and investment abroad was a confused one. That expansion through export of capital was necessary and desirable was generally accepted but the manner in which this was to be done was sharply debated, continuing through the first decade of the 20th century. The possession of outright colonies was favored by commercial interests in particular, which envisioned colonies as protected markets free from competitors; also the acquisition of cheap raw materials interested some industrialists.

Among the opponents of colonial seizure were those who argued that the cost of administering and defending such possessions would outweigh the benefits extracted. One of their most vocal spokesmen was the steel monopolist, Andrew Carnegie, who became a member of the Anti-Imperialist League: he felt that the sheer industrial might of U.S. capitalism would force the way to a dominant position in the market and investment areas of the world. Most of those who aligned themselves with the Anti-Imperialist League were not against expansionism but felt that it could be carried on without costly territorial acquisition or the subjugation of other peoples.

Associated with these groups were U.S. domestic agricultural producers who raised the same crops as grown in the Philippines—sugar and tobacco in particular and also dairy products—which would have to contend with the competitive importation of these items produced with cheap labor in the colony. These interests proved in the long run to be the most effective opponents of a Philippine possession.

Anti-colonial sentiment extended beyond the crusading Anti-Imperialist League. Other groups not prepared to be linked with that radical-sounding organization joined another movement, the Philippine Progress League, alternatively called the Philippine Independence League, which projected the slogan, "Treat the Philippines Like Cuba," i.e., permit it self-government as a dependency, under U.S. "protection," with a U.S. right to intervene if it was felt necessary for the U.S. interest.

Due to the contradictions among the U.S. imperialist and sectoral interests, it took a decade from the time U.S. ownership of the Philippines was proclaimed to work out a definite relationship between the U.S. and its colony. In addition, Philippine trade concessions to Spain in the Peace Treaty extended for a decade, impeding immediate full U.S. economic control. The Payne-Aldrich Free Trade Act of 1909 finally granted duty-free entry to the U.S. for a specific quota of Philippine sugar (300,000 tons annually), while giving duty-free entry to unlimited U.S. commodities in the Philippines. (The preferential arrangement for U.S. products achieved the effect of shutting out other imperialist powers, especially Britain, from the Philippine market.)

The controversy over colonial trade policy precipitated by U.S. domestic producers had wider ramifications: it shaped the land laws in the colony, which limited land acquisition by a corporation to 1,024 hectares (2,233 acres), with individual holdings obtained from public lands kept to 16 hectares (33.2 acres). These provisions of the U.S.-written Organic Act of 1902 were deliberately designed to prevent the development by U.S. investors of a plantation economy capable of large-scale output of agricultural products that might compete with those in the U.S. A move by the U.S. American Sugar Refining Co. in 1910 to get around the colonial land laws by buying on the sly a 22,484 hectare estate that had belonged to a Spanish religious order and to use it for sugar cane growing, produced such a furor, mainly by U.S. beet-sugar producers, that other such imperialist land grabs were barred during the colonial period.

DIVIDING A NATION

While the ways of exploiting the Philippine colony were being worked out in that first decade of U.S. possession so as to reconcile the conflicting interests of various sectors of U.S. capitalism, the interests of the Filipino people were callously shaped to fit U.S. designs. Lines were drawn in Philippine society in accordance with attitudes to U.S. rule. Broadly speaking, three main groupings were dealt with. Of these, only two relatively thin strata benefited in any way from the U.S. colonial system: the landlords who were able to produce for the

U.S. market along with the refiners and exporters linked with that process, and the middle-class elements who were brought into the administrative and civil service system needed to run the colony. The rest of the population, the working people who were the vast majority, far from benefiting, were the main victims of colonialism.

The top strata were the wealthy landlords who produced export crops (sugar, coconuts, abaca [hemp], and tobacco) and the urban real estate owners who often doubled as money lenders in the Spanish colony. These almost to a man had not rebelled against Spain, and when Spain was ousted promptly transferred their loyalty to the new U.S. colonial masters, expecting rich pickings from trade with the U.S. From this sector the U.S. drew its first collaborating local officials, using them to help achieve the submission of those who resisted. Once free trade arrangements had been worked out, the interests of the export producers were satisfied.

The Filipino sugar "barons" in particular benefited. They shipped 29,315 metric tons of sugar to the U.S. in 1903, with a value of $1,135,826. In 1910, the year after the Payne-Aldrich free trade act, the quantity had risen to 100,700 metric tons, worth $6,214,226. By 1925 sugar exports to the U.S. market had jumped to 463,989 metric tons, worth $41,416,841. Over one million tons were reached in the early 1930s and the sugar barons, rolling in wealth, were less than enthusiastic about the Philippine Independence Act being presented to the U.S. Congress. After independence, they fought for a continuation of the colonialist free trade.

All told, Philippine exports to the U.S. by the landlord-*comprador* strata as a whole, virtually all in raw material form, vaulted from $10,154,087 in 1909 to $109,044,943 in 1925; even in the depression year of 1937 exports to the U.S. attained $139 million. Preservation of the preferential tie with the U.S., independence or no independence, was the overriding concern of Filipino export producers, conditioned by the U.S. colonial policies.

Secondly, the Filipino middle-class sector provided, in the main, the colonial administrative and civil service system devised by the U.S. This grouping included the ambitious educated elements known as the *illustrados* who had sought, unsuccessfully, for social advancement and political positions in the old Spanish regime, a frustration that led many of them to join the revolution against Spain and to help set up a Philippine Republic in which they could hold leading posts. Their capitulation to U.S. conquest was influenced, in a great many cases, by the desire to take advantage of lucrative posts in the U.S. colonial government. Although briefly, as revolutionists, they had fought the collaborating wealthy Filipinos who sided with the colonial rulers—Spanish or American—as politicians in the U.S. colony they found it expedient and profitable to become allied with and to serve the interests of the landlord-*compradores* who had economic power in the mainly agrarian Philippines. This class alliance was desired and nurtured by the U.S. colonial regime.

The third section of the population, comprising the vast majority, was made up of the landless or very small-holding peasantry plus the embryonic urban working class. These had been the mass base of the revolution and of the resistance struggle against U.S. conquest. The ideal of independence, of national freedom, was strongest in this main sector. These groups had least to gain from the colonial situation and their exploitation as extremely low-paid labor provided, basically, the profits of the wealthy landlord, the careerist politician and, of course, the foreign imperialists. The U.S. directed its most ruthless policies of suppression against this mass sector, following the military suppression with more subtle and comprehensive methods of instilling acceptance of a colonial status.

In general, U.S. colonial policy relied on divide and rule methods that were typical of imperialism. At the beginning, the Filipino wealthy strata were drawn, willingly, into an alliance and pitted against the resisting middle-class and working-class forces. The middle class, forced or enticed into submission, were then encouraged to align with the wealthy against the masses, among whom rebellious tendencies would continually tremor. As a rule, the semi-feudal landlord and the self-serving politician feared the people and welcomed the protective presence of a U.S. army and a U.S.-officered paramilitary Constabulary. The effect on the Philippine nation has been disastrous. Development of a united movement of genuine national unity for real independence consistently failed to make headway both during and after U.S. rule, due chiefly to U.S. manipulation of Filipino class fears and interests. Philippine history in the 20th century is a series of disunited, sectional, and often sectarian struggles to throw off the foreign imperialist. At every point the U.S. has maneuvered to divide the country, especially striving to nurture the delusion that the revolutionary nationalism of the masses is a subversive threat, when it is actually the blood and sinew of the nation itself.

EDUCATION IN SUBJUGATION

In the "Instructions" of President William McKinley to the First Philippine Commission of U.S. officials sent in 1899 to investigate the colony and make policy recommendations, Filipinos were urged to receive Commission members as the bearers of "the richest blessings of a liberating rather than a conquering nation." When it arrived, the Commission issued a proclamation that assured Filipinos the U.S. purpose was "to encourage them in those democratic aspirations, sentiments and ideals which are the promise and potency of a fruitful national development." In practice, however, the aspirations were severely curtailed; the U.S. democratic model was to be looked up to but certainly not emulated because any real nation-building would have to originate with independence.

To mask imperialist intentions and methods, the slogan of "education for self-rule" was projected as the alleged aim of U.S. rule. This implied that Filipinos (who had fought for and established a functioning republic and government of their own that was crushed by the U.S.) were not yet fit to govern themselves and had to go through an indefinite period of tutelage by a civilized power, i.e., the United States. The education was many featured. A complete educational system was introduced from *barrio* primary school to university, with the English language the mandatory medium of instruction, and with U.S. textbooks that oriented Filipinos toward a U.S. way of life that was made to seem superior. In the colonial legislature another type of teaching went on in the political arts of patronage and personal gain and of how to seem one thing while being another. The latter art became best manifested in seeming to stand for independence while accommodating one's self to U.S. colonial rule. In addition to that political education, there was the education in economics: the wealthy landlord export producers quickly learned the lessons of free trade, which meant that the colonial relationship was profitable to them. The duty-free entry of U.S. goods educated/conditioned Filipinos in their use, making "stateside" products preferable to any manufactured locally, helping to prevent the growth of Filipino industry.

Above all, this was education in a colonial mentality, creating a feeling of inferiority and of dependence, which was likely to be perpetuated after an act of independence itself. While speaking of educating Filipinos in how to rule themselves, every means was employed to suppress or to inhibit any nurturing of national pride or of the militant nationalism that can produce the drive and enthusiasm on which nations can be aroused to develop.

An aspect of the U.S. educational system was the selection and elevation of national heroes. Among the Filipino masses the figure of Andres Bonifacio—the founder of the revolutionary *Katipunan*, which had led the great Revolution of 1896 against Spain—was of towering stature, standing for genuine struggle for freedom. U.S. officialdom, in the military governorship that was first installed and in the civil Commission that replaced it in 1901, made Bonifacio an object of denigration. The textbooks introduced in the new schools portrayed him as a terrorist and an advocate of force and violence destructive of democracy. The Commission under Governor-General William Howard Taft projected instead, counter-figure Jose Rizal, the moderately nationalist writer and doctor who was a reformist and who had denounced the revolution of 1896 at its beginning. It was the U.S. colonial regime that made Jose Rizal the national hero, proclaiming a Rizal Day as a national holiday and installing his statue in countless town plazas across the country. This is not to say that Jose Rizal was not an outstanding Filipino (his novel, *Noli Me Tangere*, written in condemnation of friar-dominated Spanish rule, is one of the great anti-colonial novels); his execution by the Spaniards, at friar insistence, when the revolution began made him a martyr figure, but he was selected as the national hero to deflect Filipinos from the path of militant struggle for independence. Typical of the way this issue was injected into the education system was a history textbook introduced in 1905, which said:

> Cruel and wicked deeds have often been done under the name of liberty, and the methods of the Katipunan were not those of honorable men ... No people ever fought its way to freedom by assassination and massacre ... The Filipinos were robbed and ill-treated by their own people ... Rizal, whom so many Filipinos love to honor, was a man of a different sort from Bonifacio ... [1]

MAKING NATIONALISM A CRIME

U.S. patriotic holidays, not those of Filipinos, were implanted in the Philippines as soon as U.S. authority was established. However, Governor-General Taft forbade the reading of the U.S. Declaration of Independence at 4th of July celebrations! During the first years of U.S. rule the advocacy of independence was made illegal, the Commission adopting a Sedition Act on November 4, 1901 which declared that "such agitation directly tends to stimulate and promote the insurrection and to continue it."[2]

Although the Sedition Act was supposed to have expired with the official termination of the Fil-American War on July 4, 1902, it continued to be applied until 1905, long after Filipino political parties of the elite were allowed to form in preparation for the election of a Filipino legislature, the national assembly, in 1907. When the fledgling Nacionalista Party and others sought to include a call for independence in their election platforms, it was prohibited by Taft. Not until persisting forms of armed resistance were considered to have been snuffed out and the middle-class leaders of the permitted political parties had accepted U.S.-dictated terms of agreeing to seek independence or to advocate it only through gradual legal processes was the issue of independence allowed to be voiced in election campaigns.

For the first two decades of U.S. rule, American officials and businessmen in the Philippines made known strongly their displeasure over any expression of sentiment for independence. It was their view that Filipinos holding office in the colony should devote themselves solely to work for the interests of the colonial regime. This was emphasized by President Theodore Roosevelt:

> It seems to me that what is important to cultivate among the Filipinos at present is, not in the least 'patriotic national sentiment' . . . but the sober performance of duty.[3]

James F. Smith, who became Governor-General on September 20, 1906, brusquely tried to smother the raising of the independence issue by Filipinos. "This question is one which can only be determined by the American Government," he proclaimed in his inaugural address, adding "a good deal of valuable time and energy is lost by able men which might be more profitably employed in perfecting the existing government."[4]

His successor, W. Cameron Forbes, Governor-General from 1910 to 1913, refused to discuss independence with any Filipino, claiming that they had nothing to do with it because it was a matter that concerned only the American Congress.[5] "I don't write or speak in favor of independence, as I don't believe in it for them," he confided in his diary. He didn't mind if Filipinos harbored a "desire" for it but only so far as it provided a motive force for "material development" under American rule.[6]

Even the slightest display of a Philippine patriotism brought antagonism boiling to the surface of the U.S. community in Manila. A notorious incident occurred just after the first Assembly election in 1907, when enthusiastic supporters of victorious Nacionalista candidates staged a parade through northern Manila, Caloocan and Navotas.

They carried large Philippine and *Katipunan* flags at the head of the procession and relegated a small American flag to a secondary place toward the end of the line of march.

Within a few hours outraged American businessmen called a mass meeting in the Manila Opera House, where over 3,000 Americans filled the auditorium and thousands more overflowed into the streets.[7] Typical of the speeches was one that shouted: "I believe in peace and harmony. I always did, and when I had a battalion of volunteers behind me I felt awful peaceful . . . I believe that if we could put about 100,000 American troops here it would be very peaceful, exceedingly so, and you wouldn't see any more *Katipunan* banners."[8]

The Philippine Commission, on the very same day, responded to the demands of this gathering by passing a law (Commission Act No. 1696) "to prohibit the display of flags, banners, emblems or devices used in the Philippine Islands for the purpose of rebellion or insurrection against the authority of the United States and the display of *Katipunan* flags, banners, emblems or devices for any other purposes."[9]

In the subsequent period, the "Flag Law" was applied with a vengeance. A typical case was that of Juan Panganiban, a resident of the town of Antipolo, Rizal, who fastened a tablet on a post to commemorate a mass meeting held for independence on June 27, 1907. The tablet was bordered by the colors of the flag of the Philippine Republic and bore the rising sun and three stars in a triangle as had appeared on that flag. Panganiban was convicted in the lower court and fined P500. On appeal, the Supreme Court upheld the conviction, contending that if the tablet did not have an exact replica of the "insurgent flag," it did have "an exact reproduction of the most prominent features" and the "exposing to the public view of such a sign or printing was for the exact purpose of exciting the people and stirring up hatred in their minds against the constituted authorities." The Court stated that if Panganiban could not pay the fine due to insolvency (his plea), he must suffer corresponding imprisonment.[10]

In another case (14 Phil. Rep., 128) a store owner, Go Chico, was convicted for having in his store window a small button with the face of Emilio Aguinaldo, president of the suppressed Philippine Republic, and a tiny image of the "insurgent flag."[11]

Suppression of nationalist sentiment went further than this. In 1909 an entire band was sent to prison for playing the Philippine national anthem in a fiesta in Quiapo, Manila.[12] A Filipino sculptor, Marcelo Nepumuceno, had his entry for an exhibition of Philippine art rejected because of its nationalist theme: a Filipino woman brandishing a bolo at a lion and an eagle.[13]

The prohibition on displays of nationalism had one of its most ruthless applications in the censorship and banning of dramas written and produced in the Philippine language, Tagalog. Dramas were an extremely popular cultural form among Filipinos. Spanish authorities had channeled this into two types of performance: the *moro-moro,* a pantomime of Christian-Moslem conflict that served the divisive policies of the Spaniards, and the *zarzuela,* a sentimental musical drama that was close to operetta. Early in the U.S. regime a group of Filipino dramatists—Juan Abad, Aurelio Tolentino, Mariano Sequera, Honorio Lopez—rejected the *moro-moro* type of play as anti-Filipino and the *zarzuela* as trivial. They began to write nationalist, patriotic dramas.[14]

Between 1900 and 1906 many such dramas were produced: *Malaya* (Freedom), *Hindi Ako Patay* (I Am Not Dead), *Tatlong Pung Salapi* (Thirty Pieces of Silver—referring to the U.S. offer during the war of resistance of 30 silver pesos for every gun turned in to them, and depicting Filipinos who did this as Judases); *Ang Tanikalang Guinto* (The Golden Chain), *Kahapon, Ngayon at Bukas* (Yesterday, Today and Tomorrow). All of these dramas were suppressed as soon as they were performed, and their authors as well as the actors were prosecuted for sedition and sentenced to prison.

Juan Abad, author of *Ang Tanikalang Guinto,* was convicted in 1903, sentenced to two years in prison and fined $2,000, by an American judge of the court of first instance in Batangas, Paul W. Linebarger. Aurelio Tolentino, author of *Kahapon, Ngayon at Bukas,* was given the savage sentence of life imprisonment in 1906; through appeals this was reduced to 15 years then to 8 years, but a pardon didn't lift the penalty from Tolentino until 1912.[15]

Governor-General Taft, when criticized for imprisoning writers and actors, insisted that "suspension by arrest of the instigators is no violation of the [U.S.] Bill of Rights."[16]

One of the clearest evidences of the effect of U.S. colonial policy on the Philippine nation and society was the smothering of a socially conscious and nationalistic literature. In the latter decades of the 19th century, such a literature of protest and of liberation arose against Spanish rule, written partially in Spanish, partially in the Philippine dialects. That literary tendency continued into the early years of U.S. conquest and consolidation, when it was snuffed out by a combination of suppression and cultural imperialism. A key feature of this was the imposition of the English language in the educational system and in most of the media and publishing fields. From the first years of U.S. rule until the 1930s, when the Commonwealth was instituted as the transition period to independence, virtually no significant Philippine literature was produced.

A NATION SUBORDINATED

The physical, legalistic and supposedly moralistic measures employed by the U.S. in the Philippines were the more obvious features of the suppression of a nation. These U.S. colonial policies were harmful enough in producing a colonial mentality and a divided nation, but one of the worst effects upon Filipinos came from the shifting circumstances, alternating interests and uneven global role of U.S. imperialism. The Filipino people have been the helpless victims of the changing power position and the changing interests of the ruling groups in the U.S.

A U.S. naval attack force came to the Philippines imbued with the theories of Admiral Alfred Mahan, who was an advocate of naval power as the principal means for advancing the manifest destiny of great nations on a global scale. The securing of naval bases, coaling stations and other support facilities across the Pacific and on the rim of Asia was important in Mahan's theory, and U.S. commercial interests saw these as stepping-stones for a trade drive to secure preferential entry to the great market of China. The Philippines were first viewed as a naval base and a stepping-stone. That the islands were populated with people desiring freedom was merely an irritating irrelevance.

A concept of the Philippines as a colony soon emerged, but what to do with it, what resources it had, and how to exploit them were little understood. Survey parties were sent to get information and these focused almost wholly on the country's products and resources; the people were secondary, a problem to be dealt with by the U.S. army. The disputes that arose over possession and use of the colony between U.S. economic interests had to do with the products and resources, the naval base and strategic factors, with the fate of the people of less importance. As influence over policy-making by the U.S. government swung from one economic interest group to another, the fortunes of the Philippine nation swung with them.

The lives and future of the Filipino people were, as a consequence, at the mercy of whatever interests were temporarily in the ascendency in the U.S. Seizure and retention of the Philippines had been carried out by Republican Party administrations, linked with the more aggressive imperialist interests; anti-imperialist tendencies at the turn of the century were mainly centered in the Democratic Party, which had a major base among domestic agrarian producers. In 1912 a Democratic administration with Woodrow Wilson as president was elected and the pendulum swung toward cutting the colonial tie. In 1916 a law was enacted by the Democrat-controlled Congress, the Jones Act, promising independence to the Philippines and granting increased Filipino participation in the colonial government (an elected Senate replaced the Philippine Commission).

At this point it seemed that the Philippine nation was about to come into its own. However, by the time supporters of independence had managed to get the Jones bill through Congress, the pendulum was poised to swing again. Opponents of independence inserted conditions into the Jones Act. Its preamble declared "the purpose of the people of the United States to withdraw their sovereignty over the Philippine Islands and to recognize their independence as soon as a stable government can be established therein." This was little more, in effect, than the earlier "education for self-rule" declaration, putting independence in a nebulous future in which "stable government" would be defined and determined not by Filipinos but by the U.S. Congress.

The Jones Act, as it happened, was adopted in a developing international climate that was deeply affecting U.S. imperialism. World War I, a war of colonial redivision, was at mid-point; the U.S. had taken sides and was being drawn in. U.S. industry, gearing for war production, had use for Philippine raw materials. Coconut oil, for example, was used in the production of glycerine for explosives. Global factors, too, were affecting the U.S. outlook in regard to its Asian colony. Japan had taken advantage of the major powers' concentration on the war in Europe and had seized German-held territory in China, at Tsingtao, using this action as the springboard for presenting its notorious Twenty-one Demands on China in 1915, which amounted to a virtual ultimatum to China to surrender sovereignty to Japan. By the end of World War I, Japan had become the strongest power in Asia, threatening to close its market to other powers.

For the U.S., therefore, the Philippines had acquired a renewed significance. At war's end the expansionist Republican Party had returned to power as spokesman of a U.S. that had emerged from the war as a much stronger imperialist country. It appointed a Governor-General of the Philippines, General Leonard Wood, who had been one of the commanders of the army of conquest early in the century and who now was of the belief that a withdrawal from the Philippines "would be very disastrous to American prestige, trade and the Eastern situation," because it would encourage Japanese penetration of China.

Wood felt that a naval base in the Philippines was indispensable for maintaining the U.S. position in the Pacific and Asia.[17]

Once again the Philippine nation and its independence became subordinate to U.S. imperialist interests. The Republican Harding administration and that of president Coolidge which succeeded it pushed aside the prospect of independence projected in the Jones Act and put a firm hand of control upon the Filipinization of the colonial government. A commission headed by Wood and ex-Governor-General W. Cameron Forbes, sent by Harding to the Philippines in 1921 to re-examine the conditions there, included as one of its recommendations:

> We recommend that under no circumstances should the American Government permit to be established in the Philippine Islands a situation which would leave the United States in a position of responsibility without authority.[18]

The attitude of the U.S. government throughout Republican rule in the 1920s and until the Democrats regained office in 1932 was expressed in numerous reports and presidential statements, consistently declaring the Philippines unfit and unready for self-rule, incapable of stable government. One such report by Col. Carmi A. Thompson, sent to the Philippines as envoy by President Coolidge in 1926, flatly declared: "independence is impossible now and for a long time to come." One of his reasons was:

> From the standpoint of American commercial interests in the Far East, it would be unwise to relinquish control of the Philippines at the present time. Our trade with the Orient has been expanding year by year and all indications point to an increased volume of business for the future. We need the Philippines for a commercial base, and the retention of the Philippines will otherwise be of great benefit to our eastern situation. Abandonment of the Philippines at this time might complicate international relations in the Orient.[19]

During the 1920s, the U.S. economy was able to absorb Philippine duty-free products, particularly sugar, at a much higher level. Coupled with the modernization of the sugar industry that had been achieved by then, this tied Filipino producer-export interests closer to the U.S. market, acting as a dampener on the ardor of Philippine independence missions. This was the heyday of the landlord-*comprador* groups in the Philippines, marked by the heightening of their political power in the colony through control of the ruling Nacionalista Party and of its relations with the U.S. authorities.

All of this changed during the Great Depression of the 1930s. Not only did the depressed U.S. market shrink, but a decisive factor came into play: the strong resurgence of the U.S. domestic producers as a lobby for Philippine independence. Hard hit by the economic depression that in itself was driving farmers into bankruptcy, sugar beet and dairy producers had additionally to compete with the duty-free entry of Philippine exports. A Democratic administration under President Franklin Roosevelt, supporting of these interests, had been elected in 1932 with a platform including a call for Philippine independence. In these circumstances, a Philippine Independence Act, the Tydings-McDuffie Act, was passed by the U.S. Congress in 1935, with independence set to take place in 1946.

This time it was the U.S. Congress, reacting to pressures and demands from U.S. sectional interests, and not an irresistable nationalist movement in the Philippines itself, that decided the issue of Philippine independence. Without a crisis of U.S. capitalism, which had nothing to do with possession of the colony, Philippine independence may well have been put off indefinitely. Revolutionary Filipino nationalism, in fact, was undergoing another period of repression at the time. As for the dominant Filipino landlord-*comprador* groups, they had been enjoying unprecedentedly rich returns from their preferential position in the U.S. market and were not welcoming independence.

As with so much of Philippine history, independence and its course were decided by factors outside the will or means of the Filipino people. That history of foreign domination was not at an end: the most tragic subordination of the Philippine nation still lay ahead.

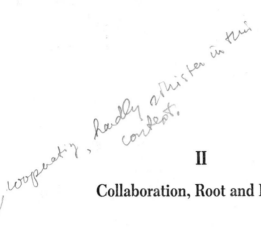

cooperating, hardly sinister in this context.

II

Collaboration, Root and Branch

The denial of self-determination and basic features of nationhood to the Filipino people was initiated by armed force, but U.S. colonial rule did not rest on the gun alone. It was maintained over the long run by support from within the Philippine nation itself, provided by the cancerous phenomenon of collaboration, the origins of which lay in class behavior developed during the preceding Spanish regime.

Arrival of a U.S. army of conquest coincided with the breaking-up of the Spanish colonial system, an antiquated mercantilism featured by restriction of trade, commercial monopolies tightly held by Spaniards, and exclusion of Filipinos from any political or significant economic role. In 1834 liberalism in Spain began the abandonment of mercantilism, opening the port of Manila to foreign trade. The consequence was the growth of export crops—sugar, copra and hemp—and setting in motion new Filipino class forces.

Foreign merchants, especially British and American, financed export crops and directly stimulated the prosperity and ambitions of many Filipino landowners, and of a middle strata of jobbers and subsidiary trades. Newly well-to-do Filipino families began to send their sons to universities in Europe, where they came in contact with liberal thought. A restless desire developed for an increased Filipino share in the restricted political life of the Philippine colony. The demand was not for independence but for representation in the parliament of Spain, the Cortes.

The outlines of the emerging class composition of Filipino society was clearly discernable by the 1880s. Although Filipino landholdings at this time were not exceptionally large, few reaching or exceeding 1,000 hectares and an estate of 250 hectares considered big,[1] wealth was being concentrated in the hands of such owners of landed estates in the provinces and also of an urban group of real estate owners, money lenders and speculators.

16

A strong sector of the landowners was produced by the boom in export crops. They were concentrated in Negros, in Iloilo and in some regions of Luzon—the sugar barons. As many as 3,000 estates were involved in the expansion of sugar production in the 1880s and 1890s.[2] The Araneta, Lacson, Yulo, de la Rama, Ledesma, Luzuriaga and Regalado sugar fortunes were launched on Negros, where the Yulo family owned 45 estates totalling 7,000 hectares, the Lacsons owning 15 estates.[3] In Pampanga province on Luzon the Henson, Dizon, Hison and deLeon sugar families became entrenched, as did the Cojuangco family in adjoining Tarlac province. In Cebu the Jacosalem and Cui families benefited.

In Manila, the families of wealth were both Chinese *mestizos* (Chuidian, Limjap, Yangco, Tuason, Lionjua, Lim) and Spanish *mestizos* (Roxas, Legarda, de Tavera). Luis R. Yangco was engaged in coastwise shipping. A small minority of 62 persons or firms owned 30 percent of all taxable Manila real estate, with 15 owning 16 percent.[4] Some became wealthy from rents on real estate, others were intermediaries between foreign merchants and Filipino planters, or were engaged in money lending, chiefly to farmers at usurious interest rates (usury was a major source of wealth).[5] The most wealthy Filipino families, especially the *mestizos,* had achieved the distinction of being accepted in Philippine Spanish or insular colonial society, a circumstance that led them to identify themselves closely with the Spaniards and Spain.

Another landowning sector owed a position of subsidiary power more to its association with the framework of colonial rule than to market relations, although the distinction was sometimes blurred. These were the *caciques,* those who played the part of the tax collector or of the petty dispenser of justice in the provinces, who "served, in brief, as points of contact between the Spanish civil and ecclesiastical officialdom and the peasantry."[6] The system of the *cacique* had been transferred from Spain, where he was "generally a large landowner who in exchange for certain unwritten privileges organizes the district politically on the government's behalf."[7]

Next in the scale of emerging classes was a variegated, more numerous middle stratum that stemmed in the main from the intermediate landowning or land-renting group with holdings ranging from 10 to 300 hectares. Some grew export crops (much sugar was produced on farms of 25 hectares or less), but the majority grew crops for home consumption—rice, vegetables or fruits. Of the property-owning or managing groups, this was the most insecure and the most ambitious.

At the mercy, on the one hand, of money-lenders or of aggrandizement from more powerful landholders they were, on the other hand, excluded from the colonial social life in towns and cities. They were the most eager, therefore, to send their sons to universities, in the Philippines or in Europe, to attain social standing through the professions of law, medicine, pharmacy, teaching or the priesthood.

The question of land ownership, which was the principal factor in the shaping of Filipino class structure, was exacerbated by the role of the Spanish Catholic religious orders, the friars, which had developed as the biggest and most exploitative landowners. These Dominican, Augustinian, Franciscan and Recollect friars eventually owned 420,000 acres of the finest agricultural land, which they operated by a feudalistic tenancy system. Innumerable Filipino families who rented friar land and couldn't meet onerous payments were evicted or suffered humiliation from the friars.

Spain, which was reputed to have won its colonial empire by "the cross and the sword," leaned increasingly on the Church and its religious orders to maintain its rule, the friar becoming landowner, governing authority and spiritual ruler rolled into one. Filipinos aspiring to the priesthood and to a secularizing of the parishes had their ambitions repressed: at the end of the Spanish regime, out of 967 parishes, 817 were in the hands of friars.[8] It was particularly the friars who stood in the path, both economically and politically, of the emerging middle stratum of Filipinos.

The vast majority of the people, however, belonged to the poor peasantry, as small proprietors or agricultural laborers. Holdings of small proprietors were among the smallest in the world, averaging barely two hectares (5 acres). Because of their marginal existence, they were the gravest victims of the usury practiced by bigger landlords or by money lenders. As a result, most small proprietors sank into sharecropping tenancy.

From the point of view of number, the propertied classes in general, from the wealthy to the middle strata to the small proprietor, were a small minority. Those known as the *principalia* (the leading propertied and educated) comprised no more than 12 to 14 families in a town of 12,000 people, a large community in the Philippines of that time. The vast majority of the population were of the laboring classes. Wrote a U.S. official:

> In the country, the laboring man is known as a "tao," a term that carries with it implications half-way between serf and peasant—possibly the

Russian "moujik" is the nearest equivalent in another language. Manual labor imposes among the natives a certain social stigma, a degradation in rank unknown in America or Europe.[9]

It was an attitude worsened by the friars, who said that laborers on the land "are fit only to tend carabaos, to pray and to follow blindly the instructions of the friars."[10]

In the concluding decades of the 19th century, the beginnings of a class of artisans and wage-workers emerged, composed of unskilled laborers and semi-skilled workers on the docks and in the warehouses of Manila, Cebu and Iloilo, employees on the first railroad (the British-built and owned Manila-to-Dagupan line opened in 1892), cigar makers, workers in the shipyards surrounding Manila Bay, printers, carriage makers, carpenters and masons.

In the rough spectrum of Filipino class differentiation in the decades just prior to U.S. conquest, there was discernable a small grouping of the wealthy based on relatively large landholdings who were conservative and inclined to resist change; a somewhat more numerous range of middle and small proprietor groups who were restive and becoming vocal about political status; and the great mass of the working people who had yet to articulate their desires.

THE REVOLUTION AGAINST SPANISH RULE

By the time the U.S. forces appeared on the scene in May 1898, these class groupings had been shaken by a revolutionary outburst from below against Spanish rule. Its beginnings were in a reform movement in the 1870s for secularization of the Catholic parishes. The friars' answer to this was the execution of three reformist Filipino priests, Jose Burgos, Mariano Gomez and Jacinto Zamora. It provided martyrs for the movement, which broadened and spread in the 1880s to Filipino students and intellectuals in Spain. They founded a nationalist newspaper, *La Solidaridad,* in 1889, copies of which reached the Philippines to stir others. One of its adherents was Jose Rizal whose powerful anti-friar novel, *Noli Me Tangere (Touch Me Not),* also had an impact among educated Filipinos.

Called the Propaganda Campaign, it was not a movement for independence but for reform within the colonial system, calling for Filipino representation in the Spanish parliament and greater liberty in the colony, for the expulsion of the friars from the Philippines and the return of land appropriated by them. The movement and the newspaper foundered in a few years, however, due in the main to refusal by wealthy Filipinos to finance it.

In 1892 Jose Rizal helped set up an organization in Manila which went a bit further, *La Liga Filipina*, a kind of mutual fund association that made a call (for the first time) "to unite the whole archipelago into one compact vigorous and homogeneous body" and proclaimed "encouragement of instruction, agriculture and commerce."[11] *La Liga Filipina* was banned at once by the Spanish authorities, and subsided.

These trends all stemmed from the restive Filipino middle-class elements who were being increasingly squeezed, especially by the friars. Filipino secular priests who held 181 parishes in 1870 were being driven out and replaced by friars, only 150 parishes remaining to Filipinos by the 1890s. In these years, on their huge estates, the friars steeply raised the rents of their tenants and evicted many who could not pay. Only one or two of the Propagandists saw revolutionary solutions as necessary, however, Marcelo del Pilar in particular. It is notable that although the Filipino groups of intellectuals abroad moved about the capitals of Europe where Marxism and other socialist ideologies were then gaining influence, none of them were attracted in the slightest. One, Isabelo de los Reyes, was subsequently influenced slightly by syndicalist ideas but that came later in other circumstances. Jose Rizal typified the attitude toward revolutionaries in his portrayal in his novel *El Filibusterismo* (the sequel to *Noli Me Tangere*) of the revengeful central character, Simoun, as a caricatured, cloaked bomb-thrower.

The wealthy Filipinos, export producers, money lenders and others who spurned the middle-class movements, far from being dissatisfied with their lot, were actually enjoying increasing prosperity in the latter decades of Spanish rule. Sugar growers whose exports were but 47,704,105 kilos bringing $2,225,022 in 1854 had increased exports to 341,469,536 kilos worth $11,808,688 in 1895.[12] Hemp growers were experiencing a boom: exports of 14,050,400 kilos worth but $1,626,746 in 1854 had quadrupled to 51,441,486 kilos worth $7,494,195 in 1890.[13] A wholly new market had been found in Europe for coconut products, created by the development of a French process for extracting oil; exports of copra that were worth a mere $13,284 in 1880 had jumped to $1,171,721 by 1894.[14]

When the revolutionary upsurge came it was from the oppressed majority of the people. In the same year, 1892, that *La Liga Filipina* was founded and extinguished, one of those on its fringes, Andres Bonifacio, a wage employee in a Manila warehouse, together with a group of other salaried employees, clerks and artisans, set up an underground organization called the *Katipunan*. (Its full name was *Kataastaasan Kagalanggalang na Katipunan ng mga Anak ng Bayan*, or, Highest and Most Respectable Society of the Sons of the People.) It had the avowed revolutionary purpose of working for the complete independence of the Philippines from Spain. Unlike their middle-class reformist predecessors, they undertook the mass recruiting of urban workers and of the poor peasantry in the provinces around Manila. One of the most remarkable of all underground movements, by 1896 the *Katipunan* had reached a membership variously estimated at 123,000 to 400,000. As the movement grew, Bonifacio and his companions decided on the necessity of armed struggle to win independence.

Approached for support, the wealthy Filipinos reacted with horror, flatly refusing financial assistance. Jose Rizal and other middle class *ilustrados* had the same response. However, the *Katipunan* did attract some adherents from among discontented *caciques* and small land-owning groups suffering friar abuses in the provinces near Manila.

On August 26, 1896, following premature exposure to the Spaniards, the armed revolution began with a call for throwing off Spanish rule. In essence it was a revolt of the masses and it alarmed the other class groupings in the Philippines as much as it did the Spaniards. Wealthy Filipinos rushed to the Spanish authorities to vow loyalty, many paying large sums of money to buy security from arrest, which didn't stop indiscriminate arrests from occurring. Jose Rizal, one of those arrested, issued a public manifesto denouncing the revolution and declaring that he had "spontaneously offered not only my services, but my life, and name as well, to be used in the manner they [the Spaniards] thought best for the purpose of stifling the rebellion."[15]

These divisions among the Filipino people at a critical historical juncture, especially the opposition by the rich to a revolt from below, were neither unexpected nor considered fatal. More important was unity within the *Katipunan*, but as the armed struggle developed, class differences cropped up there as well.

It was a confused struggle of indecisive engagements, but the Spanish regime was made aware that they could not suppress it. Real *Katipunan* successes were scored in Cavite province where forces of the people led by Emilio Aguinaldo were able to expel the Spanish troops. Aguinaldo had been the *cacique*-like mayor of Kawit, Cavite. He headed the property-owning *Katipuneros* who came from the ranks of the *ilustrados* and *principalia* in the provincial towns. They disliked having as leaders the semi-working class Andres Bonifacio and his group.

At a meeting of the movement's leaders in Tejeros, Cavite on March 22, 1897, the group around Aguinaldo scorned and insulted Bonifacio as lacking the education to lead, the *ilustrados* looking down upon him and the founding group as socially inferior. In the contest that developed, Bonifacio was out-maneuvered and at Aguinaldo's order was arrested and executed. The man who had given the mass, semi-proletarian character to the revolution was removed from the scene.

For the revolution this brought irreparable damage. The way was opened for the unhindered influx of conservative class forces into the leadership of the struggle. Having begun as a revolution of the masses, led by men who rejected reformism, it came increasingly under the influence of those whose limited goals could be satisfied by compromises that neglected the needs of the masses.

The question could be raised as to why the Bonifacio-Aguinaldo struggle and its outcome did not become an issue among the masses of the revolution. In part this was due to the immaturity of Filipino working-class forces, which had not yet acquired a clear structure or a class-conscious ideology. In part it was due to the peculiar role of the *ilustrado*, the educated elite in Philippine society, a personage looked up to with respect who exerted a somewhat paternal influence over unlettered peasants and workers.

As the armed struggle stretched through 1897 and it became obvious that it would be protracted, irresolution developed in the Aguinaldo faction. Spanish resistance stiffened. The moneyed class in Manila was eager for an end to the conflict, which was cutting into their incomes: with planting and transportation disrupted, a sharp drop occurred in the export of sugar from Manila—97,705 tons in 1896 to 57,383 tons in 1897.[16] By August the Manila wealthy, in collaboration with the Spanish authorities, sent a representative, Pedro A. Paterno, to Aguinaldo to mediate an end to the revolt. (Paterno asked the Spaniards for a Dukedom in Spain and a large sum of money for his services.)

On December 14, 1897 Aguinaldo and his dominant conservative group in the *Katipunan*, overriding the objections of the militant wing, made a compromise settlement with the Spanish regime. Accepting P400,000 in return for surrender of the arms he commanded, he and his group left the country by agreement and went to Hong Kong. Although Aguinaldo later claimed that he intended to use the money to renew the struggle, in effect the Revolution of 1896 was sold out by this act. (However, it did not end the struggle, which was resumed within two months by the *Katipunan* militants. On April 17, 1898 one of these, Francisco Makabulos, formed a provisional Executive Committee in Central Luzon with a Constitution that provided for raising an army and setting up town governments. This was less than two weeks before a U.S. fleet arrived in Manila Bay.)

COLLABORATION WITH THE U.S.: FIRST PHASE

By historical coincidence Admiral George Dewey and the Filipino exiles reached Hong Kong around the same time. Dewey's representatives and U.S. consular officials directed from Washington contacted the Aguinaldo group and came to an unwritten deal: to transport them back to the Philippines to resume their warfare against Spanish forces, in conjunction with the U.S. attack. According to Aguinaldo later, Dewey made vague promises of guaranteeing Philippine independence.[17] It was obvious that he was concerned only with making use of Filipinos to assist the U.S. in the war. When, after Aguinaldo was landed and had met with revolutionary leaders, Philippine independence was proclaimed, that momentous step for the Filipino people was ignored by Dewey and his staff. The Filipino leaders were held at arm's length and negotiated with merely to gain time for U.S. infantry to arrive, accept Spanish surrender and occupy Manila.

By that time a full-fledged republican Philippine government was functioning in most regions, joined by the middle-class groups that had campaigned for representation and broader rights. With Spanish rule ended, including the driving out of the friars, opportunities that went with power opened up, while the republic was supported with enthusiasm by the masses of the people.

Once Spain was defeated and the Philippines ceded to the U.S., a Philippine republic was viewed as a hostile obstacle to that "legal" possession. A two-phased policy secured U.S. rule: military suppression of resisting Filipinos, and the simultaneous organization of a new colonial regime. The latter step was made possible by the ready compliance of the wealthy Filipinos who opposed the desire of their countrymen for freedom and independence.

There was no problem in establishing relations with that grouping. On the staff of General Elwell Otis, who became military governor in August 1898 as soon as the Spanish army surrendered, was a man named Frank Bournes, who had visited the Philippines before the revolution and had become acquainted with many wealthy and influential Filipino families. Ostensibly a major in the medical corps, he was appointed chief health officer in occupied Manila, but he was actually the head of Otis's spy system. He made full use of his former contacts.

It did not, in fact, require much persuasion from contact men like Frank Bournes to win the wealthy elite to the U.S. side. A number of them were staying in Hong Kong in refuge from the revolution at home, and as soon as news of the destruction of the Spanish fleet in Manila Bay reached them they hastened on May 6th to U.S. Consul Rounseville Wildman, who immediately afterward cabled Secretary of State Day in Washington that he had been given signed statements by Doroteo Cortes, Maximo Cortes and his wife Eustaquia, Gracio Gonzaga and Jose Maria Basa, "All very wealthy landlords, bankers and advocates of Manila," who were tendering "their allegiance and the allegiance of their powerful families in Manila to the United States."[18] (Jose Maria Basa was a member of the Aguinaldo group of revolutionary exiles.) On May 14 Wildman cabled similar statements from Severino Rotas, Eugenia Plona, Claudio Lopez and A.H. Marti, "all wealthy and prominent landholders from Negros and Panay."[19]

Basa then sent his own manifesto to the Philippines on May 16, 1898:

> This is the best opportunity which we have ever had for contriving that our country, all the Philippine archipelago, may be counted as another star in the great republic of the United States. Now is the time to offer ourselves to that nation . . . With America we shall be rich, civilized and happy.[20]

The expression of such views and such obeisant approaches continued through the period of Spanish defeat and surrender and the beginning stages of U.S. occupation. An extreme example of the attitude of the wealthy occurred on the island of Negros where the Filipino sugar planters set up their own government on November 6, 1898 and kept it separate from the government of the Philippine Republic. A leading Negros sugar planter, Jose Luzuriaga, as soon as warfare started between the U.S. army and the Philippine army, negotiated with the U.S. commander in the central Visayan Islands, Col. James Smith, for U.S. troops to be sent to Negros where the planters' regime would be put under U.S. military government. This was done. Smith became military governor and Luzuriaga served under him as head of an appointed "Constituent Assembly." Another sugar planter, Aniceto Lacson, acted as the subordinate "civil governor."

In the Instructions written by President William McKinley to the civilian Commission sent to the Philippines in April 1900 to serve as the colonial governing body, its members were told to "give especial attention to the existing government on the Island of Negros, constituted with the approval of the people of that island (sic)" and "after verifying, as far as may be practicable, the reports of the successful working of that government, they will be guided by the experience thus acquired, so far as it may be applicable to the conditions existing in other portions of the Philippines." Approval of the people of Negros, in truth, went to the revolutionary forces fighting for independence, which persisted on that island for one of the longest periods of the Fil-American War. American authorities were themselves appalled at the way in which the planters' government proceeded to use power. "The difficulty about the government of the island of Negros," later testified Commission head and Civil Governor William H. Taft, "was that they had so many officers . . . that the $200,000 of revenue was all consumed in salaries."21 In order to forestall rising popular discontent, the central U.S. regime had to abolish the separate Negros government and reduce it to provincial status under tight U.S. control.

In Manila the behavior of leading wealthy families impressed itself even more on U.S. authorities. These rich Filipinos had been scornful when approached for contributions by the *Katipunan,* and they had denounced the Revolution of 1896 when it came. Mostly of Spanish *mestizo* extraction, they swore loyalty to Spain when war with the U.S. broke out. Their leading representatives, T.H. Pardo de Tavera, Cayetano Arellano, Benito Legarda and Gregorio Araneta accepted appointed posts in a paper "Consultative Assembly" set up by the Spanish authorities to try to rally Filipino support. As soon as the Spanish forces were defeated, however, and a Philippine Republic was proclaimed with a declaration of independence on June 12, 1898 and an acting Congress set up, the wealthy elements began to shift to the victors.

For Emilio Aguinaldo and the middle-class leaders heading the revolution, it was tactically correct to win this class to the cause of independence. This was urged by the leading revolutionary theorist and tactician, Apolinario Mabini, who saw the need to harness the talents and money of the wealthy, although he advised Aguinaldo to keep them merely in advisory posts. Aguinaldo, however, who invariably bowed to the wishes of the wealthy, went far beyond. He appointed them to key positions in the Philippine government and allowed them to carve a dominant role for themselves in the crucial months of 1898 when U.S. power was being built up in Manila. Thus, Cayetano Arellano, who was actually offered the presidency by Aguinaldo, was made Secretary of Foreign Affairs, with Pardo de Tavera as Director of Diplomacy. The Congress itself, literally taken over by landlords and money lenders, elected as its president Pedro A. Paterno, who had persuaded Aguinaldo to surrender to the Spaniards in 1897. Felipe Calderon, a reactionary landlord chosen to draft a Constitution, wrote into it provisions that made President Aguinaldo subordinate to a Congress and a powerful Permanent Commission controlled by the wealthy. Benito Legarda became vice-president of the Congress, Gregoria Araneta its First Secretary. Florentino Torres, who had held a judicial post under Spanish rule, was made head of a commission to negotiate with the U.S. military governor, General Otis.

Otis later declared:

> Until possibly the middle of November (1898) I had more influence in Aguinaldo's cabinet than he had himself. Members of his cabinet reported to me what was being done, and I sent members of the cabinet up there [to Malolos, Bulacan, seat of the Philippine government] quite frequently to ascertain what his congress was doing and to report to me.[22]

Between December 1898 and January 1899, from the Peace Treaty signing in Paris that transferred the Philippine colony to the U.S. to the opening of the war of conquest, all of the above-mentioned wealthy Filipinos abandoned the Philippine Republic and went over to the U.S. masters. All subsequently held leading posts in the U.S. colonial regime.

In March 1899, soon after the outbreak of the U.S.-Filipino conflict, the McKinley administration dispatched a fact-finding Commission to Manila under Cornell University president Jacob Schurman. The Schurman Commission held hearings in Manila with testimony from "hundreds of witnesses . . . uniform in testimony." The uniformity — condemnation of the Filipino revolutionaries and welcome for the Americans — was unsurprising: except for a few foreign businessmen, the witnesses were made up wholly of Filipino well-to-do landlords, money lenders and businessmen. No serious effort was made to obtain the views of those resisting U.S. occupation.

Cayetano Arellano told the Commission he didn't know the cause of the Philippine Revolution and didn't think the Filipino people capable of forming a government themselves. He agreed with a Commission suggestion that the power to vote should be given only to "people who had certain property qualifications." A prosperous Manila physician, Enrique Lopez, concurred, wanting the vote reserved for "people with a good station in life, well-known people, people who have property. I do not mean the peons and lower classes." He thought voting should be limited to no more than 200 people in Manila. Tomas G. del Rosario, who had deserted a top post in the Philippine Congress, favored autonomy, which he defined as "The government of the Philippines by the Filipino people under the direction or intervention of the Americans," with a cabinet appointed by the American governor-general. Benito Legarda, who boasted "I am a capitalist, I have property here and businesses" (he owned large tobacco and distillery firms), used his testimony to paint a lurid picture of the revolutionary army as a collection of robbers who, he said, had a plan to plunder Manila, "to rob the whole city." Carlos Palanca, a Chinese *mestizo* middleman who handled sugar, rice and drapery goods and who was the chief contractor in Manila for laborers for the U.S. army and for transportation for U.S. troops in their military operations against the Filipinos, came out strongly in favor of U.S. rule.

Felipe Calderon, who had drafted the Philippine Constitution and then fled to the U.S. lines, gave the Commission this portrayal of his people:

> The archipelago as a whole is composed of three classes of individuals: the rich and intelligent element; the poorer element of the country—the element that is willing to devote itself to work—and an element that may be called intermediary, made up of clerks and writers, who have a habit of stirring up the town. The first of these elements, the wealthier class and the diligent class, that by their work produce sugar, tobacco, etc. . . . wishes, by whatever means, peace and quiet . . . The third, or intermedial class, do not wish for peace under any circumstances, because it goes against their interests, and, apart from that, they also have these wrong impressions of Americans.

He recommended a policy of attraction for such elements.[23]

Based on its limited investigation, the Schurman Commission, in its report to President McKinley, asserted in conclusion:

> The United States cannot withdraw from the Philippines . . . The Filipinos are wholly unprepared for independence, and if independence were given to them they could not maintain it . . . There being no Philippine nation, but only a collection of different peoples, there is no general public opinion in the archipelago, but the men of property and education, who alone interest themselves in public affairs, in general recognize as indispensable American authority, guidance and protection . . . The greatest care should be taken in the selection of officials for administration. They should be men of highest character and fitness, and partisan politics should be entirely separate from the government of the Philippines.[24]

It was from "the men of property and education" that the first Filipino officials were chosen, by the military governors General Otis and General Arthur MacArthur and by civil governor W.H. Taft, although with their opposition to the Philippine Republic the selectees could hardly be said to be free of "partisan politics." Cayetano Arellano on May 29, 1899 accepted appointment as Chief Justice of the U.S.-designed Supreme Court. Florentino Torres and Victorino Mapa, a propertied Filipino lawyer, joined him as Associate Justices. Arellano, under U.S. direction, organized the lower courts in the colony. "It was not only a work of organization, but also of orientation of the course which the force of circumstances required our laws to take," commented Mapa.[25]

General Otis and General MacArthur were against political activity by any Filipinos and employed their wealthy allies merely as pawns to negotiate the surrender of revolutionary leaders. William Howard Taft, who arrived in his capacity as civil governor on June 3, 1900, had other ideas. He assigned Frank Bournes, the intelligence operative, to organize the wealthy into a political party to assist in establishing U.S. control. This was the Federal Party; Pardo de Tavera was made the head. It was launched on December 23, 1900, at a meeting "attended by some 125 pro-American upper class Filipinos."[26]

In its platform the Federal Party stood for "the recognition of the sovereignty of the United States." It stated that

the founders of this party promise to cooperate with the established government, using all the means in their power to procure the pacification of the country, in that the Filipinos in arms may acknowledge said government.[27]

One of the points in the platform anticipated that "The territory of the Philippine Islands may be considered one of the states of the Union."[28] Taft and other U.S. officials later denied having directly encouraged Federal Party leaders in the latter belief; if so, the deception lay in not having discouraged it.

The Federal Party prepared the basis for Provincial and local government in areas cleared of resistance by the U.S. army: it organized party committees among the *principales* of towns, and from these the Taft regime appointed provincial and town governing bodies. Between January and April 1901, a total of 283 committees were set up.

For their collaboration, Federal Party adherents were rewarded with appointments to choice political posts, as provincial governors, judges in courts of first instance, Manila municipal board members, heads of municipal organizing committees. A good example of the concept of public service that motivated such appointees was provided by Pedro Paterno—who defected from the Congress of the Republic—and who, on appointment to the Manila municipal board, delivered a speech in which he urged that members of the board receive $1000 per month instead of the $4500 per year authorized by the Taft Commission; that each should receive more than $5 for each meeting attended, and that they should get $100 for each memorial presented by the board; contending furthermore that it was entirely proper for decorations and orders of nobility to be bestowed.[29]

The cream of appointments went to those who played the leading roles in organizing the Federal Party. Arellano's Chief Justiceship was such a prize. On September 1, 1901 Pardo de Tavera, Benito Legarda and Jose Luzuriaga, the Negros sugar planter, were placed, as members, on the top-level Philippine Commission, becoming part of the colonial regime itself.

In the critical period of U.S. conquest, between 1898 and 1902, when the vast majority of the Filipino people were in resistance and supporting their own republic, the minority of wealthy Filipinos provided the narrow base on which U.S. colonial rule was initially established.

COLLABORATION WITH THE U.S.: SECOND PHASE

It was impossible, however, for U.S. imperialism to set up an administration and control system with such a thin stratum of the population; only a limited number of posts of government could be filled from this sector. To staff the colonial system, and in particular to do so as cheaply as possible without bringing in a large number of much higher paid American officials and employees, it was essential to win over the middle-class elements who were actively engaged in or supporting the war of resistance. A policy of attraction was developed, therefore, to go hand-in-hand with the policy of brutal suppression.

From an early date the U.S. authorities had a shrewd grasp of the divisions that existed in the ranks of the Philippine forces opposing them. Such information came in large part from the wealthy members of Aguinaldo's cabinet and of the Congress, who kept one foot in the American camp until hostilities began in January 1899 and then leaped into it with both feet. It was well understood that there were conservatives and radicals among the Filipinos, that Aguinaldo's advisers included both the capitulation-minded conservative Felipe Buencamino and the militant, determined radical Apolinario Mabini, and that radicals were to be found especially in the army, which was the revolutionary body closest to the people. The commander of the army, General Antonio Luna, had developed into a leading radical nationalist.

Mabini and Luna were middle-class *ilustrados* who allied themselves with the interests of the masses. They favored a kind of revolutionary military dictatorship with Aguinaldo holding supreme authority, in contrast to a wealthy-dominated Congress having control over the executive of the government. At the time the Philippine Republic had adopted the forms of democracy but its substance was far from attained: the army spoke for the ordinary people and the Congress for the propertied wealthy, and the struggle between them was an aspect of the thread running through the Philippine Revolution of an inarticulated class struggle between the masses and the middle-class elite, a struggle that had had its first serious consequence in the murder of Andres Bonifacio. Aguinaldo had dissolved the *Katipunan* as an organization as early as July 15, 1898 but it remained alive in minds and hearts of the members of the army.

On June 4, 1899, as the war of resistance was settling into a prolonged struggle, Luna was assassinated in Cabanatuan, Nueva Ecija in an ambush prepared by the conservative group around Aguinaldo, headed by Felipe Buencamino who took part in the murder. Circumstances pointed to a complicity of Aguinaldo in the act. Luna, who favored an uncompromising war for independence against U.S. aggression, had strongly opposed moves by Buencamino and his associates to negotiate an agreement with the U.S. His assassination was a parallel to the earlier murder of Bonifacio. In both cases the conservative circles around Aguinaldo had carried out the elimination of revolutionary leaders with Aguinaldo's assent. In both cases the Philippine Revolution was purged of uncompromising leadership at a critical moment.

This was well understood by U.S. authorities. General Otis, then commanding, wired Washington on June 13:

> It is believed that the killing of Lt. Gen. Luna on the 8th instant [*sic*] near San Isidro [*sic*], by Aguinaldo's guard, will be attended with important results not derogatory to U.S. interests.[30]

In another wire the next day he said:

> [Luna] was uncompromising for continuation of the war; influenced lower and robber classes . . . His death received with satisfaction by all influential Filipinos.[31]

When Buencamino and other conservative figures came into American hands soon afterward, their quick collaboration helped shape U.S. policy toward this class grouping. Buencamino, one of the most shameless turncoats in Philippine history, had once been an ardent defender of Spanish rule and of the friars and a commander of the militia set up by Spain to fight the Americans. Captured by Filipino revolutionary forces, he had immediately become Aguinaldo's adviser and speech writer. In U.S. hands, he promptly turned into their total ally, becoming one of the main founders and the program-drafter of the Federal Party, winning for himself the directorship of the important Board of Civil Service in the colonial regime, responsible for screening those it employed. Buencamino's religious commitments duplicated his political loyalties, shifting from ostentatious Catholicism to enthusiastic Protestantism and high-degree Free Masonry. He was one of the most assiduous in negotiating surrender of his former companions.

With most of the leading middle-class conservatives surrendered or captured, the radicals who included the military leaders resorted to prolonged guerrilla warfare. Against them the U.S. authorities adopted two-pronged pacification measures: 1) ruthless military suppression through orders issued by General Arthur MacArthur, especially in a Proclamation of December 10, 1900 that relegated Filipino resistance to the status of brigandage and outlawry, terming Filipino combatants "war traitors against the United States" who "if captured are not entitled to the privileges of prisoners of war"[32]; and (2) a policy of attraction implemented by the Taft Commission.

Taft and his civil commission arrived on June 3, 1900 with presidential instructions that were aimed essentially at winning over the middle-class elements who were holding out against U.S. rule. Those instructions included setting up a governing system with provincial and municipal governments, an educational system, a civil service, courts, and administrative departments, in all of which "natives of the islands are to be preferred" and "natives of the islands, both in the cities and in the rural communities, shall be afforded the opportunity to manage their own local affairs to the fullest extent of which they are capable, and subject to the least degree of supervision and control." A resolution of the friar land question, and the protection of property rights were pledged. Within the scope of Taft's instructions, the Filipino wealthy and middle classes both were given the possibility of realizing the reforms demanded from Spain, and more.

The enactment of laws by the Taft Commission for the setting up of all these features of government was accompanied by the promulgation of its Act No. 78 on January 26, 1901. This shrewd measured declared:

By authority of the President of the United States, be it enacted by the United States Philippine Commission, that:

Section 1. All persons who on the first day of April 1901, or thereafter, shall be in arms against the authority and sovereignty of the United States in the Philippine Islands, and all persons aiding or abetting them on or after said date, are hereby declared ineligible to hold any office of honor, trust or profit in the Philippine Islands.

Section 2. Section fifteen of the Civil Service Act is hereby amended by inserting after the last word of the said section the following "provided, however, that no person shall be eligible for examination or appointment under the provisions of this Act, who shall be, on or after the first day of April 1901, in arms against the authority of the United States in the Philippine Islands, or who shall thereafter give aid and comfort to the enemies of the United States, so in arms.

Section 3. This act shall take effect on its passage.

Enacted January 26, 1901.[33]

Act No. 78 was the stick part of Taft's attraction drive; the carrot was in the simultaneous acts providing for provincial and municipal governments. At the same time, the Federal Party was assigned to step up contacting the middle-class rebels and persuade them to surrender and take advantage of the lucrative opportunities being offered.

As this was in progress, Emilio Aguinaldo was captured in Palanan, Isabela. The capture itself was of less import than the behavior of Aguinaldo in U.S. hands. Seized on March 23, 1901 and brought to Manila, he took the oath of allegiance to the U.S. on April 1, and then signed a widely circulated proclamation in which he called on his erstwhile comrades to accept peace "united around the glorious and sovereign banner of the United States." He said that he was "acknowledging and accepting the sovereignty of the United States throughout our entire archipelago."[34] As soon as he arrived in Manila, Aguinaldo was seen by Cayetano Arellano, who pressed him to take such steps. Aguinaldo also promptly made personal contact with rebel leaders close to him, while the Taft Commission extended the deadline in Act No. 78 to enable his capture and conversion to take effect.

The results of these combined efforts were a turning point in the independence struggle. Many of the major figures in the Philippine Republic capitulated in this period, the first half of 1901, hurrying to avoid exclusion from advantageous positions. Even before Aguinaldo's capture, such ranking leaders as Mariano Trias, a former secretary of war in Aguinaldo's cabinet, and Severino de las Alas, a former secretary of the interior, had surrendered in Cavite province on March 14, when approached by the Federal Party. Within three months Trias had been appointed governor of Cavite. Manuel Tinio, Juan Cailles, Tomas Mascardo, Memerto Natividad, and Ambrosio Mojica gave up in May and June: Tinio became governor of Nueva Ecija province, Cailles of

Laguna. In Iloilo, General Martin Delgado, head of the revolutionary forces, surrendered in March and was made governor of Iloilo on April 1.

Within six months of its launching in December 1900, operating in conjunction with Act No. 78 and Aguinaldo's cooperation, the Federal Party claimed to have brought about the surrender of 14 generals, 28 colonels, 20 majors, 6 guerrilla chiefs, 46 captains, 106 lieutenants and 2640 soldiers.[35]

Aguinaldo, whose sense of *amor propio* prevented him from accepting a lesser post after having savored the position of president, was not averse, however, to being enabled to acquire 300 hectares of choice friar lands adjoining his home town of Imus, Cavite. It was sufficient to elevate him to the property-owning landlord class.

This widespread opportunist phenomenon marked the second stage of collaboration with the U.S. regime, begun by the wealthy Filipinos. Swayed by Federal Party promises of patronage on the one hand and by threats of the U.S. authorities on the other hand to bar from any office those who continued to resist, the middle-class leaders settled for the political rewards of collaboration.

EDUCATION FOR SELF-RULE—AND SELF-ADVANCEMENT

On July 2, 1902 the Philippine Organic Act, adopted after much debate by the U.S. Congress, was made effective. It marked the formally declared end of the Fil-American War and established full-fledged civil government in the colony. The Act laid down a legal system for a colonial economy with laws on business franchises, bond issues, land ownership and taxation, mainly designed for the operation of U.S. investment and trade and in consideration of the contradictions between U.S. domestic producers and like interests in the Philippines.

As far as Filipinos were concerned, one of the principal features of the Act set out the steps to an elected national assembly. This was of keenest interest to the middle-class elements, creating a major field of opportunity, regardless of the fact that it would be a Filipino legislature subordinate to the U.S. Commission. It opened up an arena of colonial politics and electoral contests that would take place entirely within the context and according to the rules of the U.S. regime.

A national assembly was predicated on the U.S. claim that Filipinos were not ready for self-government and had to pass through an indefinite period of "education for self-rule." Filipino leaders who had served in their own Congress of the Philippine Republic and who may have found it difficult to swallow such a characterization nevertheless did so, accepting the U.S. terms, their acceptance marking their final abandonment of revolutionary means to gain independence. Except for a handful of principled individuals, they turned away from that alliance with the masses that had featured the great national struggle begun in 1896, which had led to the founding of a Philippine Republic, and sought full accommodation with U.S. imperialism.

The political parties formed to take part in the assembly election had to bow to the Taft Commission's edict forbidding the inclusion of a call for independence in their platforms. Taft relentlessly imposed on them his Sedition Act of November 1901, Section 10 of which made it

> unlawful for any person to advocate orally or by writing or printing or like methods the independence of the Philippine Islands or their separation from the United States, either by peacable or forcible means, or to print, publish or circulate any handbill, newspaper or other publication advocating such independence or separation.[36]

Several groups of former supporters of the Republic attempted to set up political parties from 1901 onwards, all with a call for independence in their draft platforms and all were made to remove it by Taft, who told one group in December 1902 "to forget politics for two years and to take steps only to the uplifting of the agricultural prosperity of this country."[37] Not until the election year of 1907 were the parties free to mention independence. No party, in fact, could present itself to the Filipino people and have credibility if it didn't have independence at the top of its platform. Most middle-class groups finally coalesced in a Nacionalista Party which proclaimed "immediate independence" as its goal. The Federal Party of wealthy collaborators felt it necessary to call at least for "ultimate independence" and to cloak its record by assuming a new name, the Partido Nacional Progresista (Progressive Party). The issue had been made semantical, however, because in both cases it had been submerged in the commitment by both to peaceful, legal, parliamentary processes that limited an independence struggle to petitions and resolutions.

What was relevant in the colonial politics agreed to by both wealthy and middle-class Filipinos was the narrow electoral base on which it was to operate. Voting was limited to those with these qualifications: holders of office under the Spanish regime, ability to read, write and speak English or Spanish, and ownership of land or property to the value of P500 (a sizeable sum at the time). The most who had been able to register as voters, in local municipal elections, were 150,081. For the 1907 national assembly election of November 1907 the total registered was only 104,966, of which 98,251 voted. In the census of 1903 the Philippine population was 7,635,426. Philippine politics was shaped from a thin layer of the propertied and educated elite.

The character of colonial politics can be further judged from the distribution of voters. There were about 1200 municipalities. Spreading the 150,000 eligible voters among these would average around 125 voters in each, approximating the number of *principales*. A middle-class candidate would not actually be appealing to the masses for support but to the landowners, money lenders and other propertied ones, to whom he would have to commit himself.

This was the inevitable consequence of excluding all but a tiny fraction of the people from the voting process, and it was an outcome that became increasingly pronounced. At the grassroots level, in the countryside where the bulk of the population lived, the old *cacique* system of the Spaniards continued, in effect, to function. This was assured by the fact that the U.S. colonial regime provided no government or political organization for the *barrio* or village, leaving the local landlord or landlords fully in control. They appointed a *barrio* lieutenant as their authority. As an education system was developed by the U.S. regime, it was theorized by some liberal observers that as literacy grew, *barrio* inhabitants could gradually fulfill the literacy qualification. "Popular education . . . is the greatest enemy of caciqueism . . . As the schools enter, the *caciques* and their domination must go on disappearing."[38] It was a mistaken assumption. The *barrio* lieutenant marshalled the vote in the *barrio*, even into the years of independence, when it came; the minimal education received by the ordinary Filipino under the U.S. education system meant nothing in the face of land ownership and the privileges that went with it. In time, it was not an educational system, but class struggle movements against landlordism that ended *cacique* rule.

Election of the national assembly and the consolidation of the colonial political structure were major steps in satisfying the political ambitions of the middle-class groups. Economic demands from this layer of the population had been less clearly projected. The nature of the Filipino *ilustrado*, for one thing, had been influenced by the disdainful attitude of the Spanish colonial rulers toward work and business activity. Land ownership, equated with political privilege, was more in the minds of the middle-class elite than freedom for business enterprise.

Once the U.S. regime had established its land ownership arrangements—limiting U.S. land acquisition under the Organic Act as demanded by U.S. domestic agricultural producers—it was not difficult for this middle-class ambition to be realized. The land tax introduced by the U.S. Commission as the only available means to raise greatly needed revenues also caused a considerable forfeiting of lands through failure or inability to pay. Disposal of forfeited lands was put in the hands of local officials who were former revolutionary leaders. The U.S. Commission turned a blind eye to the shady property acquisitions that occurred. At the provincial and municipal level, where amnestied former leaders of the Filipino revolutionary forces were often office holders, certain provincial governors, board members and mayors of towns who were not formerly proprietors quickly became so. Many of the provincial governors who had been generals in the revolutionary army became influential landlords.

An example of the trend was Manuel Tinio, who had been a major general in the revolutionary army under Aguinaldo and who had been one of the first to give up under the deadline of Taft's Act No. 78. Tinio became governor of the province of Nueva Ecija in central Luzon and quickly built up a political bailiwick founded on landed wealth.

> Tinio controlled the entire government: the courts of first instance, the justices of the peace, the chiefs of police and the police forces, the mayor and the councils. These, together with a tremendous money power, were in his hands. No one dared to stand up against him.[39]

His rise was duplicated in numerous provinces all over the Philippines. Such an elevation into the circles of wealth by way of political position was achieved by the more prominent middle-class leaders, but the satisfying of ambitions went on at all rungs of the political ladder. The U.S. colonial regime brought a great expansion of the administrative apparatus which opened up new opportunities for professional and *ilustrado* elements who were the most vocal spokesmen for this section of the population.

In the insular government there were civil service posts for 2,697 Filipinos in 1903 and these had grown to 6,791 by 1914. In the 39 provinces, at least three or four of the five provincial offices in this period were open to Filipinos. On the municipal level the number of officials ranged between 10 and 20, depending on the size of the municipality, and there were from 800 to 1200 municipalities (the number changing in the various stages of organization and reorganization). To these categories could be added justices of the peace, teachers, clerical and technical personnel employed in private foreign firms, legal counsel engaged in government or corporation activities. At the outset of the civil regime, a low figure of perhaps 20,000 professionally trained Filipinos were absorbed in employment connected with the colonial government. The number approximately doubled within a decade.[40]

From 1907, 80 of the most publicly active Filipinos were the members of the National Assembly, which absorbed a considerable number of secretarial and other office personnel. Also in 1907, the office of Resident Commissioner in the U.S. was created, the two Commissioners appointed also having their assistants.

The extent to which the ramifications of the colonial regime absorbed the professional or middle-class categories in the Philippines can be seen from a breakdown of the composition of these groups when U.S. rule began. According to the census of 1903 (which was the most accurate in regard to educated strata), the total number with superior education—i.e., anything above primary education—was 76,627, of which 17,607 were women who played virtually no part in political life, leaving 59,020 men. Those engaged in any kind of "professional service" were, however, .8 per cent of the gainfully employed, or only 24,303. This figure included a fairly large number of foreigners (for instance, out of 1,604 physicians and surgeons, 278 were foreign, as were 476 out of the 1,153 listed as clergymen and 137 out of the 862 lawyers).

In the "professional service" figure were included 5,950 government officials of all types, 12,360 clerks, 457 accountants and bookkeepers, 50 "literary and scientific personnel," 725 lawyers, 41 architects, 79 notaries. The overwhelming number of these people became part of the framework of U.S. rule.[41] Add to these the officers in the police forces, the intelligence service and the paramilitary Philippine Constabulary, which were used to enforce order and to put down rebellious tendencies.

The Taft administration introduced a *pensionado* system in 1903, under which Filipino students were sent to the U.S. to study in U.S. universities. A first batch of 100 left in that year. By 1912 there were 200 who had U.S. degrees and, invariably a deeper commitment to U.S. purposes. Although not under firm contract, an obligation to serve the colonial system on return was understood. Most rose to prominent positions in that system. *Pensionados* were drawn from high school graduates from well-to-do families who could afford the high school tuition. This class character of the high schools persisted until 1923.

It might be argued that Filipinos could accept posts in the colonial regime and still retain a nationalist, anti-imperialist and dedicated pro-independence outlook. Conceivably this may be true, but all civil service employees and holders of political-administrative positions had to take the oath of loyalty to the United States and to its possession of the Philippines.

Only two of the ranking leaders who had been in the government of the Philippine Republic—Emilio Aguinaldo and Apolinario Mabini—did not accept or seek posts in the colonial regime (and Aguinaldo accepted the virtual grant of an estate to become a landed proprietor). Thirteen of the Republic's leading personalities sat in the first Philippine Assembly. Only two surviving Filipino military leaders of consequence—Miguel Malvar and Artemio Ricarte—declined any position under the Americans (Ricarte fled to Japan, from whence he kept up opposition to U.S. rule). No organized body of Filipino nationalists from either the wealthy or middle class strata took up a position of challenge outside the system of imperialist control.

This situation as a whole was of great importance to U.S. retention of the Philippines as a colony. One of the issues in the debate between the anti- and the pro-imperialists in the U.S. was the cost of administering a colony, and a principal objective in winning the Filipino middle class to participation in the regime was to minimize the number of U.S. officials and civil service employees, whose pay scales were far higher than those of Filipinos. It is arguable that if Filipinos who were ready to resist U.S. conquest on the battlefield would have been just as ready for passive resistance to acceptance of colonial civilian posts, it could well have tipped the scales toward the anti-imperialist side. For Filipinos, at that point, such a nonviolent struggle of civil disobedience might have yielded all the fruits of self-rule within a relatively short period of time.

Having accepted the limitations imposed on campaigning for independence, the Filipino middle-class groups that were previously a breeding ground of nationalism centered much of their attention now not merely on occupying government posts but on the amount of their salaries. While the benefits of free trade were agitating the wealthy, the "Filipinization" issue of replacing American personnel with Filipinos and especially of equalizing American and Filipino salaries occupied the colonial politicians.

In the U.S. colonial system, Filipinos appointed to top-bracket posts (as members of the Commission, or justices of the Supreme Court) received salaries on a par with their American counterparts. Below, in the civil service, it was different. The average American salary in 1907 was $1,504.06, that of a Filipino $419.46. By 1915 the gap had become wider, with $1,899.50 the average for Americans, and $499.12 the average for Filipinos.[42]

Under the Commission there were 30 executive bureaus. Of these, only four were headed by Filipinos at any time between 1902 and 1913, and these were the most minor ones with low salaries and little or no staffs (Weather, Archives, Patents and Copyrights).

In these circumstances, Filipinization of the civil service became one of the main issues in the colonial politics, being one of the principal means for middle-class elements to advance themselves. This was not a question of ousting the U.S. regime itself, which was not the issue raised. It was just that the willingness of many Filipino leaders to be drawn into the colonial system established by the Americans was based on the expectation of social and economic advancement.

As soon as the Assembly was inaugurated, its members immediately moved to reward themselves for the duties they were rendering. The third bill passed by the Assembly increased the amount of per diem payments to members of legislative committees, which were then enabled to sit even when the Assembly was not in session. Initially the colonial regime had set per diem at $10 per day; this was raised by the Assembly to $15 per day. "Although it was a form of graft," said one of the American members of the Commission, "the Commission joined in appropriating the money."[43] It was recognized as part of the process of corrupting Filipino leaders. However, it was not viewed with the same tolerance by many Filipinos at the grassroots: widespread protests came to the Assembly and to the Commission from municipalities throughout the country against this move by Assembly members to line their own pockets at the expense of public funds.

It was a tendency not limited to people at the top. There were so many cases of municipalities in which all or most of the local income was used for padding the salaries of officials and their staffs that the Commission intervened to correct the situation, out of fear of popular disaffection. Over the five year period from 1902 to 1907, in 80 municipalities all income was spent on inflated salaries, with nothing left for public works or for purchasing even essential office supplies; in 63 others less than 1 per cent of income went for public purposes, and in 163 more over 90 per cent of income was spent on salaries. All told, in 685 municipalities or about two-thirds of the total at the time, most public funds were diverted in this way.[44] Finally, on August 20, 1907 Commission Act No. 1691 put a limit on the amount that could be expended on salaries of officials (50 per cent in first class municipalities, 60 per cent in second class, 65 per cent in third class, 75 per cent in fourth class).[45]

SHAPING THE COLONIAL RULING CLASS

At the outset of the colonial politics there were still a number of the participants and adherents of the crushed Philippine Republic who retained their sense of integrity and nationalism and who were offended by the rush to collaboration by their compatriots. Such men as Rafael Palma, Felipe Agoncillo, Teodoro Sandiko and others sought to adhere to the independence goal and to a noncomformist spirit. They were not the ones who rose in the ranks of the Nacionalista Party which became dominant.

The two who climbed to compete for Filipino political leadership in the colony, Manuel Quezon and Sergio Osmena, could do so only with the blessings of U.S. officials who had confidence in their loyalty to the U.S. regime. Manuel Quezon had been a lieutenant in the Filipino resistance forces and had surrendered in response to Aguinaldo's proclamation in 1901. He became a protege of Pardo de Tavera, head of the Federal Party, and of the American head of the Philippine Constabulary, Col. H.H. Bandholtz, who together obtained his appointment as a prosecuting attorney in the province of Tayabas. The chief task of Quezon in this post was the prosecution of "bandits"—i.e., persisting Filipino rebels—captured by the Constabulary. His assiduousness in this work against mainly peasant revolutionaries won him the backing of Bandholtz's successor in the Constabulary, Col. J.G. Harbord, for governorship of Tayabas in 1905. "I was already a convert to the policy of cooperation with the Government of the United States," said Quezon later of these steps, which led straight to the National Assembly.[46] When a millenarian revolutionary movement, the *Ejercito Libertador Nacional,* arose in Tayabas in 1906, "Mr. Quezon took the field in person ... and assisted the constabulary in breaking up this thing before it had time to gather headway."[47]

Sergio Osmena had an early political career almost identical to that of Quezon, except that he did not join the revolutionary army of the Republic but merely wrote in support of it as a journalist. He, too, was made a prosecuting attorney by the U.S. authorities, in his native Cebu province, from which he was elevated to the Cebu governorship in 1905. During his term, in 1905-1906, a peasant-based rebellion developed for independence, and Governor Osmena "shouldered a gun" (which he didn't do for the Republic) and "in cordial cooperation with the Constabulary" put down the rebellion, for which he won great praise from the U.S. Commission for having "completely cleared his province of the organized bands of fanatical outlaws which had infested it."[48] Osmena was regarded with such favor by U.S. colonial officials that, with their approval, he became the leader of the National Assembly, as its Speaker.

The Nacionalista Party rapidly came under the leadership of these men and others like them whose grasp and manipulation of politics developed out of their subordinate relationship with the U.S. Commission. It was not that they and others in the Assembly did not devote themselves to needs of the Filipino people; they passed a good many laws contributing to national development, such as the building of *barrio* schools and the provision of public works, but these were adopted within the circumscribed policies of the U.S. Commission.

One of the outstanding features of Philippine politics in the decade after the inauguration of the Assembly was the relatively quick rise of the Nacionalista Party to virtual one-party dominance. In the 1907 election it had been split into petty factions that together won 58 of the 80 Assembly seats; in 1909 it took 62 out of 81 seats, repeating that same majority in 1912; by 1916, by which time an upper-house Senate replacing the U.S. Commission had been established in the Jones Law, the Nationalistas swept up 74 seats in the lower house and all but one in the Senate. What this represented was an absorption of the Progresista Party, its support base among the big landlords and urban wealthy, and its voters.

It was inevitable that the main landowning groups would seek to work through the party effectively in power, which dealt with the U.S. regime and had a voice in Washington in the Resident Commission, and would endeavor to have their interests furthered in the Assembly as well as in the U.S. Commission. This was assured by the control of the local organizations of the political parties by the largest and most influential landlords. A landlord desire to have their interests looked after by the dominant party was matched on the other side of the coin by the desire of Nacionalista leaders to obtain the financial and electoral backing of the landlords.

From its first session onwards, the Nacionalista-controlled Assembly acted in behalf of these interests, with a plethora of bills passed for the reduction, the remittance, or the abolition of the land tax. As the main municipal and provincial revenue-raising means introduced by the Commission, it fell chiefly on the landowner. One Assembly bill (No. 352) exempted all uncultivated land from the tax, a measure that could benefit most the large landowner. Such measures were approved by the Nacionalistas despite the fact that the land tax was the main revenue source from which schools and public improvements were financed. In addition, the Assembly, responding to the demands of wealthy urban Filipinos, undertook to cut sharply the taxes imposed on distilleries and the tobacco industry.

Within a few years it was plain that a predominantly one-party rule was developing, with a unification of the main ruling class sectors under the banner of the Nacionalista Party. This trend, in which the various class groupings in the Philippines were finding it possible to exist harmoniously beneath a common political cover, epitomized a growing arrangement between middle class and wealthy landed circles, in which both could have ambitions satisfied without contradictions. Inevitably, the landlord-*comprador* groups made increasingly wealthy by free trade held the purse-strings and determined the central policies of the Nacionalista Party.

The Nacionalista-controlled colonial legislature reciprocated with extensive aid to the landlord-*comprador* interests. In 1916, the boom period of World War I, it established the Philippine National Bank to finance export producers who wanted to take advantage of the expanded U.S. market. Loans were dispensed without credit consideration, principally to sugar centrals (extraction and refining mills) and coconut oil plants, far exceeding the lending limits. Investigations eventually uncovered up to $37,544,500 in losses, from unsecured loans not repaid. The Philippine National Bank, in essence, was the funding channel for the Philippine side of free trade for the rest of the colonial period.

The common ground between the landlord-*comprador* groups and the aspiring politicians of the middle class was demonstrated in the Assembly and later in post-Jones Law Congress by two predominant legislative trends: for financial and taxation arrangements that would benefit agricultural producers and related interests, and for "Filipinization" which would put civil service, judiciary and other posts in Filipino hands. Such strivings for greater opportunity within the structure of American rule was acceptable to all Filipino ruling groups, and it had a pronounced effect on the nature of Filipino nationalism and on the independence movement.

An increasing domination of Philippine colonial politics, and of the chief political party, by conservative landlord-*comprador* interests, which was the logical outcome of this development, meant that the brand of nationalism and independence projected by Nacionalista leaders would be used principally as a device to gain concessions for these groups. Landlord producers who had gained access to the U.S. market nevertheless continued to chafe under the strictures of an American colonial system that taxed them in a way not experienced under Spain and that, due to pressure from competing U.S. domestic producers, put restraints on agricultural loans and credits. To the extent that obtaining relief from these problems involved a struggle against relevant policies of the U.S. colonial administration, their maneuvers at times had a semblance of nationalism. They soon found it convenient to have their interests taken care of through the budding Filipino politics of the colony, and the vocally intense nationalism of those who fought the Filipinization battle in the Assembly and other political arenas was not disturbing to the free trade producers because they realized that it would place Filipinos in positions of greater power, over whom they would have more influence than over American officials.

This process reached its full development during the second decade of U.S. rule, which was highlighted by two significant developments. One was the passage of the Jones Act by the U.S. Congress in 1916, extending Filipinization of the colonial regime further and promising Philippine independence in the long run. The other was the expansion of the U.S. free trade market for Philippine export products, caused by World War I, coupled with the increased Filipino capacity for taking advantage of it by modernization of its sugar and coconut industries.

An episode soon after the end of World War I illustrated, and was a comment upon, the process. The Jones Act had been supported in its four-year course through the U.S. Congress by Manuel Quezon, who served as Philippine Resident Commissioner in Washington from 1909–1916, but it had actually been drafted by members of the Anti-Imperialist League, particularly Moorfield Storey, and the AIL had given much attention to Quezon and other Filipino political leaders as the presumed spokesmen of the independence movement. However, the independence pledge in the Jones Act had been virtually nullified by the insertion of the provision making "stable government" a condition. At this point leading figures in the Anti-Imperialist League began to part company with Quezon and his associates, who expressed satisfaction with the Jones Act as it stood. The AIL was not content with it, "but had to be satisfied because the representatives of the Filipinos were."

In 1919 the AIL, concerned that an expansionist Republican Party would return to power in the U.S. election of 1920 and would postpone indefinitely any hope of an independence pledge being carried out, strongly urged Quezon and other Filipino leaders to press an independence step upon the Wilson administration while it was still in office. Quezon declined to do so, claiming it was "not opportune." This led Erving Winslow, secretary of the League, to make a bitter attack on Quezon for betraying the cause of independence. The Resident Commissioners in Washington at the time, Jaime C. de Veyra and

Teodoro Yangco, were also condemned for failing to make the independence demand. AIL leader Fisher Warren

> doubted the sincerity of some of the Filipino leaders in their demand for
> immediate independence. He feared that they were asking for it only
> because it would mean political death in the Philippine Islands to waver in
> its advocacy. The Filipino people, the anti-imperialist leaders declared,
> were steadfast in their demand for freedom even though these political
> leaders hesitated for fear of the effects of immediate separation from the
> U.S.[49]

Those effects would be upon the profits of the landlord-*comprador*
groups enjoying greater access to a free trade market.

III

Undying Resistance

The most authentic account of Philippine history during the past century is being told by contemporary Filipino historians and researchers with a nationalist outlook. These are inclined to emphasize the role of those left out of the usual U.S. records of Philippine-U.S. relations, or else minimized or condemned—the rebels, the dissidents, the militant workers and peasants, the resisting nationalists and anti-imperialists, the revolutionaries, the Filipino people who never yielded to colonial or neo-colonial rule and never stopped resisting it.

In an important sense, U.S. policy toward the Philippines, past and present, is better judged by its attitude toward the ordinary Filipino people and their aspirations than toward the wealthy and elite. The struggles of Filipino working people and the leaders they have produced comprise one of the main forces in Philippine history and the popular base for the only real alternative to the partnership with imperialism that has characterized Philippine government up to now.

There has been a consistent strand of revolutionary opposition to foreign domination and of working-class struggle against Filipino landlords and capitalists. Filipino historians point to over 200 recorded episodes of armed uprising—some brief, some of long duration. If most of these were isolated or localized, particularly in the Spanish period, it was chiefly because nationhood, national consciousness and a sense of national unity had not been fully attained. With the creation of the *Katipunan* and its assumption of leadership of a more or less organized revolution against Spain, the revolutionary strand became a maturing force with a national character.

The *Katipunan* is considered the starting point for the left in the Philippines. Its founder and original leader, Andres Bonifacio, is the national hero of the Filipino labor and peasant movements. He was an artisan and wage-worker in Manila and those whom he recruited to

45

organize his movement were from the nascent working class. The movement had a strong base in the *gremios,* the guild-like embryonic workers' organizations of printers, carriage-makers, railroad workers, cigarmakers and others. The American army officer with an anti-Filipino bias who compiled the captured records of the Philippine Revolution, Captain John Taylor, wrote of the *Katipunan*'s rise: "In two years its lodges were the controlling factor in every Tagalog town. Its officers, as well as members, were drawn from the uneducated classes."[1]

Middle-class and wealthy Filipinos approached for contributions to the *Katipunan* recoiled in fright because it sprang from "the great unwashed" and, because its declaration of principles called the working people the creators of wealth and the mainspring of society, they denounced it as "socialistic." Actually, Bonifacio's movement was not consciously class-based, its main shortcoming being a lack of ideology or program. Its principles spoke vaguely of brotherhood and mutual help, while its ceremonies and oaths drew inspiration from those of the Masonic Order. Working people joined it in large numbers because the *Katipunan* opened its doors to them and strove for mass membership — and because it proposed the direct action of armed revolution to win national freedom.

Class attitudes were not introduced by the *Katipunan,* which focused its appeals on nationalism. The class factor emerged from the behavior of the middle-class personages who joined when the movement's strength became evident and who, when armed struggle began, engineered the capture of its leadership, including the ouster of Bonifacio from a leading post and his murder when he protested the takeover. Emilio Aguinaldo and the group that conspired with him to seize control were all from the elite strata who had served as mayors of towns, justices of the peace, lawyers and in other non-laboring posts.

Representing the ambitious middle class, Emilio Aguinaldo, first as president of the revolutionary government and then as president of the First Philippine Republic, made his alliances with the traitorous wealthy Filipinos, on whom he bestowed the key positions in his government. To appease the wealthy he dissolved the *Katipunan* in July 1898. These were steps on the path to betrayal.

The masses of the working people, on the other hand, were steadfastly loyal to the revolution and persisted in the struggle for independence. In the revolutionary army recruited from the masses, the spirit of national liberation was strongest. General Antonio Luna, commander-in-chief of the army in the early stage of the war against U.S. occupation (until he was murdered by those around Aguinaldo who wanted to negotiate a deal with the U.S. authorities), wrote of the people's attitude:

The Filipino people want independence, and I shall defend to the last the cause of my country, thus complying with my oath to my flag. Without talking in the superlative, I sincerely believe that it is better to die in the battlefield than to accept foreign domination . . . I feel that I am speaking the truth, for in a sort of plebiscite I have asked the people if they want autonomy. Do you know their answer? "Long live independence! Down with autonomy!"

This was the answer of either central provinces with which I communicated. I asked the fleeing refugees if they were discouraged, if they wanted peace, or wished to return to their towns, and the women, the old people and the children all answered: "We have begun the fight for independence; let us go ahead; better to lose everything than to live under a ruler that annihilates and destroys us!"[2]

It was this popular sentiment that caused the war of resistance to continue long after the middle-class leaders had surrendered and accommodated themselves to U.S. rule. Initially the army had been officered by these men of the educated elite, and for a time they carried on with the guerrilla warfare to which the struggle was forced to shift in November 1899. As soon as the guerrilla stage set in, many of those who had been associated with Bonifacio undertook to revive the *Katipunan*. On December 6, 1899 an instruction to recreate the *Katipunan* was circulated by General Luciano San Miguel who was in command in Central Luzon. In one of his communications San Miguel wrote.

It is almost certain that this society will bring us victory. Had not the Katipunan been abolished, the war would have been terminated and there would now be no small independent or disaffected parties.

According to San Miguel, the town people had not been responding while the *Katipunan* was out of existence.[3] This state of affairs changed dramatically as the guerrilla struggle developed, and as the *Katipunan* was reconstituted, a fact attested to by the U.S. military governor, General Arthur MacArthur, at the end of 1900, reporting that

the towns, regardless of the fact of American occupation and town organization, are the actual bases for all insurgent military activities ... The success of this unique system of war depends upon almost complete unity of action of the entire native population. That such unity is a fact is too obvious to admit of discussion.[4]

Although the last overall Filipino leader in the field, General Miguel Malvar, was forced by brutal suppression methods to surrender on

May 6, 1902, to decree an end to the war, and to call on Filipinos still fighting to yield, this was not the position of the *Katipunan* or of the majority of the people. For nearly a decade after the official termination of the war by Filipino leaders and the U.S. government, armed revolutionary struggle continued against the new colonial order. Sometimes called the "second wind" of the struggle, it had a different character than that conducted under the banner of the middle-class rebels. A few of these remained with the people, but the leadership of the resistance now came largely from the peasant masses and the artisan elements who had predominated in the original *Katipunan*, and the struggles were directed against both American colonialists and Filipino collaborators-exploiters, combining features of nationalism and class struggle.

On May 6, 1902, the same day General Malvar issued his call for Filipinos in arms to surrender, a manifesto was circulated by General Macario Sakay from his headquarters near Morong, Rizal. It proclaimed:

> It has been seen that during the revolution in the Philippines, all our countrymen have no unity, and this lack of unity is caused by love of money, wealth and knowledge; courage is lacking in all, only self-interest is paramount . . . Everybody is reminded that as of this date, upon the proclamation of this Order, anybody who contributes or gives aid and comfort to the Government of the United States of America will be considered a traitor to this native land, and is, therefore, within the preview of the Order known as Martial Law.[5]

Macario Sakay, a former Manila carriage-maker, had been a member of the original *Katipunan* nucleus and was close to Bonifacio. Together with fellow *Katipunan* members he undertook to recreate the Philippine Republic (which was termed the "Tagalog Republic"). Sakay himself became President and Commander-in-Chief, Francisco Carreon Vice-President and executive secretary, and Luciano San Miguel, overall commander of operations in the field.[6] A reinvigoration of the *Katipunan* accompanied this step and in the latter half of 1902 alone the organization was reported to have spread extensively from Rizal and Cavite to Bulacan, Pampanga, Zambales and Pangasinan, and to be strong in the city of Manila.

San Miguel was killed in action in March 1903 but the new phase of the guerrilla struggle went on unabated for four more years, with obvious popular support. The U.S. colonial regime dealt with it not as a legitimate revolt but as criminal activity. U.S. military and civilian authorities had been ruthless enough in dealing with the Philippine

Republic and its forces, but the fighters and supporters of the renewed Republic were treated like outlaws and hunted down.

The Commission Government of William H. Taft, with the approval of its three Filipino members, adopted a law known as the "Bandolerismo Statute" on November 4, 1902, which termed those in arms as "brigands" and "robbers" and provided the death penalty or imprisonment for not less than 20 years for those apprehended. Wealthy and middle-class Filipinos who had accommodated themselves to U.S. rule joined in the repressive measures. One of a number of anti-guerrilla laws adopted was one authorizing provincial governors (Filipinos) to reconcentrate civilians in order to deny guerrillas support.[7] Provincial jails and the American-run Bilibid prison in Manila were crammed with "brigandage" suspects in these years, with a soaring death rate from overcrowding and malnourishment, 72 per 1,000 in 1902, 99 per 1,000 in 1903, 118 per 1,000 in 1904, and by September 1905, 438 per 1,000.[8]

Sakay, in April 1905, addressed a circular to all foreign consuls in Manila:

> We, the Tagalogs, now in the mountains of our native land, fighting against the United States of America for the independence of our country, do hereby proclaim the following in order that truth and justice be known and given to us: 1st, We, the true and loyal sons of our beloved country, love and cherish the independence of our land. 2nd, We, the true revolutionists, in truth and in deeds, are not *tulisanes* [bandits], as the government of the United States calls us. We cannot be *tulisanes* as our enemies think we are, for we have our own government and constitution. We fight for the sake of our land and we uphold the spirit of justice in our war with the enemies . . .

The foreign consuls were urged to "acquaint the rest of the world with our true intent and aims."[9]

In 1906 the U.S. authorities, unable to suppress by force of arms a revolt that had become an obstacle to a stabilized colony, put pressure on Filipino leaders who had submitted and were getting ready for the Assembly election. They were told there would be no election until the revolt was ended. A group of elite figures aspiring to office tricked Sakay, his ranking officers and many of his men into surrendering with a pledge of guaranteed freedom. ("We will not allow the Americans to torture you or harm you and we will liberate you from prison. We will protect you from any punishment whatsoever.")[10]

Promised to be able to conduct the fight for independence in other ways, Sakay and the others surrendered on July 20, 1906. Shortly afterward they were all treacherously arrested by Constabulary troops headed personally by their commander, Col. Bandholtz, tried under the "Bandolerismo Statute," and given maximum sentences. Macario Sakay and one of his officers, Lucio de Vega, were sentenced to death and hung in September 1907, two months before the Assembly election. Sakay, on the scaffold, called out:

> Death comes to all of us sooner or later, so I will face the Lord Almighty calmly. But I want to tell you that we are not bandits or robbers, as the Americans have accused us, but members of the revolutionary force that defended our mother country, the Philippines. Farewell! Long live the Republic and may our independence be born in the future! Farewell! Long live the Philippines![11]

Armed revolts continued to take place throughout the first decade of the century in many parts of the Philippines, for independence and against the abuses of collaborating Filipino ruling elements, in the provinces of Central Luzon, Albay, Tayabas, Samar, Cebu, Negros, Mindanao. Attempts to revive the *Katipunan* persisted in the Luzon provinces. As U.S. rule with Filipino collaboration became more firmly established, however, Filipino workers and peasants turned to other ways to press demands for independence and social justice.

THE TRADE UNIONS, BORN IN THE INDEPENDENCE STRUGGLE

The movement for independence took a number of inter-related forms. It was an issue that gripped the Filipino people and compelled even the most thoroughgoing collaborators with the new colonialism and their nascent parties to give lip service to it. A more forthright and principled expression of unquelled nationalism was the Philippine Independent Church, founded and led by the former Catholic Bishop, Gregorio Aglipay, who broke with Rome and the Spanish friars during the revolution, launched his church in 1899 and served as a guerrilla general as well. More worrying to the U.S., however, was the growth of a trade union movement capable of bringing organized masses into open opposition to U.S. imperialism.

Philippine trade unions had their origin in the *gremios* or guilds which developed in the Spanish colony. The printers' *gremio* was a loyal part of the *Katipunan.* Later, its members comprised the printing staffs of all the newspapers, American-owned or otherwise, that sprang up in Manila at the outset of U.S. rule. In June 1901, the first formal trade union was created out of the *gremio* in the plant of the U.S.-owned paper, *Manila Times,* calling itself the *Union de Impresores.* It quickly spread to other printing establishments and on December 30, 1901 an integrated *Union de Impresores de Filipinas* (UIF) was formed.[12]

The successful launching of the UIF stimulated the calling on February 2, 1902 of a labor congress which brought together other *gremios* to establish a labor federation, the *Union Obrera Democratica* (UOD) or Democratic Workers Union. Included were tobacco workers, carpenters, cooks, mariners and laborers.

This fledgling labor federation had more of the character of a mass movement than of a trade union. Its strongly nationalistic program made the freedom of the Philippines and the encouragement of Filipino nationalism central. Consistent with this, the UOD chose Isabelo de los Reyes, an *ilustrado* nationalist who had been arrested (wrongly) as a *Katipunan* suspect in 1896 and deported to Spain for imprisonment in Barcelona's Montjuich prison. There he became acquainted with incarcerated anarchists and their ideas and with some Marxist works, a few of which he brought back to the Philippines in October 1901. Through de los Reyes a strong syndicalist influence was injected into the UOD and subsequent labor organization, combining trade union and political demands.

Choice of Isabelo de los Reyes as president was part of an inclination by Filipino working people to turn to *ilustrado*-type figures as leaders. On the other hand, nationalist political leaders like de los Reyes and others who followed him associated themselves with the organized workers and peasants because of the mass base they constituted.

On July 4, 1902 the UOD, choosing as symbolic the U.S. Independence Day, called a mass meeting of its members and of workers and employees. In response, 50,000 turned out for a demonstration in Manila. Speakers demanded independence. It alarmed the U.S. authorities who stationed troops in the city. Taft called the UOD leaders "radicals, subversives and anarchists" and put them under police surveillance. It set the pattern of U.S. colonial policy toward Filipino trade unions.

With this curtain-raiser the UOD moved to larger goals, presenting a set of demands on August 2, 1902 for wage increases to all the firms where it had members, many of them U.S. companies which reacted with rage, calling the UOD "seditious." When the demands were rejected, a general strike was called. Taft called out the U.S. cavalry to parade and intimidate workers and to be posted at struck plants. When this didn't work, de los Reyes was arrested and charged with sedition. Under pressure, he resigned from the UOD presidency. Much of the pressure came from Filipino collaborators. The strike was broken, and the UOD itself began to disintegrate.[13]

Most of its members, however, remained firm and sought out another leader to replace de los Reyes. This was another *ilustrado* nationalist, Dr. Dominador Gomez. He, too, had recently returned from Spain, where he had supported the revolution, the Republic, and the resistance against U.S. conquest. Accepting the presidency of a reorganized and renamed labor federation, now called *Union Obrera Democratica de Filipinas* (UODF), Gomez aroused the workers with a fighting speech, calling on them to "oppose our countrymen who want us to be cowards and afraid to fight!" He told them to "fight with me with heads up" and urged them

> Do not be like some of our countrymen who are wise and able but have no courage to fight our masters and oppressors. They are timid and would like always to retreat. The banner of the UODF is dynamic nationalism against any form of imperialism, against oppression.[14]

With this kind of leadership the federation was reinvigorated and expanded. By the first anniversary of its founding, on February 2, 1903, the UODF had the affiliation of 150 unions and 20,000 organized members. It campaigned for an eight-hour day and for May 1st to be proclaimed a workers' holiday. It fought the move by U.S. businessmen in Manila to import low-paid labor from China and Japan in order to break UODF unions, using strike action to force wage rises.

Defying the Taft regime's refusal to declare May 1st a holiday, as well as denial of permits for demonstrations in favor of it, the UODF on May 1, 1903 called the biggest demonstration held to that time, 100,000 workers and supporters turning out from Manila and its suburbs. They converged on the colonial government residence at Malacanang Palace, shouting: "Down with American imperialism! We want freedom! Give us an eight-hour day!" At the gates U.S. troops with fixed bayonets and a small cannon confronted them. Dr. Gomez addressed the throng:

> "We were told that America is the mother of democracy, but the American governor in Malacanang is afraid to talk with the people who want democracy. The Americans say they are for freedom, but why is it that they want to curtail our freedom by displaying fixed bayonets? . . . In our struggle for better working conditions, we must at the same time struggle for the liberation of our motherland."[15]

The U.S. regime arrested Dr. Gomez, charging him with "sedition and illegal association." The complaint filed against him in the Manila court of first instance on May 29, 1903 by U.S. prosecuting attorney Charles H. Smith charged him with "founding, directing and presiding over an illegal association, the purposes and circumstances of which are contrary to public morals and whose object is to commit certain crimes punished by the Penal Code." Among the "crimes" was propaganda for "the development of a hostile feeling and a formal movement of men and women against the U.S. Government in the Philippines." Furthermore, it was charged that Gomez, "in pursuance with said regulations and purpose of said organization," had

> regularly and continually communicated, corresponded, advised, confederated and conspired with Faustino Guillermo and other officers, agents, representatives and members of certain armed bands and certain combinations of men in the Philippine Islands organized to commit, and committing, the crimes of theft, rape, robbery and murder in the said islands, and further, to commit the crimes of sedition and treason therein.

Dr. Gomez was found guilty of the charges by the American Judge John G. Sweeney, whose decision read: "The facts and circumstances of this case established beyond a reasonable doubt that the defendant entered into a conspiracy with others, which resulted in the formation of this association, *Union Obrera*. The defendant caused himself to be elected president thereof and prepared the regulations ostensibly as a labor union, but the secret and real purpose of the defendant and his co-conspirators and the purpose of the organization being to resist the Administration and overthrow the American government in the Philippine Islands, and to this end he conspired and confederated with Faustino Guillermo, Luciano San Miguel and others in the Philippine Islands who were and are engaged in the crimes of theft, rape, robbery and murder." Sweeney sentenced Gomez to four years and two months at hard labor and fined him P3,250.[16]

This case was appealed to the Philippine Supreme Court, which took four years to rule—on September 28, 1907—that, despite "much suspicious proof," the evidence adduced was insufficient, and lifted the sentence from Gomez. It is impossible not to link that leniency with the fact that it was Gomez who persuaded Macario Sakay to surrender, promising him security and freedom, and who pressed Sakay to plead guilty at his trial in groundless expectation of clemency. Gomez found his place among the middle-class aspirants to an Assembly seat, to which he was subsequently elected in 1909 (reportedly with the support of Americans in his Manila constituency to whom he promised appointments). He retained the respect of workers, however, for his organizational achievements and for continuing to defend labor interests.

With the arrest and harassment of its leaders, and with its members under pressure from American and Filipino businessmen who threatened dismissal and wage cuts, the UODF was effectively destroyed as a federation. Affiliated unions withdrew one by one.

The pressure was combined with another repressive device. Governor-general Taft brought from the U.S. a representative of Samuel Gompers' American Federation of Labor "to advise Filipino labor leaders in matters relating to organization and propaganda." The man provided by the AFL, Edward Rosenberg, immediately contacted and invited the leaders of unions in the UODF to attend a conference to set up a new federation. This met on June 13, 1903 and agreed to Rosenberg's proposal to launch the *Union del Trabajo de Filipinas* (UTF), and to a pre-written constitution and rules.

The UTF constitution had to be submitted to Taft for approval, which was given with the comment that "I believe that some advantage may be derived from an association such as yours, if it is intelligently directed and confines its mission to proper labor ends" (i.e., no political aims). Said Taft:

> "Your society should teach him [the laborer] to work constantly for the time he has agreed, to work in the interest of his employer, in other words, to be a laborer worthy of his hire, and if your society has furnished the capitalists who wish to invest their money here workmen who do well the work for which they are paid, you will have accomplished all that can be hoped of an association in this community. You may rest assured, gentlemen, that as long as you pursue the legal object of your society, and only exercise the rights that the law grants you, the Commission, the civil government, and the entire government, will stand at your side to protect your rights."[17]

Imposing limits on Filipino trade union activity meant the denial of the right to call for and to campaign for independence, duplicated the limits placed at the same time on political parties and their activity, which were made to confine themselves to the legislative and administrative role of running a U.S. colony. In essence, Rosenberg's assignment was to set up a labor organization for supplying U.S. companies with disciplined and submissive workers. One of the rules of the UTF, demanded by the U.S. business community, was that a strike had to be approved by a *nine-tenths* vote of the striking union and approved formally by the executive of the UTF.

To ensure the complete captivity of the emerging Philippine trade unions, the Taft-Rosenberg measures included setting up rival unions wherever an existing union resisted the U.S. controls, the establishment of craft unions in place of the industrial unions that Filipino workers were developing, and the attaching of Philippine unions as branches or locals to unions in the U.S. As an official of the U.S. Bureau of Labor wrote in a 1905 study of labor conditions in the colony:

> The best influences of American trade unionism can probably be brought to bear in the Philippines by organizing the skilled trades followed or supervised by Americans and Europeans . . . These unions become locals of the parent organization in the U.S., and keep aloof from native complications.
> . . . it is probable that the Filipino labor movement has come to stay. It can be destroyed only by force, and such a recourse will hardly be adopted even by the most conservative government. As a movement ultimately to be reckoned with, it is much preferable that it should be governed by American rather than Southern European ideals, and that its organizations should be assimilated to trade unions in the U.S. This might lessen the probability that a political labor party will arise, with great influence in the local government and in the popular house of the insular legislature. Persons familiar with the Filipino character consider that the existence of such a party, if it commanded a large and well-organized body of voters, might greatly hamper the authorities in maintaining peace in case of strikes or other labor difficulties, as well as embarrass the general administration of the government.[18]

Craft unionism of the AFL type, however, although attempted, had little lasting success. The major effort made was to split up the printers' union, the UIF, with the forming of a rival "typographical union." It failed. UIF members rejected the craft union idea and instead gave even stronger emphasis to organizing a union of all workers in the printing trades. At a conference in 1906 the UIF proclaimed itself a national industrial union. Elected as general secretary was Crisanto Evangelista, who was to become the outstanding trade union leader.

No Filipino trade union ever submitted to being a mere branch of a U.S. union.

For a time, U.S. tactics of suppression, harassment and splitting disoriented Filipino workers, but not for long. On May 1, 1913 a labor congress was held in Manila with delegations from 36 full-fledged trade unions. It established a new authentic federation, the *Congreso Obrero de Filipinas* (COF). The primary resolution adopted by the congress declared support for the movement for independence.

Mainly a federation of industrial unions, the COF marked the failure of the U.S. imperialist attempt to control and shape the Philippine labor movement. Splitting methods were resorted to, several COF unions with conservative leaders being persuaded to break away to set up a rival federation, the *Federacion del Trabajo de Filipinas* (FTF). It became a center for company unionism and no-strike agreements. The COF, however, had the principal impact and growing influence. Set up shortly before the outbreak of World War I, in which the Philippine economy was made an adjunct of the U.S. war effort, it had to confront a war boom when U.S. companies and Filipino landlord-*comprador* groups made large profits while Filipino workers had to shoulder inflated prices for basic commodities. Alongside the rapid growth of sugar centrals, lumber mills, coconut-oil mills, shoe factories, cigar and cigarette factories and others, union organization and strike struggles were led by the COF. Whereas there were six strikes in 1913 involving only 1,182 workers, there were 17 in 1916 involving 4,485 workers, 50 in 1917 with 5,842 strikers, 84 in 1918 involving 16,289 workers, 67 in 1919 bringing out 4,150 and 68 in 1920 affecting 11,138.[19] Two major strikes were of particular importance for development of the Filipino trade unions: one by the UIF in 1918 which won extensive demands and raised the stature of UIF, and the other a bitter struggle by workers in the U.S.-owned Manila Electric Company (Meralco) during which picketline violence occurred when the Constabulary was brought in against the strikers, several of whom were killed.

A NEW PERIOD OF STRUGGLE MATURES

The end of World War I and the beginning of the third decade of U.S. colonial rule saw the convergence of several significant historical trends. Emerging from the war as a much stronger imperialist power, the U.S. made plain its intention to retain the Philippines as a colony, ignoring the independence pledge in the Jones Act and rejecting Filipino independence petitions. Paralleling this was the increase of power and reactionary influence of the Filipino landlord-*comprador* groups that were enriched further by the war boom, especially the sugar barons, who benefited from and favored the prolongation of free trade colonialism. For Filipino workers and peasants, however, the combination of these two forces caused intensified exploitation.

Within Philippine society a number of trends converged as well. The landlord-*comprador* groups nurtured by free trade consolidated their dominance in the political parties. At the same time the failure of the U.S. regime to conduct land reform, and the pattern of land ownership it encouraged (the acquisition of land by many of the collaborating middle-class elements), contributed to the deeper impoverishment of the peasantry and the plunging of greater numbers of them into onerous conditions of share tenancy. Suffering worsening conditions of deprivation and exploitation, the peasantry moved toward another stage of rebellion with the organization of militant peasant unions. In general, the alliance that had tended to form at the turn of the century between middle-class revolutionaries and the nascent working class movement dissipated as the former found accommodation in the political and economic life of the colony, while a maturing labor movement was increasingly able to produce its own working-class leaders.

Along with these developments were others outside the Philippines that had a growing impact on currents moving among the Filipino people. Most important of these was the October Revolution in 1917, which produced the Soviet Union and the building of the first socialist state. As elsewhere in the colonial part of the world the Socialist Revolution and its message of national liberation seeped inevitably into the Philippines and inspired militant workers and peasants. In addition, the development of the revolutionary left in the United States, spurred by the October Revolution and the creation of the Communist International, produced a new anti-imperialist force acting to support Filipinos in their struggle for independence.

The growth of a revolutionary movement among Filipino workers and peasants in the 1920s was not implanted from outside, however, but had wholly native origins in Philippine colonial conditions. Neither workers nor peasants shared in the prosperity of the landlord and *comprador*. There was an extreme widening of the gap in their incomes, which changed little relatively for the great majority. In 1926 the cost of living for a city worker's family was officially put at P2.32 per day, far in excess of the average wage. In the countryside the cost of living for a farm laborer's family was set at P1.82 per day, more than twice his average wage (not taking account of the extreme poverty of tenant farmers, most of whom were in life-long debt to landlords).

An analyst of the period of U.S. rule up to World War II commented:

> It is probable that the actual consumption level of the Filipino people *as a whole* rose greatly owing to free and preferential trade with the United States. However, the popular belief that the Filipino *working class* enjoyed a higher level of living under the American regime than under the Spanish regime does not agree with facts and figures.[20]

Manuel Quezon, speaking as president of the Commonwealth in the 1930s, made the same point:

The men and women who till the soil or work in the factories are hardly better off now than they were during the Spanish regime. Of course, wages have increased as compared with those paid when we were under the sovereignty of Spain, and those wages are higher than in any other Oriental country, with the possible exception of Japan. But it should be remembered that money could buy more in those Spanish days than it can now, and furthermore, in the relationship between employer and employee in the days of old, there was a consideration of higher value to the employee than the monetary compensation itself.[21]

Quezon's latter comparison applied particularly to the Filipino peasants for whom U.S. rule brought more hardship and misery than were experienced by any other section of the population. The land question and revolt against abusive exploitation by the Spanish friar religious orders had been the engine of the Revolution of 1896. Landless or poor peasants composed the overwhelming majority of soldiers who fought in defense of the Republic against the invading U.S. army, a war in which the right to land was mingled with the right to independence. One of the factors contributing to the "second wind" of the War of Resistance was the widely circulated report that the U.S. regime would allow the friars to return and reclaim their estates. So damaging was that report that the Commission government took steps to dampen down the issue by purchasing the bulk of the friar estates and converting them into public lands for sale. Of broader significance were the colonial government's land laws which supposedly enabled the landless to obtain land. In actuality, combined with the land tax and the non-provision of assistance to poor peasants who might obtain a grant, the U.S. land laws resulted in reinforcing the landlord system, the perpetuation of large land holdings, the loss of land by peasants unable to sustain payments of purchase, and the spread of tenancy with all its evils.

The first census conducted by the U.S. colonial regime in 1903 had shown the existence of 815,000 farms of which 19 per cent or around 160,000 were worked by tenants. This was prior to the purchase of the bulk of 200,000 hectares of friar land that accounted for 60,000 of the tenants. Theoretically, these lands were to be sold to the tenants or to others. In addition, the U.S. regime's Homestead Act was designed to open up new lands. The next census of 1918 did show an increase in the number of farms, to 1,955,000. However, it also showed an increase in the rate of tenancy to 22 per cent: 435,000 farms were now under tenancy conditions. From this it was obvious that U.S. colonial land policies were not solving the basic land problem, the tenancy question. Furthermore, the increase in the number of farms concealed the fact that the vast majority were very small, less than two hectares in size, while the process of family land inheritance tended to split these up into smaller fragments. Concealed in the figures, too, was the minority of large landholders who were unaffected by the U.S. land laws. They were able to grab the land of debt-ridden small owners, converting them into tenants. This was made evident by the census of 1939 which revealed the process during the 1920s and 1930s: the number of farms worked by tenants had risen to 575,000, or 35 per cent of the total. The agrarian problem and peasant poverty had become massive. As for the landlord-tenant relationship and its deterioration, hinted at by Quezon, it was featured by obscenely extreme conditions of usury with interest rates of up to 300 per cent exacted on tenants forced to borrow rice or funds to survive after being compelled to turn over most of their harvest as the landlord's share.

First signs of peasant rebelliousness came in 1919, with the formation of the first Philippine peasant unions. In Bulacan province the *Union de Aparceros de Filipinas* (Union of Philippine Peasants) was organized by Jacinto Manahan. Another, called *Anak-Pawis* (literally, Sons of Sweat), was set up in Pampanga province, in the barrios of the town of Mexico and surrounding towns, by Estanislao Garcia. Both unions set out to fight debt slavery, evictions, unfair crop-sharing, low wages and other landlord abuses.

By 1922 the UAF was renamed the *Confederacion de Aparceros y Obreros de Filipinas* (Confederation of Peasants and Agricultural Laborers of the Philippines) as it spread into other Central Luzon provinces. By 1924 it had expanded into Southern Luzon and its name was changed to *Kalipunang Pambansa sa mga Magbubukid sa Pilipinas* (KPMP, or National Association of Philippine Peasants), a name retained for the next 18 years. Its shift from Spanish to the Philippine language was significant, reflecting the resurgence of nationalism among the people.

The early 1920s were a time of ferment and revolutionary stirring. Along with a growth of class struggle consciousness, the failure of the political parties of the collaborating bourgeoisie to achieve or to lead a real fight for independence had led to a loss of faith in them by many people. Semi-mystical peasant movements called Colorums developed in various parts of the country, with millenarian desires of freedom from foreign rule and of wealth redistribution. A peasant revolt with this inspiration broke out in the province of Surigao on the island of Mindanao in 1923–1924, and a secret society with armed features was discovered in 1924 by the authorities in Nueva Ecija province, leading to the imprisonment by the U.S. regime of its leader, Pedro Kabola, and 76 members for "conspiracy and sedition."

Among the urban workers in the COF there were also militant stirrings, bringing about the election of Crisanto Evangelista as COF president in 1924. Evangelista's rising prestige came from his leadership of the UIF in successful strikes that won demands including the right of collective bargaining. Quezon, head of the colonial Senate—always with an eye to buying off or winning over opposition leaders—had appointed Evangelista as a member of the 1919 Independence Mission to the U.S., representing labor. That Mission was a failure and the way it was conducted led the Anti-Imperialist League's Erving Winslow to condemn what he perceived as Quezon's insincerity on independence. However, for Evangelista it was a seminal trip. Part of his role was to contact the U.S. labor movement for support of independence. His approach to the AFL was without success; Samuel Gompers expressed opposition to independence. As it happened, the militant Industrial Workers of the World (IWW) held a convention in 1919 and Evangelista attended it. The convention responded to his appeal and adopted a strong resolution calling for Philippine independence. It was a watershed year for the U.S. labor and revolutionary movements, the year of the founding of the Workers (Communist) Party of the USA, to which many leaders and members of the IWW transferred. A ferment of discussion—on the October Revolution, on the formation of the Communist International, and of Marxist ideology—impressed Evangelista.

Although a mood of militancy existed among many Filipino workers and peasants, it tended to be sporadic. This was largely due to the absence of a working class political party or political movement that could provide a program or ideology. The COF was an example. It had remained a loose federation of left-leaning and conservative unions, with most of its leaders maintaining membership in the Nacionalista Party. Militant strike action by affiliated unions, like the UIF, did not always win the full support of the COF. The October Revolution stirred interest, but the COF convention in 1920 adopted by a large majority a resolution of opposition to "Bolshevism" out of a belief that it was "against a democratic form of government." This was obviously the Nacionalista and U.S. regime influence. As the new temper grew in the early 1920s that view changed. In the COF convention of 1924 the question of endorsing a Labor Party termed "Bolshevik" lost by only one vote.[22]

U.S. COMMUNISTS OPEN THE INTERNATIONAL DOOR

In 1924 a development of major significance for the left in the Philippines occurred. It was initiated by the Workers Party of America (later Communist Party), acting as an affiliated section of the Communist International. Two years earlier in March 1922 the CI had made a policy decision for affiliated parties in imperialist countries to establish contact with revolutionary or potentially revolutionary organizations in colonies. In the latter part of the same year the CI's trade union wing, the Profintern, decided to hold a congress of transport unions of Pacific rim countries, eventually setting June 1924 as the time and Canton, China as the place. The Workers Party of America was "assigned the duty of sending a representative to the East" in connection with this step.

Sent was Alfred Wagenknecht, a Workers Party member who was also in a leading capacity in the left-wing Trade Union Educational League. Wagenknecht's assignment was to go to the Philippines and to arrange for a delegation of Filipino trade unionists to attend the Canton conference. He took the pains of obtaining a letter of introduction from the Resident Commissioner of the Philippines in the U.S., Pedro Guevara, addressed to the executive secretary of the Philippine Independence Commission in Manila, Teodoro M. Kalaw.

The letter introduced Alfred Wagenknecht as representing the Workers Party of America and as going to the Philippines "to have connection with the labor unions and study the political conditions prevailing over there in order that his party may start a campaign in favor of Philippine independence." Asking Kalaw to put him in contact with the labor unions, Guevara went on to say: "The Workers Party in the United States has been campaigning for our independence since I arrived here. Said party has been holding public meetings and adopting resolutions in favor of our independence and their organ in the press The Daily Worker has been publishing almost daily editorials in our favor."[23]

It took some effort for Wagenknecht to find his bearings among the relatively loosely organized trade unions in Manila. He finally managed to obtain a delegation of five for the Canton conference: one from the International Seamen's Union (Jacinto Salazar), one from the New Seamen's Union of dockers, harbor and river launch workers (Eugenio Enorme), one from a railway workers union (Eliseo Alampay), and two from the Legionarios del Trabajo (mutual society with lodges among trade unionists)—Domingo Ponce and Jose Hilario.

The Canton conference focused on transport union problems but it adopted a resolution on independence for the Philippines which called on Filipino unionists "to strive for the improvement and perfection of their organizations so that they could . . . advance their struggle for independence and their ambition that the government of the Philippines should be completely in the hands of the workers and peasants." A general resolution against imperialism, which the Philippine delegation endorsed, urged struggles "against native feudalists, militarists and capitalists who compromise with the imperialists."[24]

None of the Filipinos who attended the Canton conference went on to play any significant part in the Philippine labor movement. However, the episode was like the opening of a door for the Filipino left. It established a link between the Pan-Pacific trade union body subsequently set up by the Profintern in Canton and the Filipino trade unions, and it established a connection between the U.S. Communists and the Filipino labor leaders moving to the left. Of particular importance was the carrying out by Alfred Wagenknecht of the other half of his assignment: exploration of the possibilities for a communist movement in the Philippines that would "perform its tasks as part of the labor and independence movement of the Philippines." In his "Final Report on the Situation in the Philippine Islands, and Recommendations," Wagenknecht wrote:

> The independence movement of the Philippine Islands is buried in [a] morass of bourgeois ideology. It is a movement composed of all classes and is led by those who consider parliamentary democracy and independence as their only aim. These leaders make a concerted effort to discourage most of the struggles of the workers and peasants because these leaders fear that such struggles will prove the instability of the Philippines to the rulers in the United States. They oppose firmly the organization of a workers' political party (an attempt was made to organize one) on this same ground. This opportunist character of the independence movement is not only a source of danger to the workers and peasants of the Islands, but also the the revolutionary nationalist movements of the colonies and semi-colonies of the Far East. The interests of the workers and peasants of the Philippines are subordinated to this opportunistic nationalism . . .
>
> The opportunism of the Independence Commission of the Philippines leads it to eschew mass support in the United States and contact with the organized workers and peasants in the Philippines. It opposes making the movement for independence a mass movement and places its whole trust in an honorable and gentlemanly petitioning of the United States Congress by the leading politicians of the Philippines.

Wagenknecht found at that time "not even the vestige of an organization of enlightened and revolutionary proletarians," but he did find "a group of Filipinos who sympathize strongly with the revolutionary wing of labor, for whom nothing seems to be too revolutionary. This revolutionary spirit must receive communist direction and undertanding for unless it does it will lead to anarchism." It was recommended that literature be sent to prepare the ground for organization. Wagenknecht's list of names of people to be sent literature included Crisanto Evangelista.[25]

In point of fact, a move by Filipinos had already been made, as Wagenknecht mentioned, to establish an independent party of labor. Called the Labor Party, it had been launched two years previously, in 1922, with Antonino D. Ora as its president. Ora was a well-to-do property owner who had close ties with trade union leaders in the COF. He was one of a dwindling group of Nacionalista Party members who retained a sense of allegiance to the *Katipunan* spirit, and who saw the Nacionalista role in the colonial regime as an abandonment of the real struggle for independence. However, those whom Ora sought to draw into a Labor Party were still unready to break with the Nacionalistas who ruled in the legislature and controlled patronage. The initial Labor Party venture subsided.

It was undoubtedly of no coincidence that in 1924 soon after the Wagenknecht visit, Antonino Ora called a meeting at his home in the Tondo district of Manila and undertook the re-launching of the Labor Party. The basic issue of severing the link with the Nacionalista Party and of taking an independent path was not immediately decided, but by 1925 a significant change had occurred: the entry into the Labor Party of left leaders in the trade unions. Most decisive was Crisanto Evangelista, who became the new party's secretary in July 1925. No less important was the affiliation of the peasant union, the KPMP, its leader, Jacinto Manahan, being appointed the Party's representative in Central Luzon. Selected as the date for a public announcement of a new orientation for the party was Bonifacio Day, November 30, 1925. A manifesto that called ringingly "Workers of the Philippines, Unite!" at once stated an anti-colonial aim:

> The Philippine Revolution of '96 that gave birth to a new concept of Justice and freedom on this side of the world, was organized and successfully led by a proletarian, Andres Bonifacio, expresses the truest sense of Democracy for it had the support of the people and whose aim was fully consecrated for the emancipation of the people. After this epoch-making organized movement that awakened the popular consciousness from years of lethargy, the toiling mass of the Philippine Islands has undergone many a lesson and experiences in their political, economic and aocial lives.
>
> They realized that they have been taught by imperialists and their tools

in this country to forebear the yoke of foreign domination by suppressing their most emphatic expression of protest against it; they have been misled and forced to believe that their freedom and independence could never be attained unless it be the will of their foreign master; they have been systematically lured to adapt themselves into a new environment foreign to their own with one final purpose in view to eliminate from their hearts and souls that burning desire of all ages and all subjugated people: Freedom and Independence.

The Labor Party then declared its break with bourgeois leadership, saying that Filipino working people

were gradually convinced by the tactic heretofore displayed by the Nacionalista and Democrata parties in fighting for our right to be free are but a shameful maneuver staged solely to capture the sympathy of the people, concealing thereby the utter failure of their organized efforts; they are being compelled to believe that these parties, judging from cold facts, should they be let alone shall become the people's antagonists whose principal object is not to fight earnestly for the emancipation of the people and for the establishment of a democratic and independent Philippine Republic, but merely for the sake of monopolizing all government jobs in order to satisfy the most shameful ambitions of their constituents; they realized that the Nacionalista and Democrata parties, before their failures, have failed to amend their wrongs, and judging from the passive attitudes of their stands, clearly proved that these parties can never lead the people in a successful fight for their freedom and independence.

First among the demands in the Labor Party program was "immediate, complete and absolute independence for the Philippine Islands." Other demands were for the withdrawal of the U.S. army and the institution of a "People's Army," radical reform of the judicial system because the courts had become "the instrument of the bourgeois class against the laboring people," nationalization of all lands combined with a liberal agrarian reform, nationalization of all banks and transportation, "fostering of new industries under government initiative and control," and the amalgamation of worker and peasant unions and youth organizations so as to "line them up into one united front to stand against their common foe: imperialism."[26]

In this manifesto an historic position was taken by the advanced section of the Philippine labor movement, repudiating the leadership of what it saw as the discredited Nacionalista Party and proclaiming independent working-class political action. In effect it declared that the leadership of the independence struggle was now being assumed by the working class. On that manifesto the Labor Party ran independent candidates in the election for Manila councillors in 1925; they won 19 per cent of the vote, 6,000 votes out of 34,000 cast, a showing that startled Nacionalista leaders and the U.S. regime.

Although the Labor Party manifesto had a Marxist ring and was undoubtedly influenced by the literature and communications from the U.S. and Pan-Pacific links maintained by its leaders, neither the party nor its leaders were then Marxist. Despite the initial electoral success, the party did not advance much further. This was mainly because it had little alternative but to base itself on the COF, which was a mixture of left and conservative trade unions. The Nacionalista influence remained strong in the COF and the police agents of the U.S. colonial regime were ever-active as a disuniting element. The party lacked a clear-cut ideology, its organizational structure was weak, and it did not conduct systematic education and propaganda among workers to whom it appealed.

However, a significant development was the growth of worker-peasant unity. The COF and the peasant union, KPMP, displayed solidarity during much of the 1920s by holding their congresses at the same time in Manila. In 1924 the KPMP became affiliated to the COF as well as to the Labor Party. The spirit this brought to both is indicated by the creed expressed in the preamble of the KPMP's program:

> We believe that the emancipation of the peasants and workers must be accomplished by the workers and peasants themselves.
> We believe in mass action.
> We believe in real peasants' and workers' government.
> We believe that the time has come for the peasants and workers in the Philippines to express themselves and make more effective and extensive campaigns for immediate, complete and absolute independence for the Philippines.
> We believe that unity, good understanding and cooperation among peasants and workers in different countries of the world is absolutely needed for the emancipation of the proletariat and for peace on earth.[27]

Between 1924 and 1928 the links of Filipino workers and peasants with the international labor movement increased and became relatively strong. U.S. Communists played an important part in this. The visit of Alfred Wagenknecht was followed by visits from Harrison George, Earl Browder and Sam Darcy, who successively represented the U.S. Trade Union Educational League, led by the CPUSA, at the Pan-Pacific trade union center, located variously in Canton, Hankow and Shanghai.

A large Pan-Pacific Trade Union Conference held in Hankow on May 20–27, 1927 established a permanent Pan-Pacific Trade Union

Secretariat. Invitations sent to all Filipino trade unions and federations, and to the Labor Party, to attend this conference were delayed in delivery by the U.S. colonial authorities, preventing the sending of a delegation, but the conference adopted a resolution on the Philippines. It was introduced by the U.S. delegate Harrison George in behalf of the TUEL. George said in his introductory remarks that

> it is well that this historic conference hear something of the story of the Philippines, since none other is here to speak but we, the revolutionary workers of the United States, who regard the struggle of the Filipino people as our struggle and who are in every way possible under the circumstances in which we have to work, trying to aid them.

Adopted unanimously, the resolution said that the conference delegates

> take especial notice of the fact that American imperialism nearly thirty years ago began its policy of imperialist expansion and domination of weaker peoples and nations in the Pacific with the violent and bloody conquest of the Philippines... The workers and peasants of the Philippines, suffering under the rule of American imperialism with its irresponsible and autocratic military dictatorship, are by that fact inevitably at one with the oppressed peoples and exploited classes of the Pacific countries. Their struggles are our struggles, their defeats our defeats, and their victory will be our victory, even as our advances will bring to them help and hope in their struggle against tyranny.[28]

When the COF held its 15th Convention on June 30–May 1, 1927, it adopted a resolution in reply which proclaimed that due to "the necessity of proletarian unity in the Pacific area for the liberation of oppressed peoples and exploited classes, and the campaign against the danger of a new imperialist world war, the *Congreso Obrero de Filipinas* declares its adherence to the Pan-Pacific Trade Union Secretariat."[29] The KPMP also affiliated itself to the PPTUS and took the further step of affiliating to the Krestintern, the Peasants' International that was a branch of the Comintern.[30]

The movement to the left in the Philippine trade unions was hastened by this step. In the following March 1928, Crisanto Evangelista headed a Filipino delegation to attend the 4th Congress of the Red International of Labor Unions, and Jacinto Manahan of the KPMP similarly attended a conference of the Krestintern, both held in Moscow. On this occasion Evangelista formally affiliated the COF to the RILU, a step causing consternation among U.S. authorities in the Philippines. That alarm was increased when the 1928 COF convention passed a resolution over the opposition of right-wing representatives calling for the setting up of a new Labor Party that would be transformed into a revolutionary workers' party.

PHILIPPINE TRADE UNIONS TAKE A REVOLUTIONARY PATH

In the sharpening of class and national struggle that these developments reflected, both the U.S. colonial regime and its Filipino collaborators reacted in a suppressive manner. Manuel Quezon summoned Evangelista and other COF leaders and demanded that they cut their links with the international labor movement. The demand was rejected, but it was only the start of a concerted campaign against the leftward trend.

The U.S. and *comprador*-owned Manila press conducted a virulent anti-communist propaganda assault which provided a background for the traditional U.S. tactics of dividing workers. Company union and class collaboration leaders in the COF, headed by Ruperto Cristobal, Isabelo Tejada and others close to Quezon and U.S. businessmen, conspired to oust the left from its positions of leadership in the federation. Although unable to prevent the adoption of the decision to support establishment of a new Labor Party, they did succeed at the May 1928 COF convention in maneuvering the removal of the left-backed president, Francisco Varona, and his replacement by Cristobal, which led to right-wing control of COF machinery.

At the 6th Congress of the Communist International in Moscow in July 1928 a delegate of the CPUSA, Dixon, reported

> the [Filipino] masses are deeply determined upon independence. They are filled with hatred against American imperialism and are seething with revolt. So far this has not found effective leadership, but soon it must smash the old political alignment in the Philippine Islands and find expression in open struggle.

Dixon stressed that this was essential because "the nationalist bourgeoisie has surrendered to American imperialism under the slogan of 'cooperative efforts for industrial development' . . . not only without a struggle but actually with the cooperation of the so-called nationalists."[31]

By the latter part of 1928 a high point of militancy was reached by both urban workers and the organized peasantry of Central Luzon. A one-day general strike of tobacco workers occurred in December in Manila, 10,000 walking out of 13 tobacco factories in protest against imprisonment of a leader of the Cigar Makers' union for allegedly striking a scab in an earlier strike. It coincided with strikes in woodworking plants, lumber mills, transport, boot and shoe industries and sugar mills. In the countryside the KPMP led bitter struggles against the mass eviction of tenants on big landlord estates—3,000 evicted on the Jesuit-owned San Pedro Tuason estate in Laguna province, 1,000 from the Borja family's Jalajala estate in Rizal province, 500 from the Dinalupihan estate in Bataan belonging to the Roman Catholic Archbishopric of Manila. At the KPMP's 3rd Peasants' Congress in December, the Platform of Action adopted called for

> Abolition of all semi-feudal forms of exploitation and oppression of the peasants and agricultural workers, arising from a) concentration of lands in the hands of the land-owning class, b) special privileges whether legal or customary of the landlords, and c) usury.

The KPMP adopted a coincident resolution at the same Congress urging

> a more effective campaign of the KPMP together with the workers, for complete, immediate and absolute independence for the Philippines, and to organize public meetings in different barrios, towns and provinces in the Philippine Islands, but absolutely independent from the movement of the two major political parties, Nacionalista and Democrata, which are the leaders of the rich and land-owning class of the bourgeoisie.[32]

As the 17th Convention of the COF approached, held on May 1, 1929, both left and right trade union groupings maneuvered for control of the proceedings. Although the Evangelista groups succeeded in gaining a pre-convention executive body decision for a collective leadership, which would negate the presidential position of Cristobal, the right had control of the credentials committee and packed the convention with illegal delegates (one right-wing leader increased his authorized delegates from 54 to 188, and a single stevedores' union of only 250 members was allotted 65 delegates). In the American-owned Manila press the Cristobal group published statements declaring it would use its "majority" to cut COF international ties with the PPTUS and RILU, which, charged Evangelista, "shows the hand of American imperialism which seeks to isolate the Filipino workers and peasants."[33] The right was poised to use its fake delegates to oust all left leaders from posts in the COF.

Before this could occur, the entire left body of delegates, headed by Crisanto Evangelista, denouncing the convention as fraudulent, walked out. On May 5, 1929 they met and established a new trade union federation, the *Katipunan ng mga Anak Pawis ng Pilipinas* (KAP or

Proletarian Labor Congress of the Philippines). It was composed of 21 unions, of printers (the UIF), tobacco workers, woodworkers, railroad workers, slipper makers, barbers, workers in button and crystal factories, public utilities workers, hat makers, docks and warehouse workers, abaca strippers, peasant organizations in eight provinces, six Philippine-Chinese craft unions and others. Elected as secretary was Crisanto Evangelista, and as president Antonino D. Ora.

The launching of the KAP was welcomed in the U.S. by the Communist-led Trade Union Unity League, which was linked with the Philippine labor movement through the Pan-Pacific Trade Union Secretariat. At the TUUL convention held in Cleveland on September 2, 1929 a resolution of some length was adopted pledging to "reserve a seat on our National Executive Committee for a representative of the Philippine Proletarian Labor Congress," and to work in solidarity with Filipino workers and peasants for absolute and immediate independence for the Philippines. The resolution declared:

> The Philippine bourgeoisie, which is allied with and bound to the land-lord class that—protected by the imperialist-ruled courts and constabulary—robs and enslaves the peasants without mercy or limit, must no longer be considered as spokesman for the independence movement of the masses, but as traitors to it and the enemies of the interests and aspirations of the toiling millions . . . only the rising resistance of the masses of workers and peasants, in close alliance, in which alliance the organizations of the city proletariat must play the guiding role, can be effective, either in the effort to maintain and improve economic standards or in the struggle for independence. The Filipino masses cannot successfully fight for better economic conditions without fighting American imperialism, nor can the struggle for independence be triumphant without a fight against the ruling economic class—American capitalists and their native agents.[34]

In this resolution the TUUL pointed to the political significance of the KAP, marking the repudiation of class collaboration in the labor movement and of the bourgeois political parties that stood behind the Cristobals and Tejadas. One of the first steps of the KAP, in fact, was to set up a committee to prepare for the launching of a genuine working-class party of a revolutionary vanguard type. Members of the committee were Crisanto Evangelista, Antonino D. Ora, Arturo Santiago, Jacinto Manahan, and Jose Quirante.

The groundwork for such a party had actually been laid at least two years before; a Marxist group was set up around Evangelista and Ora in 1927 with that aim. The U.S. delegate to the PPTUS, Harrison George, had visited the Philippines in September of that year and discussed the perspective with the Filipino group, after which he proposed to the Comintern that one of the group be invited to Moscow to discuss the question.[35] It was Evangelista who made the trip, in March 1928, combining it with attendance at the RILU 4th Congress.

Comintern records show that the question of a Philippine Communist Party was discussed in April 1928 by the political secretariat of the Comintern Executive Committee and that a resolution "The Main Task of the Communists in the Philippines," was adopted by it on April 20, 1928. It was neither a directive nor an organizing brief but was in the nature of advice to Filipinos who themselves were moving in the direction of establishing a Communist Party. "The primary and the necessary condition for the establishment of a Communist Party," it said,

is the formation of an initiating Communist group that has educated itself in the spirit of revolutionary Marxism-Leninism, that has studied the principal lessons of the experiences of the international Communist movement, that has learned how to apply that experience to the particular conditions of the working class movement in the Philippines, and that has undertaken to transform gradually the Labor Party into a party of the masses, into an effective Communist Party.[36]

Evangelista, Ora and their group began the transformation with care, gradually selecting the members of a revolutionary core, during the latter half of 1928. These were chiefly factory workers. By January 1929 forty members had been recruited. Recruiting went on through 1929 and by June 1930 a nucleus of 96 members had been enrolled. Of these, 50 per cent were industrial workers, 25 per cent handicraft workers, and 25 per cent peasants and clerks. In the main they were drawn from KAP unions.

At the KAP's convention on May 29–June 3, 1930 the final preparatory step was taken with a resolution on "the formation of a mass Political Party of the Workers and Peasants." It set the date for the founding convention: August 26, 1930. From KAP unions 60 delegates were chosen to attend.

The founding convention met on August 25, 1930 at the Temple del Trabajo in Manila and decided to initiate the new party on the following day. Various names were proposed—"Proletarian Labor Party," "Socialist Party," even "Bolshevik Party"—but Evangelista's proposal of "Communist Party" was finally approved. Its Philippine language name, Partido Komunista ng Pilipinas (PKP), was proclaimed.

In its origins and initial composition, the PKP was unique among Communist Parties in Asia or in most colonial and semi-colonial countries, springing wholly from the organized working class movement.

In most other cases revolutionary intellectuals had played an initiating role. The 35-member PKP Central Committee, headed by Crisanto Evangelista as general secretary, had wholly working class composition: four printers, seven tobacco workers, four woodworkers, four peasants, two cooks, two slipper-makers, two seamen, two electricians, a plumber, two journalists, a clerk, a railroad worker, and three worker representatives of the Chinese Labor Federation in the Philippines.[37]

In a sense, the Philippine working class had not yet reached a very high stage of development. Industries were small-scale, no basic industry existed, and labor concentration was not significant. Nevertheless, a high degree of class consciousness prevailed, responding to left unionism. This was undoubtedly related to the class features of the revolution against Spain and of the revolutionary war of resistance to U.S. conquest, both of which were still in the memory or the family background of most workers, especially those who had come to the city from the agrarian provinces around Manila where the revolutionary struggles had been most intense. The peasant union members who were affiliated to the KAP had an even more intimate association with that relatively recent past. Many urban workers and rural peasants still had fathers or grandfathers who had been *Katipuneros,* and the *Katipunan* was regarded as a proletarian movement with a proletarian hero, Andres Bonifacio, as its leader. Those who joined the new Communist Party were stirred by its call to "follow in the steps of Bonifacio."

This, in fact, was a strong motivation in the PKP founders, who selected August 26 as the party's founding date because August 26, 1896 was the day when Bonifacio made "the cry of Balintawak," i.e., proclaimed the start of the revolution against Spain in the barrio of Balintawak near Manila. The choice of date demonstrated the revolutionary nationalism of the PKP.

The public launching of the party, however, was made on November 7, 1930, the anniversary of the 1917 October Revolution which established the world's first working-class state with the orientation of constructing socialism. It has remained as the PKP's anniversary. At a public meeting of 6,000 people in Plaza Moriones, in the working class district of Tondo, Manila, speeches by the party's leaders declared the unity of Filipino workers and peasants with the working people of all countries in the common struggle against imperialism and the capitalist ruling class, and linked the gaining of independence with the building of a socialist Philippines. Revolutionary nationalism and proletarian internationalism have been interwoven in the ideology of the PKP.

Over 3,000 applications for membership were made at the November

7 meeting alone and this enthusiastic response continued in the following weeks as the party brought its program to the people in numerous public rallies.

Establishment of a Communist Party in the Philippines was the first real political challenge to U.S. colonial rule, the first organized movement for independence since the suppression of the 1898 Philippine Republic, one that U.S. imperialism knew that it could not buy off or make subservient to its colonial structure. With the PKP, the left trends and forces in the Philippines came to full maturity.

For the U.S. colonial regime this was a serious threat that it would not tolerate. PKP leaders spoke at public meetings in the various Manila districts and in towns of Central and Southern Luzon virtually every day from November 1930 to February 1931, calling for immediate, absolute independence and denouncing the bourgeois Filipino parties participating in the colonial political system as betrayers of the people and of the national interest. At first permits to hold such meetings were granted by local Filipino officials but the U.S. authorities intervened and compelled the denial of permits. When the Communist leaders continued to address crowds without permits they were arrested and charged with sedition.

First to be arrested early in January 1931 was the chairman of the PKP, Antonino D. Ora. For no clear reason the U.S.-officered constabulary ordered his transfer to a provincial jail in Cabanatuan, Nueva Ecija, far from Manila. En route a mysterious alleged car accident occurred, resulting in Ora's death. The PKP charged that he had been murdered and in defiance of a government ban held a funeral ceremony, parade and demonstration in Manila of more than 10,000 workers.

Virtually every PKP leader was arrested successively in February 1931, charged with sedition for reading the PKP constitution and by-laws in public, the charge alleging that their "words and speeches constitute scurrilous libels against the Government of the United States and of the Philippine Islands, and are highly seditious in that they suggest and incite rebellious conspiracies."[38] Finally on March 6, 1931 the Manila mayor banned all PKP meetings.

The PKP sought to run candidates in the June 1931 election in Manila but the candidates were arrested when they sought to address meetings. Even the annual May 1st parade of the KAP was forbidden by the mayor of Manila, but a permit was granted by the mayor of suburban Caloocan. When the parade reached the Manila boundary it was attacked by the constabulary using fire hoses. Evangelista was arrested but the workers pierced constabulary lines to release him and marched with him into Manila to the site where the KAP was holding a congress.

Defying bans, striving to assert its right to legality, the PKP organized and held its first congress on May 30, 1931. It was concluding its proceedings when the gathering was raided by U.S.-headed secret police who arrested the entire 400 delegates and held them incommunicado. Finally 27 PKP leaders were accused of "illegal association" and tried in "criminal" cases in Manila. They were found guilty and given sentences of one to four years in prison.

Of this group, 20 were given the further sentence of banishment from Manila, to exile for eight years in provinces distant from the Manila political and trade union center. Crisanto Evangelista was exiled to Mountain Province, Mariano Balgos to Tarlac, Jacinto Manahan to Pangasinan, others to Nueva Ecija, Tayabas (now Quezon province), Laguna, Batangas.[39]

The cases were appealed to the Philippine Supreme Court but in decisions rendered by that Court on October 26, 1932 the convictions were upheld and put into effect. At that time the nine-member Supreme Court had a majority of five Americans and the decisions were written by two of the Americans, J. Ostrand and J. Street, without a dissent from the four Filipino members. These decisions declared the PKP an "illegal association," thus outlawing the party and driving it underground.

In these decisions it was not claimed that the PKP was an agent of a foreign power, saying merely in passing that it "insisted that it was the duty of the laborers to bring the government into their hands and to run by themselves and for themselves, like the laboring class in Russia." The American-controlled Supreme Court was mainly concerned with condemning the PKP for its historic links with the *Katipunan* and Bonifacio, declaring that "the purpose of the CPP is to promote the struggle and antagonism of classes, and to establish an independent Philippines; that a revolution like that initiated by Andres Bonifacio is necessary . . . " At a later point this was reiterated:

> The evidence is conclusive that when the appellants and the Communist Party advocated revolution, they did not mean peaceful revolution, but specifically said that they meant a revolution like that initiated by Andres Bonifacio which led the *Katipunan* to take arms, against the advice of Doctor Rizal who advocated peaceful means in the fight for independence.

The issue of collaboration versus resistance echoed in these decisions, the U.S. colonial regime up to the end refusing to acknowledge Bonifacio as a national hero.[40]

As in every other country, colonial or independent and advanced, illegalizing the Communist Party did not end its existence or stop its activity. Although for a time the PKP, deprived of its leaders and with membership made a criminal offense, suffered demoralization, a new underground leadership, decided upon before the convicted leaders entered confinement, quickly took over and resumed recruiting as well as giving direction to the KAP, the KPMP and other organizations.

In its outlawing of the PKP the U.S. colonial government sought to forbid an independent political voice to the worker-peasant majority in the Philippines, and to keep the colony's political life wholly in the hands of the collaborating landlord-*comprador* groupings.

There were other reasons for U.S. suppression of a revolutionary working class party at that time. The Great Depression of the 1930s, the worldwide crisis of capitalism, was having a serious effect in the Philippines. Economic decline had set in rapidly. In 1930 Philippine exports dropped 16 per cent compared with 1929 and imports fell by 13 per cent. A steep fall in the prices of sugar, copra, hemp and tobacco occurred, contributing to a 44 per cent drop in the value of Philippine trade. Landlord-*comprador* groups passed the effects of this on to the workers and peasants, to retain their free trade profits. A mass dismissal of workers, wage cuts, and the eviction of peasants on big landed estates were taking place. On January 10, 1931 there was a peasant revolt in the town of Tayug, Pangasinan which shook the colony: the rebels beseiged the constabulary garrison, occupied the town and destroyed land records. A PKP declaration of support for the participants in the Tayug uprising was one of the reasons for the step by the U.S. authorities to suppress the PKP. In 1931, too, the discovery and arrest occurred of secret revolutionary movements, the Tanggulan in Central Luzon and Colorums in the Visayas and Mindanao, engaged in plans for revolt to achieve independence and land redistribution. U.S. imperialism feared a general upsurge of revolutionary nationalism, with the PKP, as an organized vanguard, in a position to lead it.

Furthermore, at this time the U.S. had reached a critical stage in its relations with the Philippine colony. The Depression had revived and aggravated the historical debate in the U.S. over retention of the colony and had strengthened the arguments of the opposition, while the growth of Japanese power in Asia had enlarged the strategic problem of being able to hold onto what amounted to, in the military sense, a U.S. outpost in that part of the world. In the U.S. Congress the independence advocates had growing support and an independence bill, the Hare-Hawes-Cutting Act, was in the process of approval while the colonial Philippine Supreme Court was upholding the conviction of the PKP leaders and illegalizing the party. The terms of an independence were about to be negotiated and U.S. imperialism wanted to deal only with the Filipino political leaders it had nurtured, without an anti-collaboration left-wing presence on the scene.

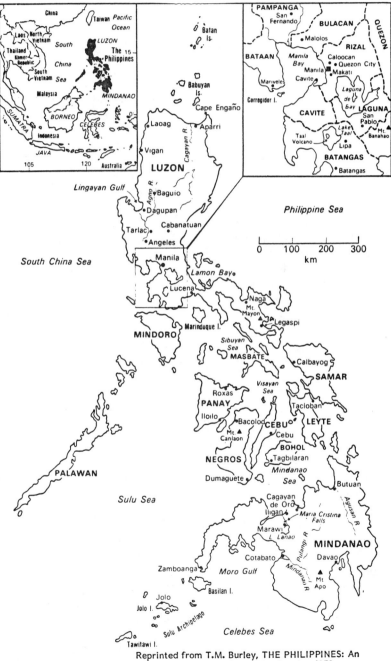

Reprinted from T.M. Burley, THE PHILIPPINES: An Economic and Social Geography, London, 1973.

IV

Independence: For Whose Benefit?

One of the major features of the century-long relationship of the United States and the Philippines has been the manner in which Philippine independence took place. In a good many historical accounts the end of colonial possession has been given an aura of U.S. benevolence, pictured as a voluntary handing over to the Filipino people of their national freedom, after a magnanimous education in self-government. It is a myth. The train of circumstances that led to Philippine independence neither began nor ended in benevolence.

At the level of simply stated historical fact, on March 24, 1934 the Tydings-McDuffie Act, which had been approved by both houses of the U.S. Congress, was signed into law by Democratic President Franklin D. Roosevelt. It provided for independence for the Philippines, to take final effect on July 4, 1946. This Act was accepted and approved by the Philippine legislature on May 1, 1934, making it absolute. A Filipino Constitutional Convention was then prepared and held, drawing up a Constitution for an independent republic which was accepted by an overwhelming vote in a referendum on May 14, 1935. Under it, a Filipino government was elected in September 1935 to head a transitional Commonwealth. As stipulated, Independence was indeed handed over on July 4, 1946.

Ostensibly the Filipino people thus achieved their long-sought aim of liberation from foreign rule that had begun in armed struggle but was now completed, it seemed, through peaceful parliamentary procedure. The real picture, however, was quite different.

The Filipino people themselves had never ceased to call, from below, for independence. Left-wing trade unions and peasant organizations placed independence foremost in their constitutions and resolutions. The Partido Komunista ng Pilipinas was outlawed by the U.S. colonial regime primarily because of its militant advocacy of independence.

76

Peasant revolts in the 1920s and early 1930s, incoherent as they were, invariably included a clear call for freedom from U.S. rule. On February 22–26, 1930 a broadly based Independence Congress with nearly 2,000 delegates met in Manila and unanimously adopted a resolution for independence. In the colonial politics no candidate for office could hope to be elected who did not give at least lip service to the known popular sentiment for independence. From the Philippine Congress itself Independence Missions were regularly sent to lobby the U.S. Congress in Washington.

All such Missions were fended off by the Republican administrations from 1920 to 1932. When the Philippine legislature in 1927 passed a bill for a plebiscite on immediate independence, and then re-passed it over a veto by then Governor-General Leonard Wood, U.S. President Calvin Coolidge vetoed the bill on grounds that such a plebiscite vote by the Filipino people would be "unconvincing, it might create friction and disturb business . . . "[1] He said that unless such a plebiscite was requested by the U.S. Congress, it would be harmful to good relations.

As far as the sentiments and demands of the ordinary Filipino people were concerned, the U.S. attitude was constant—to put down revolt with force, to outlaw militant nationalist movements, and to ignore resolutions—however mass-based. As for the recognized Filipino political leaders nurtured under U.S. rule, their public declarations for "immediate, complete and unconditional independence," often delivered in the ringing tones of the crusader for the benefit of Filipino audiences, contrasted with the confidential tones with which they spoke in private to U.S. officials. There are too many memoirs and testimonies relating privately expressed sentiments against complete independence by those same top-level Filipino politicians to dismiss these accounts as untrue, particularly in the light of such public statements as that by Manuel Quezon to a gathering of New York bankers and businessmen in 1927, coincident with the Coolidge plebiscite veto:

> "The natural resources of the Philippines offer a rich reward for investors, but the Filipinos lack capital and American capitalists hesitate to invest capital in the islands because they fear the movement for national independence makes future American domination and therefore American investments, insecure. It is true the Filipino people profoundly wish their independence, BUT for the sake of 'progress' are willing to accept a dominion status, such as Canada's relation to Great Britain. We will guarantee the United States a permanent naval and military base in the Orient, and give security to American capital and thus the uncertainty

which hinders industrial development at present can be brought to an end."[2]

Present-day Filipino historians, in fact, accept that many of those who put themselves publicly in the forefront of the Independence Movement sought behind the scenes to sabotage it, to water down independence legislation, and to perpetuate a protectorate status for the Philippines. After three colonial decades, U.S. interests were quite content with the behavior of the upper strata of Filipino political leaders, civil servants, landlords and businessmen their policies had produced.

INDEPENDENCE AND THE UNITED STATES

At any rate, the attitudes among the Filipino people were not the determining factor in the passage of the Tydings-McDuffie Independence Act. It was the attitude among U.S. interests that determined the Act's introduction and approval.

Philippine independence had always been somewhat of a political football in the U.S., kicked forward and back between the Democratic and Republican Parties and the varying imperialist policies they represented. An expansionist Republican administration had seized the Philippines, acting for those who believed that possession of such a colony served imperialist aims in Asia. The Republican Party election platform of 1904 (which boasted of having "suppressed insurrection") explicitly stated: "By our possession of the Philippines we were enabled to take prompt and effective action in the relief of the legation at Peking [in the Boxer rebellion], and a decisive part in preventing the partition and preserving the integrity of China." That is, U.S. penetration of China was furthered. At no time did the Republican Party advocate or support independence for the Philippine colony. The only mention of the question was in the party's 1924 election platform which said, " ... if the time comes" when the U.S. Congress felt it would be better for the Philippines to be independent and if the Filipino people would desire it, independence would be given, but "A careful study of the conditions in the Philippine Islands has convinced us that the time for such action has not arrived." The Republican election platforms of 1928 and 1932 did not even mention the Philippines.

The Democratic Party did not oppose the extension of U.S. interests abroad. "We favor expansion by every peaceful and legitimate means," said its election platform in 1900, "but we are unalterably opposed to seizing or purchasing distant lands, to be governed outside the Constitution, and whose people can never become citizens." It was stated that "we favor an immediate declaration of the nation's purpose to give to the Filipinos first, a stable form of government, second, independence, and third, protection from outside interference, such as has been given for nearly a century to the Republics of Central and South America." In other words, there was no objection to a protectorate status. The 1904 election platform made this plain: "We insist that we ought to do for the Filipinos what we have already done for the Cubans." Cuba had been made a dependency.

Although the Democratic Party regularly called for Philippine independence throughout U.S. colonial rule, modifications crept in. In both 1908 and 1912 its platform attached the condition "as soon as a stable government can be established," the stock phrase for compliance with U.S. desires. In addition both of those platforms contained the following: "In recognizing the independence of the Philippines our Government should retain such land as may be necessary for coaling stations and naval bases." This fitted the Mahan prescription for naval power. In the Tydings-McDuffie Act adopted by a Democrat-controlled Congress there is a provision for the retention of U.S. naval base facilities.

The position of the Democratic Party was a more complex one than that of the Republicans. It served the interests of both domestic producers who wanted to be free of low-cost duty-free Philippine exports and U.S. commercial and investment groups who wanted protected expansion overseas. At the same time it adopted a moral position that appealed to various shades of anti-imperialism. The Democratic Party has had the capacity to present a reformist image but it has also headed the administrations that have led the U.S. in the two huge world wars of the 20th century from which the U.S. emerged as a dominant imperialist power without the need of a colonial empire. Once the issue of Philippine independence was out of the way, and in the light of U.S. power after 1945, the differences between the two U.S. parties over imperialist policy became minimal and confined more to the question of style than of form or substance.[3]

Whether or when Philippine independence should occur was decided in the U.S. boardrooms and legislative chambers. The catalyst for it was the Great Depression that began in 1929 and ravaged the U.S. and other capitalist countries through the 1930s. That crisis of U.S. capitalism greatly accentuated one of the main contradictions of possessing the colony: the conflict between the free trade entry to the U.S. market permitted to Philippines sugar, copra, coconut oil, tobacco and other products, and U.S. domestic production of beet sugar, dairy products, tobacco and other items. U.S.-owned sugar plantations and mills in Cuba and Puerto Rico were also affected by the Philippine trade. As the Depression deepened and cut into the sales of these U.S. producers, the demand for the competitive Philippines to be cut loose increased.

In committee hearings and debates on Philippine independence held in the U.S. Senate and House of Representatives in 1930 and 1932, the relative advantages and disadvantages of retaining the colony were argued. Although members of a Philippine Independence Mission testified at the hearings, the main debate was between two U.S. interest groups: those that profited from the colony and were opposed to independence, and those whose interests were adversely affected by the colonial relationship and wanted it ended.

1. The former grouping included: those Americans resident in the Philippines who had built a stake there including in land, businesses and investments, the American bureaucratic officials in the colonial administration who would lose their posts with independence, the U.S. manufacturers engaged in duty-free export trade to the Philippines, importers in the U.S. of Philippine duty-free products which cost more coming from tariff-paying countries, and Americans who had absentee overseas investments in the Philippines.[4]

Taken as a whole, this grouping did not comprise as powerful a force as might have been suspected after more than three decades of U.S. rule. According to the Philippine Census of 1939, the total Americans in the colony were only 8,709, of which but 1,026 were employed in Philippine industries controlled by U.S. capital.[5] (In contrast, there were 30,000 Japanese and 117,500 alien Chinese.) Officials and employees in the colonial civil service numbered only 494 Americans in 1930.[6] The export trade to the Philippines was more significant: in 1934 the Philippines ranked 9th among the principal U.S. export markets and for certain exports it was 1st, including cigarettes, galvanized iron and steel sheets, ready-mixed paints, canned milk and cream, soap and a few other more minor items, while it ranked 2nd for cotton cloth, wheat flour and canned fish.[7] The extent of U.S. investments in the Philippines was summarized in the report made in 1938 by the Joint Preparatory Committee on Philippine Affairs:

Total American investments in the Philippines in 1935 have been estimated at approximately $200,000,000. Of this amount, nearly 20 per cent consists of investments in bonds issued by various Philippine political entities, private companies and religious organizations; the remainder represents direct investments in a wide variety of industries operating in the Islands ...

The value of investments held by citizens of the United States in Philippine industries on June 30, 1935 approximated $163,500,000. Of this amount, nearly $111,250,000 represented the book value of investments in land, and the book value of other fixed assets less depreciation. Current assets, such as receivables, advances, and inventories accounted for the remainder. American commercial investments are represented in all of the principal Philippine industries and thus are widely diversified. Mining, which accounted for 23.2% of total American investments (other than in bonds) in 1935 is probably the most important. Other prominent industries from the standpoint of invested American capital in 1935 are public utilities which represented 19.5% of the total; the sugar industry, 12.5%; plantations, 12.2%; and merchandising concerns, 10.8%. These five industries accounted for 78% of the American capital directly employed in Philippine industries in 1935; the remaining 22% was invested in a large number of varied industries.[8]

It is surprising that despite the great advantages enjoyed by U.S. interests over other foreign investors in the Philippines, barely half of all foreign investment was American. At the end of 1941 the U.S. total was P537,000,000 and the combined total of Chinese, Japanese, Spanish and other investment was P550,000,000.[9]

When the U.S. investment stake is seen in relation to the overall picture of U.S. overseas investment at the time, its relatively low significance can be appreciated in the debate taking place. U.S. investments in Cuba, Chile and Argentina were all larger than in the Philippines. U.S. capital was flowing mainly to areas closer to home: about $4 billion invested in Latin America, $3.5 billion in Canada; even in Europe as a whole the total was only around $1.3 billion. In all of Asia, Africa and Australia combined U.S. investments had reached but $913,000,000. The great dream of the China market had never been realized, and the U.S. now had to face an aggressive rival in Asia—Japan—which posed a threat to the Philippines itself, raising the question of a huge military outlay to defend the colony, if it were retained.

It must be stressed that independence for the Philippines did not mean the loss of the existing U.S. economic stake. U.S. interests had a strong preferential position even if the special colonial advantages and privileges were terminated, and the peaceful non-acrimonious manner in which independence was to be carried out added to the conditioning of Filipinos to continuance of a "special relationship" with the U.S.

2. In conflict with the investment interests opposing independence were the U.S. groupings that supported an Independence Act. They included: the three major national farm organizations (the American Farm Bureau Federation, the National Grange, and the Farmers Educational and Cooperative Union of America), the National Cooperative Milk Producers' Association, the National Dairy Union, the organized producers in 19 beet sugar and 8 cane sugar states, American investors in Cuban sugar production, the American Federation of Labor, and certain groups that objected to the permitted entry of Filipinos, on racial grounds.

From the standpoint of the various agricultural organizations, colonial possession of the Philippines and the free trade arrangement that went with it constituted a competitive threat, not only in regard to prevailing quotas but in the capability of the Philippines to increase agricultural production greatly and more cheaply and to press for expanded quotas. The two export products drawing most protest were sugar and coconut oil. Philippine sugar was an obvious competitor for U.S. cane and beet sugar growers and for the U.S. investments in the Cuban sugar plantations and mills; coconut oil was considered a threat by U.S. cottonseed oil producers and by the dairy industry whose milk and butter were undercut by a coconut oil-based margarine selling for 17 cents to butter's 37½ cents. To a lesser extent, U.S. tobacco interests opposed the tariff concessions given to importation of Philippine cigars and filler tobacco. In addition to these various interests, organized labor favored independence because it would end the unhindered immigration of Filipino workers who became cheap labor competitors in the U.S. labor market, a factor aggravated by the huge numbers of unemployed in the Depression years.

Representatives of these groups testified in Congressional hearings on independence. Not testifying, nor sought after to do so, were left-wing movements such as the Communist Party, the Trade Union Unity League, the surviving elements of the Anti-Imperialist League, and others who consistently demanded the freedom of the Philippines from imperialist colonial rule.

The pro-independence forces among U.S. capitalist sectors had greater weight at this point in the early 1930s because the Great Depression was ruining both domestic and world markets, creating mass unemployment, and making more acute competition in both commodities and labor. They also happened to have greater voter strength in the Southern, Southwestern and Middle Western states, exerting a powerful congressional influence.

That influence was demonstrated in two Acts providing for Philippine independence passed by the U.S. Congress after debating the issue: the Hare-Hawes-Cutting Act approved on January 17, 1933 and the Tydings-McDuffie Act signed into law by President Franklin D. Roosevelt on March 24, 1934. The latter Act was the one finally accepted by the Philippine legislature but was virtually identical to the former, the dispute over the two being chiefly a matter of personal leadership rivalry between the two dominant Filipino politicians, Manuel Quezon and Sergio Osmena. Osmena was identified with Hare-Hawes-Cutting, Quezon with Tydings-McDuffie, but in truth the hands that wrote the independence terms were not Filipino but American, the key provisions tailored to the pressures of the conflicting U.S. lobbying groups.

The Independence Act set a ten-year transitional period, to terminate on July 4, 1946, during which the Philippines was designated a Commonwealth with a degree of political autonomy. In that time gradual adjustment from dependence to independence was supposed to occur. The economic adjustment was fundamental; it involved the termination of the free trade relationship, the goal of the U.S. agricultural interests.

During the first five years of the transition period the existing free trade relations were to prevail, except that the standard U.S. tariff duties would be collected on all Philippine unrefined sugar in excess of 800,000 long tons and on all refined sugar in excess of 50,000 long tons, on all coconut oil in excess of 200,000 long tons, and on abaca (manila hemp) or other fiber in excess of 3,000,000 pounds. In the sixth year tariff rates of 5 per cent would begin on the quota amounts and increase by 5 per cent for each of the remaining transition years. As soon as independence would take effect, full U.S. tariff duties would be imposed on all Philippine exports entering the U.S. Independence would thus eliminate the Philippines as a competitor of U.S. domestic producers.

This was the overriding concern of the U.S. Congress in passing independence legislation. Another question that preoccupied the Congress and was given extensive attention in the text of the Act had to do with the payment of the principal and interest of the bonded indebtedness of the Philippines. Bond issues by the Philippine colony had been strictly limited by the Organic Act of 1902 and by the Jones Act of 1916. The former had provided for a bond issue to pay only for the friar lands that were purchased from the Catholic religious orders; the latter limited indebtedness of the Philippine government to $15,000,000, while no province or municipality was allowed to exceed a bonded debt in excess of 7 per cent of the aggregate tax valuation of its property. The bonds were held by U.S. banks and private hands. As mentioned earlier, bond holdings were classified as part of the U.S. investment stake in the Philippines and amounted to about $50 million.

Determined to be left with no obligations for what had transpired in the course of its colonial rule, the U.S. insisted that during the Commonwealth decade the Philippine government must collect an export tax on all Philippine articles exported to the U.S. between 1941 and 1946, the amount to go into a sinking fund to be used to pay off as much as possible of the debt. Another provision stated that whatever debts remained had to be paid by "the free and independent government of the Philippine Islands," and that "such obligations shall be a first lien on the taxes collected in the Philippine Islands."

These features of the Independence Act that imposed conditions favoring the U.S. were added to by a provision giving U.S. goods unrestricted free entry to the Philippines throughout the ten-year transition. Like the bond payments, this trade imposition embodied squeezing out every last drop of profit from the colony to the last day. Grossly unequal as the trade terms were, they also inhibited the establishment of Philippine industry that might produce many of the imported goods.

The U.S., in other words, took care to protect and maintain its own interests as it withdrew from the colony. It could not be said to protect the interests of Filipinos whom it would have controlled for half a century. The Independence Act did virtually nothing to assist the Philippines in launching into the difficult, depression-racked world of the time. Far from readying the country to stand on its own feet, the Act, in effect, cut the colony loose in a sink or swim manner.

During nearly half a century the U.S. had done very little to prepare the Philippines for an independent existence. On the contrary, it had nurtured a dependent economy relying heavily on preferential "free trade," its principal exports leaning on the cushion of duty-free quotas. Those exports were not diversified, limited to a few raw or semi-raw products—sugar, copra, coconut oil, tobacco. There had been no perspective on finding alternative markets for these, or for developing other exports to broaden or supplement them. As for an industrial base for an independent economy, that had been almost wholly prevented. U.S. rule fostered no development program and gave no economic aid. Whatever little infrastructure was built was done through government corporations set up by the Filipino legislature, necessarily having meager funds. The ten-year Commonwealth transitional period, with these circumstances, merely made the severance a bit gradual without creating the means for an independent economy.

This relative indifference to the fate of Filipinos caused complaints to develop against the trade provisions of the Independence Act. Filipino producers and exporters who had been the beneficiaries of free trade, and who were lukewarm if not antagonistic to the idea of complete independence in the first place, protested about the application of U.S. tariff duties even on smaller exports like cigars and filler tobacco, pearl buttons and embroideries, contending that the 5 per cent annual increase in duties beginning in the sixth transition year would make it prohibitive to continue exporting to the U.S. Other complaints came from fledgling small Philippine industries and hopeful Filipino entrepreneurs who welcomed independence for the diminishing of the privileges of big U.S. companies with which they had to compete at a disadvantage. There was no provision whatsoever in the Independence Act either to assist this aspect of the economy or to help in setting up new industries.

Finally in 1937 the unfairnesses of the Act caused the Roosevelt administration to set up a Joint Preparatory Committee on Philippine Affairs, composed of U.S. and Philippine representatives, to study the situation and recommend improvements. Despite the avowed aim of making adjustments that would benefit the Philippines, the recommendations that emerged, and the Tydings-Kocialkowski (Philippine Economic Adjustment) Act of 1939 that followed, did virtually nothing to resolve the problem.

Complaints of the threatened Filipino exporters were answered not by reducing or postponing the 5 per cent annual increase of tariffs from 1940 onwards but by reducing their duty-free quotas by 5 per cent each year from 1940. This meant that by the end of the transition period their duty-free exports to the U.S., and earnings from them, would be cut by 25 per cent. All that was conceded to them was the opportunity to keep exporting to the U.S., at a diminishing rate, up to independence day.

The Tydings-Kocialkowski Act, however, then included a significant provision, for a Philippine-U.S. trade conference to be held at least two years before independence (by 1944) to review the situation that might exist by that time—in other words, holding open the prospect of an extended form of free trade. To pro-independence forces this provision had an ominous ring: it appeared at a time when signs of recovery from the Depression were affecting the outlook of U.S. interests, and when an actual call for a "reexamination" of independence itself was being made.

Long sections of the Tydings-Kocialkowski Act were concerned with an amendment to the Independence Act which gave detailed instructions to the Philippine Commonwealth government on how to use its export tax to pay up on its bonded indebtedness. It was obvious that the U.S. lawmakers were more concerned with seeing to it that their bondholder lobbyists got their money back with interest than with the fate of the Filipino population whose economic future was infinitely less certain.

INDEPENDENCE AND THE PHILIPPINES

Under U.S. colonial rule an important distinction had grown between the political and economic aspects of independence. The U.S. policy of "education for self-rule" nurtured a colonial political system from which developed a demand for political independence, while the economic system of free trade and of smothering the growth of Philippine manufacturing industry developed a dependent economy and a demand from collaborating groups for continued dependence. Colonial politics, of course, could not exist apart from the colonial economy, so that political leaders proclaiming their independence avowals at the same time worked for the interests of the producers and exporters dependent on the imperialist power's market.

The Independence Act preserved the distinction. It provided quite clearly for Filipinos to govern themselves fully in the political sense, including stipulations for calling a constitutional convention and writing their own constitution for self-rule, but its economic provisions gave no such assurance of independence, the amendments to the Act even proposing negotiations implying the continuing of some form of dependence after the handing over of political independence.

In the Philippines itself a telling commentary on the Independence Act and on the colonial political system to which it gave a nod of recognition was the artificial controversy that was created over the initial measure approved by the U.S. Congress, the Hare-Hawes-Cutting Act. This was passed while an Independence Mission headed by Sergio Osmena was in the U.S., and Osmena returned to the Philippines in the role of the leader who had won the freedom of his country. He had the support of a Nacionalista wing called the "Pros" (pro-Hare-Hawes-Cutting). Manuel Quezon, however, could not abide the triumph of his rival who might thereby edge him out to become the first president of the Commonwealth and of the forthcoming Republic. Therefore he launched a campaign of opposition to Hare-Hawes-Cutting, denouncing it as unacceptable. His argument was minor, centered particularly on a sentence that gave the U.S. the right to retain land for "military and other reservations." Quezon said the Act was "inconsistent with true independence." Heading a Nacionalista wing called the "Antis" (anti-Hare-Hawes-Cutting), he maneuvered its rejection by the Philippine legislature.

Quezon himself then went to Washington with another Independence Mission and secured the adoption of the Tydings-McDuffie Act. It was virtually identical, word for word, to Hare-Hawes-Cutting, except for a slight alteration in the paragraph on military reservations which now provided for negotiations to be held within two years after the proclamation of independence "for the adjustment and settlement of all questions relating to naval reservations and fueling stations of the United States in the Philippine Islands," with existing reservations and stations remaining "in the present status" until that time. Waving this version of the Independence Act, Quezon staged his own triumphant return to the Philippines, won its approval in the legislature, and secured his political leadership.

The petty squabble of the Antis and Pros tended to devalue the U.S.-made independence instrument in the eyes of many Filipinos. When elections were held in July 1934 of delegates to the constitutional convention provided for in the Independence Act, scarcely 40 per cent of qualified voters bothered to cast a ballot. In Manila, reputed to have an electorate more sophisticated than in the rest of the country, only 28,000 voted out of the 71,000 qualified.[10]

Virtually all delegates to the Constitutional Convention were from the well-to-do Filipino elite that was the breeding-ground of collaboration, mostly products of the U.S. educational system and adherents of the form of government it taught. The document they wrote and adopted drew heavily on the U.S. organic acts that established and elaborated colonial government in the Philippines. As in the Independence Act, it was interlarded with provisions conceding rights to Americans and declaring obligations and deference to the U.S.

Upon independence, it said, "all existing rights of citizens and corporations of the United States shall be acknowledged, respected and safeguarded to the same extent as property rights of citizens of the Philippines." Most onerous, an ordinance was appended to the Constitution which listed 20 points of continued U.S. authority to prevail throughout the ten-year Commonwealth period. These included: obligating all citizens and officials of the Philippines to owe allegiance to the U.S., establishing Philippine public debt limits to be fixed by the U.S. Congress and forbidding the contracting of loans from foreign countries unless approved by the U.S. President (both of which prevented the Commonwealth from taking economic development steps on its own); pursuing an education system conducted primarily in the English language; putting foreign affairs "under the direct supervision and control of the United States," directing that military forces organized by the Commonwealth can be called into service with U.S. armed forces by order of the U.S. President; making Philippine court decisions subject to review by the U.S. Supreme Court; declaring the right of the U.S. to intervene in the Philippines for a wide range of reasons; obligating the Philippine government to submit Constitutional amendments, laws, contracts and executive orders to the President of the U.S. who would have the right to suspend their operation.

Indifference by the majority of the Filipino electorate to the way in which independence was being enacted and implemented reflected a distrust of the political leaders who had negotiated it. That distrust was deepened by the opposition expressed by important groups of the comprador bourgeoisie to the severing of the colonial relationship. A petition was signed by 200 Filipino exporters, landlord producers and leading politicians, headed by the prominent spokesman of the sugar bloc, Salvador Araneta, and addressed to the U.S. President, calling for a far longer period of transition and for the Philippines to be given dominion status instead of actual independence. In the United States the Philippine Resident Commissioner, Pedro Guevara, told the U.S. Congress that a ten-year transition period was not long enough and that the U.S. should remain in the Philippines for 25 more years at least.

For the underground Partido Komunista ng Pilipinas and the left in general the whole scenario of independence as initiated and conducted in the first half of the 1930s was permeated with fraud. The Hare-Hawes-Cutting/Tydings-McDuffie Act with its design of protection for U.S. interests, the Commonwealth Constitution with its features of submission to U.S. control, the Quezon–Osmena unprincipled fight that put personal power ahead of national freedom, and the efforts by the comprador-landlord groups to stave off independence indefinitely were believed to have all the ingredients of deception and betrayal. When the Antis and Pros proceeded to form a coalition to run Quezon and Osmena as president and vice-president of a Commonwealth government, it drew sharp attack from the PKP.

Both Nacionalista groups, said a PKP leaflet that was distributed on May 10, 1935 ("Fight Against the Coalition and Struggle for Immediate Independence!") "have always played with independence, peddling it to the masses in order to hide the fact that they really do not want the country to be free but to make it a perpetual slave of the imperialists. Due to this fact, the question of the independence of the country is again in danger."

The PKP leaflet assailed in particular the establishment under the Commonwealth of a National Defense Force to be under the command of U.S. officers. General Douglas MacArthur, previously a chief of staff of the U.S. army, had been assigned to command the Force. Citing the Tydings-McDuffie/Commonwealth Constitution provisions enabling the U.S. President to order the Philippine armed forces to be joined with the U.S. army in certain circumstances, including U.S. intervention in Philippine affairs, the PKP condemned the authorized use of Filipinos to protect U.S. interests. (An American official in the U.S. colonial regime at the time wrote confirmingly: "The Constabulary is always standing by and not infrequently is ordered to take over the police functions of a municipality in times of emergency. The Philippine Army is in the background and behind that looms the Philippine Division of the U.S. Army. No revolt has any prospect of success in the Philippine Commonwealth.")[11]

This critical attitude of the Filipino left toward the nature of the independence steps arose in one respect from the working class awareness of the betrayal of the Philippine Revolution by the wealthy groups and the consistent collaboration of those groups and their ambitious middle class allies with U.S. colonial rule. It was also based on the existing situation in which the PKP had been outlawed, with its leaders imprisoned and given internal exile, and in which the organized labor movement was harassed and persecuted. In general, the Filipino masses had not been drawn into any national movement for independence and were treated as subversives when they sought to raise a demand for freedom from colonial rule; they had not been consulted on the independence issue in any way and apathy toward the Constitution and the Commonwealth was widespread.

While independence was being shaped in the U.S. Congress and in the top circles of colonial business and politics, it was raised in quite another manner by Filipino peasants and workers. In a number of uprisings and acts of revolt in the early 1930s, demands of land for the landless and justice for working people were invariably linked with demands for independence from foreign rule which was seen as the basic cause of exploitation.

Leaders of the secret peasant society that staged the Tayug uprising in January 1931 conceived of it as the spark to achieve independence for the whole country. It was condemned as fanaticism by Manuel Quezon and the Speaker of the Assembly, Manuel Roxas. However, the same theme appeared in numerous semi-religious secret societies that sprang up and clashed with the authorities in most of the provinces of Central and Southern Luzon, Leyte, Cebu and Mindanao from 1930 onwards, most often influenced by impoverishment worsened by the Great Depression.

In the movement called the Tanggulan, headed by Patrico Dionisio, reputedly 40,000 members were spread across the provinces of Nueva Ecija, Bulacan, Bataan, Pampanga, Tayabas, Laguna and Cavite. Its declared aim was to achieve independence through an armed uprising, but was exposed in December 1930 before taking action, its leaders arrested. In 1934 a trade union leader, Teodoro Asedillo, evading arrest for participation in a major Manila tobacco workers' strike, took to the Sierra Madre mountains of Laguna-Tayabas where he recruited an armed group, led a year-long guerrilla struggle and won extensive support from villages of the region. A call for independence was made, as well as for an end to unjust taxation and poverty. Asedillo was killed by the Constabulary. Both he and Dionisio were members of the PKP, but the party did not support their actions.

Largest of the revolts at this time was that of a movement called the Sakdal. Organized by Benigno Ramos, a clerk in the Philippine Senate, in 1933, it was set up as a political party. It contested the 1934 congressional and local elections, electing three representatives to Congress (from Laguna and Tayabas), a provincial governor (Marinduque), and a number of municipal officials in Laguna, Rizal, Cavite, Bulacan and Nueva Ecija. The Sakdal program was headed by a call for "complete and absolute independence" to occur by December 31, 1935. It opposed the Tydings-McDuffie Act and the establishment of the Commonwealth. It attacked what it termed the colonial education system, the control of the economy by U.S. interests, and U.S. military bases. When the Sakdals called for a boycott of the referendum on the Commonwealth Constitution they were termed seditious by the U.S. Governor-general. On May 2-3, 1935, ten days before the holding of the referendum, the Sakdals attempted an armed insurrection, nearly 60,000 peasants marching on 14 towns in Central and Southern Luzon, entering them and engaging the Constabulary. Poorly-armed and ill-led, they were easily suppressed by the Constabulary, which killed 57 and wounded hundreds. The Sakdal movement was tainted by a connection with Japan, through Benigno Ramos who was in Japan seeking support when the revolt broke out, apparently prematurely organized by impatient lower-ranking leaders.

The implication that stands out from these outbursts of revolt, in which an independence demand was mingled with social protest and class-based rebellion, was that Filipino peasants and workers did not have faith in those who had negotiated an independence or were implementing its terms and did not believe that the independence arranged over their heads held any benefit for them. They did not see that the independence in the offing would change anything in their lives; the same collaborating officials, landlords, and others of wealth would remain in their positions of power, including even the foreign imperialist who would be guaranteed his "rights."

To the revolutionary left, the independence being prepared, and the Commonwealth Constitution, were not for the people but were a facade for imperialism to continue in control of the Philippines with the aid of traitors. Said the PKP,

> under the Constitution, if the agents of imperialism are the ones to govern, the right of the workers and peasants to organize and defend themselves is lost forever. This is the prelude to the establishment of a dictatorial form of government which is really against the interests of the workers and peasants . . . We don't want a fake independence! We don't want leaders who are only the miserable agents of the imperialists![12]

Such a viewpoint was in keeping with the sharp class struggle conditions then prevailing in the Philippines, in which the Constabulary was increasingly used against rebelling peasants and striking workers. Both U.S. and Filipino officials termed peasant union and trade union leaders who called for "complete and immediate independence" as "agitators" and "Bolsheviks." Not surprisingly, the PKP saw the Tydings-McDuffie and the Constitutional provisions for the right of the U.S. to intervene and to call Filipino armed forces into service with those of the U.S. as intended for putting down struggles of the people for social justice.

In the election of a Commonwealth government held on September 17, 1935 the movements of the left did not support Manuel Quezon or Sergio Osmena, who ran as presidential and vice-presidential candidates of the Nacionalists Party claiming credit for independence. A Coalition of the Oppressed Masses was put together, comprised of the Republican Party (headed by Bishop Gregorio Aglipay of the nationalist Philippine Independent Church), the Socialist Party, and the Toilers' League (a legal front for the outlawed Communist Party). The Coalition ran Bishop Aglipay for president and Norberto Nabong of the Toilers' League for vice-president. Its program, headed by the demand for complete and immediate independence, included removal of the U.S. army from the Philippines, the extension of civil rights, the release of political prisoners, and nationalization of key industries and haciendas. In the election, Bishop Aglipay received 147,951 votes to

Quezon's 694,104; Emilio Aguinaldo, running as a third candidate to draw opposition votes from the left, had 179,390.

Left opposition to the Commonwealth government continued after its installation.

INDEPENDENCE AND THE FASCIST THREAT

The independence issue, and the Commonwealth period, were deeply affected and had a different light thrown upon them by the course of world events in the 1930s.

One development was the shift toward capitalist reform by the dominant business and political circles in the U.S. The New Deal program of Franklin D. Roosevelt brought enactment of a social security system for the people, unemployment insurance, a minimum wage, laws that enabled trade union organization and collective bargaining, state-provided work for the unemployed and other democratizing measures, all demanded and fought for by the American left. A New Deal liberal, Frank Murphy, was appointed as Philippine governor-general in 1933, becoming High Commissioner in 1935 when the Commonwealth came into effect.

The U.S. reform trend influenced the policies of Quezon soon after he assumed the presidency of the Commonwealth. In 1936 his government passed a series of reform laws that amounted to a response to demands of the labor movement: a Minimum Wage Act, an 8-Hour a Day Labor Act for at least some industries, the expansion of public education, the establishment of a national language. In 1937 he proclaimed the implementation of a Rice Share Tenancy Act which had originally been passed in 1933 but blocked with a nullifying rider by the landlords; now to be unblocked, it provided for 50-50 crop sharing, a guaranteed 15 per cent share of the harvest to a tenant regardless of his debt to the landlord, and for landlord-tenant contracts to be in writing and in the local dialect so peasants could understand them. Also in 1937 the right to vote was extended to women. Quezon called this his Social Justice Program.

This move to reform was one factor in a reassessment of Quezon by the Philippine left. Another, deeper factor was the rise of aggressive fascism which had become seriously felt in the Philippines by the mid-1930s. The triumph of Hitler and the Nazi Party in Germany in 1933 was a distant warning, but a much closer threat came from Japan, where militarist fascism had gained full control by the middle of the decade, embarking in 1937 on the conquest of China and proclaiming the establishment of a New Order in Asia, accompanying this with an unrestrained naval buildup that pointed to expansion southward.

At first the PKP took the position that a threat of war and Japanese attack was due to the U.S. military presence in the Philippines and that the U.S. would use Filipinos as cannon fodder in an imperialist war with Japan. However, by 1935 the international Communist movement had developed a clear-cut anti-fascist stand which Filipino Communists soon adopted. A delegation of the PKP attended the 7th World Congress of the Communist International held in Moscow in July–August 1935, bringing home the message of a united front of all democratic forces against fascism.

That attendance was arranged by a representative of the Communist Party of the USA, Isabelle Auerbach, who was sent to the Philippines with the clandestine mission of contacting the underground PKP, obtaining a delegation of six, and then escorting them over a difficult route by way of China and Japan and the Trans-Siberian railway to Moscow. The six Filipino communists remained in the Soviet Union for study after the Comintern Congress.

The anti-fascist policy, its ramifications, and its call for new class alliances to contend with the fascist threat were not easily accepted and implemented by the left in the Philippines, which was being suppressed and denied any real benefit in the independence process by U.S. imperialism and its Filipino collaborators.

However, in August 1936 another American Communist initiative helped to clear the way for the change. Isabelle Auerbach returned to the Philippines with her husband, Sol Auerbach, who became better known under his pseudonym, James S. Allen. Part of their mission was to work for the freedom of the imprisoned and exiled PKP leaders. Bearing also an assignment from *The Nation* magazine to write a series of articles on the Philippines, James Allen obtained a long interview with President Quezon in which a wide-ranging discussion of the fascist question was developed, climaxed by his urging Quezon to grant amnesty to the PKP political prisoners, as evidence that an independent Philippines would be founded on democracy and justice as the best counter to fascism. The interview took place on November 23, 1936, and on New Year's Day of 1937 Quezon issued an amnesty proclamation restoring freedom to the Filipino communists.[13]

Quezon's amnesty step contributed further to a reassessment of him by the left but it was still insufficient to establish him as an ally against fascism. Although moves to build a democratic front were undertaken, the Commonwealth government continued to be denounced as reactionary and a call continued to be made for complete and immediate independence. A PKP change of policy, of moving away from a relatively sectarian attitude to a broadened position, was occurring, but slowly. On September 7, 1937 the PKP submitted a statement to the Joint Preparatory Committee on Philippine Affairs holding hearings in the U.S. It persisted in the demand for immediate, complete and absolute independence," for the immediate complete severance of the U.S.-Philippine trade relationship, and for the immediate withdrawal of all U.S. armed forces from the Philippines.[14]

Within three weeks a letter was sent to the Philippines by James S. Allen and was published in the Manila press on November 1, 1937. In a fraternal manner it sought to throw a fresh light on the national and international situation. While agreeing with the correctness of the PKP slogan "An independent republic and the building of a democratic nation," the letter warned that in carrying it out "we must guard against any tendency towards any revolutionary romanticism and substitute for it a solid revolutionary-nationalist realism."

That realism had to do with a correct appreciation of the fascist threat. "During the last few years the international situation has changed so radically that a change in the traditional attitude on the part of the Filipino Marxists and radicals has become necessary." The change arose from the aggressive actions and designs of Japan. "Today, not the United States but Japan appears as the main obstacle to Philippine independence." To confront this menace "by no means implies that the aim of obtaining complete independence from the U.S. is to be sacrificed nor are the related questions of liberating the Philippines from the bondage of feudal remnants to be lost sight of."

The core of the argument advanced by James Allen, who was voicing the antifascist united front position of the CPUSA, was the need for a change of attitude toward the United States which, in view of the new alignment of forces in the world, had to be seen as part of the democratic front against fascism; ("the defense problems of the Philippines coincide with the defense problems of the United States in the Pacific area"), and, together with this, the need for a change of attitude toward Quezon:

> In the fight between democracy and fascist tendencies, which is assuming such important forms in the Philippines also, the policy should be to direct the main blows against the most reactionary forces. In the case of the Philippines, those reactionary forces are the pro-Japanese elements and the sugar barons. Every effort should be made to prevent driving Quezon into their hands, and in drawing him toward the democratic front. Quezon is still far from being a Mexican Cardenas or an American

Roosevelt. But the important thing is that he can be made to go toward that direction. He will go in that direction, i.e., in the direction of democracy, if he is made to understand that he can get the support of all the so-called opposition elements on really democratic and progressive measures.[14]

This fraternal contribution helped to crystallize the ideas of a national democratic front that were growing within the PKP by this time. It was concluded that an essential part of such a front should be the attainment of the legality of the outlawed PKP. An Extraordinary Plenum of the Central Committee of the party was held on August 28-30, 1938 which decided on the bold step of forcing the issue by holding an open, public Congress of the PKP, at which the democratic, anti-fascist position would be central. A Memorandum prepared for the Plenum said:

The central problems now facing the Filipino people are: improvement of the living standards, security of welfare and democratic rights of the people against the encroachments of reaction and monopoly capital inside the country as well as against the outside intervention and aggression of fascist powers, especially Japan, and expansion of the political freedoms and democratic rights of the people. This is the way to give a firm and strong foundation to the gaining of complete independence.

It was then asserted that Japanese military fascism

is the main obstacle to the establishment of an independent democratic Republic of the Philippines and to the securing of its security. Under the present conditions, the immediate and complete severance of *all* relations with the United States will enable Japan to convert the Philippines into a new Formosa, Korea or Manchukuo, into a new military base for aggression against the Pacific Ocean peoples.[15]

The 3rd Congress of the PKP, to which this change of political position was presented, was held on October 29-31, 1938. Held openly and given wide publicity in the Philippine press, it proved to be a landmark in the development of the left in the country and of the substance of a national democratic front. It was attended by James S. Allen, who was sent to the Philippines once again to cement further the solidarity of U.S. and Filipino Communists and anti-fascists. Commonwealth government agencies did not interfere with the Congress and in effect acknowledged the PKP's legal status. No opposition to this was expressed by the U.S. authorities who had illegalized the party six years earlier, an attitude undoubtedly reflecting the fact that the

Communists in the United States itself were then playing an important part in support of Roosevelt's New Deal reforms.

Among numerous political statements and resolutions approved by the 3rd Congress of the PKP was a central statement, "Independence, Democracy and Peace," which dealt with the salient question of the national struggle for independence. Asserting that "We cannot separate the destiny of our country from the destiny of mankind," it pointed out that "The development of our democracy, the preservation of our national integrity, the well-being and prosperity of our people, the attainment of our complete independence are inseparable from the world-wide struggle of democracy against fascism."

Said the statement:

> Our only hope of maintaining the right of independence and securing our freedom rests, not in reliance upon the Japanese military-fascists and their allies but in our continued and firmer cooperation with the forces of world democracy. The emphasis should not be upon immediate separation from the U.S. but the interest of the Filipino people lies in establishing their unity with the democratic and progressive forces in the United States and with other democratic people, and not in attitudes which would favor the projects of fascism and place the Philippines under the heel of the Mikado.

Such a position was in no way a retreat from nor an abandonment of the independence struggle. While declaring that "The well-being of our people, the preservation and extension of our democratic rights and advancement of the cause of complete independence can best be attained, under the present circumstances, within the form of relations established under the Independence Act," the PKP stated firmly that it was "opposed to any form of permanent retention by the United States" and condemned the moves by both U.S. and Filipino monopoly groups to obtain acceptance of "perpetual American sovereignty."[16]

One of the most important features of the PKP's 3rd Congress was the sealing of a merger of the PKP with the Socialist Party. Organized in 1933 in Pampanga province of Central Luzon, where semi-feudal land tenancy was most widespread and oppressive, the Socialist Party was a militant, fighting organization, not at all a social-democratic party as its name might imply. Founded by an elderly nationalist lawyer from a Pampangan landowning family, Pedro Abad Santos, who had been a Nacionalista Party stalwart until disillusioned by its collaborationist record, it had a syndicalist character, with virtually no distinction made between the party and its amorphous trade union, the *Aguman ding Maldang Talapagobra* (General Workers Union) .

However, Abad Santos and the Socialist Party worked closely with the underground PKP in united front activity and the positions of the two parties on independence and working class demands were almost identical. The merger, combining the leaderships under the name of the PKP, considerably strengthened the core of the left, democratic forces in the country.

In the period that followed the concept of a democratic front against fascism did not acquire much substance and was never formalized in agreed positions of the left or broad democratic movement with President Quezon. However, Quezon continued to project his Social Justice program, did not reverse his allowance of legality to the PKP, and increasingly took an anti-Japanese posture as Japan's aggressions in Eastern Asia mounted. The left supported whatever democratic steps were taken by Quezon but at the same time reactionary forces and tendencies exerted strong pressure on Quezon to curtail concessions to the left. Furthermore, pro-fascist activities grew.

Pro-fascism in the Philippines came from two sources. One of these was within the remnants of the Spanish colonial groups, especially the Spanish-dominated Dominican religious order and others in the hierarchy of the Catholic Church. During the civil war in Spain that began in 1936 the main sections of the Catholic Church sided with General Franco and his fascist Falange movement and conducted an international campaign against the Spanish Republican government, of an anti-Communist character. It was carried on in the Philippines as well, with the PKP the target. The Church was not alone in pro-fascist sentiment: the owner of the big San Miguel brewery in Manila and related interests, Andres Soriano, then a Spanish citizen, had close ties with the Falange, as did other Spanish businessmen and landowning families. They played an important part in the Philippine economy and wealthy social life.

The other pro-fascist groupings were pro-Japanese and were of greater direct menace. Japanese commercial activity was growing and a sizeable Japanese colony had been implanted in the Davao region of the island of Mindanao, engaged chiefly in cultivating banana plantations. More of a problem, however, was a pro-Japanese (and to some extent a pro-Falangist) influence in Philippine opposition political parties, especially the Sakdal Party and a small National-Socialist Party.

Aside from the direct fascist threat there were other anti-democratic tendencies that disturbed progressive Filipinos. Jose Laurel, an Associate Justice of the Supreme Court, published a book, *Forces That Make a Nation Great*, which voiced authoritarian concepts close to the fascist ideology. Laurel was appointed Secretary of Justice in the

Quezon cabinet. Quezon himself, instead of moving toward an expansion of democracy and of civil rights for the people in keeping with social justice, came out with a proposal for "partyless democracy," an idea born of his ambition to become president of the future independent republic; it would have meant the elimination of all opposition political parties and the installing of dictatorial rule by Quezon's own political organization. Widespread criticism, including a PKP attack on the concept as a variant of fascistic government, caused Quezon to drop the proposal.

Relations of the left with Quezon became increasingly under strain. They nearly reached breaking point in 1939 when Quezon began to lend endorsement to the slogan of "realistic reexamination" of Philippine independence. The "reexamination" move emanated on the one hand from U.S. interests that were feeling confidence in a revival of world trade and in signs of recovery from depression linked with the outbreak of the World War II in Europe and therefore saw benefit in a more indefinite retention of the Philippines, and was supported on the other hand by Filipino landlord and *comprador* groups that wanted a perpetuation of their preferential colonial ties with the U.S. market. In the Commonwealth years from 1936 to 1941 these Filipino groups, instead of actively seeking new markets in preparation for independence, had maximized exports to the U.S., gaining a favorable balance of trade for the Philippines in that time totalling P401,800,000, which went almost wholly into the pockets of the sugar barons and other export producers, the main financial backers of the Nacionalista Party. Nationalist sentiment among the Filipino people, including PKP protest against backtracking on independence, proved stronger and "reexaminationism" subsided.

In April 1941 the Commonwealth government began setting up a civilian defense system to meet the threatening war emergency, a step that dovetailed with intensified training of a national army. Neither of the defense measures had a democratic content. As part of its call for a national democratic front, the PKP had urged the creation of a people's army and for the involvement of the people's organizations, including trade unions and peasant unions, in national defense. The call was ignored by the Quezon government and by General Douglas MacArthur, who assumed command of the combined U.S. and Philippine armies. Instead, the civil defense program, which had an authoritarian character, included instructions for suppressive steps against left-wing organizations considered "subversive."

As the fascist threat loomed larger from outside the country (in 1939 Japanese forces occupied Hainan and the Spratley Islands and in

1940 moved into Indo-China in the wake of the capitulation of France to Nazi Germany), class conflict and anti-democratic tendencies intensified in the Philippines. Initially, Quezon, pursuing his Social Justice policies, gave concessions to the militant labor movement, his tactics being to try to contain and control them. He created a National Commission of Labor and a National Commission of Peasants in which the left-wing organizations were included and given board posts (although conservative or right-wing organizations were carefully given majority representation). However, when an upsurge of working class organization occurred in the latter 1930s and beginning of the 1940s, reactionary landlord and business groups clamored for laws restricting worker and peasant organization and for re-imposing illegality on the PKP.

In 1938 there were 188 recognized trade unions (i.e., registered with and recognized by the Department of Labor, a total that did not take account of unrecognized unions) with 46,456 members; by 1941 the number of unions had jumped to 438 with 100,907 members. Trade union-led strike struggles numbered 57 involving 4,667 workers in 1937 and increased to 203 involving 27,559 workers in 1940. By 1941 the Communist-led peasant organization, KPMP, had more than doubled in the same period, to 60,000 members. Peasant struggles against semi-fuedal tenancy conditions rose from 663 involving less than 2,000 tenants in 1937 to 1,374 involving 4,691 tenants in 1940.

In Central Luzon the peasant-landlord disputes became especially sharp and the Constabulary was called on to put down strikes in the fields. Quezon was put under strong pressure from reactionary landlords, and from urban business interests, to suppress worker and peasant organizations. Anti-Communist propaganda from these groups became intense, combining with that disseminated by the pro-fascists. In Pampanga province, where peasant struggles reached their peak, a right-wing strike-breaking organization, *Cawal ning Kapayapaan* (Knights of Peace), was set up to terrorize peasants. The anti-Communism and the suppressive measures did not stop the mass movement. In the municipal elections of 1940 PKP/Socialist mayors were elected in a dozen towns of the Central Luzon provinces of Pampanga, Tarlac and Nueva Ecija (including the town of Arayat, Pampanga where Quezon himself had a home and an estate), and PKP councillors were elected in other towns.

However, as urban and agrarian strike struggle grew, Quezon yielded increasingly to landlord and capitalist pressure. In September 1940 he appointed as Secretary of Labor the arch-reactionary and active anti-Communist, Leon Guinto, who was one of the leading members of the

Cawal ning Kapayapaan. At landlord demand, Quezon put Pampanga under Constabulary control in mid-1941, and in the latter part of that year the Constabulary was authorized to take control of the municipal police forces in a great many towns of Pampanga, Nueva Ecija, Bulacan, Tarlac, Pangasinan, Bataan, Zambales, Laguna, Cavite, Batangas, and Rizal provinces. This was the increasingly tense situation on the eve of the Japanese attack on the Philippines.

Throughout this period the Filipino left tried hard to preserve the semblance of a national democratic front and to give substance to it. A significant development, influenced in part by the growth of an anti-fascist awareness and in part by national feeling stirred by the prospect of independence, was a spread of a left nationalism among many Filipino intellectuals. From the mid-1930s onward, for the first time, a growing number of intellectuals joined the PKP. This incidence of unity between the working class movement and a segment of the middle class was the first such trend since the conquest and collaboration era early in the century.

It was far, however, from representing the national unity indispensable for a country nearing its independence. In general, as the transitional Commonwealth stage to independence passed its halfway mark, the basic conflict in Philippine society, the deep and unbridged class division, remained and was tending to worsen. The approach of independence day furthermore was made problematical by the coming into the open of some of those who preferred the colonial relationship and had not been resigned to its ending. By all indications the national unity that was essential for the balanced launching of Philippine freedom was very far from realization. Doubts existed, too, about the intentions of the U.S., as colonial ruler and as future influence. Over everything, over the prospect of independence itself, had spread the cloud of uncertainty from the menace of Japanese militarist fascism. Once again the destiny of the Filipino people was a hostage of outside forces.

V

World War II and Independence: The Fateful Intervention

The consequences of World War II were the most profound historically of all the outcomes of military conflict. In their attempts to conquer and dominate virtually the entire globe, Nazi Germany and Japanese militarist fascism had shattered the structures of rule in numerous countries, and the restoration of that rule proved impossible in the wake of fascism's defeat. Far-reaching change took place, in Eastern Europe under the protective arm of the Soviet Union's victorious army, and in Asia through popular liberation movements led by Communists and revolutionary nationalists.

Japan's drive of conquest in Asia drove out the colonial regimes of France, Britain, the U.S. and the Netherlands. Japan's own defeat opened the way for the victory of the Chinese revolution, and for the successful independence struggles in Indo-China, Indonesia, Malaya, India and Burma. In all those countries the colonial system was ended and governments of varying forms of nationalism won power.

In the Philippines it was different. Although Japan defeated and drove out the U.S. colonial rulers and occupied the country for over three years, a similar profound change did not occur. Independence had already been legislated and it took place, as laid down, in 1946. By all implications of the war's significance, however, the nature of that independence should have been transformed to a more democratic state but unlike the rest of colonial Asia, it was the imperial power, the United States, that returned to dictate and to reshape the Philippine future.

Elsewhere, liberation followed World War II. In the Philippines the victory was far from complete.

THE EXPENDABLE COUNTRY

For U.S. imperialism the Japanese factor had been a looming menace almost from the moment the Philippine colony had been acquired. At the outset that acquisition had had a military motivation, to gain a naval base close to the Asian mainland to serve as a support for the commercial penetration of the China market. Also, it fitted the concept of the naval power theorist, Admiral Mahan, of building a string of naval bases across the Pacific as the support structure for a U.S. Pacific fleet. That concept, however, which envisaged a fleet in the Atlantic as well, had to be severely scaled down out of cost considerations. It was one of the issues, together with the opposition of domestic producers in the U.S. and of anti-imperialists acting on practical and moral grounds, which determined the character of the U.S. relationship with the Philippines. What aggravated the military issue was the fact that, no sooner had the U.S. declared its conquest of the Philippines complete, in 1902, than a menacing Japanese military power appeared on the scene.

That factor had materialized before the U.S. arrival in the Philippines, in the Sino-Japanese War of 1894–95, one result of which was the ceding of Formosa to Japan by defeated China. The full Japanese threat was demonstrated, however, in the Russo-Japanese War of 1904–05, fought in Manchuria and Korea, in the course of which Japan destroyed a Russian fleet in the Battle of Tsushima, fought numerically superior Russian land armies to a stalemate, and in a significant episode beseiged and captured the supposedly impregnable fortified Russian naval base of Port Arthur.

With a militarily strong Japan looming as a rival in the markets of China and other Asian countries, U.S. fears persisted that the Philippines was a logical target for Japanese expansionism. U.S. military plans for the Philippines had centered on constructing a fortified naval base on the western side of the island of Luzon, either at Subic Bay or Manila Bay. The lessons of the battle for Port Arthur forced realization that almost identical questions of defense against attack and seige figured for the contemplated Philippine base. It was decided that the Philippines could not be defended against an attack by a power like Japan, nor could a Philippine base be reinforced in time and sustained at the end of a logistic line extending across the Pacific.

In the argument over a military strategy for the Pacific, the idea of building a major naval base in the Philippines was abandoned, the main base for the strategy being located at Pearl Harbor, Hawaii. Bases were constructed in the Philippines but appropriations for them by the U.S. Congress were limited and they were relegated to a lesser category.

In the secret Taft–Katsura Agreement in 1905, the U.S. sought to secure Japanese assurance of non-infringement on U.S. colonial possession of the Philippines in exchange for U.S. recognition of a Japanese protectorate in Korea, but a few years later, in World War I, Japan's seizure of the German holdings of Kiaochow Bay and Tsingtao in China and its attempt to impose its notorious 21 Demands on China itself made it obvious that no agreements could be relied upon to deter the Japanese drive to be dominant in Asia. Western powers gradually retreated before Japan's ascendency. In 1922, in order to obtain Japan's agreement to a five-power naval treaty that put limits on its building of battleships and aircraft carriers, the U.S., Britain, France and Italy agreed that in Asia "the status quo . . . with regard to fortifications and naval bases shall be maintained." For the Philippines this meant no further U.S. fortification of bases, which increased their vulnerability to a Japanese attack.

Although the U.S. press in the 1920s was filled with alarmist reports of Japan's aggressive intentions, featured by the racist warning of "the yellow peril," U.S. War Department plans did not contemplate a serious effort to engage Japan in Asia, or to defend the Philippine colony. U.S. War Plan Orange, designed for the Philippines, dating from 1925, was not a plan for resolutely defending the country as a whole or the Filipino people, but was limited to a holding action of not more than six months around Manila Bay, particularly on the little rocky island of Corregidor. No more than token resistance was involved. As the former U.S. governor-general in the Philippines, William Cameron Forbes, said in 1927:

> I doubt very much if any real effort will be made to defend the Philippine islands as such. They are indefensible and from a military point of view not worth defending. The main thing is to make interference with them as costly as possible.[1]

War Plan Orange was maintained as the official U.S. military policy up to World War II, including while Philippine independence was being approved and set on course with the Commonwealth. It was maintained despite the mounting of Japanese military aggression in Manchuria and China in the 1930s and down the Asian coast to Indo-China. During the threatening 1930s, no increase of appropriations for defenses in the Philippines were made by the U.S. Congress.

Missing from U.S. military planning was any serious effort to provide for the defense and security of the Philippines. Only when the

Commonwealth was established and Filipino leaders had the authority to do so were such steps taken, by them. Significantly, the first act of the Commonwealth's National Assembly was the creation of a National Army. However, not a single factory for manufacturing arms or other military equipment existed in the Philippines, and the U.S. did virtually nothing to fill the gap.

The chief but small act of U.S. military assistance to the Philippines was the assignment in 1935 of General Douglas MacArthur, a former chief of staff of the U.S. army, to President Quezon's Commonwealth government as military adviser. Even this was given only at Quezon', pressing request. Assuming the grand title of Field Marshall (and demanding an $18,000 salary that equalled that of the U.S. governor-general), MacArthur, who privately considered the Philippines indefensible, projected a grandiose plan that went far beyond War Plan Orange, proposing an extravagant scheme for the defense of the entire country from attack. The enemy would be met at the beaches of every obvious invasion point.

MacArthur called for the creation, over the ten-year transition period to independence, of a large citizen's army, with a regular army of 11,000 plus the training of 40,000 reserves each year. To finance this, he asked the Philippine government to provide a total of P16,000,000 ($8,000,000) to be spread over the ten-year plan. To be included was a 250-plane air force and a 50-torpedo boat navy. Huge as it was for the Philippines to muster, not only was the sum hopelessly inadequate for what MacArthur proposed but the U.S. War Department considered the Field Marshall's plan wholly unfeasible and would not provide even obsolete equipment for it. Although MacArthur went on talking about defending the entire islanded country, little was done to create the army needed to do it.

When President Franklin Roosevelt, reacting finally to the Japanese advance southward, resorted to his powers under the Philippine Independence Act and on July 27, 1941 ordered the integration of the Philippine army into the U.S. army, making Douglas MacArthur commander of the United States Armed Forces in the Far East (USAFFE), the combined total of the U.S. and Filipino troops was only 22,550 officers and men. Ten Filipino reserve divisions were supposed to be included, but these existed for the most part on paper.[2] Many of those able to be called up lacked guns or uniforms. MacArthur, however, persisted in his bombast, claiming that his defense measures would cost an invading enemy half a million casualties and $5 billion, which he said he was confident would deter an attack. Despite the talk about such a powerful defense, on November 30, 1941 the total of the

U.S.-Commonwealth armed forces were 31,095 officers and men, of which 11,957 were Philippine Scouts.[3]

To Filipino government leaders it became increasingly obvious that the MacArthur defense plan had no real substance. Both President Quezon and Vice-President Osmena, seeing no army taking shape, began to voice criticisms. Osmena in particular called the plan a failure, charging it with giving Filipinos a false sense of security. (MacArthur never forgave Osmena for his sharp criticism, resulting in serious consequences later.) Quezon took the course of urging the U.S. to advance the date for independence to 1940, which would enable the Philippines to proclaim its neutrality in the conflict that seemed inevitable. The idea of an earlier independence and neutrality was rejected by Washington as well as by MacArthur. It ran counter to U.S. war plans for the Philippines to serve as a delaying point to hold a Japanese attack while the U.S. mobilized its response.

President Quezon went further. On a trip to Japan in 1937 he sought a guarantee that Japan would respect the neutrality of an independent Philippines. The Japanese foreign minister gave him an assurance that Japan would sign such a treaty.[4] Quezon's effort reflected the fact that many Filipinos didn't share the U.S. imperialist attitude toward the Japanese. It was recalled that during the resistance war against U.S. conquest, Filipino envoys had been sent to Japan to obtain arms; a shipload was provided but it had unfortunately sunk en route to the Philippines.[5] One of the Filipino resistance leaders, General Artemio Ricarte, refusing to live under U.S. rule, chose Japan for exile. Any pro-Japanese sentiment arose mainly from a hatred of U.S. colonialism. Ricarte returned with the Japanese invaders to find that history had passed him by, and to be regarded as a traitor instead of a liberator.

When the Japanese attack finally came on December 7, 1941 (December 8, Philippine time) it struck on the same day at Pearl Harbor, Hawaii and at U.S. bases in the Philippines. It was quickly plain that the MacArthur defense plan for the whole of the country was indeed an illusion. The crowning blow to the ill-prepared defense was the destruction of MacArthur's entire air force, caught on the ground by Japanese planes despite a nine-hour warning interval between the Pearl Harbor attack and the invaders' appearance over the Philippines.

Filipino reserves called up with virtually no training, equipment, arms or officers were unable to resist Japanese invasion forces at any point. MacArthur's USAFFE fell back hastily on the old War Plan Orange strategy of a Manila Bay delaying action, retreating to Bataan peninsula bordering the Bay and to fortified Corregidor Island in the Bay. Even for this move, sufficient stockpiled supplies had not been accumulated. The Pearl Harbor disaster, the near-destruction of the U.S. Pacific Fleet, put finish to the theory of a supposed U.S. reinforcement/ rescue operation hurrying to save the Philippines from the enemy. This myth, however, was kept up to the U.S.-Filipino USAFFE troops until their surrender, on April 9, 1942 on Bataan and on May 7 on Corregidor.

President Quezon, holed up on Corregidor under Japanese bombard-ment, developed a sudden clarity about the interests of the Filipino people at this point. In his subsequent autobiography he wrote of his concern over "the possible useless sacrifice of the Philippine Army," which led him to question the situation of his invaded country. "At last," he wrote,

> I thought I found the key to the problem. I would ask the President of the United States to authorize me to issue a public manifesto asking the Government of the United States to grant immediate, complete and absolute independence to the Philippines; that the neutralization of the Philippines be agreed at once by the United States and the Imperial Japanese government, that within a reasonable period of time, both armies, American and Japanese, be withdrawn; that neither nation should occupy bases in the Philippines; that the Philippine Army be demobilized, the only organized force remaining in the islands to be the Philippine Constabulary for the maintenance of law and order; that Japanese and American noncombatants who so wished be evacuated with their own army under reciprocal and fitting conditions.

Quezon sent such a communication to President Roosevelt, winning the approval of his Cabinet by arguing that the Japanese might move to declare Philippine independence themselves and win over the Filipino people by doing so.[6]

The reply of Roosevelt which turned away the call of Quezon was a good example of the rhetoric employed by the U.S. in its wartime policy toward the Philippines. Claiming that under the terms of the Tydings-McDuffie Act "we have undertaken to protect you to the uttermost of our power until the time of your ultimate independence has arrived," it pledged to marshall U.S. forces to "return to the Philippines and drive the last remnants of the invaders from your soil." Pointing out that the "brutal sway" of the Axis partners (Germany, Italy and Japan) in every country they occupied negated any indepen-dence promises the Japanese could make, the letter of the U.S. presi-dent soared rhetorically: "For over forty years the American Government has been carrying out to the people of the Philippines a pledge to help them successfully, however long it might take, in their aspirations to become a self-governing and independent people, with the individual freedom and economic strength which that lofty aim makes requisite," an aim which "towards another people has been unique in the history of the family of nations." Quezon in retrospect professed to have been overwhelmed by the message but his answer had the subdued tone of the colonial politician: "We fully appreciate the reasons upon which your decision is based and we abide by it."[7]

THE REAL U.S. WAR AIMS

Out of the Bataan-Corregidor defense a legend was woven not of American-Filipino unity but of Filipino loyalty to the U.S. In truth, U.S. colonial and military strategy was not based on protecting and upholding the interests of the Filipino people but on preserving U.S. colonial interests which Filipinos were expected to defend. MacArthur, ordered out of the Philippines in March, ahead of the surrenders, to command allied forces in the South West Pacific Area, sought to prolong the myth with his proclamation, "I shall return!" At that time the date set for Philippine independence was barely four years distant and a Filipino president was accompanying MacArthur on his outward flight and would logically also return, but no "WE shall return" was announced. MacArthur's pompous words meant, in essence, that U.S. colonial rulers would return, to reclaim the colony from Japan.

As it happened, during the three years of Japanese occupation the Filipino people were left only with the making of a grim contrast between the foreign rule of the United States and that of Japan. Over 40 years of U.S. occupation and indoctrination had had their effect. Most Filipinos as a result were sympathetic to the U.S. and looked to the victory and re-arrival of the U.S. forces. The Japanese appeared harsh and ruthless in comparison, although the contrast becomes less extreme when the Japanese record is set beside that of the U.S. conquerors at the turn of the century, with its atrocities and prohibitions.

Undoubtedly the hope of Quezon and others that Japan would recognize the neutrality of a Philippines then made independent was illusory. If the Philippines had had an early freedom, an invasion by Japan of the kind made necessary by the U.S. military presence would probably not have been needed, but Japan would still have wanted the food and raw materials of the Philippines and would have obtained them. An independent Philippine government would have had to yield to Japanese demands and perhaps accept some form of dependency status. Nevertheless, it would have been a Philippine decision, and Filipinos opposed to it would have dealt with their own capitulating leaders. A struggle of resistance would have likely occurred, and those who fought would have been allied with the U.S. and the other powers in the anti-fascist camp.

The differences, however, would have been fundamental. It would have been a national liberation struggle, in defense of an independent country, with the clearest nationalist ideals rallying the population, leavened with the democratic aims of an anti-fascist war. The eventual victory, even if aided by an arrival of U.S. forces, would have enhanced and solidified Philippine independence.

For the majority of Filipinos, World War II and resistance to the Japanese were not waged in that spirit. The wartime resistance movement in the Philippines was one of the most widespread of any occupied country. Groups of a guerrilla or underground character sprang up all over the country, on virtually every island, and they had the support or sympathy of most of the population. However, only one such organization of major importance, organized and led by the Partido Komunista ng Pilipinas, had full Filipino leadership and an orientation toward national-democratic freedom. With only a few exceptions, the rest were U.S.-led or directed, subordinated to U.S. war aims.

In most cases the guerrilla units were headed by USAFFE officers, American and Filipino, who had evaded capture or had refused to surrender, going into hiding in mountains, forests or rural areas distant from the main towns. As soon as General MacArthur reached Australia after evacuating from Corregidor, he and his staff set up radio contact with the USAFFE officers left behind and assumed control of their activities. These guerrilla forces from that time onward functioned as a subordinate section of the U.S. armed forces.

A number of the USAFFE-led guerrillas were eager for action against the Japanese enemy. During the early months of the war some of them recruited Filipino fighters and began attacks on Japanese patrols and vehicle convoys. Such tendencies, however, were soon checked by MacArthur. A group led by a U.S. officer in Northern Luzon, Colonel Martin Moses, was for example instructed in October 1942 by MacArthur from Australia "to limit hostilities and contact with the enemy to the minimum amount necessary for safety" and to "concentrate on perfecting organization and on developing an intelligence net."[8]

This was the standard order of the U.S. commander in the South West Pacific Area as far as the Philippines was concerned. The message in December 1942 to the Filipino USAFFE officer on Panay island, Major Macario Peralta, further elaborated the policy: "Your primary mission is to maintain your organization and secure maximum amount of information. Offensive guerrilla activity should be postponed until ordered from here."[9] Overall, a lie-low policy was imposed on the U.S.-controlled guerrilla groups whose main role was made one of collecting and relaying intelligence information to MacArthur and his staff. Filipino guerrillas were instructed to wait until the U.S. army returned before taking offensive action against the Japanese. Some action did occur but not enough as far as the USAFFE was concerned to comprise a major military problem for Japanese occupation forces.

Behind this policy was the U.S. aim to regain the Philippines as the colonial ruler, in control of the Filipino political and military forces that the war might engender. Above all, the U.S. did not want a liberation movement to emerge in which leaders with nationalist aspirations might come to the fore. No national guerrilla directing body was allowed to develop. From MacArthur's headquarters in Australia and then in New Guinea, direction was given to all USAFFE-connected groups which were divided up on a regional basis into ten military districts, the local commanders of which were appointed and authorized by MacArthur.

On MacArthur's staff the man put in charge of directing, organizing, supplying and keeping a tight rein on Filipino guerrillas was Courtney Whitney, a resident of the Philippines from 1925 to 1940 as corporation lawyer and president of several U.S. mining firms. Elevated to the rank of brigadier general, Whitney, a close friend of MacArthur during his field marshall years (he was MacArthur's lawyer), was appointed head of the Philippine Regional Section under the G-2 (Intelligence) wing of staff but actually reported directly to MacArthur. Whitney had intimate knowledge of and links with Filipino political leaders, particularly those from the most conservative collaborating elite, and he saw to it that the guerrilla network was as much as possible in touch with those Filipino sectors.

Whitney was but one of a coterie of officers on the MacArthur staff who had pre-war business interests in the Philippines and close ties with the wealthy Filipino elite. The head of MacArthur's G-2, General Charles Willoughby, had held that position on MacArthur's pre-war staff in the Philippines and had become closely related to Andres Soriano, the Spanish Falangist businessman. Willoughby admired Franco. Another, who had become a Navy Commander, was Charles "Chick" Parsons, an owner of the Luzon Stevedoring Company which had a near-monopoly on port services. He sat on the boards of four banks in

Manila. Parsons, working in coordination with Whitney, ran a number of clandestine missions to the Philippines by submarine to contact guerrillas and perfect communications. His reports, however, concerned not only military matters but also estimates of Filipino political forces and figures who could play a part in the postwar period.[10]

Also on the MacArthur staff was Joseph McMicking who, like Parsons, was among the wealthiest businessmen in the Philippines, an executive of both the Ayala and Soriano corporations which ranked high in *comprador* interests. Andres Soriano himself, the leading personage in the Philippine branch of the Spanish fascist Falange, owner of the highly profitable San Miguel Brewery in Manila, joined MacArthur in 1944 shortly before the re-invasion of the Philippines was to begin. During most of the war Soriano was in Washington acting as Secretary of Finance in Quezon's cabinet-in-exile. His closeness to Quezon demonstrated the interlocking of the colonial politics with the most reactionary business circles in the Philippines. When Quezon in September 1943 attempted to renew his effort to have Philippine independence proclaimed as a wartime measure (it was evidently intended to negate the effect of the puppet independence the Japanese were preparing to announce, which occurred on October 14, 1943), asking U.S. Senator Millard Tydings to manage it through a congressional resolution, it was Soriano who intervened to persuade Tydings to withdraw the resolution. Soriano was afraid that independence at that time, when the U.S. was not on the ground in the Philippines to control affairs, might endanger his extensive business interests. His transfer to MacArthur's staff put him in a position to protect his holdings. Significantly, the San Miguel Brewery compound was one of the few sites in Manila that was not destroyed or badly damaged by U.S. bombing and ground fighting in the retaking of the city, enabling it to resume production almost immediately to satisfy the thirst of U.S. troops.

This group with special interests in the Philippines, made up of top businessmen who had been close associates in the colony and who favored either "reexamination" of independence or the perpetuation of a colonialist relationship with the U.S., worked as a team in the U.S. command structure, with the close cooperation of MacArthur, mapping out the policies for a "liberated" Philippines. In particular attention was paid to re-installing or rebuilding the political structure, from town level on up, making use of the intelligence information supplied by lie-low guerrillas.

The role of the Philippines in the Pacific war strategy of the U.S. and allied forces against Japan is of particular interest for an understanding of imperialist aims in the war. Seizing the Philippines was a major triumph for Japan over its U.S. rival. In the strategy to defeat Japan, however, its recapture was of debatable military importance.

Japan's offensive drive reached its limit in New Guinea and the Solomon Islands, where U.S. and Australian troops checked the advance and enabled the buildup of forces for a counterattack. The campaign to dislodge the Japanese from their South West Pacific conquests was assigned to MacArthur and he directed it with panache, in "island-hopping" operations that were featured by the cutting-off of Japanese garrisons along the route from the Solomons, to the Admiralty Islands, up the coast of New Guinea, to the East Indies.

This was but one phase of the Pacific war. On a grander scale was the counterattack across the central Pacific, under the naval command of Admirals Ernest King and Chester Nimitz. After sweeping up the numerous islands the Japanese had captured and fortified—Tarawa, Kwajalein, Guam, Saipan—a direct strike at Japan itself was planned. By the middle of 1944 both prongs of the Pacific campaign had reached jump-off points for major assaults—MacArthur's forces on the approaches to the Philippines, the King-Nimitz forces poised to attack the Japanese islands themselves. At this point a dispute occurred over where the next and main blow was to be struck. King and Nimitz favored a direct assault on Japan proper, preceded by the invasion and capture of Formosa, to be used as a base for air attacks on the Japanese homeland. This would mean by-passing the Philippines and its Japanese garrison.

MacArthur insisted on first employing U.S. sea, air and ground power to regain the Philippines. His arguments were made more on alleged moral than military grounds, saying that he had promised the Filipinos he would return, that they looked upon the U.S. as the "mother country," and that they would feel "sold out" if bypassed. It would "cause all Asia to lose faith in American honor." The Filipino people, furthermore, would suffer, left in Japanese hands.

The issue was resolved in a showdown meeting with President Roosevelt in Hawaii, on July 26, 1944. MacArthur's rhetoric prevailed and the die was cast for a Philippine invasion.[11]

Behind the rhetoric were the real motivations for the military reconquest of the Philippines. By the time the decision was made to conduct a full-fledged Philippine campaign (the actual instructions for MacArthur to go ahead were not issued until September 14, 1944), the outcome of the war was very plain: Japan was being defeated and the U.S. would emerge as the dominant power in the Pacific and eastern Asia. For the power-conscious this would mean the attainment of all the strategic objectives with which the drive across the Pacific at the turn of the century, including the seizure of the Philippine colony, had been made. The logistical flood of supplies and equipment on which the U.S. armed forces rode toward victory was a forerunner of the export tide to wide-open Asian markets that could be expected, to follow. With that prospect the Philippines re-acquired its strategic value as a secure base for a resurgent imperialism.

There were fears that if the Philippines were bypassed with Japanese forces left to "wither on the vine," it would be much less submissive to U.S. designs when the war ended. Even the resistance movement so carefully controlled by Whitney and the Philippine Section might throw off U.S. restraints and pursue its own course of fighting for liberation, thereby acquiring an independent outlook. MacArthur and Whitney had their eyes on the Communist-led guerrilla movement on Luzon that was conducting a people's war including the political organization of its mass base. In the absence of U.S. control, a unity of resistance movements was not inconceivable and could confront returning U.S. forces at war's end with a provisional governmental authority capable of gaining nationalist demands. The fact that a well-supplied guerrilla army—a feasible achievement—could tie down the Japanese forces in the Philippines and thus aid an attack on Japan was not even considered. There was greater concern that the occupying Japanese army, in defeat, might surrender to or otherwise facilitate the recognition of Philippine authority.

Not to be lost sight of is that the independence date set in the Tydings-McDuffie Act was but two years distant from the 1944 decision to re-invade the Philippines. There could have been no more auspicious start for that independence than with Filipinos at the helm who had fought to throw off a foreign occupation. A U.S. government sincerely desirous of assisting in the launching of that independence should have done everything possible to help generate the national sentiment and the leadership embodying it. The independence legislation was the main consideration that set the Philippines apart from the other countries of South East Asia—colonies of European imperialist powers—occupied by Japan during the war. There was less reason in the case of the Philippines than elsewhere for the U.S. to fear Filipino resentment against the "mother country" for not storming onto its beaches because the "mother country" was leaving anyway in the very near future. Indeed, any resentment that Filipinos might have felt for being left on their own would have been all to the good in encouraging them to stand on their own two feet.

As it happened, the Philippines was the only South East Asian colony occupied by Japan where a large-scale military campaign of reconquest was mounted. It was not done in the Netherlands East Indies, Malaya or Indo-China, where Japanese forces were left on the vine and where they did not thereby take revenge bloodily on the inhabitants, as MacArthur claimed they would do in the Philippines. In those countries, of course, the war resulted in the success of independence movements and the loss of colonies to the Netherlands, Britain and France. In Indo-China decades of bitter struggle were to follow before full independence was achieved, but this was due in large part to the retention by the U.S. of its strategic position in the Philippines, which was enabled by the MacArthur military reoccupation policy.

NEW MASTERS, BUT THE SAME SERVANTS

Collaboration was a phenomenon in all of the countries overrun and occupied by the fascist powers, in both Europe and Asia. It had various motivations, the most reprehensible being ideological affinity, as fascists, with the invaders. Those with a fascist mentality were the "fifth column" of the enemy, taking an active part in occupation rule. Others collaborated out of opportunism, fear, or the desire to be on the side of the winner and to benefit materially from it.

In the Philippines the Spanish Falange movement had an estimated 10,000 members, including the backing of prominent figures in some of the richest families of Spanish origin—Soriano, Zobel de Ayala, Elizalde. The business interests of some members of these families were linked with U.S. capital or were free trade *compradores,* causing them to throw in their lot with the U.S. Andres Soriano was the principal example of these, aligning himself with Quezon and MacArthur. The Falange members in the Philippines, however, collaborated with the Japanese, who gave them privileges.

The pre-war Sakdal movement of Benigno Ramos, which disintegrated after its abortive uprising in 1935, had looked to Japan for aid. Ramos, who had fled to Japan at the time, returned in 1939 to found the Ganap Party, which conducted such rabid pro-Japanese propaganda, with an anti-American theme, that he was imprisoned for subversion. Released by the Japanese on their arrival, he played a very active collaborationist role. The Ganap was dissolved by the Japanese in 1942 along with all other political parties, to be incorporated in the fascistic mass organization, the KALIBAPI (Kapisanan sa Paglilingkad sa Bagong Filipinas, or Association for Service to the New Philippines) which functioned as a principal arm of Japanese rule. As the U.S. re-invasion started, Ramos, at Japanese behest in November 1944, organized the Makapili, an armed force of Filipinos, drawn from lumpen elements among his old Ganap members. The Makapili engaged in fighting against U.S. troops but also committed atrocities against Filipino civilians.

Active fascists were an extremist minority among those who collaborated with the Japanese. More important was the political and economic collaboration which was engaged in by a large proportion of the elite elements in Philippine society, among them most of the prominent political leaders developed by the U.S. colonial system.

This phenomenon was little different from the behavior of the *illustrado* and wealthy groups who found accommodation with the U.S. conquerors early in the century, shifting from the Spanish regime and then from the Philippine Republic to accept positions and lucrative opportunities in the new U.S. dispensation. World War II collaboration in the Philippines had this difference from the cooperation with the Nazis that occurred in occupied Europe: it had historical precedence and was in a pattern of class behavior conditioned by previous foreign rule. The readiness of Filipino bourgeois leaders to accept a compliant if not puppet role under the Japanese was intimately related to the real essence of the "education for self-rule" inculcated by U.S. officials.

It was obvious as Japanese invading forces swept from their Pangasinan landing point toward Manila in December 1941 that the Commonwealth government and its members were likely to fall into the hands of the enemy. To prevent such a total victory for the Japanese, the U.S. government, through MacArthur, insisted that President Quezon and Vice-President Osmena evacuate to the Corregidor fortress. They were accompanied only by Quezon's two aides and his family, and by Chief Justice Jose Abad Santos, Major General Basilio Valdez, Manuel A. Roxas, and Serapio Canceran, who was private secretary to Quezon. Bidding farewell to his cabinet members who were left behind in Manila, Quezon exhorted them: "Keep your faith in America, no matter what happens, She will never let you down."[12]

From Corregidor, Quezon and his party were evacuated on February 20, 1942 to the Visayan Islands and then to Mindanao, from where U.S. B-17 bombers flew them to Australia (except for Abad Santos and Roxas who were left in Mindanao). By May they had been transferred to Washington. From that time until the Philippines was re-invaded in October 1944 the semblance of a Commonwealth government in exile was maintained in Washington.

Quezon did not live until the order to reconquer the Philippines was issued to MacArthur. He died on August 1, 1944. Osmena immediately succeeded him as president. When MacArthur waded ashore at Leyte on October 20, President Osmena landed with him.

As a government-in-exile, the Commonwealth figment had a nebulous character. It was permitted token representation on the U.S. Pacific War Council but it played no part in shaping the policies of the Pacific war, including the Philippine re-invasion. Behind the scenes Quezon kept urging that Philippine independence be granted much earlier as a wartime measure but this was ignored. It might be thought that a Philippine government would have an active role in directing and encouraging the resistance against the Japanese, but neither Quezon nor Osmena were permitted to have a finger in that MacArthur-controlled area. Quezon's tendency, at the same time as urging independence, was toward increasing dependence on the U.S., especially for the reconstruction and rehabilitation of his country after the war. Thus Quezon gave virtually no attention to devising a program of postwar planning. The importance of this was tremendous because it had to do not only with overcoming war damage and dislocation but with launching the country on an independence that would be solidly based. Not until September 1943, after insistence by his cabinet members, did Quezon finally set up a Postwar Planning Board, with Osmena as chairman, but then rendered it ineffective by providing no funds for it.

After becoming president, Osmena undertook a belated planning program. Reinvasion, with all its enormous problems of reestablishing governmental authority and of reorganizing a state, was by then under way. The planning contemplated was bound narrowly by the colonial thinking that had been engrained in the Filipino political leaders developed under U.S. rule: it was focused almost exclusively on the retention, extension and expansion of free trade relations with the U.S. Discussions were begun with U.S. officials on such a perspective.[13]

The Philippine government-in-exile represented the sectors of the Filipino landlord-*comprador*-bureaucrat strata which remained firmly pro-American during the war, mainly because they were physically with American officialdom. They were the pro-U.S. wing of wartime collaboration, who were able to get away from the Philippines ahead of the Japanese occupation. The rest—landlords, businessmen, politicians, intellectuals, petty officials—remained to live under the Japanese. A few, very few, went to the guerrillas and refused to submit to the invaders. Some others endured the occupation while preserving their pro-American sentiment, keeping silent as they waited for the U.S. to return.

Of much greater concern to the Filipino people, however, were the sectors of this part of the population who made accommodation with the Japanese.

When Quezon left the Philippines he took the correct diplomatic step under conditions of belligerency of leaving behind a representative of his government to deal with the occupying power in regard to Filipino interests. He chose for this his executive secretary, Jorge B. Vargas. The U.S. High Commissioner, Francis B. Sayre, took the same step, leaving behind his Executive Assistant, Dr. Claude Buss.

By strict diplomatic procedure, Vargas was not obliged to do anything more than to make representations to the occupying forces in behalf of the Filipino people and of the Commonwealth government. To provide him with an official capacity, Quezon appointed Vargas to be Mayor of Greater Manila, but he was given no detailed instructions. The only other official left in Manila given an assignment by Quezon was Jose Laurel who was appointed Secretary of Justice as well as acting Chief Justice of the Supreme Court, and who was told to "help Mr. Vargas," presumably with legal advice. No appointments or directives were given to any other cabinet member, political leader, or other Filipino.[14]

Except for the rather vague order to Vargas, Filipino leaders were left on their own as to how to conduct themselves with the new conqueror. The issue that confronted them bore comparison with that posed by the U.S. conquest, when a refusal by Filipinos to cooperate or to accept posts in the U.S. colonial regime could well have made U.S. retention of the colony too costly to be viable. Refusal to serve the Japanese may not have meant the same problem for the Japanese who would have certainly ruled with a military government, but it would have made Japan's occupation more burdensome and would have contributed much to the national spirit of the people.

From the outset, however, Vargas and the group of cabinet members, congressmen and other leaders with whom he consulted thought only in terms of forming a council of state, chosen from among them, to be an administrative body under the Japanese. The idea of refusing to serve the new conqueror was not considered. Discussions on the form this would take began on January 4, 1942 with the Japanese command within two days of the occupation of Manila. By January 26 a Philippine Executive Commission, as demanded by Commander-in-Chief General Masaharu Homma, was formally proclaimed. At that time the fighting was at its height in Bataan and President Quezon was on Corregidor under bombardment.

The Executive Commission went beyond the instruction given to Jorge Vargas by President Quezon. It was the vehicle and embodiment of collaboration. As a critical Filipino historian has termed it, "it was a model of that elite continuity which had characterized every change of government and master since the last days of Spanish colonialism."[15]

Included in the Commission were most of the top political leaders and elite figures developed during U.S. colonial rule. Department heads under the Commission, comprising a cabinet were: Benigno S. Aquino, Secretary of Interior; Jose P. Laurel, Justice; Antonio de las Alas, Finance; Rafael R. Alunan, Agriculture and Commerce; Claro M. Recto, Education, Health and Public Welfare; Quintin Paredes, Public Works and Communications; Teofilo Sison, Auditor General and Budget Director; Serafin Marabat, Executive Secretary.

These were but a few of the elite who joined in the parade of collaboration, agreeing to take and to implement Japanese orders. The "letter of response" to the demand of General Homma for an Executive Commission to be created was signed by 32 persons who were the top strata of Filipino political and business circles. In addition to the cabinet members they were: Jose Yulo, Jorge Bocobo, Leon Guinto, Eulogio Rodriguez, Sotero Baluyot, Emilio Aguinaldo, Vicente Madrigal, Ramon J. Fernandez, Elpidio Quirino, Jose Zulueta, Dominador Tan, Francisco Lavides, Ramon Avenceña, Miguel Unson, Alejandro Roces, Pedro Sabido, Melecio Arranz, Pedro C. Hernaez, Jose Osamiz, Jose Veloso, Ricardo Navarro, Prospero Sanidad, and Eugenio Perez.[16]

As chairman of the Commission, Vargas had the authority to appoint the members of the Supreme Court, the Court of Appeals and all the lower courts. In doing so, he actually had to make few changes, the existing members proving to be readily compliant. The Commission theoretically had legislative authority but this was limited chiefly to removing or rendering inoperative existing laws which prohibited Japanese or "aliens" from owning or exploiting Philippine natural resources.

Having taken the initial step of submission and readiness to obey or conform to the invaders' orders, the collaborating Filipinos fell easily into line with succeeding moves and directives of the Japanese. One of these was the launching in December 1942 of the Kalibapi. Having dissolved all political parties and civic organizations, the number of which made control over them inconvenient, the Kalibapi was designed as a single organization for everyone, through which control and political indoctrination could be effected. Agreeing to head the Kalibapi as its director-general was Benigno Aquino, who relinquished his post as Commission secretary of the interior. His chief aide, acting as

Kalibapi secretary-general, was an extremist pro-Japanese former congressman, Pio Duran. Benigno Ramos, the Sakdal-Ganap organizer, was on the Kalibapi executive body. Together with these men, Aquino conducted vigorous tours of the provinces, setting up Kalibapi chapters and speaking to mass meetings at which he extolled the "new order," hailing it as permanent. One of his main themes was denunciation of "pernicious guerrilla activities."

The Kalibapi was the chief vehicle for carrying out Japanese directives and policies. It served as a labor recruitment agency, particularly for constructing military installations. The Japanese had initially set up a Neighborhood Association system to serve as a policing and informing network, and this was taken over by and placed under the Kalibapi.

Between May and October 1943 the Kalibapi carried out one its main purposes, the preparation and establishment of Philippine "independence" and of a Philippine "Republic." It wrote and ratified a new constitution and created a National Assembly as its legislative body. The National Assembly was made up of 54 provincial governors and city mayors (all appointed by Vargas' Commission) and 54 elected members, one from each province and city, not elected by popular suffrage but by Kalibapi members who were declared to be "the voice of the people." The National Assembly elected Benigno Aquino as its Speaker. He was replaced as Kalibapi director-general by Camilo Osias.

Elected as President of the "Philippine Republic" by the Assembly was Jose Laurel, who was inaugurated on October 14, 1943. The oath of office was administered by Chief Justice of the Supreme Court Jose Yulo. Catholic Bishop Cesar Ma. Guerrero delivered the invocation. The Philippine flag was raised by Emilio Aguinaldo and Artemio Ricarte. The Laurel government's first act, on the same day, was to sign a pact of alliance with Japan.

The government headed by Laurel supplanted the Executive Commission, Jorge Vargas being dispatched to Japan as its ambassador. In the Laurel cabinet were: Claro M. Recto, Foreign Affairs; Antonio de las Alas, Finance; Teofilo Sison, Justice and commander-in-chief of armed forces; Quintin Paredes, Justice; Rafael Alunan, Agriculture and Natural Resources; Camilo Osias, Education; Jose Paez, Public Works and Communications; Emiliano Tria Tirona, Health, Labor and Public Welfare; and Minister Without Portfolio, Manuel Roxas.[17]

In the immediate postwar period the question of collaboration with the Japanese became a major issue, with furious debate at the center of Philippine politics over its reasons and motivations. Among the self-justifying excuses of those involved were: 1) collaborators were obeying the orders of Quezon and MacArthur, a flimsy claim because no such orders were given except the vague and non-specific representation assignment to Vargas by Quezon; 2) they were allegedly protecting the people by interposing themselves between the harsh Japanese and the population; 3) they really had remained loyal to the U.S. and were actually helping the guerrillas in secret ways; 4) if they hadn't agreed to cooperate the Japanese would have chosen worse puppets to do their bidding; and 5) they were acting under duress with their lives at stake if they did not.

In truth, the collaborators acted with a minimum of direction or suggestion from the Japanese military administration. Virtually the entire Commonwealth cabinet of Quezon joined in the rush to cooperate. From the pre-war Commonwealth Congress, 14 out of 24 senators and 35 out of 98 representatives participated in the puppet Republic. In its National Assembly, the 54 elected from and by Kalibapi members included 9 former senators, 18 former congressmen, and 6 former provincial governors. A handful managed to remain passive. A tiny few became guerrillas, notably the congressman from Camarines Sur, the youthful Wenceslao Vinzons, who led a guerrilla force in his home province and was killed in fighting, and the pre-war governor of Iloilo, Tomas Confesor, who headed a guerrilla unit and survived.

Claro Recto, in his defense against a postwar treason charge, published in part as a book with anti-imperialist features, *The Law of Belligerent Occupation,* argued that collaboration with the Japanese by responsible Filipino leaders was no different from the cooperation given to the U.S. invaders at the turn of the century by the Arellanos, de Tavera, Luzuriaga and others. In both cases, he said, Filipinos had acted as they did "to stop the hand of the cruel and merciless soldiery" of the occupying power and they should not be accused of treason if they failed to do so. Recto, as one of the elite, was blind, in this instance, to the historical pattern that was illustrated in both periods, of the political and economic elite being ready to collaborate with the invading enemy in order to retain a share of power and to preserve their property and social position.

Laurel and some others did intercede with the Japanese in a few cases to prevent an execution or imprisonment, but it could not be shown that the Filipino population suffered less or were less deprived because of the collaboration of their leaders. The argument that they were protecting the people and alleviating their conditions evades the example they set that was followed down to the lowest provincial and town level where large numbers of regional and local officials acted for the Japanese. Most inexcusable of all were the economic collaborators who were found at all levels—those who made fortunes from selling war materials to the enemy, through unscrupulous "buy-sell" operations, or landowners who diverted rice and other food crops to the Japanese at inflated prices, leaving markets bare and the people hungry. A notorious case was that of the son of the exiled Vice-President Osmena, Sergio Osmena Jr., who became a "buy-sell" millionaire. Some of the leading Filipino businessmen—Vicente Madrigal, Ramon Fernandez—thrived while holding top posts in Laurel's Council of State.

Many collaborators were to claim that they were merely pretending, that they remained basically loyal to the U.S.—i.e., to the preceding colonial collaboration—and that they secretly aided or had ties with the guerrillas. If this was ever the case, and little proof could be offered for it, it merely showed the readiness of the political elite to keep one foot in both opposing sides and to take out insurance with those who did resist. As long as the Japanese seemed able to win, collaboration laid the basis for a profitable future. It was only when the war swung the other way, the U.S. counterattack began and returning U.S. aircraft appeared over Philippine territory, that a rediscovery of loyalty to the U.S. occurred. This was just the shifting nature of colonial loyalty, of siding with whatever foreign conqueror is stronger, to preserve personal fortunes.

The behavior of the Laurel government, inaugurated with fanfare in October 1943, as the tides changed in 1944, was a case of trying to face both ways. By September 1944 the Japanese authorities began to press for their Philippine Republic to declare war on the U.S. and to conscript an army to fight beside Japan. Laurel's Proclamation No. 30, issued September 22, 1944, was a careful, legal two-faced document, an attempt to sidestep the issue, announcing that a "state of war exists between the Republic of the Philippines and the United States and Great Britain." The wording, attempting to make a fine distinction between a declaration of war and a declaration of a state of war, was the work of the foreign minister, Claro Recto. In his public statement elaborating on the Proclamation, Laurel said: "This declaration of a state of war is an official confirmation or recognition of an existing condition. This war is not of our own making. We did not will it." He then announced that the Republic would give every aid and assistance to the Japanese Imperialist Government "short of conscription of Filipino manhood for active military service."[18] The signs could scarcely be more clear that Laurel and his cabinet, seeing the end of the collaborationist road (the Proclamation was made the day after the first U.S. air raid over Manila on September 21, 1944), took a position that fell short of what the Japanese wanted and that could be used technically to avoid a charge of treason by the re-conquering Americans, as the beginning of the process of shifting back to collaboration with the previous colonial ruler.

There was also the collaborator claim of acting under duress, which had virtually no evidence to support it. While it was true that early in the occupation the Japanese had executed Chief Justice Jose Abad Santos on May 7, 1942 after he had refused to collaborate following his capture on Mindanao, this was an isolated case perpetrated by a lower command and contrary to decision at the top.[19] As the occupation was consolidated there was little likelihood or reason for Japan to make such executions general, except in the case of resisting Communists or as punitive measures against armed or underground opposition. The fact is that no collaborator could produce evidence that he was personally threatened or put under duress to serve the Japanese. Actually, far more people came forward voluntarily to take part in the commissions, committees, assemblies and other aspects of the puppet government structure than were needed. They relieved the Japanese of the burden of administration in the same way that the Filipino collaborators early in the century relieved the U.S. of the costly burden of colonial rule.

From the historical standpoint a blanket condemnation of all those who accepted posts under the Japanese has not been wholly proper. Filipino anti-imperialists and progressives have made a distinction between the more obvious self-servers and those with nationalist attitudes that were to become more accentuated as their careers developed in later years. A few, like Artemio Ricarte, Leon Villafuerte and Andres Villanueva, had been *Katipuneros* and generals in the revolutionary army that had fought U.S. occupation; they were motivated more than anything else by an enduring hatred of the U.S. imperialists. Even the Sakdals and Ganaps had many in their ranks who were misled nationalists lacking contact with the revolutionary left and coming under the spell of reactionary demagogues.

Jose Laurel himself was a complex figure in whom the compromising tendencies of the elite were mixed with a nationalistic impulse that had been accentuated by an episode of conflict with U.S. colonial officials in the early 1920s that damaged and interrupted his political career. It had led to a pre-war gravitation toward friendship with Japan as an advanced Asian culture. As the puppet president, Laurel exuded a certain independence of spirit. Although one USAFFE-linked guerrilla group (Hunter's Guerrillas) wounded him in an assassination attempt, Laurel convinced some Filipinos that he had stood up to the

Japanese. It is significant that in the postwar Philippines this leading collaborator became identified with the nationalist forces and staged an amazing, rapid recovery from the collaboration taint to become a popular presidential candidate in 1949.

Among the collaborators, however, Manuel Roxas provided the most historically important case. Roxas, educated as a lawyer and developed as a political leader under the U.S. colonial administration, was a pre-war Speaker of the House of Representatives, a joint head of Independence Missions to the U.S. (including the one in 1933 that worked for the Hare-Hawes-Cutting Act), a senator, and a member of the Quezon cabinet. He was a prime example of the colonial politician who merged his political career with a law practice serving big business: he was the senior partner in the law firm handling the Soriano interests. He had a close association with Douglas MacArthur.

At the outbreak of war Roxas was commissioned a major and made the liaison officer between Quezon and MacArthur. One of the very few Filipino leaders allowed to go to Corregidor, he was appointed executive secretary by Quezon two days before the President's departure from the island fortress. Fearing that he and Osmena might be intercepted and killed during their flight, Quezon signed a decree making Roxas in line to Osmena to succeed to the presidency. He was left behind in Mindanao when Quezon flew from there to Australia, and authorized to represent the president as Jorge Vargas had been instructed. Ostensibly he was supposed to join a guerrilla force.

The record of Manuel Roxas from that point onward was virtually indistinguishable from that of other collaborators. By April 1942 he was already in the hands of the Japanese, whether through capture or surrender is unclear. The difference in his fate from that of Abad Santos, captured in the same region around the same time, is marked. He was treated well and released after a short time. The Japanese, well aware of Roxas' development and ranking in colonial politics, are believed to have offered him the presidency of the puppet republic before selecting Laurel for the position. Roxas, however, evaded deep involvement publicly for some time, claiming that he did so because he was pretending to be sick. While briefly in detention he wrote a letter to U.S. and Filipino USAFFE officers who were in resistance calling on them to surrender: "Your presence in the hills is causing grave concern and is greatly delaying the return of the people to their normal occupations."[20]

The motivations of Roxas need to be viewed in the light of a career closely tied to U.S. nurturing which had virtually assured him the presidency in succession to Quezon. A calculating man, he sought to avoid holding top posts under the Japanese which could endanger his relations with a victorious U.S., while keeping on good terms with the Japanese who, after all, might win the war. Although Roxas refrained from playing a top role in the puppet government, he is believed to have been the chief adviser of Laurel. Complete disassociation could be detrimental in case the Japanese won, an outcome in which his presidential prospects were bright. By playing his cards right, Roxas could be president whoever won the war. In June 1943 he accepted membership in the preparatory commission that wrote the constitution of the puppet republic. He was, in fact, the principal author of that constitution. Finally, in 1944 he agreed to be a member of the Laurel cabinet, as Minister Without Portfolio, to be chairman of the Economic Planning Board and to be head of the *Bigasang Bayan* (BIBA), the rice procurement and distribution agency which had as one of its chief activities keeping rice from coming under guerrilla control. Of all Roxas did during the occupation, his role in the BIBA discreditied him most in the eyes of many Filipinos because BIBA was the instrumentality for taking the staple food from the mouths of the people and channeling it to the Japanese.

Roxas remained at work in the Laurel cabinet until the end. As the U.S. reinvasion forces neared Luzon in December 1944 Laurel and his cabinet fled from Manila to Baguio, in the northern mountains, and Roxas went with them. In April 1945, with U.S. troops advancing on Baguio, Roxas, together with Jose Yulo, Quintin Paredes, Antonio de las Alas and Teofilo Sison, crossed over to the U.S. lines. At that point the whole issue of collaboration and of its relation to Philippine politics acquired a different complexion. In the report of the incident released to the press by the MacArthur command, Yulo, Paredes, de las Alas and Sison were referred to as "captured"; Roxas, it was reported, had been "liberated."

Flown at once to Manila to be re-united with MacArthur, his old friend, Roxas quickly was built up as a hero and as the ablest Filipino leader. Around him a political party was shaped, heavily staffed with prominent collaborators. To Filipinos who had fought for true liberation in the war this forecast the character of the postwar Philippines, the nature of Philippine independence, and the intentions of U.S. imperialism.

In no other country that had taken part in the anti-fascist World War II were the collaborator with the enemy, the quisling, the traitor to the national interest made the leaders and the heads of government, as occurred in the Philippines. Wartime collaboration, in fact, helped create the ideal compliant ally for U.S. imperialism, the threat of prosecution for treason used as the perfect lever for obtaining agreement to whatever U.S. interests wanted, economically, militarily, politically or culturally. Collaboration with the occupying Japanese was the logical consequence of a history of elite alliance with the colonial master; it was also the logical progenitor of the next stage of collaboration, the neo-colonial independence finally granted to the Filipino people.

THE PEOPLE'S WAR

For the Philippines the course of history during and after World War II would have been far less controversial, the issues far less clearly defined, if the capitulation of the ruling elite and U.S. control of lie-low guerrilla groups had been the only features of significance. The U.S. might have managed the transition to the kind of independence arrangement it wanted quite smoothly with a minimum of resistance As it happened, however, a sizeable section of the Filipino people chose to uphold the true national interest and to fight for their country. That struggle was led by the Partido Komunista ng Pilipinas.

With its anti-fascist position and its lack of illusions about a U.S. defense of the country, the PKP held inner-party discussion two months before the Japanese attack on the organization of guerrilla warfare. A circular sent to all party nuclei proposed organization along military lines, into squads of 12 with a commander and under-officer for each Communications and food supply systems were outlined. To the PKP, resistance was the only outlook conceivable.

As soon as the first Japanese air raids occurred on December 8, 1941 the PKP political bureau met and decided to put guerrilla organization into effect. At the same time a 12-point memorandum was drawn up and sent to President Quezon and U.S. High Commissioner Francis B. Sayre. It was built around a PKP pledge of all-out support to national unity around an Anti-Japanese United Front, and of loyalty to the existing government, declaring that "All people and all strata of the population must organize, secretly if necessary, to assist the Philippine and American government to resist Japan." The memorandum asserted that "All patriotic rich elements must contribute their wealth, all intellectuals contribute their knowledge to the common cause of national defense," and that "questionable elements will commit acts of treason at the expense of their lives." It was proclaimed that the people must be armed and that underground organizations of the people must be formed.[21]

Although this memorandum was printed in the Manila press, no reply to it was ever made by President Quezon or Commissioner Sayre. (The attitude of the U.S. authorities toward the Filipino Communists was indicated in the weeks just before the war by the activity of U.S. intelligence agents in the areas of Pampanga province near the U.S. bases at Fort Stotsenberg and Clark Field; they arrested and interrogated party members and peasant leaders as if they were fifth-columnists in the same category as pro-Japanese.) In none of the proclamations and orders issued by Quezon, Sayre and MacArthur was any mention or hint made about arming the people or organizing guerrilla resistance. *and other ?*

Regardless of the attitude of colonial officials, PKP-led labor and peasant unions undertook voluntarily to form labor battalions to help construct military defenses. Over 50,000 workers and peasants were organized by the PKP and put at the disposal of the U.S. Corps of Engineers. Among the defenses they built were those at the key Calumpit crossing point on the Pampanga River, which enabled holding up Japanese forces while the USAFFE retreated to Bataan for its strategic holding action.

On January 2, 1942 the Japanese army entered Manila. Its top command declared at once that the Communists were their "first and last enemy." Unlike the soft treatment given to the compliant members of the elite, the invaders went after Communists with ruthless intent, using spies and informers who had supplied lists well in advance. Although most PKP cadres had left Manila for the countryside to begin carrying out guerrilla organization, the party's leading organ had remained over-confidently in the city, vulnerable to informer activity.

A Japanese raid on January 24 captured the entire first front PKP leadership including Crisanto Evangelista, Pedro Abad Santos, Agapito del Rosario and others.

At first the Japanese tried to win over those arrested by claiming to be also against U.S. imperialism and by saying independence would be given. Crisanto Evangelista, rejecting all enemy overtures, was tortured and killed, as was Agapito del Rosario. Pedro Abad Santos refused to collaborate but, very old and sick, had his life spared. Imprisoned, he was released in a general amnesty declared by Jose Laurel in October 1943 on inauguration of the puppet republic, but died in 1944 before U.S. re-invasion. Other Communists fell into Japanese hands in the course of the resistance struggle but none were persuaded by either torture or enticement to collaborate. In general, the behavior of the Filipino communists was in utter contrast to the ready collaboration of the elite.

Early in February 1942 the PKP's second front leadership, with Vicente Lava as general secretary, called a meeting of party and mass organization leaders in barrio Bawit, Cabiao, Nueva Ecija. (Vicente Lava, a scientist who specialized in coconut derivatives, was much wanted by the Japanese, who were after his formula for deriving alcohol.) At the Bawit meeting some participants argued that the Commonwealth government had ceased to exist, with most of its members collaborating with the enemy, and therefore an underground government should be established that would declare independence and a people's republic. This was rejected by the majority who adopted a proposal for development of a broad united front, to attract all sectors of the population prepared to resist and fight the invader, regardless of class interests.

In the broad united front tactics put into effect, class struggle features were set aside. The PKP's mass base in the Central Luzon provinces had been built in leading bitter struggles of poor peasants against landlords. At first, as Commonwealth government collapsed along with police that supported the owner class, incidents occurred of people taking vengeance against abusive exploiters. The PKP quickly acted to halt such acts that would antagonize well-to-do or middle-class Filipinos. To show good faith to those sectors, the KPMP and AMT were dissolved. Filipinos might be fought against *not* because they were landlords or capitalists or erstwhile corrupt politicians but because they might be collaborators with the Japanese enemy. The slogans "All Anti-Japanese Our Friends, All Pro-Japanese Our Enemies" and "Anti-Japanese Above All" were projected. United front efforts were conceived as a national as well as local policy, and unity relations with all other anti-Japanese guerrillas, groups or individuals were sought.

This policy enabled the building of a broad mass base for the main feature of resistance—the guerrilla army for striking and destroying the invader. A special military conference was prepared by the PKP and held during the last week of March 1942, in the forest near Bawit, Cabiao. Several hundred potential guerrilla fighters, mostly young members of the KPMP and AMT, attended, many bringing arms obtained or confiscated from landlords or from USAFFE stragglers. The form and program of a guerrilla force to be known as the *Hukbo ng Bayan Laban sa Hapon* or People's Army against Japan were worked out. It was abbreviated to Hukbalahap.

On March 29, 1942 the Hukbalahap was formally inaugurated. A Military Committee was elected: Luis Taruc, a Socialist leader of the merger with the PKP, now a PKP political bureau member, as Commander; Casto Alejandrino, also Socialist and now PKP central committee member, as Vice-Commander; Bernardo Poblete and Felipa Culala, both PKP members. Felipa Culala, a woman peasant leader, had already led the first attack, an ambush, against Japanese forces. Later Mateo del Castillo, of the PKP political bureau, was added as political advisor.

Subsequently a further addition was made, to the Military Committee and to the armed force. This came from the Chinese Communist Party organization that existed among the large Chinese population in the Philippines. It was also a target of the Japanese and many of its members came to Central Luzon for security and to fight. Their leaders were given places on the PKP political bureau. A separate Chinese Hukbalahap unit, called Squadron 48 or Wa Chi after the 4th Route and 8th Route armies of the Chinese Red Army, was created, not out of ethnic separatism—its relations with Filipino were very close—but to serve as a model military organization, some having fought the Japanese in China.

A guiding document, "The Fundamental Spirit," was adopted which included this principle:

> A revolutionary army struggles for the realization of a political aim. For example, the fight against Japan aims to defeat the Japanese and achieve national emancipation. This struggle will not stop until its aim is realized. Only by struggling and fighting to the end can the objective be reached. Even if there is only one man left the struggle must still be carried on. To sign any agreement with the enemy without victory means we have lost faith in the revolution, and humble ourselves before the enemy. To capitulate is treachery and is a shameful crime.[22]

As a statement of national pride and resolution, this was poles apart from the collaborationist attitude, marking the sharp differences between the ordinary people and the well-to-do elite when it came to defending the national interest.

The "Fundamental Spirit" also called for relations of love, protection and help between the Hukbalahap and the people. It was a relationship very different from the way in which the U.S.-directed USAFFE and other guerrillas operated, which invariably was a confiscatory way of living off the people that bordered often on banditry. No organization of the people was done by these groups, which condemned the Hukbalahap and PKP for doing so. In U.S. intelligence reports the Hukbalahap was charged in hostile terms with setting up "Communist government."

As built by the PKP, the anti-Japanese resistance movement was a people's movement in every sense of the word. Forms of barrio organization had sprung up as soon as colonial authority evaporated with the

USAFFE retreat to Bataan. Bandits and other criminal elements had soon emerged to rob and abuse the barrio people. In the barrios of Pampanga and Nueva Ecija where the AMT and KPMP had been strong, with virtually 100 per cent organization of the population, spontaneous self-protection systems arose, called *Bantay Nayon* or Barrio Guard organizations. These quickly cleaned out the bandits, but remained as a form of authority.

A stimulus to more complete self-government came from the experience of creating the guerrilla army and leading it into battle against Japanese troops. Attacks were pressed throughout 1942. The consequence was a well-organized large-scale counter-guerrilla operation by the Japanese army in March 1943 which caught the PKP and Hukbalahap off guard. Their main base in the forest near Cabiao was surrounded and pierced. Most PKP cadres and guerrilla soldiers escaped or fought their way out, but a number were killed or captured.

From this experience the greatest lesson was in the need to give major attention to representative barrio organization and the involvement of the whole people in the resistance. The Japanese surprise attack had been possible due to skillful use of spies and informers. It had been a failure of intelligence and of safeguards against infiltration, caused especially by an insufficient delegation of responsibility among the people.

Set up in barrios all over Central Luzon from that time onward was the Barrio United Defense Corps or BUDC (it was also known by its Tagalog name, *Sandatahang Tanod ng Bayan* or STB). This rapidly became a highly developed organ of local democratic government. It was a profound, new experience for the barrio people, who had never known democracy. The U.S. colonial system extended elective government only down to the central town or *municipio* level; in the outlying barrios, numbering up to twenty in some town areas, some with several thousand inhabitants, the *cacique* system perfected by the Spaniards had been preserved in which a barrio lieutenant, usually appointed by landlords, was the sole authority. This system was replaced by the PKP with elected local councils, the BUDC introducing self-government of the broadest democratic type.

Depending on the size of the barrio, BUDCs had from five to twelve elected members: chairman, vice-chairman, secretary-treasurer, director of intelligence, directors of recruiting (for the Hukbalahap), education, transportation, communication, agriculture and sanitation, and a chief of police. All residents over 18 years of age could vote, a far wider extension of ballot rights than under the colonial government. The only limitation on ballot rights was their denial to anyone with a pro-Japanese record of sympathies, and to anyone committing acts against the interests of the people.

Cases concerning the latter were dealt with in BUDC courts, a system of justice, with juries, being one of the most important democratic innovations. All types of cases were handled, except those of spies, traitors or major collaborators. In ordinary cases any punishment meted out was limited as a rule to courses of improvement, forms of public disapproval, and criticism. The more serious cases of spies or traitors in which execution might be the decision were handled by Hukbalahap military courts, so that the barrio people could not be held responsible in the future by vengeful elements.

The new democratic system affected as well the economic life of the barrio. Consistent with the united front policy of moderating class struggle, existing tenant-landlord relations were not essentially altered, but in the case of friendly anti-Japanese landlords, peasant-landlord committees were set up to regulate the sharing of the harvest. No confiscation of land or actual land reform was attempted, but the BUDC did organize the cultivation of unused land in a communal manner, the profits going to the barrio treasury, and wherever feasible cooperatives were organized, especially in fishpond areas and in the growing of fruits and vegetables.

Economically, the most important BUDC activity was the Harvest Struggle. Beginning with the harvest season in 1942, the PKP mobilized the widest number of people to keep the rice harvest from falling into enemy hands. As soon as it ripened it was harvested, threshed and rushed to remote places or hidden in any kind of cavity. Destruction of Japanese or collaborator threshing machines, trucks or other transport was carried out. If rice was seized by the enemy, the *bodegas* (warehouses) where it was kept were raided and the rice captured, or were burned. A day and night guard system warned of any sudden arrival of Japanese harvesting teams and quickly informed Hukbalahap fighters so the enemy could be attacked. The entire barrio population, including small children, took part.

Harvesting was but part of the struggle. Control was exerted also over every step of the marketing system. Release of rice to the market was regulated. All rice agents and market operators had to carry a license issued by the resistance movement. A system of patrol and check-up was strictly maintained. Any diversion of rice to the black market was blocked. Anyone caught violating the licensing system or engaging in black market activities could be turned over to the barrio courts for trial and punishment. Each year of the war the Harvest Struggle became more effective, until the rice industry and trade were tightly sewed up. Unlike unorganized regions of the country, the people of Central Luzon were guaranteed rice without inflated prices.

This control aspect of the Harvest Struggle led to conflict with a good many landlords who either collaborated with the enemy and tried to sell rice to them at profiteering prices or tried to channel rice to the black market. The prevention of this kind of unpatriotic enrichment caused landlord resentment and class enmity that were to be harbored for the future.

Through 1942 most attention was given to organizing and staffing the Hukbalahap and to acquiring arms, many of which were gleaned at first from the Bataan battlefield; later they were captured from the enemy in ambushes and raids. The major Japanese attack on the Cabiao forest base in March 1943 temporarily interrupted the guerrilla campaign. A policy called "retreat for defense" was adopted in haste, to play down aggressive guerrilla attacks to avoid provoking heavy Japanese retaliation, until the armed force and its mass base were strengthened. This policy was devised and insisted upon by the leading Chinese cadres who had been integrated with the PKP political bureau. "Retreat for defense" was approved out of respect for Chinese experience in fighting the Japanese, but it was not followed by Hukbalahap commanders who not only continued but intensified attacks during 1943. For the PKP, "retreat for defense" became a dead letter in no time.

The main unit in the Hukbalahap was the squadron. Composed on average of 100 fighters, it had a commander, vice-commander, political officer, supply officer and intelligence officer. A squadron was subdivided into platoons and squads; two squadrons comprised a battalion, two battalions a regiment, for deployment in large operations. Some squadrons were known by nicknames, most by numbers relating to their district. At first squadrons were directed simply by the PKP's Military Committee, but as squadrons multiplied districts were set up, eventually numbering five, and the Military Committee became the GHQ Hukbalahap.

Districts were: 1st Military District, embracing southern Pampanga and the fishpond and swamp areas around Masantol, Minalin and Macabebe; 2nd Military District, south east Pampanga and part of northern Bulacan, covering Baliwag, Apalit, San Ildefonso, San Simon, San Luis, Candaba, Santa Ana and part of Arayat; 3rd Military District, northwestern Pampanga and southeastern Tarlac, around Mount Arayat; 4th Military District, all of Nueva Ecija; 5th Military District, western Pampanga, from Mexico to Bacolor, Lubao and Floridablanca.

These were the initial district areas. They expanded: the 1st under

Bernardo Poblete (Banal) expanding southwest into Bataan and southeast into Bulacan, the Bulacan section subsequently becoming so strong it was made separate, under Fred Laan; the 3rd under Eusebio Aquino spread northwestward through all of Tarlac to Pangasinan; the 4th under Jose de Leon (Dimasalang) built such a large military force it had to be divided into eastern and western subdivisions; the 5th under Abelardo Dabu grew westward into the Zambales mountains.

The Hukbalahap was not confined to Central Luzon. One of the first PKP guerrilla units was set up around Tanay, Rizal, to the east of Manila. Further south an entire very active district was developed in the Laguna-Tayabas region, including the towns of Santa Maria, Paete, Longos, Nagcarlan, Cavinti and Mauban along the Sierra Madre Mountain range and in the lowlands from Santa Cruz to San Pablo. Leading PKP cadres who gave direction to this southern district and its Talban Guerrillas as they were known were Pedro Villegas, as military commander, Felicissimo Macapagal, Jesus Lava and Jorge Frianeza.

In Manila the PKP maintained a partially-armed force of about 300 members, called the League for National Liberation. It was limited to the liquidation of informers and collaborators and had its main role as a security force for united front work, for which Manila was the chief contact point for diverse groups.

All told, around 100 squadrons had been organized and were operating against the enemy by war's end, comprising over 10,000 armed fighters, with 10,000 others trained and rotated in active units, kept in reserve in the barrios. The Hukbalahap fought over 2,000 encounters, large and small, with the enemy and killed at least 20,000 Japanese and puppet troops. (Much of the pre-war Philippine Constabulary, augmented by collaborator officers trained by the Japanese in a constabulary school, was employed against guerrillas.) Developed into a tough and skilled fighting force, the Hukbalahap was the only Filipino guerrilla force that fought the Japanese throughout the war, refusing to lie low or to subordinate the national interest it upheld to U.S. aims or authority.

At no time, however, did the Hukbalahap seek to compete with the other anti-Japanese groups, to oppose them or to dominate them. The united front policy was adamantly adhered to, including in relations with American-officered USAFFE groups that had a hostile attitude toward the PKP-led guerrillas. At the beginning of the war the PKP sent a mission headed by Casto Alejandrino to Bataan while fighting was still in progress, which met with the U.S. officer assigned by MacArthur to be in charge of U.S.-led guerrilla activities, Major Claude Thorpe. At first Thorpe argued that the PKP-led guerrillas should come under

U.S. command, but the PKP mission insisted on a united front arrangement in which the Communist-led forces would have independence of organization. Thorpe agreed to this and also agreed to supply the Hukbalahap with arms. Unfortunately Thorpe and his team were captured and killed before the end of 1942.

The only other American officer who worked in a relatively cooperative and unbiased way with the PKP-led guerrillas was Colonel Bernard Anderson who held a command position in Southern Luzon. Anderson, who maintained a clandestine submarine link with Mac-Arthur, helped coordinate Talban Guerrilla operations with those of other guerrilla groups—Markings, Hunters ROTC, President Quezon's Own Guerrillas (PQOG), Blue Eagles, Red Lions and others. The Hukbalahap developed close ties with some of these that continued into the postwar period. That this was feasible in Southern Luzon was due in large part to the less acute problems there of tenancy and class struggle.

In Manila, the PKP's League for National Liberation and the PKP had one of the best of the united front successes in ties with the Free Philippines, an independent group without U.S. control of about 100 leading Filipino intellectuals, progressive and nationalist-minded lawyers, writers and others, which acted as the intermediary connecting body for contacts of diverse guerrilla groups.

It was in Central Luzon, however, where the PKP-led resistance had its most testing united front role. This was remarkably successful in relations with fellow Filipinos, in barrio organization and in work with anti-Japanese landlords and rural middle class elements. However, a serious problem arose from the attitude of U.S. officers who headed small lie-low groups in territories adjacent to the Central Luzon provinces. A Lt. Robert Lapham and a pre-war mining engineer in a U.S. mining company named Mackenzie who operated together along the Pangasinan-Nueva Ecija border spread slanderous, lying stories in barrios about the Hukbalahap, claiming it was composed of bandits and rapists who abused the people and who were imposing lawless and Godless communism in the barrios. It caused difficulties for Hukbalahap expansion. The Lapham-Mackenzie groups did not stop at propaganda but made armed attacks on the Hukbalahap as well. Similar attempts to create antagonism against the PKP-led resistance and its organizing of the barrio people, and to make armed attacks on its expansion teams, were made by units under Lt. Col. Edwin Ramsey in parts of Bulacan province. Ramsey had an unsavory reputation of being in league with collaborating Filipino landlords and politicians who were reaping fortunes from black market activities; he resented the PKP and Hukbalahap because they put a stop to such collaboration wherever their organization spread.

The behavior of these MacArthur-connected USAFFE elements did not alter the PKP's basic adherence to the wartime anti-fascist alliance. In the latter part of the war, as the return of U.S. forces developed, U.S. air crews on missions over Luzon were given warnings in their flight briefings that if they fell in Huk-controlled territory the Huks could not be trusted because they were "anti-American." A number of U.S. planes were shot down over Central Luzon. Hukbalahap squadrons rescued 30 U.S. pilots and crew members and gave them exceptionally hospitable treatment before returning them safely.

As the first returning U.S. air raids struck Luzon in September 1944 the PKP held an enlarged central committee meeting in Central Luzon, to discuss the policies of the party in the coming critical period. It was attended by nearly fifty of the cadres who had grown into leading roles in the anti-Japanese struggle, heading a party that had grown greatly in membership and experience. The meeting's agenda was mainly concerned with the nature of the future government of the country and how it was likely to be shaped.

It was fully agreed that U.S. imperialism and the *comprador*-landlord allies with which it had ruled would quickly move to re-establish their control along with the colonialist exploitation that had prevailed previously. The war, however, had brought changes: the Commonwealth government of Manuel Quezon had disintegrated and a new president, Sergio Osmena, would return without a constituted government to assume authority. Most of the former principal political leaders had collaborated and faced possible treason charges. Aside from a very few of the ruling elite who had resisted and set up a semblance of local guerrilla authority—Tomas Confesor in Iloilo, Alfredo Montelibano in Negros, Tomas Cabili in Mindanao, Roque Ablan in Ilocos Norte—the only force filling at least part of the political vacuum was the PKP and the BUDCs of Central Luzon.

The PKP meeting debated what to do in this situation. Suggestions that an overall central united front provisional government be set up to proclaim a people's democratic republic were dismissed as unrealistic. A PKP mission had been sent to Negros to discuss united front prospects with Montelibano but he had displayed no interest in unity with the PKP. The possibility of regional provisional united front governments in Central and Southern Luzon where the PKP-led movement was established was examined and also rejected. Finally a more realistic decision was made, to set up provincial and local united front governments where the movement was strong.

Provincial governments were thus established in Nueva Ecija, Tarlac, Pampanga, Bulacan and Laguna, and local governments were set up in virtually all of the towns in these provinces. They were in being and functioning with support of the people when the U.S. forces arrived. The PKP, however, had no illusions about the postwar future. Vicente Lava put this plainly to the meeting:

> If the Filipino bourgeoisie obtain the hegemony, since they are essentially *comprador* in character, we should expect immediately after defeat of Japanese fascism a reversal to the former colonial status under U.S. imperialist domination with perhaps nominal independence, a strengthening of the native bourgeois-landlord state dictatorship over the broad masses far more brutal and terroristic than that of the former Quezon regime, the continuation and aggravation of the semi-feudal conditions in the country, and a progressively worsening economic condition of the country as a whole and of the workers and peasants particularly.[23]

Indeed, as the signs of a U.S. return multiplied during the latter half of 1944, reactionary landlord-*comprador* groups in the Central Luzon region which had tended to be subdued in their class hostility out of fear of an armed people at a time when the state supporting them had collapsed, and who had had their fears heightened by the growing strength of the BUDCs, had become emboldened to the point of subsidizing anti-PKP and anti-Hukbalahap acts. In Pampanga the landlord representative and collaborator Sotero Baluyot and his lieutenant, Jose Lingad, organized the perpetration of killings and other atrocities against Hukbalahap supporters. In alliance with these elements, USAFFE guerrilla groups engaged increasingly in attacks on Hukbalahap squadrons. These were omens of the future.

THE RETURN OF U.S. IMPERIALISM

On October 20, 1944 reconquest of the Philippines began with the invasion of the island of Leyte, in the central Visayan islands. Only at this point, when direct U.S. command could be exerted, were the lie-low guerrillas ordered into action, attached to U.S. forces. With Leyte as a base, Mindoro was invaded on December 15. The major assault, on Luzon, started at Lingayan, Pangasinan on January 4, 1945. Other operations were launched on Palawan (28 February 1945), Zamboanga (10 March), Panay (18 March), Negros (29 March), Cebu (26 March), Bohol (4 April), Mindanao (12 April). The campaign was long and bitter, the Japanese fighting tenaciously, particularly on Luzon, where they retreated to fortified mountain positions. They were still fighting when Japan finally surrendered on September 1, 1945. In that campaign, fought to restore U.S. control of the Philippines, a Japanese army had to be destroyed that could have been left inactive and useless, as in the Netherlands East Indies, to surrender when the Japanese homeland did. It was the Filipino people, however, who suffered the most as a result of the U.S. reconquest. The number of civilians who died has never been fully ascertained; an estimate of 200,000 has been made that includes USAFFE troops, a figure that equals the number who died in the initial U.S. conquest at the beginning of the century.

For the country as a whole, the reinvasion was catastrophic: it was left in a state of utter devastation. The destruction was caused overwhelmingly by the U.S. bombing and shelling. Innumerable cities, towns and villages were reduced to ruins, the worst example being Manila, which U.S. troops took by assault, the Japanese making a last-ditch defense in the old Spanish walled district, Intramuros. In Manila the entire business district was destroyed, along with 70 per cent of public utilities, three-quarters of factories and stores, and 80 per cent of the finest residential areas. In the Visayas, Cebu City, the country's second ranking city, was completely destroyed.[24]

The original damage estimate for the whole country, made by the U.S. army itself, was $1.5 billion. A study by the Philippine Bureau of Census and Statistics shortly after the end of the war, which was only a partial survey, arrived at P5,589,580,005 ($2,794,790,002). (The Philippine government eventually made an itemized reparations claim upon Japan of P16,000,000,000 ($8 billion) but that included losses in trade and production.) In terms of values at the time the destruction was enormous.[25]

For most Filipinos, not aware of U.S. aims or of issues of military strategy in the Pacific war, the return of the U.S. to their soil in the manner it did was an acceptable price to pay for what was considered liberation. The majority of the people hated the Japanese occupation, which took away their rights and reduced them to poverty and hunger. Whatever the destruction that accompanied the driving out of the invader, it was fatalistically thought worth it. U.S. soldiers for the most part were greeted enthusiastically as liberators. In comparison with the Japanese Imperial Army and its military-fascist objectives, they were a democratic army, returning with a way of life to which the Filipino people had been conditioned for half a century. Furthermore, any tendency for them to look upon the re-invading U.S. army as the instrument for restoring past colonial rule was negated by the fact that

independence was within their grasp, just around the corner of the
year. As they saw it, Filipinos had reason to feel liberated.
The reality, of betrayal, had yet to be seen through the battle-smoke.
That reality set in as soon as the Leyte invasion occurred. In the
special landing party that waded ashore after beaches were secured
for the benefit of the cameras and posterity, General MacArthur was
well to the front and Sergio Osmena, President of the Philippine
Commonwealth, was barely to be noticed, behind him. It was a
symbolic tableau. It was MacArthur who was in command throughout
the "liberation" period, directing the reestablishment of U.S. control.
The U.S. army had the funds, the equipment, the food and other
supplies, and the manpower to begin reconstruction. President Osmena
had virtually nothing, and MacArthur, who had a long-nursed resentment against him for criticizing the grandiose, useless pre-war defense
plan, gave Osmena virtually no assistance and made no effort to help
put the Philippine government on its feet.

MacArthur, arriving with his staff team of men with special Philippine interests—Willoughby, Whitney, Soriano, Parsons, McMicking—
proceeded to put in place the political structure that would serve the
transformed postwar interests of a more powerful U.S. imperialism. A
Philippine Civil Affairs Unit (PCAU, or "Peecow" as it was called) was
set up, with Courtney Whitney at its head and staffed by U.S. personnel,
which acted ostensibly as the main relief agency. It had other powers,
however: it was first into areas cleared of Japanese resistance and
established civil government in the towns, selecting who were to be
the town and provincial officials. In a great many cases these were
drawn from the USAFFE guerrilla rosters and their contacts who included
collaborators and black marketeers as well as the most conservative of
landlord and local elite elements. Invariably, selection of officials was
based on their estimated readiness to support the U.S. choice of
national leaders in the postwar Philippines.

Aiding PCAU in its work of installing a pro-U.S. civil administration
was the U.S. army's Counter-Intelligence Corps (CIC). The CIC undertook to screen not only officials but all people who had been politically
active on one side or the other during the war. In Central and Southern Luzon lists were drawn up of members and supporters of the
Hukbalahap, who were excluded from any post or even employment
in U.S. army camps. The principal role of the CIC, however, was the
handling of the collaboration issue. It was the CIC which arbitrarily
rendered judgment on whether a person should be regarded as a
collaborator. In truth, the criterion was collaboration with the U.S.,
which cancelled out collaboration with the Japanese. The Filipinos

who wound up as chargable on the CIC collaboration lists were those who had openly proclaimed an anti-U.S. position as their reason for serving the Japanese or who had behaved in a nationalist manner in the pre-war decades.

MacArthur and his team were most of all concerned with the least possible dislocation or transformation of Philippine society by the war, and with putting back into power the political elite which had been molded into a colonialist posture under U.S. rule. This was endangered by the extent to which the collaboration phenomenon had encompassed most of that very stratum. Some new prospective pro-U.S. politicians had come forward in the USAFFE guerrilla groups but they were not yet fully tested in their loyalty as the established leaders were. Consequently MacArthur through his CIC and PCAU set about rebuilding a reliable political structure while at the same time excluding or keeping out of power those who were likely to resist imperialist demands.

President Osmena had returned with an anti-collaborationist outlook, shaped in part by his close association with President Franklin Roosevelt's secretary of the interior, Harold L. Ickes, who was strongly in favor of prosecuting collaborators. Ickes, who also distrusted MacArthur, warned Osmena against the dominance of the U.S. military command, which would leave him without power. Osmena, hampered at every turn by MacArthur, who kept him immobile by not even providing him with transportation from the vast U.S. vehicle stores, was able only to re-inaugurate a government in March 1945. His cabinet, which was free of collaborators, included the prominent non-USAFFE guerrilla leaders Tomas Confesor, as secretary of the interior, and Tomas Cabili, as secretary of defense. Osmena called for the reconstitution of the legislative branch by "all duly elected members of our Congress [i.e., in the last 1941 election] who have remained steadfast in their allegiance to our Government during the period of the enemy occupation."26

This was wholly to the displeasure of MacArthur, who could not oust the Osmena government but who moved to create an alternative political grouping to which the support of his imperialist coterie could be swung. The opportunity for this presented itself in mid-April when cabinet members of Laurel's puppet government who had fled with the Japanese from Manila to Baguio surrendered to the advancing U.S. army. With that group was Manuel Roxas. As we have discussed, the MacArthur press office released a highly significant communique of this incident. It referred to the "capture" of Jose Yulo, Quintin Paredes, Antonio de las Alas and Teofilo Sison, but it played up the "release" of Roxas. Roxas was separated from the rest of the collaborators and was classified as a captive, not a collaborator of the Japanese. This was the first step in absolving Roxas from a collaboration charge. MacArthur personally cleared him, sending a special plane to fly him immediately to Manila for an ostentatious "reunion," then restoring Roxas to the rank of brigadier-general and assigning him to the U.S. army's GHQ to serve in the G-2 (intelligence) section under General Willoughby. As soon as President Osmena convened the Philippine Congress on June 9, MacArthur permitted Roxas to return to civilian status, including taking up his pre-war seat in the Senate. At the same time, the large number of arrested and detained collaborators were released on bail to resume their former posts. Many flocked back into congressional seats in disregard of the Osmena policy preference. In the opening session of Congress on June 9 Roxas was elected president of the Senate and another collaborator, Jose Zulueta, became speaker of the lower House of Representatives. Roxas had been put in a key position to challenge Osmena and to build a political base for contesting the Philippine presidency itself. One of the first steps of the Roxas-collaborator dominated Congress was the rejection of the Osmena appointments of Confesor and Cabili to his cabinet. This stripped the Osmena government of the key figures for an anticollaboration policy.

Above all, the U.S. interests represented by MacArthur needed to eliminate the entire collaboration issue which threatened to be the nemesis of their favored allies. This was done on the one hand by enabling the re-seated collaborators in Congress to enact legislation making prosecution of collaboration hopelessly difficult, and on the other hand by the CIC and the MacArthur headquarters deliberately withholding dossiers and other assistance from the People's Court set up by the Osmena government to try such cases. Few collaboration cases thus ever actually came to trial and only one top collaborator was convicted (Teofilo Sison, who had been defense secretary in the Quezon cabinet). Sent to prison finally were merely rank and file members of the Makapili.

Manuel Roxas, in December 1945, quit the Nacionalista Party and, in close consulation with the MacArthur team and that of the new U.S. High Commissioner, Paul McNutt, set up his own political party, the Liberal Party. It became at once the rallying center for collaborators, USAFFE guerrilla leaders, and the most reactionary landlord and *comprador* elements. The U.S. Congress, eager to install a Philippine government to its liking prior to the long-fixed independence date of July 4, 1946, had set a general election for April 20, 1946. The Roxas candidacy for president was declared in January, and at once a well-oiled and funded U.S.-backed campaign to elect this chosen son as the head of the government to which independence could be handed swung into action.

While this blatant, treacherous manipulation of Philippine politics was occurring at the top level, the betrayal of the liberating and democratic character of the anti-fascist war was being carried out more ruthlessly at the level of the people's movement. In the intelligence reports doctored in MacArthur's headquarters by Courtney Whitney, the Hukbalahap had been continually referred to as "anti-American" and as having fought USAFFE groups (a reversal of the actual attacks by the USAFFE on the Hukbalahap and BUDCs). The Hukbalahap was described as a "semi-political, semi-bandit organization" allegedly intending "the establishment of a communistic government in the Philippines after the war." It was called "a distinct potential threat to the Commonwealth government and the future peace of the Philippines."[27] This was preparation for the steps to be taken in regard to the Hukbalahap on the return of the U.S. forces: it became an immediate target of repression as soon as the CIC came within reach of it.

The path of the U.S. army had, in fact, been swept clean of Japanese troops by the Huk squadrons all the way from the invasion area of Pangasinan to Manila. Central Luzon was in virtually every respect a functioning liberated area, with government, commerce, agricultural production, and policing in order. Provisional government up to provincial level was established. Juan Feleo was acting governor of Nueva Ecija, Casto Alejandrino in Pampanga, Alejandro Simpauco in Tarlac, Jesus Lava in Laguna in Southern Luzon. Both the Hukbalahap and the people who overwhelmingly supported it greeted the U.S. forces as allies, in friendship.

That friendship was not reciprocated at U.S. command level. The provisional governments, provincial, town and barrio, were promptly ousted, called illegal. They were replaced by the PCAU with USAFFE officers and men who had fought the Hukbalahap, reactionary landlords or even known collaborators. The BUDCs were simply abolished or ignored. Under CIC direction, the disarming of squadrons was attempted. In the most notorious case, Squadron 77 which had spearheaded the U.S. drive into Manila, was disarmed at gunpoint in the city suburbs and forced to walk back to Central Luzon. Its unarmed 108 fighters were seized in Malolos, Bulacan and all massacred by a USAFFE band under Colonel Adonais Maclang, who was then appointed the mayor of Malolos by the PCAU.

Attempts by the Hukbalahap commander and vice-commander, Luis Taruc and Casto Alejandrino, to meet and confer with responsible U.S. officers were received coldly. They were channelled to intelligence officers who expressed disapproval of "civilians with guns." On February 22, 1945 Taruc and Alejandrino, along with other members of the Hukbalahap GHQ were arrested by the CIC in San Fernando, Pampanga and confined in the town jail. A protest demonstration of 40,000 peasants filled the town and forced their release. However they were re-arrested on April 8 and brought to the Iwahig penal colony on Palawan island, where they were confined with the detained top collaborators. This time protests and demonstrations were held all over Central Luzon, culminating in a massive march of 50,000 people to Malacanang presidential palace in Manila on September 23. At the end of September Taruc and Alejandrino were set free, but other Hukbalahap leaders were kept in prison for months longer.

These steps of repression were all taken before the war against Japanese fascist aggression was ended and while many Hukbalahap squadrons were still in action against the Japanese army, steps that negated the people's war features of the conflict and made it plain that the U.S. command in the Pacific theater was not concerned with a democratic outcome for the Filipino people or their genuine independence, but wanted the reimposition of a U.S. control as repressive and dominating as any stage of the colonial period.

The campaign for the pre-independence election began in January 1946 with the launching by Manuel Roxas of the new Liberal Party, at a convention which selected Roxas for the presidency and Elpidio Quirino as his vice-presidential running mate. Quirino was chosen largely because of his low collaboration profile, his only public post under the Japanese being his chairmanship of Laurel's Economic Planning Board. Meeting a few days later, the Nacionalista Party convention chose the team of Osmena and Eulogio Rodriquez to contest the top posts.

From the outset Roxas had a commanding lead in the campaign. His Liberal Party machine was bolstered by a wholesale desertion of the Nacionalistas by regional and local political leaders who opportunistically went with the U.S.-backed party. These were, in fact, mostly people who had played ball with the Japanese and who had been "cleared" by the PCAU and CIC. Osmena, who had had little choice but to rely on such elements in the first place, was hard put to fill in the gaps in the Nacionalista organization.

U.S. backing for the Liberal Party was particularly noticeable in the important area of propaganda. A proliferation of pro-Roxas newspapers appeared in Manila, the newsprint supplied from U.S. army stocks at Clark Field. From the U.S. the publishers Randolph Hearst, Henry Luce and Roy Howard shipped newsprint and financial aid to

Roxas while boosting him in their press, giving Osmena scanty mention. The public relations officer of High Commissioner Paul McNutt, Julius Edelstein, worked simultaneously as the PRO of Roxas.[28]

For most Filipinos the differences between the two parties were not clearcut. Collaboration with the Japanese, which could have been a powerful issue, was virtually smothered by the clearing of Roxas and the entire grouping around him. When the Osmena team sought to use the collaboration issue to claim that a Roxas presidency would wreck hopes for U.S. rehabilitation aid, it backfired. "Americans have sacrificed much in this war and they are not going to help a man who actively aided the Japs," declared Tomas Confesor.[29] He was promptly refuted by a statement from Paul McNutt: "The U.S. Government will carry out its promised aid to the Philippine people regardless of whom they choose for their next president."[30] Roxas seized on this to assert that he was the man who could get large-scale U.S. aid, proceeding to make extravagant promises of what he would do for the people, while Osmena could promise nothing, his government struggling with an empty treasury.

A more significant feature of the 1946 election was provided by the participation of a political party of the left. For the first time since the beginning of the century such a people-based party was able to inject into Philippine national politics the basic issues of anti-imperialism and a national-democratic program.

As soon as Central Luzon and Manila were free of the Japanese army, early in 1945, the PKP had begun discussions with other non-USAFFE resistance groups on building a broad progressive unity. Besides the PKP and the Hukbalahap, these included the Free Philippines, the Blue Eagle guerrillas who had operated in Cavite and Batangas, sections of the USFIP guerrillas in Bulacan, and the League for National Liberation. By May the projection of Roxas had started and the vacillations of the Nacionalista Party made it evident that it would not conduct a strong principled fight for genuine independence or for the basic interests of the working people. It was decided, therefore, to set up a new party, comprising a united front of working people and middle-class groups, to be called the Democratic Alliance. Launched formally in July 1945, its founding organizations were subsequently added to by the affiliation of the Civil Liberties Union, the Philippine Lawyers' League, the Democratic Youth League, Llanes Guerrilla Veterans, League for the Defense of Democracy, the Manila Railroad Union, and the Rural Transit Employees Union.

The mass base of the Democratic Alliance, however, lay in the re-created trade unions and peasant unions. In May the *Pambansang*

Kaisahan ng mga Magbubukid (PKM) or National Confederation of Peasants was set up in a convention in Central Luzon, unifying the pre-war KPMP and AMT. Its president was Mateo del Castillo, a PKP political bureau member. Its membership rapidly grew to 500,000. Also in May a Committee of Labor Organizations began the building of a new federation based on the trade unions that began to be reformed while the battle for Manila was still in progress. In July a Manila convention inaugurated the Congress of Labor Organizations (CLO), almost all the officers and leading personalities of which were PKP trade union cadres. By the end of 1945 the CLO had 35,000 members in Manila and another 45,000 in the provinces. Both the PKM and the CLO affiliated to the Democratic Alliance.

It was the DA which called the mass march to Malacanang in September 1945 which presented demands to Osmena, its 50,000 participants demanding: for the resolute carrying out of independence, the removal of collaborators from public positions and their prosecution, the protection and extension of democratic rights including an end to U.S.-landlord inspired persecution in Central Luzon, an agrarian reform program with a 60-40 crop sharing law, and an industrialization program for national economic development. Included foremost was a demand for the immediate release of Hukbalahap leaders arrested by the U.S. army. The Osmena government reacted by ordering their release on September 30, a rebuff to the U.S. military.

Within the PKP a sharp debate occurred over the tactics to pursue in the forthcoming election. At issue was whether Osmena and the Nacionalista Party should be supported through a coalition of the DA with the NP, or whether the DA should run independently. Advocates of the former position argued that while Osmena and the NP were not really progressive, for the most part they were not inclined to be as fascistic, ruthless and ready for any service to imperialism as Roxas and the Liberals, and could be supported as the lesser evil. Supporters of the latter position insisted that Roxas and Osmena were two sides of the same coin, should be exposed to the masses, and that the DA should present its own program to the people.

Initially the latter view was favored by a majority in the PKP political bureau who won the adoption at a June central committee plenum of a resolution declaring: "The Democratic Alliance should be made the rallying point of all the democratic forces and groupings fighting against reaction and fascism. It should present a complete election ticket from the president down to the lowest elective office."[31] However, the course of events resolved the issue. By January 1946, when the LP and NP held conventions to nominate candidates, it was clearly evident that a general shift of landlord and *comprador* groups to the Liberals had occurred with a puppet-like readiness to serve U.S. wishes, while those with a relatively nationalist inclination remained with the NP, whose delegates authorized the party directorate to negotiate with the DA for a "tactical" coalition. Osmena himself, opposed at the outset to any coalition with the left, but impressed by repeated demonstrations of 50,000 to 60,000 under DA auspices, made a nomination speech with sections directed toward the DA, assailing "the backward economic practices which make the rich richer and the poor poorer" and urging "a more equitable sharing of the crop between tenant and landlord."[32]

The debate within the PKP was settled at a DA convention on January 27, 1946 which decisively backed the political bureau minority stand for coalition. This decision was quickly followed by an NP-DA meeting on February 1 which was joined by elements of the pre-war Popular Front and Philippine Youth Party. All signed a joint resolution to coalesce in the election to fight "the sinister forces of reaction, including re-examinationists, collaborators, vested interests, and imperialist agents."[33] On February 26–28, 1946 the PKP held its Fifth Congress at which the coalition was endorsed and all-out support given to 24 DA congressional candidates running in 13 provinces and the city of Manila, three of whom were widely known as PKP leaders.

The NP-DA coalition was the first of its kind in Philippine politics, projecting anti-imperialist and national-democratic issues. However, it did not please many of the traditional elite elements in Osmena's party, especially the landlord-controlled local branches. Osmena, to curry the support of the sugar bloc and win sections of it away from the Liberals, had made one of its prominent figures, Alfredo Montelibano of Negros, his secretary of the interior. Montelibano, who had headed a guerrilla organization on Negros during the war, had rejected PKP overtures in 1944 for unity around a provisional government. As the political realignments took place, his tendency was to favor an Osmena coalition with Roxas rather than with the DA. As secretary of the interior he had under his authority the paramilitary national police force. Set up as the Philippine Constabulary by the U.S. colonial regime, it had become so discredited for its collaboration role, including anti-guerrilla operations, under the Japanese that its name had been dropped in the immediate postwar period. Re-established as the Military Police by the U.S. army, its ranks were nevertheless filled with collaborators, including officers, and it was commanded by U.S. officers until well past the date of independence. In coordination with the U.S. CIC it participated from mid-1945 in the arrest, raiding and

harassing of the Hukbalahap, PKM members and PKP cadres. Montelibano, in January 1946, reinforced the MP in Central Luzon with the
issuance of 5,000 submachine guns supplied by the U.S. army, and in
Nueva Ecija alone, a strong Hukbalahap-PKM province, increased MP
companies from six to twelve, totalling 2,000 men. Montelbano then
issued orders for the use of terroristic measures against the PKP-led
mass movement.[34]

This was nothing less than sabotage of the NP-DA coalition. It
constituted backing for the most reactionary landlords and the fascistic
"civilian guard" units that they set up all over Central Luzon to destroy
the PKM and the PKP. These landlord groups were ardent supporters of
Roxas and the Liberal Party. An insidious alliance was in operation, of
the U.S. authorities, the Liberal Party, the reactionary semi-feudal
landlords, the collaborator-ridden Military Police, and Montelibano's
interior department. Throughout the election campaign in March and
April 1946 a continual wave of attacks occurred against DA candidates
and their election teams. DA offices were repeatedly raided and their
equipment smashed. MPs fired upon peaceful meetings and into homes,
and their armored cars constantly roved through towns and barrios
with threatening machine guns. MPs openly campaigned for Roxas and
warned that anyone voting for the DA and Osmena would be regarded
as a Communist and dealt with after the election. DA supporters were
termed "bandits," "terrorists" and "criminals." MPs reported attacks on
their patrols by armed Huks that were total inventions and MP violence was credited to "the Communists," who were portrayed as
preparing for an insurrection.

A hunting down of disbanded Hukbalahap members occurred,
with ex-USAFFE members joining civilian guards and MPs in raids.
Many ex-Huks were killed and others tortured. In self-defense Hukbalahap veterans took weapons out of hiding, reformed units and
fought back against attacks by terrorists who entered their barrios.
Having resisted such attacks by the recent Japanese invader, they were
not prepared to endure the same or worse from U.S.-linked Filipino
class enemies. This was not official policy by PKP leading organs but
local party organizations upheld the right of people to defend themselves against persecution. The PKP tried to avoid conflict and violent
incident, adhering to its decision to pursue legal, peaceful, parliamentary struggle.

The terror campaign, it must be noted, took place while the Philippines was still a colony of the U.S., which had the overall responsibility
for policy. Far from intervening by act or word to guarantee a peaceful
and democratic election, no U.S. official, from the U.S. Embassy in

Manila to the Truman administration and U.S. Congress in Washington, voiced a criticism or a protest.

Landlord-backed terror had a particularly vicious purpose: the PKM, which had swiftly grown into the most powerful peasant organization in Philippine history, had immediately conducted a very effective campaign for agrarian reform. It called for a 60-40 sharing of the crop for tenants, in place of the existing 50-50 arrangement, for government acquisition and distribution of big landed estates, for an end to landlord usury, for replacement of tenancy by leaseholding, for rural banks with low interest rates, and other agrarian demands. In one of his few really important acts, President Osmena responded to the PKM petition and promulgated a 60-40 crop-sharing law. This victory for the organized peasants improved Osmena's image in their eyes and gave greater substance to the NP-DA coalition. However, it proved to be an empty victory. Not only were no funds or administrative machinery provided to carry out the law or to resolve tenant-landlord disputes, but nothing was done to halt landlord-funded civilian guard depradations against peasants or Montelibano's Military Police activity. Landlords ignored the law and went on forcing tenants to agree to a 50-50 sharing.

As election day neared the terror mounted in Central Luzon, many PKP and Hukbalahap leaders forced into hiding to escape being killed. On election eve the chairman of the DA in Pampanga, Edilberto Joven, was kidnapped together with his son, riddled with bullets, and their bodies flung on their doorstep.

In spite of all this, the Democratic Alliance won seven out of the eight congressional seats in Central Luzon, several by massive majorities. Those elected were: in Pampanga, Luis Taruc and Amado M. Yuzon; in Nueva Ecija, Jose Cando and Constancio Padilla; in Bulacan, Jesus Lava and Alejo Santos; in Tarlac, Alejandro Simpauco. Taruc had 39,289 votes to his opponent's 1,312; Yuzon 26,322 to 5,317; Simpauco 18,578 to 5,611.

For the first time in Philippine history, two known Communists —Luis Taruc and Jesus Lava—had been elected to the Philippine Congress. All told, 152,361 people voted for the 24 DA candidates, roughly 6 per cent of the total vote, gained in contesting only one-fifth of the congressional seats. It was a successful launching of a national-democratic, anti-imperialist party that had the capability of future growth.

In Central Luzon, also, President Osmena won a majority of the votes. The people's movement had carried the Nacionalista candidates, an important lesson for bourgeois nationalist political leaders.

Manuel Roxas, however, had won the election and become the first president of an independent Philippines. Despite the heavy U.S. support, his margin of victory was not great, 1,333,006 votes to Osmena's 1,129,884. By that margin the Filipino people lost the opportunity to become the masters and mistresses of their own destiny.

VI

Independence, Without Freedom

As so often before in its history, the fate of the Philippines at the end of World War II was taken out of the hands of the Filipino people and determined by an outside force. In 1945–1946 the interests and policies of the United States overrode the interests of an independent Philippines just as surely as a conquering U.S. army had smothered resistance half a century before.

By decisively defeating Japan, the U.S. emerged as the dominant power in the Asia-Pacific region. Other powers and forces had shared in the victory—the British army in South East Asia, Chinese armies both Communist and Kuomintang on the mainland, the Soviet army that shattered Japan's Kwantung elite, the guerrilla movements in the Philippines, Indo-China, Malaya and other places—but it was U.S. military might that destroyed Japan's navy, its air force, and the bulk of its army and finally its cities with fire-bombs and nuclear devastation. A U.S. supreme commander, General Douglas MacArthur presided in Tokyo like a proconsul over much of eastern Asia, including the Philippines, the southern half of Korea, and Japan itself.

As Japan surrendered, U.S. generals proclaimed to their troops that "the Pacific is now an American lake."[1] The hope of a U.S. imperial thrust into Asia—that had burned brightly at the beginning of the century and had been dimmed by anti-imperialist opposition at home and by such an obstacle as an expanding Japan at China's door—now revived in another form. This time it had little of the appearance of a naked drive for colonies, markets and spheres of interest that had frankly characterized the earlier period. The new leaders of American expansionism could mask their aims with the claims that the U.S. occupying army ruling in Japan was there as a consequence of a popular war against an aggressor and to keep the aggressor from reviving; that in South Korea U.S. forces were protecting the independence of a newly freed people, and that in the Philippines a colony was being magnanimously relinquished and Filipinos aided in building the independence for which the U.S. had prepared it. On top of all this altruism, as the wartime alliance with the Soviet Union was dissolved and transformed into cold war and as the Chinese Revolution swept to its resounding conclusion, it was claimed that a U.S. presence in Asia in strength was necessary as part of a global program of protecting the "free world" from Communist aggression.

In the new U.S. policy in Asia, opened up by victory over Japan, the Philippines was viewed in a new light. Whereas in the past it had been considered militarily indefensible, which was one of the arguments that contributed to the granting of independence, under the changed situation such a liability was lifted. A military threat to the Philippines from a rival power no longer existed. It had become a secure base. Furthermore, it could be used as a cornerstone base for an imperialist design that was taking shape while the war was still in progress: the containment and reversal of socialism and of national liberation in Asia and around the world.

COLLABORATORS' RULE

In any logical course of events, the launching of a country's independence after centuries of colonial domination would have been accompanied by a fanfare of patriotic fervor, of appeals to nationalist traditions and to the emulating of nationalist heroes. For the Philippines in its war-stricken condition such a call to national effort and for national unity to reconstruct what had been destroyed, and to build the new and free society that had long been denied, was an obvious need.

The tone of the new era was set, however, by Independence Day proceedings on the Luneta in Manila that were embarrassingly lacking in national pride. In conscienceless symbolism, Emilio Aguinaldo, who had abandoned the cause of the First Philippine Republic 46 years before, tottered forth to hand to President Manuel Roxas the same 1898 battle flag that he had handed to Laurel at the puppet ceremony under the Japanese. The newly elected Roxas (who had declared at the time of his election that "I again pledge my faith and loyalty to America. Confident in her kindly interest and assistance, I shall not fail in the expectations of the American Government and the people of the Philippines"—in that order).[2] Roxas seemed more concerned in his address with pleasing the American representatives present, including General MacArthur and High Commissioner Paul McNutt, than with arousing the patriotic spirit of Filipinos: "The Philippine people now look back with gratitude to the day when God gave victory to American arms in Manila Bay and placed this land under the sovereignty and protection of the United States." The Philippines, he said, must follow "in the glistening wake of America whose sure advance with mighty prow breaks for smaller craft the waves of fear."[3]

Only Filipino nationalists noted that Roxas and his crew paddled so closely in the U.S. wake that the July 4, 1946 Philippine Independence Day to which they agreed was made identical to the date of U.S. Independence Day, a date whose sole relevance in Philippine history was that on July 4, 1902 President Theodore Roosevelt proclaimed officially the suppression of Filipino resistance to U.S. conquest.

That independence should begin with a subservient bow to the colonial ruler rather than with a ringing call to Filipinism was wholly in keeping with the U.S. designs that had hand-picked Roxas and his group for power. It was a government predominantly made up of those who had collaborated with the Japanese and who were obligated to the U.S. authorities for not prosecuting them for treason.

Immediately the U.S. government exacted from the compliant Roxas administration the whole range of its demands that would establish a U.S. economic, military, political and cultural control as complete as that under colonial rule. In a matter of months the Bell Trade Act, a product of the U.S. Congress, had restored colonial economic ties including the "parity" suspension for U.S. investors of the Constitutional provision for Philippine corporations to be 60 per cent owned by Filipinos.

Military agreements had implanted long-term U.S. bases in the Philippines and had placed Philippine armed forces under U.S. direction.

At the outset there was actually no organized section of the ruling groups in Philippine society that had a coherent program for an independent development in the interests of the nation or that was prepared to lead a struggle of any kind against U.S. control. The Nacionalista Party headed by Sergio Osmena had contested the 1946 election with Manuel Roxas and the Liberal Party, but the basic issue of nationalism versus collaboration with imperialism was not clearly projected. Some Nacionalistas attacked Roxas for collaboration with Japanese imperialism but not for collaboration with U.S. imperialism. An issue that tended to be debated was whether the Liberals or the Nacionalistas were better able to obtain U.S. aid. Only the Democratic Alliance condemned the subservience of Roxas to both imperialisms and put forward a program of unequivocal support for independence, for expansion of democracy, and for agrarian reform and industrialization, but the DA, with just a few progressive middle-class figures, was overwhelmingly a peasant-worker alliance.

Any economic grouping of a manufacturing or other industrial character was miniscule in the Philippines at the time and not capable of significant financial or other backing to candidates. The predominant factor in a country still overwhelmingly agrarian—its population in 1946 around 80 per cent peasant—was the landlord. Failure of the U.S. colonial regime to carry out any serious land reform had resulted in the expansion and entrenchment of semi-feudal agrarian relations, spreading to 38 per cent of landholdings. The semi-feudal landlords in this relationship, particularly in rice-growing and domestic sugar production, were the most reactionary ruling sector; if not involved in export production, they were strongly allied with the landlord-*comprador* groups that were, and had looked to the U.S. colonial presence for protection against an organized peasantry demanding reform or revolutionary change. It was this grouping in Central Luzon that favored armed suppression of the PKP-led Huk movement and other mass organizations, and which worked in complicity with the U.S. army on its return to destroy the democratic structures set up by that movement during the war.

At independence, the pre-war reactionary economic elite remained in unchanged control of the levers of Philippine society. The Bell Trade Act, as one of its aspects, had carefully arranged for the Filipino beneficiaries of colonial free trade, the landlord-*comprador* groups who had always been cold to independence and who had agitated for indefinite free trade after independence, to continue to be the beneficiaries of the Bell Act system of quotas in the U.S. market. Said Section 214 (c) of the Act:

> Each of the quotas established by this section shall be allocated annually to the manufacturers in the Philippines in the calendar year 1940 of products of a class for which quotas were established, and whose products of such class were exported to the U.S. during such year . . .

This assured that the Filipino sector of the economy remained in the hands of the traditional collaborators with U.S. interests, who were dependent on the U.S. market. These elements backed the Bell Act in its entirety, including "parity" for U.S. companies because it was part of the deal that gave them a preferred status.

A possibility that Filipino industrial and manufacturing enterprises might arise to compete with U.S. interests was to be effectively smothered by the Bell Act's "parity" provision cancelling out the protective 60 per cent Filipino ownership stipulation in the Constitution. This discouragement was doubled by Section 403 (c) (1) of the Act which stated that no future Philippine articles, outside of the traditional agricultural exports (by which manufactured goods were implied) would be permitted quota entry to the U.S. market if "the President of the United States, after investigation, finds that such Philippine articles are coming, or are likely to come, into substantial competition with like articles the product of the United States."

Philippine independence had thus been delivered to a Filipino regime based on traditional landlord-*comprador* power, made up of members of the colonial-nurtured political elite who had been selected for their guaranteed collaborationist tendencies. U.S. expectations of its proteges were fulfilled by the manner in which the Roxas Liberal Party government rammed through approval of the Bell Act and of "parity." Constitutionally, an amendment was necessary to the national charter to effect "parity," and this required the approval of three-fourths of the members of both houses of Congress. Roxas did not have the three-fourths majority in either house. Most important, the seven Democratic Alliance congressmen in the House of Representatives, who opposed "parity," held the balance of power on the issues.

The Roxas tactic was to use the simple majority held by the Liberal Party in both houses to adopt a resolution refusing to seat all Democratic Alliance congressmen, plus one Nacionalista in the House and three Nacionalista senators, on spurious grounds that "peace and order" did not prevail in their election, which was allegedly due to "terror and fraud." No proof was produced for this; it did not exist. The Liberal regime then circumvented the Constitution by adopting a resolution basing the three-fourths vote not on the full composition of Congress but on members actually seated. In this ruthless manner "parity" was approved, but then only in the narrowest of means, by exactly three-fourths in the Senate and by a margin of one vote in the House.[4]

Thus, to further U.S. economic interests and demands, democracy in the Philippines, fragile at best, was literally destroyed—the elected representatives of the large majority of the people in Central Luzon arbitrarily thrown out of their seats. It was only the beginning of the obliteration of the right of the people to form their own party outside of the parties of the property-owning groups and to elect their own representatives. The Roxas government followed up the congressional ousters with an all-out drive of military suppression of the DA's mass base in Central Luzon, particularly the PKM and the Hukbalahap veterans. This began in August 1946, shortly before the parity vote in Congress. The suppressive action was designed, too, to guarantee a "yes" vote for parity in a national plebiscite on the issue, also required for a Constitutional amendment. When this was held on March 11, 1947 the ballot boxes in Central Luzon were located in the main towns and not in barrios, and were flanked by machineguns of the Military Police, for intimidating effect.

The mailed fist brought down upon Central Luzon precipitated a prolonged armed struggle and a condition of crisis and instability that has persisted in the Philippines to the present day.

The most disturbing and pervasive features of this have been the ruthless and brutal methods employed by the Filipino ruling groups to maintain their dominance and to prove to U.S. interests their capability to "govern," that they had indeed been educated for self-rule. The acts of murder, massacre, torture and destruction carried out in Central Luzon and elsewhere from 1946 onwards equalled if not exceeded the policies of conquest by the U.S. forces early in the century. It was made obvious that a democratic independent Philippines was not possible as long as collaborationist forces clinging to colonial relationships were in the positions of power.

It was most illuminating that the U.S. authorities, whether in the Manila Embassy or in Washington, uttered not a word of criticism of the ouster of legally-elected members of Congress, or of the savage use of terror by the Roxas government in Central Luzon to secure U.S. aims. At this time the U.S. ambassador was Paul McNutt, who had literally organized the election of Roxas and had played the central role in obtaining agreement of his government for all the main U.S. policy measures. Beyond any doubt, the McNutt hand and advisory voice figured in the key Roxas tactics and decisions.

Collaboration of the Roxas government with U.S. interests and desires could scarcely be ascribed to pure ideological cohesion and a common adherence to "free world" concepts. On September 11, 1946, a week before the September 18 Congress vote on the parity question, the U.S. Foreign Liquidation Commission, acting on a provision in the Tydings Rehabilitation Act, turned over to the Roxas government an enormous quantity of surplus army property that had been stockpiled in the Philippines largely for the planned invasion of Japan, made unnecessary by the war's termination. The procurement value of this was estimated at $1,121,400,000. Huge amounts of construction equipment, vehicles, prefabricated structural material, clothing, medicines, foodstuffs, and numerous other supply items were included. A "fair valuation" was set on this, or the least amount that could be realized from sale, of $137,000,000 (P274,000,000), and an additional $25,000,000 in cash was included in the deal. It was reported as "the largest single transaction in the history of the country."[5] Theoretically the money realized by the government through selling the surplus property was to go into the treasury to aid the Philippine economy. To handle the disposal of the vast stores, a Surplus Property Commission was set up. It was comprised of leading figures in the Liberal Party. Between September 10, 1946 and September 30, 1949, when the Commission was dissolved, its accounts claimed that only P73,460,208.08 ($37,000,000) had been realized by the government from the sales. In other words, at least $100,000,000 (P200,000,000) had disappeared. It had gone into the pockets of government officials and Liberal Party leaders. The editor of the *American Chamber of Commerce Journal* called the surplus property deal "the biggest windfall in Philippine history."[6]

The surplus property episode was the first major case of corruption in the Philippine independence government. Colonial politics had been a lucrative area of enrichment in the past but it was child's play compared with the uninhibited corruption that began to permeate every corner of political and public life under the Roxas regime. Collaboration and black market dealings during the Japanese occupation were contributing factors, causing moral breakdown. Any hope of this being rectified by a firm U.S. policy of holding the guilty to account was shattered by the unprincipled manner in which U.S. policy-makers installed a neocolonial structure. It is inconceivable that U.S. officialdom, particularly the McNutt staff in Manila, was not aware of what would happen to the surplus property so loosely handed over. It had all the earmarks of a pay-off, weaving one more thread into the net of imperialist control.

It also threw open the door to a pattern of general corruption that affected virtually every government department and branch, from the national administration down to the municipal level. Funds appropriated for every type of program or service were ruthlessly milked away, including those for hospitals and school equipment, road-building and construction. It became virtually impossible to expedite a claim, obtain a public document, or see an official without greasing a palm or several palms with the appropriate *pabagsak* (bribe). In the popular view, all politicians were now for sale. The Military Police/Philippine Constabulary, engaged in suppressive warfare against the Huk movement and the PKM, were a particular case of uninhibited corruption; low-paid troops looted entire barrios, homes, poultry, livestock and rice stores, besides torturing and killing their inhabitants.

Within a very short time the Roxas Liberal Party government became thoroughly discredited in the eyes of the people for its rampant corruption. That loss of faith mounted with the local elections held on November 11, 1947, for 9 senatorial posts, 45 provincial governors and 952 municipal mayors. The fraud and terror employed to retain Liberal Party control were far beyond anything experienced in the pre-independence period. The election was called by the Manila press "the bloodiest in Philippine history." Nine Senators, 37 provincial governors and 752 mayors were claimed Liberal victors. Ballot boxes were held back throughout the Visayas and Mindanao while counting was manipulated. That election made the mold for elections to come.

On April 15, 1948 President Roxas died of a heart attack while visiting the U.S. Clark Air Base in Pampanga. The irony of this was widely commented upon by Filipinos. Replacing him as president was his vice-president, Elpidio Quirino, a man whose entire career had been shaped by colonial politics. He had held posts in the House of Representatives (1918), the Senate (1925) and Quezon's Common-wealth cabinet. Although staying mostly out of the limelight as a collaborator with the Japanese, he accepted the chairmanship of Laurel's Economic Planning Board. Experienced in the maneuverings and shady dealings of the feudal-like regional bailiwick politics of the Philippines, Quirino made use of this and of the entrenched system of corruption he had inherited from the Roxas regime to build his own machinery of power. In the first post-independence national election in November 1949, his Liberal administration perpetrated the most massive campaign of fraud and terror seen in the Philippines, far exceeding the 1947 episode. This was done to negate the obvious mass shift of discontented voters to a resurgent Nacionalista Party. The popular saying, as the rigged election returns kept Quirino and the Liberals in power, was that "even the dead and the birds and the bees voted."

The first years of independence in the Philippines had shown the Filipino ruling elite in its undisguised nature after half a century of U.S. colonial conditioning—prepared to surrender the substance of sovereignty and the national interest to foreign wishes, to suppress with savage brutality the opposition movements among the people, to loot public funds and the economy in general in an orgy of corruption for private enrichment, and to violate democratic rights and processes wholesale in the struggle between rival elite groups for enjoyment of the fruits of power.

ECONOMIC NEOCOLONIALISM

Before the Filipino people had a chance to take a full breath of freedom, an all-encompassing neocolonialism was clamped upon them. Most damaging of all were economic agreements with which the supposedly independent republic was launched, like a new vessel sent down the slipway already holed below the water line.

That launching occurred for a country with a war-shattered economy, for which virtually nothing had been done to prepare it for an independent course. At the outbreak of World War II the Philippine economy was still transfixed by the free trade relationship. Section 13 of the Tydings-McDuffie Act had provided that "at least one year prior to the date fixed in this Act for the independence of the Philippine Islands, there shall be held a conference of representatives of the Government of the United States and the Government of the Commonwealth of the Philippine Islands . . . for the purpose of formulating recommendations as to further trade relations." By Filipino landlord-*comprador* groups this was taken to mean some form of free trade or special relations after independence. The Philippine government-in-exile in wartime Washington was, virtually to a man, for the continuation of free trade, for which it undertook to lobby as the war drew to a close.

Coupled with this essentially colonialist Filipino attitude was the fact that at independence, 48.1 per cent of Philippine assets were in foreign hands, including most of banking, manufacturing, foreign trade, domestic wholesale and retail trade, public utilities, transport, communications, mineral production, offshore fishing, and lumbering. Of foreign investments 60 per cent were U.S., with British and Chinese holding the larger shares of the remainder. One and a half million foreigners (mostly Chinese, with only a few thousand Americans and Britishers) owned more than did 23 million Filipinos (including those who were naturalized).[7]

Towering beside these factors at war's end was the horrific war damage, which included 1,111,938 casualties—dead and wounded Filipinos. The Philippine Bureau of Census and Statistics' damage total was $2.8 billion, while a minimizing U.S. army survey put it at $1.5 billion (which was reduced to $1 billion when U.S. responsibility for its repayment was made clear). Philippine reparations claims upon Japan came to $8 billion. The economic impact of the losses may be gauged from the fact that the total national income of the Philippines in 1946 was only P4.36 billion ($2.18 billion) and stood at only P8.3 billion ($4.15 billion) in 1956.[8]

In these circumstances only an extremely strong Filipino nationalist leadership could have projected and held out for a reparations and rehabilitation program that would have set the independent Philippines on a development path away from colonialism. That required an effort to place a greater share of the national assets in Filipino hands and a war damage approach predicated on aid to economic development rather than on piecemeal doling out of relief-like funds, which was the U.S. policy. Above all, a truly independent course would have meant the scrapping of free trade with the U.S.

No Philippine-U.S. conference, as prescribed in the Independence Act, took place to determine trade or other relations. These were laid down unilaterally by the U.S. in the piece of legislation known as the Philippine Trade Act of 1946 or Bell Trade Act after Congressman Jasper Bell of Missouri, who introduced it in the U.S. Congress. The Bell Act was probably the most unfair act of economic relations to come out of the U.S. Congress, its purpose made worse by the Rehabilitation Act of 1946 that was linked with it.

It covered a period of 28 years, from 1946 to 1974, the crucial period for a Philippine economy to develop. Completely free trade was to prevail for the first 8 years, up to 1954 — i.e., Philippine products could enter the U.S. without payment of duties and U.S. exports could enter the Philippines also duty-free. However, strict quotas were placed on Philippine products while an unlimited quantity of U.S. goods was free to enter the Philippines. After 1954 a gradual stage-by-stage application of duties on both would occur until full duties were paid by 1974.

The Bell Act had other features. It tied the Philippine peso to the U.S. dollar at the existing 2 to 1 rate. This deprived the Philippine government of the freedom to adjust its currency in accordance with true values.

Most controversial, however, was Section 341, "Rights of United States Citizens and Business Enterprises in Natural Resources." It declared: "The disposition, exploitation, development and utilization of all agricultural, timber and mineral lands of the public domain, waters, minerals, coal, petroleum and other mineral oil, all forces and sources of potential energy, and other natural resources of the Philippines, and the operation of public utilities, shall, if open to any person, be open to citizens of the United States and to all forms of business enterprise owned or controlled, directly or indirectly, by United States citizens."

The real impact of this was hammered in by Section 402 (b): "That the Government of the Philippines will promptly take such steps as are necessary to secure the amendment of the Constitution of the Philippines so as to permit the taking effect as laws of the Philippines of such part of the provision of Section 341 as is in conflict with such constitution before such amendment."

What this demanded was amendment of Article XIII, Section 1 of the Philippine Constitution of 1935 which specified that all Philippine natural resources belonged to the state and that "their disposition, exploitation, development and utilization shall be limited to citizens of the Philippines or to corporations or associations at least sixty per centum of the capital of which is owned by such citizens." The authors of the Constitution had been particularly proud of this provision which was viewed as a cornerstone for control of the Philippine economy by the Filipinos. The Bell Act now demanded that U.S. citizens have equal rights, or parity, with Filipinos in exploiting the basic features of the Philippine economy.

Furthermore, Section 404 (c) (2) of the Bell Act warned that if any U.S. citizen or business enterprise were discriminated against "in any manner" the U.S. had the right to suspend, in whole or in part, the trade agreement. This was a threat, well understood by Filipinos concerned, aimed chiefly at the concession of free trade for 8 years granted to the elite group of producers and exporters tied to the U.S. market under colonialism.

So important did the U.S. interests involved consider the "parity" provision, and so determined were they to secure its approval, that the other major measure for the Philippines adopted simultaneously by the U.S. Congress, the Tydings Rehabilitation Act, had its implementation made conditional on Philippine acceptance of the Bell Act in its entirety. The Rehabilitation Act was the war damage payment legislation hopefully awaited by many Filipinos. A penny-pinching Act that whittled war damage payment to merely $520 million, it contained a stipulation that no payment over $500 would be made unless and until parity was adopted by the Philippine Congress and amendment of the Philippine Constitution carried out. In this bludgeoning manner U.S. interests forced their way into a dominating position in the economy of the independent Philippines, able to enjoy an extreme advantage over investors and traders of other countries.

Debate on the Bell Act, introduced in the U.S. Congress in October 1945, went on for seven months, until April 1946. It had five versions, as U.S. domestic producers once again struggled to prevent a duty-free influx of Philippine products. The original bill proposed 20 years of free trade, which were finally cut down to 8 years before graduated duties were to begin. Limited absolute quotas were finally imposed on seven Philippine items entering the U.S. (including 850,000 long tons of sugar, 200,000 long tons of coconut oil, 6,000,000 pounds of cordage, 6,500,000 pounds of tobacco, and 200,000,000 cigars). Not until these terms were obtained did U.S. congressmen and senators from agrarian states finally join with investment interests to enact the bill.

Above all, the Bell Act was the imperialist instrument of the expanding and aggressive U.S. investment interests with an eye on the Pacific-Asia regions now wide open to U.S. invasion. Congressman Jasper Bell was the sponsor, but the Act was written by Paul McNutt and his economic adviser, E.D. Hester.[9] McNutt, as a pre-war U.S. High Commissioner to the Commonwealth, had tried to promote a re-examination of independence. Reappointed as High Commissioner during the Osmena government, he attempted to revive a reexaminationist campaign on his return to the Philippines in November 1945 (after setting the Bell bill on its way through Congress).

The McNutt intention with the trade bill and its parity provision was caustically commented upon during hearings on the bill by Senator Millard Tydings, who had authored the 1934 Independence Act:

> I have no right to quote the Governor [McNutt], but I think that fundamentally he is opposed to Philippine independence, and if you would ask him he would tell you so. The truth of the matter is that most of the people, outside of the Filipinos, who favor this bill are fundamentally opposed to Philippine independence. Many of them have told me so. I do not like to mention names. Their whole philosophy is to keep the Philippines economically, even though we lost them politically.[10]

McNutt himself frankly admitted the purpose of continuing free trade:

> When you say trade in the Philippines, you mean the national economy. It is a trading economy. And I might and should say here and now that we, the United States, managed it that way. We are responsible for the sole dependence of the Philippines on the American market. Our businessmen and our statesmen in the past years allowed the Philippines to become complete economic dependents of the United States to a greater degree than any single state of the Union is economically dependent on the rest of the United States.[11]

In the long or even rather short term, McNutt envisioned the consequence of the Bell Act in this design of things:

> Even those who have felt that independence was unwise at this time have come to the conclusion that the matter has gone so far that it would be necessary for them to try independence, and that with our wholehearted support and effort to help them. If they should not be satisfied, then, as a

sovereign people, they could come back to the United States and ask to reestablish political ties in some form or another.[12]

Authorship of the Bell Act was only part of Paul McNutt's pervasive role in the shaping of the nature of Philippine independence. As High Commissioner in 1945 he openly backed Manuel Roxas for president against Sergio Osmena. McNutt's public relations officer, Julius Edelstein, was simultaneously the PRO of Roxas.[13] McNutt brushed away Filipino objections to linking war damage payments to acceptance of parity, saying scornfully: "Filipinos should not look behind Uncle Sam's whiskers, because after all, the U.S. is giving the money and there should be no quibble about it.[14]

Automatically becoming the first U.S. ambassador to the Philippine Republic, McNutt used that post to oversee the ruthless railroading of the Bell Act through the Philippine Congress and the amending of the Philippine Constitution to put parity into effect. As ambassador he encouraged the Roxas mailed fist suppression policy to destroy the mass base of opposition to the Bell Act, and he negotiated the military agreements that literally stripped the Philippines of sovereignty. The Philippines has never shaken off the imperialist legacy bestowed upon it by this unrelenting agent of U.S. corporations. After his job was done as ambassador, he became chairman of a body set up to promote U.S. business in Asia, the Philippine-American Trade Council, besides holding directorships on several U.S. companies in the Philippines.[15]

It is pertinent that the parity provision of the Bell Act was not designed for the benefit of the existing U.S. business interests in the Philippines that had been built up during colonial rule, but for new, future investment by what were to develop as the transnational corporations. In fact, the publication of the American Chamber of Commerce in Manila ran an editorial opposing parity. "The United States has granted independence to the Republic of the Philippines," it said,

> and has no right to impose a provision of this nature. To Americans in the Philippines the provision is a source of considerable embarrassment. The then High Commissioner McNutt made clear on one public occasion that the provision did not originate with Americans in the Philippines, and was never asked for by them as a group or individually. In the interest of preserving the respect and friendship of Filipinos, the fullest possible publicity should be given to this fact. In the interest of honesty and fair dealing, the government of the United States should voluntarily abrogate the invidious provision at the earliest possible moment.[16]

Established U.S. businesses for which the publication spoke had all the rights they needed guaranteed by the Philippine Constitution of

1935. Its Article XVII, Section 1 (1) declared that upon proclamation of independence "all existing property rights of citizens or corporation of the United States shall be acknowledged, respected and safeguarded to the same extent as property rights of citizens of the Philippines."

Even the free trade aspect of the Bell Act contradicted the U.S. key proposals on international trade being put to Great Britain and the Commonwealth and to the United Nations Economic and Social Council, for the removal of trade barriers and of the use of absolute quotas. As an economic preserve for U.S. business was set up in the Philippines, negotiations were undertaken with Britain for relaxation of its Commonwealth sterling bloc preferences, while an Assistant Secretary of State, William L. Clayton, told a U.S. Senate committee that quotas were "without doubt, one of the most vicious of trade restrictions. Their use by other governments has been highly detrimental to American exports."[17]

The determination of the Bell Act's promoters to smother or override all opposition to its parity provision could only have stemmed from the swollen character of a U.S. capitalism that had become dominant not only in Eastern Asia but had emerged from World War II as the world's chief creditor nation, ready to put the Marshall Plan into effect in Europe and to flood all continents with the mass production of its factories and with its investment and loan capital. On top of this, the supine collaboration of the type of leaders who had been installed in the Philippines was an advantage that aggressive U.S. interests could not resist.

The roughshod U.S. policies and methods caused even such a normally compliant ally as Sergio Osmena, not given to sharp differences with U.S. colonial rulers and much in favor of prolonged free trade, to be offended. Finding it hard to swallow the virtual ultimatum of parity, Osmena cabled the U.S. House Ways and Means Committee in the midst of its hearings on the Bell bill, calling parity

A curtailment of Philippine sovereignty and a virtual nullification of Philippine independence. That act is unfair and un-American and finds no precedent in the annals of American relations with sovereign states.

Complaining that it was unnecessary, he pledged:

Consistent with our rights and obligations as an independent nation, the Philippine Government is always ready to create opportunities for Americans, now and in the future, to preserve the ties of friendship between the people of this country and the United States.[18]

U.S. interests preferred to deal with an uncomplaining Roxas. It was the extent to which U.S. interests were prepared to go to get the Bell Act accepted in its entirety that startled many people in both the Philippines and the U.S.: the arm-twisting of withholding war damage payments until approval was obtained, the ruthless steps of arbitrary ousting of legally-elected congressmen to gain approval, and of savage suppression of the mass base of opposition in Central Luzon. Despite the steamroller pressure to obtain special privileges, U.S. investment capital did not flow into the Philippines in large amounts once the enabling laws were in place. At the time of independence in 1946, U.S. direct investments of non-resident Americans stood at barely $100 million. These had climbed to only $149.2 million by 1950 and crept even more slowly to but $188 million in 1953. Considering the unrestricted entry possibilities this was a trickle. The climate of civil war and political instability that developed, coupled with enormous corruption by successive compliant Philippine governments, made investors cautious. The Bell Trade Act established the near total trade and investment domination of U.S. business in the Philippines, but its very operation during the first few years was ruinous in its effect.

THE MILITARY SIDE OF NEOCOLONIALISM

The economic arrangements desired by the U.S. in the independent Philippines were but part of the neocolonial package that the Roxas government agreed to deliver. It included wrapping-up the military aims that were integral to the new U.S. supremacy in the Asia-Pacific region.

In the Tydings-McDuffie Independence Act of 1934 were certain tentative provisions for U.S.-Philippine relations to follow independence. One of these, in Section 10 (b), was for negotiations to take place, not later than two years after independence, "for the adjustment and settlement of all questions relating to naval reservations and fueling stations of the United States in the Philippine Islands." Manuel Quezon had maneuvered the rejection of the earlier Hare-Hawes-Cutting Act because it specifically called for the retention of U.S. military and naval bases, while the Constitution of 1935 had recognized the U.S. right to maintain "military and other reservations and armed forces in the Philippines" only during the period of the Commonwealth, "pending the final and complete withdrawal of the Sovereignty of the United States over the Philippines." Quezon, having successfully out-maneuvered Osmena for political leadership, may have given private assurances to

U.S. officials about a future for the bases, but it was generally understood by most Filipinos that the wording in the Tydings-McDuffie Act and the Constitution meant the phasing out of U.S. military bases.

World War II changed the picture. Quezon, in wartime exile in the U.S. and still rankling over the failure of the U.S. to make a major defense of his country against Japanese attack, delivered an address in 1943 to the Maryland State Bar Association in which he called for a U.S.-Philippine military alliance after the war. He was obviously thinking in terms of Philippine defense against any other aggressor and it is known that he supported the making of a formal U.S. commitment to that end. On June 29, 1944, a month after Quezon died and four months prior to the U.S. re-invasion of the Philippines at Leyte, the U.S. Congress adopted Joint Resolution 93 which authorized the President of the U.S. to "withhold or to acquire (in addition to the naval reservations and fueling stations) such bases as may be deemed necessary for the mutual protection of the Philippines and the United States." Quezon's successor, President Sergio Osmena, hailed the Resolution, saying "this protection insures for our present and future generations the peaceful enjoyment of the blessings of independence."[19]

Such opinions and actions of the Filipino leaders, who had been nurtured and molded by U.S. colonialism, were undoubtedly influenced by the shock of war, exile, and enemy occupation of their country. U.S. strategists, however, had other aims than satisfying Philippine fears. Their readiness to acquire expanded bases in a Philippines once considered untenable had less to do with protection of Filipinos against an enemy now being eliminated than with the structure of a dominant U.S. position in East Asia and the Pacific.

The changed outlook on military bases was the first formal indication of U.S. postwar policy in regard to the Philippines. Significantly, Joint Resolution 93 coincided with the decision to re-invade rather than bypass the islands. General MacArthur returned bearing the assurance of a re-establishment of U.S. control. The swift, roughshod steps of PCAU and the CIC in installing local and national governing bodies of their choice, the sidelining of Osmena and his cabinet, the selection and promotion of Roxas and the smothering of the collaboration issue, the repressive steps against the Hukbalahap and the PKP, were all part of a calculated design for the retention of U.S. control after independence, a design into which the altered conception of military bases fitted. The new military bases that were contemplated had none of the half-hearted and disputed conception of the colonial years but were to be confident fortresses and launching sites of the world's strongest power.

To Filipino leaders and to the Filipino people in general the bases issue of course was not dealt with from the standpoint of U.S. strategy but as a contribution to Philippine defense. In reaction, one of the first acts of the re-opened Philippine Congress was a resolution on July 28, 1945 authorizing the Philippine president to conduct negotiations on U.S. military bases. It was done after Manuel Roxas and his fellow collaborator, Jose Zulueta, had won control of both houses of Congress. President Osmena, however, aware of U.S. hostility toward him, did not undertake such negotiations while he was in office: that was initiated by Roxas after he was elected to the presidency in April 1945. Insistent on getting the bases question settled, the U.S. pressed for talks to start while the Philippines was still a colony. On May 14, 1945 Roxas signed a preliminary statement with President Harry Truman on the general principle of a military agreement, a month and a half before Independence Day.

Despite the compliant character of the Roxas government, it took eight months of negotiations and maneuverings to produce a military bases agreement that encompassed U.S. desires. The stationing of U.S. troops in the Philippines after independence and the scope of U.S. demands were opposed by some members of Roxas' Liberal Party, and the head of the Philippine negotiating panel, Vice-President Elpidio Quirino, balked at agreeing to the whole U.S. position. Talks were stalled until the Truman administration became impatient and resorted to pressure tactics. Declared to be on the recommendation of the Secretaries of State, Navy and War and of General Dwight D. Eisenhower, then U.S. Army Chief of Staff, a message to Roxas from President Truman warned that U.S. forces might be withdrawn unless agreement was quickly reached. It said, tongue-in-cheek, "that the long-term continuance of Army forces in the Philippines would be of little value unless their retention was the result of an expressed desire of the Philippine government." At that time, as well understood by the U.S. officials, an armed struggle provoked by the Roxas government with the PKP-led mass movement was spreading. Roxas, reacting in the way of the dependent, needing military aid for his campaign of suppression, hastily informed the U.S. that his government "does desire maintenance of U.S. bases in the Philippines."

The U.S.-Philippine Military Bases Agreement was signed on March 14, 1947. Its terms would have been difficult for the most subservient of collaborators to swallow. They provided for the U.S. use of 23 bases "for a period of ninety-nine years subject to extension thereafter," 16 to be in active use immediately and 7 other sites to be held in reserve and activated as the U.S. might determine. Article I enabled the U.S.

"to expand such bases, to exchange such bases for other bases, to acquire additional bases or relinquish rights to bases, as any of such exigencies may be required by military necessity." Article III gave the U.S. the right "to construct, install, maintain, and employ on any base any type of facilities, weapons, substance, device, vessel or vehicle on or under the ground, in the air or on and under the water that may be requisite or appropriate," an unlimited provision that could include the stationing of nuclear, chemical or bacteriological weapons on the bases.

A few days later, on March 21, 1947, a second military agreement, the Military Assistance Agreement, was signed, complementing the bases agreement. Under this, the U.S. agreed to arm, equip and train the Philippine armed forces "and other services essential to the fulfillment of those obligations" (such as intelligence agencies). A key section of the assistance agreement provided for the establishment in the Philippines of a Joint U.S. Military Advisory Group (JUSMAG) "to assist and advise the Republic of the Philippines on military and naval matters." JUSMAG members, drawn from all branches of U.S. military and related services, were to be paid and their accommodation, needs, and services paid for by the Philippine government. In its operation, the Military Assistance Agreement put the Philippine armed forces effectively under the control of the Pentagon and produced an organization, tactics and general military orientation both internally and externally that suited U.S. global strategy. As developed under this Agreement and JUSMAG direction, the Philippine armed forces became not the means for defending the country from an aggressor but a counterinsurgency instrument for purposes of internal suppression of unrest.

These military arrangements bore no relation to the terms of the Independence Act from which even the word "bases" had been deleted and reference made merely to "naval reservations and fueling stations." Instead of a "naval reservation," the huge Subic Bay Naval Base was built under the Military Bases Agreement, a 14,570 hectare (32,000 acre) complex at the juncture of Zambales and Bataan provinces, which was made the main base of the U.S. Seventh Fleet. Its naval station, air station, supply depots, naval magazine, marine barracks, and enormous ship repair yards and other facilities comprised a U.S. capital investment of $327.94 million by 1975. The Clark Air Base, the second of the two main U.S. bases constructed after independence, occupied 53,492 hectares (115,482 acres) of Pampanga province. A vast extension of the prewar Clark Field-Fort Stotsenburg base, its capital investment stood at $150.6 million by 1975.

Subic and Clark were developed into the two biggest U.S. overseas bases. They were designed not for the defense of the Filipino people from a theoretical aggressor but as major components of an aggressive U.S. strategy in the Asia-Pacific regions. The U.S. Seventh Fleet in particular, with its aircraft carriers and nuclear-armed warships, has been primarily a strike force ranging over Western Pacific, East Asian, South East Asia waters, with Subic subsequently the jump-off and support base for the U.S. naval thrust into the Indian Ocean. In 1950 the Subic base had its first major role in U.S. military policy when President Truman, as part of operational orders related to the outbreak of the Korean War, drew a U.S. protective line around Taiwan (formerly Formosa) and directed the Seventh Fleet to patrol the strait separating it from mainland China and other sea approaches to repel a supposed invasion threat from the Chinese Red Army.

From Clark Air Base repeated operations were carried out by planes of the 13th Air Force and by others assigned to the CIA against neighbor countries of the Philippines. In April 1958 a CIA agent, Allan Pope, flew a B-26 bomber from Clark to the North Celebes in Indonesia in support of a rebel force attempting to overthrow the government of President Sukarno; he was shot down and captured. The full extent of such interventions in Indonesia and elsewhere is unrevealed, becoming known only when exposed and leading to incidents. Although President Sukarno sought and was given an assurance from the Philippine government that it would not permit U.S. bases to be used for intervention, CIA documents seized by Indonesian forces at a rebel base in Menado, North Celebes showed U.S. infiltration into Indonesia from a military base in the southern Philippines.[20]

In the early 1960s a U.S. campaign of military intervention in Laos was mounted from Clark, surreptitiously supporting the U.S.-backed Boun Oum government against a revolutionary liberation movement. A fleet of thirty C-130 transport planes was used in the Clark-based operation, to fly Boun Oum's troops, arms and equipment to combat areas in Laos. In addition, Laotian Royal Army units were trained secretly by U.S. advisers on bases in the Philippines.[21]

The Clark base was most extensively used, however, against Vietnam. This began in 1954 as part of a clandestine U.S. plan to conduct warfare against the Vietminh while its struggle for independence was still in progress. A Saigon Military Mission set up on June 1, 1954 and headed by the CIA's Colonel Edward G. Lansdale developed a program for supporting the puppet regime in South Vietnam by "training personnel for eventual guerrilla warfare in case the Vietminh won." A secure location was desired for this.

Plans were made with Major Bohanon and Mr. John C. Wachtel in the Philippines [both CIA agents] for a solution of this problem: the United States backed the development, through them, of a small Freedom Company training camp in a hidden valley on the Clark AFB reservation.[22]

During the subsequent major U.S. war in Vietnam, the whole complex of U.S. bases in the Philippines was brought into play in the massive program of bombing missions, logistical support, transit of troops and planes, hospitalization of wounded, and rest and rehabilitation. The contingency air base on Mactan Island, one of the 23 included in the Military Bases agreement, was activated to handle the flow of missions, troops, planes and material. U.S. bases thus involved the Philippines in a western war against a fellow Asian country.

The Tydings-McDuffie Independence Act had declared in Section 11:

The [U.S.] President is requested, at the earliest practicable date, to enter into negotiations with foreign powers with a view to the conclusion of a treaty for the perpetual neutralization of the Philippine Islands, if and when Philippine independence shall have been achieved.

Neutralization, which would remove the Philippines from entanglement and conflict with other countries, was the fond desire of most Filipinos, and the experience of Japanese occupation had intensified it.

From the moment of independence, however, neutralization vanished as an objective. A neutral Philippines did not fit U.S. aims. The presence of U.S. bases and linking Philippine armed forces with JUSMAG and the Pentagon cancelled out hopes of neutrality. A U.S. strategic aim was to make the Philippines a junior pawn in its global policy of surrounding the socialist part of the world with military blocs and bases and of intervening in and reversing national liberation revolutions.

Among the newly free and developing countries of the postwar world, the Philippines was one of the very few that became fully aligned with what was termed "the west." Its first act in that compliant role came in the Korean War in 1950, fought ostensibly under a United Nations mandate but wholly commanded and directed by the U.S. Of the sixteen countries that sent troops to fight beside U.S. forces against North Korea, the Philippines (besides South Korea) was the only formerly colonial country to do so. Five battalion combat teams, totalling 6,000 men, were sent in rotation between 1950 and 1953, suffering 488 casualties or 8 per cent of strength. The cost of this operation, over P560 million, was "reimbursed" by the U.S., which put the Filipino troops in a virtual mercenary position.

In the course of the Korean War the U.S. pressed upon the Philippines a further military agreement that could be used to align it with the U.S. in other war situations. This was the Mutual Defense Treaty, signed in Washington on August 30, 1951 and entering into force on August 27, 1952. Its key provision stated:

> Article IV. Each Party recognizes that an armed attack in the Pacific area on either of the Parties would be dangerous to its own peace and safety and declares that it would act to meet the common dangers in accordance with its constitutional processes.

This was a Treaty that a powerful U.S. could conceivably employ to pressure the Philippines and its legislative body to react supportively to any military threat or venture affecting U.S. interests, but which the Philippines had scarce chance of using to get a U.S. Congress to come to Philippine defense. It gave, in fact, no automatic guarantee of a U.S. defense of the Philippines, despite the presence of U.S. military bases, which were shown more than ever to be intended solely for protecting and furthering U.S. interests.

The U.S., however, had still not completed the binding of the Philippines into its military network. Following the French-Vietnamese Geneva Agreement of July 21, 1954 in which defeated France had to recognize an independent Republic of Vietnam, the U.S. called a seven-nation conference in Manila to draw up and sign a South East Asia collective defense treaty on September 8, 1954, which created the South East Asia Treaty Organization (SEATO), alternatively called the Manila Pact. The Philippines and Thailand were the only South East Asian countries included, the other signatories being the U.S., Britain, France, Australia, New Zealand and Pakistan (the latter brought in for the purpose of linking the Treaty body with the Middle Eastern Central Treaty Organization (CENTO), which completed a military cordon of sorts around the socialist countries from Japan to Norway).

SEATO also contained the U.S. loophole to "meet the common danger in accordance with constitutional processes," which enabled the U.S. to pick and choose whatever situations for intervention furthered its interests. Provisions of the Treaty made it applicable to "armed attack in the treaty area against any of the Parties or against any state or territory which the Parties by unanimous agreement may hereafter designate." The "treaty area" was the whole of South East Asia and thus was the instrument for intervention in Vietnam, Laos and Cambodia. It was for resisting not only armed attack but "to prevent and counter subversive activities directed from without against their territorial integrity and political stability," a provision that could be used to claim "subversion" directed from "Moscow" or "Peking" and to justify intervention against popular movements and struggles within a member state. As a consequence Philippine foreign policy, both in its own Asian region and in the world in general, was made subordinate to U.S. wishes. In particular, the Philippines became completely aligned with the U.S. in the anti-Communist postures of the cold war, which greatly distorted Philippine diplomatic relations, trade, and possible development assistance from other countries.

Thus, until 1967 Filipinos were forbidden to travel to any socialist country; trade with such countries was barred for a longer period. Not until 1973 were diplomatic relations entered into with a socialist country (the first was Yugoslavia), and formal diplomatic ties were not signed with the main socialist state, the Soviet Union, until 1976, three decades after Philippine independence. During that interval the Philippine governments subserviently supported a very anti-communist cold war position of the U.S. within or outside the United Nations. So dogmatically was that attitude pursued that Filipino U.N. delegates did not speak to the delegates who sat alphabetically beside them, from the socialist Peoples Republic of Poland.

The presence of the U.S. military bases and the nature of the military agreements with the U.S. had another effect on Philippine relations with other countries. They put the Philippines outside the community of other developing countries, which formed the Non-Aligned Movement for taking a unified stand on issues of peace, progress and fair trade or aid relations with the west.

CULTURAL CONTROL

One of the most important and indispensable features of U.S colonial rule, comparable to the colonial policy of the British in India and of the French in Africa, was the implanting of an educational system in the Philippines from 1898 onwards that oriented Filipinos overwhelmingly toward U.S. culture and the U.S. way of life, while denied its substance. That system was far from comprehensive—at independence the rate of literacy was still only 60 percent and the great majority of the people concerned had not been educated beyond the fourth grade of elementary school—but in contrast to the meager, Catholic Church-controlled, elitist education of the Spanish period, it was universally welcomed by the people. Educational attainment was so eagerly desired by Filipinos that it facilitated the instilling of a colonial mentality in most of the population.

This was accomplished to begin with by the imposition of the English language, the obligatory medium of instruction and learning throughout the school system. Tagalog and other Philippine languages persisted in the home and the street among working people, particularly in the rural *barrios;* it prevailed in a limited vernacular press, and in popular cultural forms like *zarzuela* (light operetta) performances, the *balagtasan* (poetic debate), and the *kundiman* (semiclassical love song). In general, however, Philippine culture was smothered, untaught in schools. American literature, music, films, advertising, art, history and heroes, and holidays shaped the Filipino outlook and made Philippine culture seem inferior.

Significantly, the policy of Filipinization of the colonial administration that helped nurture a collaborating Filipino political elite was never extended to the department of education, which remained with an American at its head until the Commonwealth government was inaugurated in 1935. Even then, American advisers continued to be a directing influence.

The Commonwealth government did take serious steps toward a national educational system. In the 1935 Constitution, Article XIII declared that "The National Assembly shall take steps toward the development of a common language based on one of the existing native languages." In 1936 the Assembly created an Institute of National Language which decided that Tagalog, the most developed and literary of the Philippine dialects, spoken chiefly in the provinces of Luzon surrounding Manila, should be the basis of the national language. In addition, a start was made toward Filipinizing education through introduction in the teaching materials of greater attention to Philippine history and to the deeds of national heroes. The production of textbooks by Filipino authors was programmed.

Although the war and Japanese occupation interrupted all Commonwealth work, it is interesting that the educational system carried on by the Japanese gave major attention to Filipinization. One of the first Orders of the Japanese Commander-in-Chief was a six-principled renovation of education which included the eradication of American and other western culture and the gradual diffusion of the Japanese language in place of English. Attached to this was a note for the "popularization" of Tagalog. The teaching of Japanese made little progress, but Tagalog fared far better. When the puppet government was established in 1943, President Jose Laurel, in his Executive Order No. 10, ordered the teaching of the national language as the official language in all schools from the primary level to universities. Nationalism in general was to permeate the curricula. Resistance to Japanese occupation tended to nullify its education policies but they were not without effect among many Filipinos.[23]

The whole cultural perspective was changed with the U.S. return. As in the case of economic and military relations, the entire range of education, culture and information in the newly independent Philippine republic became a target of the U.S. drive to retain the Philippines as an appendage.

Accompanying the re-invading U.S. army in 1944 was a branch of the Office of War Information. It was headed by a U.S. journalist, Frederick (Fritz) Marquardt, who had been on the staff of the leading magazine in the country, *Philippines Free Press.* Marquardt was another of the returning number of U.S. citizens with a special interest in re-establishing prewar relationships. Under him, the OWI set up a newspaper, a library and a radio station in Manila as soon as it was captured. These spearheaded and set the tone of media as it was restored.

At the end of the war the OWI was terminated by President Truman who set up an Office of International Information and Cultural Relations, later reorganized as the U.S. Information Agency. The overseas branches of this were called the United States Information Service (USIS). A USIS office was opened in the Philippines on the eve of independence, on July 1, 1946. President Roxas readily agreed to invite it formally to assist in the educational program of the republic.

The USIS branch in the Philippines was concerned only in part with propaganda and indoctrinating operations in that country. It was also the regional office for U.S. propaganda activities throughout Asia, for which the Philippines was considered the key reliable base and to which the Roxas government submissively agreed. In the latter part of 1946 a huge shortwave radio transmitting station was constructed near Malolos, Bulacan, for beaming Voice of America programs throughout Asia. In 1951 a second transmitting station was built at Poro Point, La Union, and a receiving station in Baguio City. These were administered by one of the two special divisions under the Philippine USIS branch, the Philippine Relay Station. The other division, the Regional Service Center, had the editorial office and printing plant for a vast propaganda operation through the printed word. It had one of the largest offset printing plants in Asia, comprising 18 presses capable of turning out six million sheets daily in 20 languages, for distribution all over Asia, including the Philippines. The plant's staff of 14 Americans and 225 Filipinos worked two 8-hour shifts daily to produce that flood. The Press and Publications Branch that supervised this included the press attaché of the U.S. Embassy in Manila "One feature of this branch," wrote a U.S. editor, "is an extensive mailing list of leaders in every field of Philippine life."[24] The output included magazines, pamphlets, posters, newspaper and magazine inserts, leaflets, calendars and photograph packets. Nothing of this kind and scope was done while the Philippines was an outright U.S. colony.

Two large USIS libraries were established in the Philippines, in Manila and in Cebu City. These had 30,000 volumes dealing with the U.S. way of life and policies, 364 U.S. periodicals, 3,000 recordings of American music and poetry, 1200 scores of American music. Special film programs, seminars and forums were held in the libraries. Virtually no other public libraries existed in the Philippines at this time. The National Library premises had been destroyed in the Manila fighting, its salvaged books kept for years in dilapidated warehouse conditions, relatively inaccessable to users. The U.S. cultural presence was overwhelming.

USIS activities were stepped up enormously as U.S. anti-Communist policies were intensified following the victory of the Chinese revolution in 1949, the outbreak of the Korean War in 1950, and the growth of armed rebellion in the Philippines. Between 1950 and 1953 USIS centers were increased to 18 in the Philippines and 23 USIS mobile units were sent to barrios with pamphlets, posters, films and lecturers. The Psychological Warfare Unit of the Philippine Army, engaged in the anti-Huk suppression campaign, distributed the USIS material and were advised by USIS on the preparation of its own propaganda material.

Boasted the editor of the *American Chamber of Commerce Journal,* such a "democratization" effort had never before been equalled in the Philippines, including the occupation period after 1898.[25]

The USIS was an arm of the U.S. government, serving overall imperialist policy interests. In the Philippines itself was resident U.S.-owned media that was embedded in the society, partially carried over from the colonial period. The *Manila Daily Bulletin,* most prestigious of the newspapers, was U.S.-owned and edited by Carson Taylor. It spearheaded the pro-parity campaign. An American, Dave Boguslav, edited another leading paper, Filipino-owned but pro-U.S., the *Manila Times.* In 1949 the *Evening News,* the main evening paper, was bought by General MacArthur's old intelligence aide, Charles "Chick" Parsons. The country's leading magazine, the *Philippines Free Press,* was owned jointly by an Englishman, R. McCullough Dick, and an American, Theo Rogers; Dick was the editor and an American, Robert Hendry, the associate editor. The influential *American Chamber of Commerce Journal* had an American editor, A.V.H. Hartendorp.

If the majority of newspapers, mostly of small circulation, were Filipino-owned, including one in the Tagalog language (*Bagong Buhay*, New Life), their contents were heavily reliant on U.S. news services for virtually all foreign news, which reached Filipino readers filtered through U.S. policy strainers. Furthermore, there was in operation a highly effective system of interfering in Philippine political affairs through an interrelation of U.S. and Philippine media. This was (and is) done by planting in the U.S. press stories and reports, either favorable or unfavorable, defending or smearing, on Filipino political or business leaders. Carried by U.S. news services, these have often appeared in the Philippine press with considerable impact, especially because the importance of U.S. opinion has been carefully magnified among Filipinos. The U.S. publishers William Randolph Hearst, Henry Luce and Roy Howard created support for Manuel Roxas in this way in 1946, besides providing finance and newsprint for the pro-Roxas press in Manila. In the same manner successive Philippine presidents were built up or knocked down since then. Planted stories of graft, corruption, venality or instability, published in the U.S. and reprinted in Manila, have frequently shaped the course of Philippine politics, just as the praising and whitewashing of other parties and figures have equally helped determine who rises or stays in power. An intertwining, of course, has existed of USIS and the private press.[26]

In addition, virtually all syndicated filler material—comic strips, crossword puzzels, horoscopes, beauty care hints, Hollywood gossip— was also derived from U.S. news services, so that almost everything in print that affected the thinking and imaginations of people had an American association. That effect was even more pronounced in the predominance of U.S. films in all the leading cinema houses. In the 1950s, with television programs for many years derived chiefly from the U.S., the American imagery was kept on view to an even greater extent.

The outlook of the population in general was shaped in this way, but a more telling effect was inculcated by an institution termed the U.S. Educational Foundation in the Philippines. Set up in 1948, it was an offspring of the Fulbright Act, adopted by the U.S. Congress on August 1, 1946, and of the Fulbright Agreement between the U.S. and the Philippines signed on March 23, 1948. These provided for an annual program, for 10 years, of sending Filipino graduate students and lecturer-researchers to the U.S. for specialized study and, in exchange, for American graduate students, lecturers and researchers to be sent to the Philippines.

From 1948 to 1957 a total of 504 Filipino graduate students and 21 researcher-lecturers were provided by the Educational Foundation with grants to study in U.S. institutions of higher learning. In exchange, 79 American lecturers, 9 teachers, 43 graduate students and 16 advanced researchers went to the Philippines. They were assigned to key Philippine institutions: University of the Philippines, Bureau of Education, Philippine Normal College, several provincial normal schools, Philippine School of Arts and Trades, Philippine Women's University, Bukidnon National Agricultural School, Silliman University, Ateneo de Manila, Central Philippine College. Many Filipinos in the program subsequently occupied top posts in universities, government departments, the media and business.

A second U.S. indoctrination program complemented the Fulbright awards: the Smith-Mundt Act, adopted in January 1948, which arranged for travel and field study grants for Filipinos identified as leaders in teacher education, information media (including press, radio and films), youth leadership, social welfare, Asian studies, labor, government and cultural affairs. In the five years of its operation, the Act financed sending 143 Filipinos to the U.S. to meet and confer with American authorities in their fields. American specialists, especially in labor and cultural affairs, were funded to stay for a time in the Philippines.

Apart from the Fulbright and Smith-Mundt programs, over 700 Filipinos were sent to the U.S. for training between 1947 and 1950 under a provision of the Philippine Rehabilitation Act, for the staffing of Philippine government departments, bureaus and services. These were adult employees.[27]

A U.S. source has pointed out that "Even under the 'pensionado' system adopted by the Government in the early days of the American occupation, no such numbers of Filipinos were ever sent to the United States."[28] It might be claimed that this was an altruistic set of measures to help the Philippines with trained personnel for its development in independence. They were not designed, however, to instill national pride, confidence in independence and national development, or a Philippine cultural identity, but were designed to project a psychology of dependence on the U.S. Such programs need to be seen in relation to all other U.S. policies at that time for the Philippines— economic, military and otherwise. Above all, the aim was, and continues to be, to instill an outlook of looking up to U.S. leadership in all fields, a subservient relationship that in subtle ways perpetuated the colonial mentality. The U.S. lecturers and other grantees performed a similar function in Philippine institutions, little different from the role of the American teachers during the colonial period. The generating of Filipino pride and confidence and encouragement for the people to take an independent path of development based on Philippine needs was not embodied in the principles and aims of any of the training programs.

One final, pervasive fact: the selection of Filipinos to be sent to the U.S. for study and training lay with the Office of the President of the Philippines. In charge of selection was the educational adviser of the President. He was Dr. Luther B. Bewley, an American.

THE FIGHT FOR GENUINE FREEDOM AND DEMOCRACY

No objective or rational historian of the early years of the 1946 Philippine Republic, either U.S. or Filipino, could point with admiration to the governments or to their leading figures which took on the responsibility of self-rule. Inevitably, the image of the independent Philippines that is likely to be formed is of a violent, corrupt society, led by puppets.

That, however, is the record of the neocolonial elements of the elite ruling groups. It is not the record of the people's movement which fought for genuine freedom and democracy against the Japanese fascist-militarists and which tried to realize those goals after the war, nor is it the record of a good many national-democrats among the elite who opposed the degeneration of independence.

The Partido Komunista ng Pilipinas and the Democratic Alliance in which it participated were the only organized political forces that had a program for a genuine and democratic independence. They had committed themselves fully to legal, peaceful parliamentary struggle. The PKP was prepared to accept the result of the April 1946 election and to continue to work in coalition with the DA and the Nacionalista Party, and to build patiently a mass base for the coalition in the other parts of the country to match that which had produced victories in Central Luzon.

In later decades, some left theorists, attempting to look with hindsight on the postwar period in the Philippines, have contended that the PKP should not have taken the parliamentary path but should have continued the armed struggle of the Hukbalahap and simply turned it into armed struggle against U.S. imperialism and the collaborators. The fact that the PKP and the Huk were forced to resort to armed struggle again eventually anyway, the theorists argue, shows that the legal struggle decision was an error. Such an argument ignores numerous factors. To begin with, the Huk movement at war's end was limited to Central Luzon and its fringes and to part of Southern Luzon, with no organization or base in the rest of the country. Of greater importance, the Filipino people in general, including in the Huk areas, had welcomed peace and the opportunity to express their will by ballot. Furthermore, virtually all people in the rest of the country had welcomed the returning U.S. troops as liberators and understood almost nothing of the imperialist policies that came with them. Indeed, independence was about to take place and in the popular view did not have to be fought for. To have proclaimed an armed struggle at war's end would have won practically no sympathy and would have tended to isolate the PKP-led movement. It would have disregarded the principle that the basis of any mass struggle must be the readiness of the people, or important sections of the people, to support and participate in it.

A strong, legal, left political force in the Philippines was precisely what imperialism feared, knowing that if the PKP and its mass organizations could freely and democratically bring their program to the people, they were likely to rally around an anti-imperialist, national-democratic cause. The actuality was that imperialism and its reactionary collaborationist allies wanted to drive the PKP out of the legal political arena and to force it into illegality and suppression. This had been the aim of U.S. imperialism from the time the PKP had been founded, when it had been driven underground in the early 1930s. As for an armed struggle situation developing in 1946, U.S. imperialism had crushed a Filipino revolutionary army at the beginning of the century and had been able without difficulty to put down a number of uprisings during the colonial period. Now it had a military assistance pact and a military bases agreement with which to back the Roxas government if a PKP-led armed struggle became serious.

The arbitrary ouster of the Democratic Alliance congressmen from their seats in Congress was the first step toward a forcible political isolation of the left. It was not enough, so the brutal smashing of its mass base was next.

In an effort to resolve or to take the heat and tension out of the worsening situation, DA, PKM, and, indirectly, PKP representatives met repeatedly with President Roxas in June 1946. PKM leaders Juan Feleo and Mateo del Castillo, DA Congressman Luis Taruc and DA executive member Judge Jesus Barrera on June 10 presented a memorandum to Roxas protesting the murder of more than 500 peasants and PKM organizers in the month and a half since the election. Along with this was a memorandum detailing land reform measures as the main basis for peace in Central Luzon. The seating of the ousted congressmen was demanded, coupled with broader demands for the repudiation of the Bell Trade Act and the pursuit of real independence from U.S. domination.

Roxas reacted to this with a set of duplicitous acts. He created an Agrarian Commission to look into agrarian reform; it came up at the end of June with a 70-30 crop sharing arrangement in place of the 60-40 law of Osmena, but it had the enormous loophole of allowing all landlord-tenant agreements made outside of the arrangement legal, which opened the door for landlords to use coercion to force the old 50-50 share system on tenants, a worse situation than before. Roxas also agreed that civilian guards ought to be disbanded, but not only was this not implemented, an expansion of civilian guard units occurred and they became more aggressive and ruthless.

A cruder betrayal came in the case of a third Roxas agreement: to conduct a "pacification" program in Central Luzon. Under this, the government was supposedly to restrain MP and civilian guard aggression, while PKM and DA leaders were to tour the barrios, meeting with Huk and PKM members to caution against armed encounters: Juan Feleo to Nueva Ecija, Mateo del Castillo to Bulacan, Luis Taruc to Pampanga, Alejandro Simpauco to Tarlac. As the left representatives were meticulously carrying out their side of the agreement, Roxas on July 20 abruptly dropped the "pacification" mask and ordered the surrender of all arms by Huks by the deadline of August 31. His statement, grossly distorting the true state of affairs, demanded "immediate termination of lawlessness, banditry and resistance to the peace forces of the government."

Despite this demonstration of treachery, the left forces persisted with every avenue left open to obtain a peaceful resolution of the mounting crisis. A last-ditch memorandum signed by Mateo del Castillo and Luis Taruc, in behalf of the PKM and the Hukbalahap Veterans, was presented to Roxas personally on August 17. It stressed the desire of the peasants "to live and earn their livelihood peacefully and enjoy their fundamental rights provided for by our Constitution" and blamed the disorder and strife "on the selfish, undemocratic and reactionary desire of those landlords who are feudal to perpetuate what you yourself, Mr. President, have termed 'an archaic and socially undesirable system' of agriculture." Urged the memorandum:

> We respectfully present the following concrete measures which we believe will bring about Justice and enduring peace to all:
>
> 1. The right of every citizen to keep and bear arms should, for the present, be recognized. This must be applied equally to landlord and tenant, to Huk-PKM members, guerrillas, and all other citizens of the

Philippines . . . All arms shall be registered in order that responsibility for criminal actions can be easily pinned. Arms can be kept only in the house.

2. All private armed groups should be disbanded and every member should register his firearm. Only the regular police forces of the government receiving their salary as such, shall have the right to bear arms collectively and do peace duties. There should be no such things as deputies, special agents, civilian guards, etc.

3. But, in the transition period, to protect the barrio people from the depradations of any armed bands, every barrio should be permitted to form self-defense units which should include every member of the barrio with or without affiliation and whatever his affiliation might be, and those units should be responsible to the meeting of the barrio as a whole . . .

4. All charges against members of the Huk and other guerrilla organizations for actions taken in the collective interest during the Japanese regime and up to the present, should be dismissed . . .

5. All anti-peasant local officials should removed and replaced by at least impartial elements . . .

6. So as to enable the masses of Central Luzon to voice their needs and feelings in the democratic way, all their Congressmen should be seated . . .

7. The Constitutional liberties of individuals which have been arbitrarily abolished by local officials should be restored . . . [29]

At the meeting where this memorandum was presented, Roxas agreed to permit the peasants to retain arms, to stop MP raids and to control civilian guards, to remove fascist-minded officials, and to put reforms into effect. However, Roxas then asked that the PKM-Huk memo and his reply to it not be published.

The dishonesty of Roxas in all his negotiations with the left reached its depth within five days. On August 22, Military Police troops in full battle array poured into Central Luzon where they set up mortars in the fields and began without warning to shell the most strongly organized barrios. First to be shelled were the barrios of Cabiao, Nueva Ecija. Others were raided, mass arrests occurring. The attacks were launched nine days before the expiration of the Roxas arms surrender deadline.

On August 23 PKP intelligence sources in Manila learned that Secretary of the Interior Jose Zulueta had issued an order for the killing of Feleo, Taruc and del Castillo. PKP warnings reached Taruc and del Castillo, who immediately went into hiding. However, the warning failed to reach Juan Feleo. On August 24 he was kidnapped in barrio Baluarte, Gapan, Nueva Ecija by men in MP uniforms. He was taken to a secret place and murdered.

For the peasants of Central Luzon the murder of the loved and respected Feleo was the last straw of a long series of brutal and treacherous acts against them and their leaders. The military attacks on their barrios were acts of war by the government on the people. The re-forming of Huk squadrons became general and all peasant leaders and PKM, PKP or Huk members who were on the wanted lists of the landlords and MPs "went outside" for self-preservation. This occurred also in Southern Luzon where Pedro Villegas and others were MP targets. Huk squadrons did not seek out government forces but they did not evade them when barrios were raided. In resulting encounters, the veteran Huks inflicted heavy casualties on MPs and civilian guards.

President Roxas ordered an all-out mailed fist offensive against the organized peasantry of Central and Southern Luzon.

The full-scale armed struggle that began in this fashion at the outset of Philippine independence was the choice of U.S. imperialism and its reactionary and collaborationist Filipino allies; it was the means employed for crushing the national-democratic forces that were resisting U.S. neocolonial impositions. As the main leader of those forces, the PKP strove to adhere to its strategic line of legal, parliamentary struggle, which has been its chosen course since its founding, but it had been constantly compelled, either for defending the people or for its own survival, to resort to illegal and non-peaceful methods. These were never turned to without attempting and exhausting every peaceful means.

For the PKP it was a difficult and confusing period. From the time of the presidential election campaign, many PKP members had been compelled to go underground, particularly in Central Luzon. On May 25 the former leading commanders of the Hukbalahap met in barrio Kandating, Arayat, Pampanga and reestablished the Huk GHQ so as to control and give direction to the re-assembling Huk squadrons and to prevent any anarchistic tendencies. Such a step was wholly pragmatic and did not derive from any PKP decision to resume armed struggle.

From this point, however, a majority and a minority situation developed in the Political Bureau of the PKP. The majority advocated and sought to apply tactics of negotiation and maneuver with the government in order to gain time and preserve organizations intact while working for a united front of all nationalist and democratic forces. It was insisted that there should not be a voluntary giving up of hard-won gains or of organizations of the working people in order to retreat underground. Armed self-defense was considered necessary but to serve the defense of legal struggle aims. The majority felt that the Roxas suppression policy could be overcome by standing firm and building broad support for a democratic settlement. The slogan "For a Democratic Peace" was projected. Armed struggle and militant self-defense against attack were not rejected but viewed as a lever to compel imperialism and the neocolonial government to agree to peace and democratic rights. For example, approval was given to a Huk expansion program. Decided at a conference in October 1946 in Bulacan, Huk expansion teams of up to 100 fighters were sent out of Central Luzon to Pangasinan in the northwest, deeper into Bataan to the west and to Batangas in the south (by the mountain routes through Rizal and Laguna). A combat team was dispatched to Panay and an organizing group to Mindanao. The Bataan, Batangas and Panay expansion steps were very successful, developing mass base support.

The Political Bureau minority opposed this political course, declaring that in had been proven that no negotiations could be undertaken in good faith with the Roxas government, which was instituting a fascist regime, and that there should be an immediate full-scale resumption of the armed struggle with the movement taking the initiative rather than adopting a defensive posture. This position was turned down at an enlarged PB meeting held underground in Manila in January 1947, but the leading figure in the minority, Jose Lava, was made head of the party's Organizational Department, a key post from which he continued to call for all-out armed struggle. In a remarkable display of inner-party democracy, he was permitted to bring his position down to the various organs of the party. During the course of 1947, special regional and Manila conferences of PKP cadres were held "outside" in Central and Southern Luzon and "inside" in Manila to debate the issue.

By this time the majority of PKP members and leaders were in the countryside with the re-assembled Huk forces, resisting the repressive campaigns, and were increasingly in favor of the armed struggle orientation. Support for the PB majority stand came chiefly from urban areas, especially from those in the trade unions and in Democratic Alliance work. Actually, except for Central Luzon and parts of Southern Luzon, the mass work of the PKP could still be carried on. The Congress of Labor Organizations was organizing, leading strikes, and conducting political activity, making a strong public demand for real independence and against subservience to U.S. imperialism. Much was done by the CLO toward unifying the fragmented trade unions in the country, in particular forming close unity relations with the Federacion Obrera de Filipinas (FOF) in the Visayas, headed by Jose Nava. This latter link was the main channel for the Huk expansion into the Visayas. The CLO also developed international ties, affiliating to the World Federation of Trade Unions (WFTU) in January 1948, and establishing connections with CIO unions in the U.S., especially with the longshoremens' union. Organizations of women and youth could also function, and the PKP newspaper, *Katubusan,* was published in Manila throughout 1947 and ceased to appear due not to suppression but to lack of finances.

In the 1947 senatorial and local elections the united front policy that had featured in the DA-NP coalition of 1946 was much diminished in scope. The top Nacionalista Party leadership shied away from association with the left as well as from opposition to the neocolonial direction of the Roxas government. PKP-led forces campaigned for Nacionalista candidates on a provincial or local level who were friendly with or willing to have relations with the Huk movement, and for the very few individuals prepared to run for local positions as DA candidates. On the national level, however, the 1947 election greatly aggravated the majority-minority differences within the PKP: a number of Congress of Labor Organization leaders who were PKP members associated with the majority in the Political Bureau supported, through the CLO's Political Action Committee, four senatorial candidates from each of the Nacionalista and Liberal Parties. Support for any ruling Liberal was opposed by the minority in the PB which charged three PB members (Jorge Frianeza the general secretary, Pedro Castro and Geruncio Lacuesta) with "conscious appeasement of the enemy." An enlarged Central Committee conference was called for by the minority, which succeeded by means of its control of the PKP Organizational Department in generating general approval of such a meeting to settle the strategic and tactical issues under debate.

The Roxas government caused those issues to come further to a head by intensifying repression in the wake of the fraudulent election. On February 24, 1948 hirelings of the Department of Labor kidnapped and murdered Manuel Joven, the general secretary of the CLO, a PKP Central Committee member. On March 6, 1948 Roxas proclaimed the formal outlawing of the Hukbalahap and the PKM which he termed "illegal associations organized and maintained to commit acts of sedition and other crimes for the purpose of overthrowing by forceful means our present Government under the Constitution."

Before the planned PKP conference could occur, a complication came with the sudden death of President Roxas while visiting the U.S. Clark Air Base. For U.S. interests and policies this meant no essential change: the man who replaced Roxas by succession, Vice-President Elpidio Quirino, was perhaps not as capable but was just as ready to agree to U.S. wishes. For the PKP and in particular for the ascendent grouping favoring armed struggle, a temporary problem was created: Roxas had become fully discredited in the eyes of most people for corruption and electoral fraud, but Quirino was not, as yet. Furthermore, Quirino publicly announced that he wanted a settlement of the Huk question, and privately contacted the PKP to offer peace negotiations. This could not be ignored by the PKP without being put on the defensive before the people as being unreasonable.

The PKP Central Committee conference was in progress at the end of May 1948 and when the Quirino contact was made, its basic decisions had already been arrived at. What had been the minority position won the support of the great majority of the Central Committee, and the former majority leaders in the PB were suspended and eventually expelled (except for Jorge Frianeza who accepted criticisms and was readmitted to party membership). The elected members of the new Political Bureau were: Jose Lava, Ramon Espiritu, Federico Maclang, Jesus Lava, Mariano Balgos, Mateo del Castillo, Luis Taruc, Peregrino Taruc, Casto Alejandrino, Lazaro Cruz, and Benedicto Serrano. Chosen as general secretary was Jose Lava who, together with Espiritu and Maclang, comprised the directing secretariat of a now united movement.

Among the major conference decisions was that the main form of struggle must be the armed struggle and that all other forms of struggle should be subordinated to it. Some delegates argued that a revolutionary situation existed and that the stages in a strategic plan for the overall seizure of power should be discussed, but this was considered premature and set aside. A formulation was agreed that U.S. imperialism was the main enemy of the Filipino people and that the Liberal Party was an instrument of the main enemy and a part of it. It was concluded that the Nacionalista Party constituted "the direction of the main blow," because, although in opposition to the Liberal Party, it had essentially narrow ruling class aims and would compromise with imperialism when only very limited features of those aims had been realized.

Quirino's overture, although known at the time by the new PKP leadership, was not presented to the conference, but talks began on June 1, with Luis Taruc and Casto Alejandrino representing the Huk/PKP and President Quirino's brother, Judge Antonio Quirino, representing the government. Neither side undertook the negotiations in good faith. The Quirino government, as the PKP was well aware, wanted to maneuver the PKP-led movement into a position of vulnerability to repression, while the PKP leaders aimed at exposing the

Quirino government as a repressive, undemocratic puppet regime, not seriously desiring peace.

In the negotiations President Quirino went to the extent of verbally agreeing to adopt a nationalist position of independence from U.S. imperialism, including working for abrogation of the Bell Trade Act and of the Military Bases Agreement, extending democratic rights of the people, carrying out land reform and stamping out corruption. He agreed to give amnesty to the Huks and to release up to 600 Huk and PKP political prisoners. Luis Taruc had his seat in Congress restored (which demonstrated the falsity of the reasons for unseating the DA congressmen). The PKP negotiators in turn agreed to accept amnesty, and for Huks to present themselves for registration of firearms, but to keep them.

This was a precarious set of agreements, that soon broke down. Almost at once the Quirino government displayed its insincerity and deception. Quirino failed to live up to his pledge to release political prisoners, and he publicly denied that he had agreed to any Huk terms. When the PKP began to publish in the Manila press the documents of agreement, the government imposed censorship and banned publication. The Philippine Constabulary (which had resumed its old name, discarding the Military Police label) as well as the civilian guards quickly resumed the arrest, torture and murder of Huks who surfaced for registration, and of peasant activists. The Huk leader in Southern Luzon, Pedro Villegas, died after being dined by local officials who were believed to have poisoned him. Finally the Quirino government set a deadline of August 15 for surrender of all arms, and resumed attacks on barrios. (PKP leaders acknowledged that Quirino may have wanted at least a compromise settlement, but that after the negotiations U.S. pressure was strongly exerted to compel him to back away from a real settlement.)

Proclaiming that "Legal, constitutional parliamentary methods of struggle alone cannot achieve democratic peace," the PKP withdrew from all agreements being violated by the government and began implementing its decisions on armed struggle. The name of the movement was changed from Hukbalahap (which related to the struggle against Japanese occupation) to Hukbong Mapagpalaya ng Bayan or HMB (Army of National Liberation). An extensive HMB expansion drive was launched, the best Huk fighters streaming out of Central Luzon to spread revolutionary struggle to all parts of the the the Philippines.

VII

Suppressing a Nation—2

At the outset of Philippine independence U.S. policy-makers had every reason to believe that they had put in place all the necessary instruments and controls to make continued U.S. dominance secure: a handpicked submissive government, economic arrangements heavily weighted to favor U.S. trade and investment, military agreements that gave the U.S. both powerful bases and command over Philippine armed forces, driving the left from the legal political arena, pervasive cultural influences, and dictation of Philippine foreign policy.

As complete as the neocolonial system seemed, however, it quickly proved unstable. Within three years, from 1946 to 1949, the Philippines had been plunged into such deep crisis that the government and the economy were in a state of collapse. This was in no sense evidence that the Filipino people were not ready for self-government or were not capable of managing their own affairs, as the more extreme imperialists contended. Much responsibility did lie with the corrupt Filipino collaborators who readily acceded to U.S. wishes, but the real causes lay overwhelmingly with the neocolonial economic relations imposed by the U.S., which were designed to satisfy U.S. business interests and not the well-being of Filipinos.

The crisis generated and strengthened the very forces that U.S. imperialism wanted to stifle and to hold in suppression: Filipino nationalist business interests which might grow strong enough to challenge U.S. control of the economy, and the revolutionary forces of the left which were prepared for an all-out liberation struggle to end the neocolonial system. To counter these trends and forces for the advancement of Philippine national interests, U.S. imperialism engaged in multiple acts of intervention to eliminate all opposition to its domination.

183

NEOCOLONIAL CRISIS AND IMPERIALIST MANAGEMENT

In the short period from 1946 to 1949 the Philippines accumulated a total trade deficit of P2.2 billion ($1.1 billion). Virtually all of this was with the U.S. and was due to the operation of the Bell Trade Act. Independence was launched in 1946 with the U.S. still accounting for 72 per cent of total Philippine foreign trade and for 87 per cent of its imports. In 1949 these respective figures were 77 per cent and 80 per cent. This unaltered, unbalanced trade situation, fitting the Bell Trade arrangement, had ruinous consequences, quickly leading to the near-obliteration of Philippine dollar reserves and of the whole foreign exchange position.

Ostensibly, the Philippine economy was being bolstered by a large inflow of U.S. dollar payments. War damage payments began in April 1947 and were completed by 1950: $400 million to private claimants (individuals and corporations) and $57 million for restoration of public property. In addition, the U.S. Veterans Administration paid out large sums to Philippine war veterans, widows and orphans, which amounted to $113 million through 1949, while the back pay promised to USAFFE and other pro-U.S. guerrillas came to $37,800,000 over the 1946–1956 decade. Even if earnings from exports to the U.S. are added for the period concerned, the income total just about equalled the trade deficit. In other words, in effect, the dollars flowed out of the Philippines and back into U.S. pockets as fast as they came in, acting as little more than priming for the U.S. consumer goods imports.

The Philippines needed a development program and funds designed to suit real independence. U.S. rehabilitation funds, as they were called, did not constitute development aid. A large amount of war damage money went to corporations owned by resident Americans or other foreigners. Some ordinary Filipinos whose homes had been destroyed were able to begin replacing them (the payments never covered more than a fraction of the damage). The Bell Trade Act's relentless implementation was a counterweight to rehabilitation, a recipe for neocolonial non-development.

It was not that plans for real development were not produced. In 1947 a series of surveys and proposals were made with precisely such a purpose.

Soon after independence a Joint Philippine-American Finance Commission was set up to make recommendations, belatedly, for a Philippine financial structure. Its report was published on June 7, 1947 and one of its proposals, for establishment of a Central Bank, was acted upon without delay. Included in the report was a supplement, "Philippine

Economic Development, a Technical Memorandum," prepared by Thomas Hibben of the U.S. Department of Commerce. It proposed a balanced program of restored agricultural export industries and new manufacturing and infrastructure projects. The plan suggested an expenditure of P2.18 billion ($1.09 billion) spread over five years, an estimate based on the actual U.S. funds entering the Philippines in that time. Hibben urged "domestic production, where quantities warrant, of all goods now imported for the manufacture of which the principal raw materials are now or can be made locally."[1]

Recommending iron and steel and chemical plants in the program, the Hibben Memorandum asserted that if fully carried out it would provide

> at least 75,000 homesteads, 80,000 hectares of irrigated land, self-sufficiency even with increased population and higher living standard demand in rice, corn and vegetables; self-sufficiency and possible export of fruits, nuts, fish and meats; greatly reduced import requirements in shoes, leather, chemicals, paper, glass, clay products, iron and steel; maintenance of pre-war levels and possible increase in export of sugar cane products, coconut products, abaca and other fiber products, lumber, tobacco products and mine products; increase in the output of power; and transportation and communication facilities to meet the demand of a growing industrial and prosperous agricultural economy.[2]

Also prepared in 1947 was a "Proposed Program for Industrial Rehabilitation and Development," supervised by the H.E. Beyster Corporation, Consulting Engineers, Detroit, Michigan. Requested by the Philippine government with a view to rehabilitation of pre-war industry, it went beyond that brief to call logically for the establishment of machine-tool industries, non-ferrous and other metallurgical plants, a chemical industry, power plants, textile plants, forest-product plants, and numerous other projects. This plan was to be spread over 15 years and to expend P3.2 billion ($1.6 billion).

Both the Hibben and Beyster plans came under strong criticism from the U.S.-owned press in the Philippines and in Manila from financial, industrial and business circles. Neither plan was given serious consideration in Roxas government departments or submitted to the Philippine Congress for discussion and possible implementation. The determinant was the fact that U.S. interests opposed industrialization projects for the Philippines and used every channel to minimize or discredit such plans.

A third plan, an "Electric Power Program for the Republic of the Philippines," prepared by the Westinghouse Electric International

Company in cooperation with the Philippine National Power Corporation, encountered the same obstructionist attitude. It envisioned a 12-year power development program of large hydroelectric projects. Despite the benefit that U.S. interests themselves might derive from this, the U.S. Export-Import Bank sat for five years on a Philippine loan application to implement it, until 1952.

In truth, the principal U.S. interest was not in aiding an independent Philippine path of balanced development but in the free entry to the Philippines of massive quantities of exported U.S. consumer goods. Furthermore, the great bulk of those imports, and their distribution, was handled by the big U.S. trading firms established in colonial times: Atkins, Kroll & Co., Ault & Wiborg Co., Dodge & Seymour Inc., Macondray & Co., Levy Hermanos Inc., F.H. Stevens & Co., Universal Trading Co., Philippine Education Co., Pacific Merchandising Corp., Oceanic Commercial Inc., and others.

The Joint Philippine-American Finance Commission of 1947 had foreseen the effect of U.S. policy, pointing to the adverse piecemeal way in which U.S. "aid" funds reached the Philippines, the lack of any means of focusing them on development, and the inevitable consequences of free trade. The Commission found that "the Philippine economy is in an exceptionally favorable position compared to other former enemy-occupied countries because of its abundant exchange reserves" but it expressed concern over the "wide diffusion of money incomes" due to the manner of paying out the U.S. funds which "will result in a substantially greater demand for consumer goods" than if payment was concentrated. Said the report:

> The Commission believes that there are serious potential dangers in this situation, and that measures should be taken to limit the expenditure of foreign exchange upon non-essential consumer goods which do not contribute to the development and well-being of the economy.

The Commission urged a shift in the pattern of imports to capital goods and recommended "for the immediate future a pilot program of import controls and licensing limited initially to a few commodities," to achieve that goal.[3]

It took over a year, while the drain went on, for the Philippine government to act, hesitantly, on the Commission's recommendations, and then not until President Elpidio Quirino had replaced the deceased Manuel Roxas. The hesitance was due to the Manila American Chamber of Commerce disapproval of controls. Finally, on July 15, 1948, the Philippine Congress passed Republic Act No. 330 which authorized the establishment of a system of import controls. Even then it took nearly six months more before an executive order from Quirino on December 30, 1948 began implementing that Act. By that time it was too late to prevent an extreme trade imbalance and disastrous drain on foreign exchange reserves, which continued through 1949 as imports in the pipeline kept arriving. In desperation the Quirino regime had to resort to one act and order after another curtailing hundreds of imported commodities, first non-essentials and then essentials.

The damage, however, had been done. The rapid depletion of dollar reserves, which dropped precipitously from $453 million in 1947 to $250 million in December 1949 and fell below $200 million at one point, was accompanied by a growing flight of capital. These signs of catastrophe forced the Quirino government to introduce exchange controls as well as import controls. Remittance of profits and dividends by foreign firms, mainly U.S., was put under strict licensing.

Under the terms of the Bell Act the Philippines was not free to enact economic control measures on its own: it had to have the approval of the President of the United States. So threatening was the Philippine situation, with a spreading armed revolutionary struggle adding to the restricting of U.S. interests, that President Harry Truman reluctantly agreed to the control steps as emergency measures although technically they violated Bell Act provisions.

U.S. business interests in the Philippines, however, bitterly attacked both import and exchange controls for interfering with their alleged rights. The editor of the *American Chamber of Commerce Journal*, which opposed all controls, calling them "wicked" and "control gone mad," argued that restricting the importation of U.S. consumer goods would cause "a fall in the standard of living" of Filipinos and a "lowering not only of morale but of health." He claimed that "happy consumers would not agree with" import control and called the Joint Finance Commission's recommendation for a shift in the import pattern to an emphasis on capital goods a "planners' dream" in which "the Government must take the people's money away from them so that it may finance grandiose schemes of development."[4]

The great worry of U.S. interests was that the application of economic controls would act as a form of protection for Filipino enterprises which might arise and start producing many of the U.S. commodities being excluded (as the Hibben plan had suggested). For members of the American Chamber of Commerce in Manila, the first sign of a competitive Filipino tendency was an Executive Order by President Quirino on March 30, 1949 which amended his original order three months earlier implementing import controls by providing that 20 per cent of permitted import quotas be set aside for new importers, to be "allocated exclusively to Filipino importers." U.S import companies raged against this, calling it "official discrimination on nationalistic grounds."[5]

On May 19, 1950 the hard-pressed Quirino government was driven to enact a second import control Act (R.A.No.426) which widened the range of controls to cover almost all imports. In its original wording as introduced in Congress, this measure would double the allocation for Filipino importers, setting aside for them 40 per cent of import quotas. That provision immediately brought U.S. intervention, a strong official protest from the American Embassy which threatened that the matter came within the scope of Article X of the Bell Act giving the U.S. President the right to terminate the Act in case of any Philippine discrimination against U.S. citizens or any form of U.S. business enterprise. Furthermore it was said that the Executive Agreement at independence was being violated. (According to Article VI of that Agreement "all existing property rights of the citizens and corporations ... of the United States of America in the Republic of the Philippines shall be acknowledged, respected and safeguarded to the same extent" as those of Filipino citizens and corporations.) In the face of this pressure the Quirino government backed down by inserting in the relevant section of the new import control measure a provision that "nothing contained in this section shall in any way impair or abridge the rights granted citizens and juridical entities of the United States of America under the Executive Agreement signed on July 4, 1946."

That the Quirino government was inclined to respond to the demands of nascent Filipino businessmen seeking to find substance in independence, a tendency which would cut into the lion's share of the import trade held by Americans, was not liked by U.S. interests. Friction appeared again when Quirino worriedly visited Washington in February 1950 to request a further U.S. aid program. He proposed a joint Philippine-U.S. survey team to assess the need and recommend action. President Harry Truman rejected the Quirino joint survey proposal and insisted that it be solely an American team. Quirino returned home in annoyance and procceded to appoint the Filipino half of a survey team and to press for U.S. agreement. However, by now the pressures on Quirino had become so great, with the Huk rebels able to strike at will at government forces, that by June his government backed down. When a survey group arrived and began work in Manila on July 10, 1950 it was solely an American team, and its approach and assessments were wholly as U.S. interests desired.

By this time an element of grave urgency had entered the situation for both the Philippines and the U.S. Import and exchange controls had temporarily checked the drain on the Philippine economy but the armed struggle of the PKP-led Huk movement had intensified to the point of a major threat. In January 1950, following the re-election of Quirino in the extremely fraudulent 1949 election, the PKP had declared the existence of a revolutionary situation and formally called for the overthrow of the Quirino "imperialist-puppet regime." HMB attacks of mounting strength in succeeding months caused the alarmed Quirino government, pressed by JUSMAG, to order the entire Philippine Army into the field against the Huks in place of the demoralized Constabulary. The scare thrown into Quirino—who had an escape launch ready and waiting in the river beside Malacanang Palace to speed him to safety if the HMB entered Manila—undoubtedly influenced his acceptance of an aid survey mission on U.S. terms.

For its part, the U.S. was being confronted by a challenge to its position at numerous points in East and South East Asia. The confident postwar prospect of U.S. supremacy in the whole region was fading. Instability in the Philippines, intended as a southern anchor to that position and supposedly securely neocolonial, was but one factor. The victory of the Chinese Revolution had been completed in October 1949. In December the Netherlands was forced to yield sovereignty to an independent Indonesia. In Indo-China a major national liberation movement had confronted France with a proclaimed republic. Finally, in June 1950 a revolutionary war in Korea threatened to sweep away the only U.S. foothold on the Asian mainland. In that month the Truman government reacted decisively, committing itself to an all-out war in Korea, dispatching the U.S. Seventh Fleet from its Philippine Subic Bay base to patrol the strait between China and Taiwan, and increasing the U.S. forces stationed in the Philippines. In addition, the U.S.-Philippine Military Assistance Pact was invoked with interventionist steps for the suppression of the HMB. These moves were the component parts of an imperialist policy to defeat and reverse the national liberation process in Asia.

Overriding the Quirino wish for a joint economic survey team was an aspect of that policy. The wholly American mission was headed by Daniel W. Bell, a former Undersecretary of the Treasury and now a private banker, and had four other members and a staff of 24 assistants. After more than three months of study, the Bell Report was published in October 1950. It was a wholesale criticism of the Philippine government and society since independence. It said that the Philippine economy had fundamental ills that had acquired "a more acute form" in the postwar period (i.e., after independence):

The basic economic problem . . . is inefficient production and very low incomes . . . The standard of living of most people is lower than before the war . . . The finances of the government have become steadily worse and are now critical. The Treasury has a large and mounting deficit, with taxes covering little more than 60 per cent of expenditure . . . The international payments position of the country is seriously distorted and a balance has been maintained only by imposing strict import and exchange controls . . . The opportunity to increase production efficiency and to raise the standard of living in the Philippines in the postwar period has thus been wasted because of misdirected investment and excessive imports for consumption . . . Inefficiency and even corruption in the government service are widespread.

In general, the Bell Report was a severe indictment of the Philippine government. Although it included mild admissions that the Bell Trade Act had defects that hindered the Philippines in coping with its problems and it suggested that "the present Trade Act be re-examined in the light of new conditions," the essential blame for the crisis was placed on the Filipino leaders. A solution would be found, it said, only "if the people and the government of the Philippines" would make an effort "with the aid and encouragement of the United States." The Bell Mission made the Philippine government the scapegoat of the neocolonial crisis, and absolved the U.S. from responsibility for it while giving it the image of a saviour.

A U.S. grant of $250 million, to be provided over a five-year period, was to be the core of an aid program for "economic development and technical assistance." Various reform measures were recommended for alleviating the conditions contributing to "the dissident trouble," including a minimum wage for urban workers and agricultural laborers, steps to "insure honesty and efficiency in government" (i.e., against corruption), and encouraging trade unions "free from Communist influence," but the salient feature of the Bell Report lay in the recommendation that

> The aid from the United States will be more effective if the United States retains control of the funds and their use for development purposes in the Philippines.

That control would be conducted through a United States Technical Mission to function in the Philippines throughout the five-year program,

> The members of which must be competent not merely to give general advice, but also to assist Philippine officials in the actual day-to-day operations and in the formulation and implementation of changes in policy which must be brought about.

For an independent government such as the Quirino regime was supposed to be, the Report of the Bell Mission, was a humiliating dosage, with its blunt criticisms and its terms for U.S. officials literally to run Philippine affairs due to alleged Filipino incompetence. President Quirino had no option, as a collaborator, but to accept it, as he did in the Quirino-Foster Agreement signed on November 14, 1950 (William C. Foster was head of the U.S. Economic Cooperation Administration, the agency that would direct the Technical Mission.)

The full depth of the humiliation and of the demeaning character of the conditions being forced upon President Quirino was written into the Special Technical and Economic Mission Agreement signed by the Philippine president with U.S. Ambassador Myron Cowen on April 27, 1951. Its Article III, Section 2 read:

> The Government of the Philippines will communicate to the Government of the United States of America in a form and at intervals to be determined by the latter after consulation with the Government of the Philippines:
>
> (a) Detailed information concerning projects, programs, and measures proposed or adopted by the Government of the Philippines to carry out the provisions of this Agreement;
>
> (b) Full statements of operations under this Agreement, including a statement of the use of funds, commodities and services received hereunder, such statements to be made in each calendar year;
>
> (c) Information regarding its economy and any other relevant information which the Government of the United States of America may need to determine the nature and scope of operations under this Agreement and to evaluate the effectiveness of such operations.

Besides this demand for an open window on Philippine affairs, Section 5 of the Annex to the Agreement bound the Philippines not to take protectionist measures of any kind and to "cooperate with other countries to reduce barriers to international trade and to take appropriate measures singly and in cooperation with other countries to eliminate public or private restrictive practices hindering *domestic or international* trade" [Author's italics]. Although the Bell Report grudgingly endorsed the maintenance of import and exchange controls as a necessity, it called for their "liberalization."

Most onerous of all the many U.S.-dictated terms, however, was the demand that U.S. "technical assistants" be installed in every key department of the Philippine government, not merely to advise but to formulate and implement policy. This had to do not only with the selection of projects for which aid funds were to be spent but with economic policy in general. To all intents and purposes, this amounted to a reversion to colonial-style administration in which Filipinos were ostensibly governing but U.S. officials had the ultimate and the veto power.

The control was not merely over the use of the U.S. aid funds. Another Bell condition was that the Philippines had to put up a "counterpart fund" to match the U.S. funds, i.e., two pesos for every dollar. A Philippine Council for U.S. Aid (PHILCUSA) was set up to manage these, but the allocation and direction of use were determined jointly with the U.S. Technical Mission. Final approval, however, lay with the ECA in Washington. In other words, the Philippines had to provide funds for a U.S. neocolonial program over which it had no actual control, and which was designed to divert the Philippines from a true path of development, as well as to help suppress rebelling Filipinos.

U.S. interventionist decisions had a far wider scope than the sending of economic survey and technical missions. In concert with other military steps in Asia, the 1947 Military Assistance Pact was put into full effect. Putting the anti-Huk campaign under the Philippine Army was directed by the Joint U.S. Military Advisory Group. The JUSMAG, from March 1950, carried out the reorganization of the Philippine Army into battalion combat teams designed for counterinsurgency operations. To attain more complete control of military affairs, JUSMAG insisted on the removal on September 1 of the then Secretary of National Defense, Ruperto Kangleon, and his replacement by a relatively obscure congressman, Ramon Magsaysay, a former "lie-low" USAFFE member with meager military capability but one totally compliant with the wishes of the U.S. officials who had handpicked him. These steps preparing the organizing of suppressive force was followed by the arrival in Manila on September 21 of a U.S. Military Aid Mission, headed by the U.S. Defense Department's John F. Melby. It presented Quirino with a program of military assistance for putting down the PKP-led armed struggle as well as for contributing Philippine battalion combat teams to the U.S.-commanded forces in Korea. Allocation and use of the military assistance equipment and funds were supervised by JUSMAG which in every respect gave day-to-day direction to Secretary Magsaysay and his Defense Department.

Coinciding with the Melby Military Mission was a confidential mission of the U.S. Central Intelligence Agency (CIA) which secured the placing of the Philippine intelligence bodies, in particular the Military Intelligence Service (MIS), under CIA direction. Two major developments flowed from this arrangement. One was intensified intelligence activity against the underground PKP and HMB. The other was the assigning of a CIA officer, Colonel Edward Lansdale, as the chief adviser and 24-hour mentor of Magsaysay, a move that was not merely for military purposes but was part of a longer-range U.S. plan for political intervention.

The economic aid program, including the Philippine counterpart funds linked with it under the Quirino-Foster Agreement, may be judged in its effectiveness by comparison with the Hibben, Beyster and other more genuine development plans. To begin with, the $250 million recommended by the Bell Mission was never fully provided, and the five-year period specified became extended to ten years or more. Between 1951 and 1960 a total of only $226.4 million was made available, plus a counterpart expenditure of but P172,952,000 ($86,476,000). Of the dollar aid, nearly $50 million (23 per cent) went to "military construction." For economic purposes, agriculture received the largest sum, about $45 million (21 per cent). A category termed "industry and mining" had $36.2 million (17 per cent), a bookkeeping device which obscured the fact that manufacturing industry received virtually no assistance. The expenditure reports on the U.S. aid state that $190.2 million, out of the $226.4 million, were employed for "defense support," which indicates the true nature of the aid—an amelioration and suppression program as part of the counter-insurgency campaign against the Huk movement. Road-building to assist military operations in mountain, forest and swamp areas, agrarian services to appease discontented peasants, and psychological warfare projects to "bring the government closer to the people" absorbed much of the funds.[6]

In general, economic development as a result of the alleged aid program of the Bell Mission was miniscule. Indeed, development was not its aim. It was to provide the excuse for U.S. personnel to be inserted into all levels of the Philippine government in order to prevent the unavoidable import and exchange controls from being used to foster a Filipino manufacturing sector. The development being generated by the controls, behind the protection of which Filipino enterprises were emboldened to emerge and expand, disturbed U.S. policy-makers. During the period when the aid agreement was in operation, a bitter conflict occurred between the U.S. administrators of aid, whose economic line was "agriculture first," and Filipino entrepreneurs who sought industrialization. Government counterpart funds that might have been used to support industrial development were diverted into unproductive channels.

Most glaring of all in the dissipation of overall funds from all sources that might have gone into real development programs was the huge sum devoted to "defense," the bulk of which was spent for the anti-Huk campaigns of the 1950s. Between 1951 and 1954 the total military expenditure by the Philippines and the U.S. for this purpose was P1,115,759,283 ($557,879,642), of which 40 per cent was provided by the U.S. (i.e., $223 million—three times the ECA program aid as a result of the Bell Mission provided in that same period). In those four years alone the hard-pressed Philippine government, with an economy in crisis, spent P668 million ($334 million) to suppress a movement among its own people for genuine independence and democracy. The money was spent as allocated and directed by the Joint U.S. Military Advisory Group under military agreements drawn up by and designed to serve U.S. interests.[7]

THE ARMED STRUGGLE FOR NATIONAL LIBERATION[8]

U.S. policy-makers had not anticipated the readiness and capability of the Partido Komunista ng Pilipinas in leading an armed liberation struggle in the post-independence period. It was apparently believed that the PKP and left-wing nationalists could be driven from the political arena and isolated if not destroyed. The Roxas government, in close consultation with U.S. advisers, had confidently announced when its mailed fist drive began in Central Luzon that the "peace and order question" would be settled in 60 days, indicating the low estimate of PKP strength and survivability.

Latter-day U.S., British and other historians and analysts of guerrilla warfare in the post-World War II decades have promoted a similar underestimation of left movements, claiming that they were launched in Asia in accordance with a directive for such struggles to begin delivered by the Soviet Union to a conference of Asian Communists held in India in 1948. It is alleged that the armed struggle of the PKP-led HMB was in obedience to that directive. There are so many fallacies in that story that it is laughable. To begin with, armed struggle started in the Philippines in 1946 as a reaction of self-defense against attacks on the peasantry, arising wholly from U.S.-influenced Philippine conditions. Secondly, the PKP at that time had no contact of any kind with the Soviet Union or any other part of the international Communist movement. Such relations as had existed in the 1930s had been disrupted by the war and had not been re-established. U.S. Communists in the returning U.S. army had made contact with the PKP in 1945 but this was on an individual and not an organizational basis. No PKP representative or member attended any conference in

India in 1948. An outbreak of liberation armed struggles at several points in Asia or South East Asia in that year and later years was due to common circumstances of resisting recolonization attempts by imperialist powers.

The PKP-led guerrilla forces were able to develop extensively with scanty knowledge of the government, repeatedly achieving surprise in their attacks. Election of a new PKP leadership at the May 1948 Central Committee conference and the launching of an expansion drive were virtually unknown to the Quirino government or to the JUSMAG, until the HMB suddenly appeared in new areas. Not known was that the entire country had been divided into regions, with Regional Committees (Recos) of the PKP and parallel Regional Commands of the HMB (subordinate to the political Recos) established in each. They were:

Reco 1 (Nueva Ecija, parts of Tarlac and Pangasinan, part of Quezon); Reco 2 (Pampanga, part of Tarlac, Zambales, and Bataan); Reco 3 (Bulacan); Reco 4 (Laguna, Quezon, Rizal, Batangas, and Cavite); Reco 5 (Bicol region including Camarines Norte and Sur, Albay and Sorsogon); Reco 6 (Visayas region, including Panay, Negros and Cebu); Reco 7 (Mindanao); Reco 8 (Northern Luzon east, including Isabela, Nueva Vizcaya and Cagayan); Reco 9 (Northern Luzon west, including La Union, Ilocos Sur and Norte, and Mountain Province). Subsequently a Reco 10 was created from parts of Reco 4, Batangas and Cavite, as expansion developed there. An 11th body existed for Manila, called the City Committee. Expansion extended in all of these Recos between 1948 and 1951.

The Recos were divided into party District Organizing Committees (DOCs), each paralleled by an HMB Field Command (FC). Each Reco had from five to seven DOCs and FCs. In a Field Command armed forces varied from 100 to 300, depending on the extent of organization of a base.

When this structure was set up in 1948 only Recos 1 to 4 and a City Committee were fully functioning, but by the early 1950s Recos 5, 6, 8, 9 and 10 were well organized and an organizing team was in Reco 7. A steady shift from a defensive to an offensive position occurred. The popular acceptance of HMB expansion forces was evidence of the growing revolutionary temper in the country, fed by government corruption, fraud and terror in elections, and widespread abuses by the Philippine Constabulary during anti-Huk operations. Economic effects of the Bell Act and of the failure of the Roxas and Quirino regimes to generate development were other factors. In 1948 15 per cent of the labor force, or 1.2 million working people, were unemployed, while food and other necessities were eight times the pre-war prices In the countryside hunger was common.

Up to the latter part of 1949 the PKP leadership recognized, however, that the majority of people still retained a belief in the electoral process, which held back a general rallying to the armed struggle. Furthermore, although a mass disillusionment with the Liberal Party existed, the likelihood was that people would swing support to the Nacionalista Party as the alternative rather than the HMB. With the approach of the 1949 national election, the PKP sought a position that would either draw the Nacionalista Party or a large part of it to an anti-imperialist alliance with the PKP or expose it as little different from the LP.

By this time Sergio Osmena had retired from NP leadership, which had passed to Jose Laurel, Claro Recto and others who had overcome wartime collaboration records as they took an increasingly nationalist stand in regard to the negation of independence. In 1949 Laurel became the NP presidential candidate against Quirino, whereupon the PKP undertook secret negotiations with him, proposing to place its mass following behind him if he adopted an anti-imperialist position in the election campaign. Laurel agreed and went further, also agreeing to a PKP proposal that he lead the Nacionalistas, jointly with the HMB, in an armed struggle against the corrupt Liberal regime if it resorted to fraud and terror again to win. An HMB detachment headed by a PKP cadre, Jesse Magusig, was assigned for liaison with Laurel's political lieutenant and security chief, Francisco Medrano, in Batangas province, in preparation for such an eventuality.

As the election campaign developed, however, Laurel retreated from the agreement, dropping an anti-imperialist line and ceasing to refer to a readiness to fight if cheated. There were indications that U.S. envoys had approached Laurel and that U.S. pressures had been put upon him to desist from contacts with the PKP. Although in the 1949 election Quirino and the Liberals employed massive fraud and terror to win, far exceeding any such previous episode in Philippine history, Laurel bowed to his defeat and reneged on the armed struggle promise.

Only Francisco Medrano went ahead with the agreement, proclaiming a rebellion when the fraudulent election returns were announced. His followers fought side by side with HMB forces in Batangas against Constabulary troops sent to put down the revolt. It lasted for 40 days before Medrano surrendered, abandoned by Laurel and the NP who said and did nothing to support him. Some his followers joined the HMB, which continued the struggle. (A casualty of the fighting was Jesse Magusig.)

Roxas had not seated the Huk rep's!

In the view of the PKP leadership the 1949 election confirmed the bankruptcy of parliamentary struggle in a neocolonial Philippines, and the correctness of armed struggle. In January 1950 an enlarged PKP Political Bureau meeting was held in the mountains above Longos, Laguna. It discussed the thesis that the position of the Quirino government had deteriorated irretrievably, that the disaffected masses were moving increasingly to the HMB, and that a qualitative stage had been reached in the situation. It was believed to be a classic example of those in power being no longer able to rule in the old way and of the people being no longer willing to live in the old way. Additionally, it was concluded that the non-intervention by the U.S. in China to prevent the victory of the Communist-led revolution that had recently been victorious indicated that the U.S. was inclined to retreat from the region rather than be more deeply committed and was unlikely to intervene elsewhere in Asia, including the Philippines.

Consequently, the PKP conference adopted a political resolution declaring the existence of a revolutionary situation in the Philippines and setting forth the tasks of active preparation for the seizure of power.

'49

In the course of 1950 an aggressive program of expansion and recruiting was pressed. A series of key dates was selected for concerted attacks to be made by the HMB on government forces at widely separated points—on March 29 (the Hukbalahap founding day in 1942) and on August 26 (when the 1896 revolution of the Katipunan against Spain began). The large Constabulary Camp Makabulos in Tarlac province was destroyed on the latter date. Numerous towns were entered in Central and Southern Luzon and in the Visayas.

The policy of making armed struggle the main form of struggle now received increasing emphasis, becoming one of throwing virtually everything into the military strategy of winning power. Forms of legal struggle that had continued to be possible in Manila and other places were run down. PKP members who were top trade union leaders in the CLO were sent "outside" for expansion work, Mariano Balgos to Reco 5, Guillermo Capadocia to Reco 6 in the Visayas. Legal organizations of women and youth were allowed to disintegrate, their responsible cadres removed for assignment with the guerrilla forces.

From the latter part of 1949 a significant shift of sympathy for the struggle of the HMB occurred on the part of middle class and small business sectors. Filipino businessmen who were contacted readily agreed to donate money or produce to the movement—shoes, clothing, foodstuffs, medicines, paper and other supplies. A considerable number of intellectuals were recruited into the PKP, reflecting a turning away from both Liberal and Nacionalista Parties. Within the Philippine Army disaffection began to set in; middle-ranking officers made contact with the PKP, preparing to change sides if the Quirino government collapsed. By the middle of 1950 the PKP leadership called for the "aggressive projection of the Party leadership over the struggle for national liberation and the corresponding isolation of the Nacionalista leadership and other non-Communist leaderships from the reserves of the revolution."9

Projection of the hegemony of the PKP over the revolution was a strategic decision of profound importance: in essence, it constituted a dissolving of the united front strategy of the PKP that had guided the party since the mid-1930s. It produced a gap between the nationalist-democratic leaders in the Democratic Alliance and the PKP. The non-Communist leaders in the DA remained firmly nationalist and anti-imperialist in conviction, but they rejected the PKP decision to make armed struggle the main form of struggle and its conclusion that this was the only real alternative in the Philippine situation. The DA leaders took the position that legal, parliamentary struggle had not been fully exhausted and that it could still realize the national-democratic aims of the united front, but they did not join in condemnation of the PKP and HMB as did many Nacionalistas who became afraid of the armed struggle being turned against them.

A rapid building of the PKP in order to carry out the tasks of leadership was called for. An inner-party document issued in May 1950 exhorted the movement to "hasten the tempo of recruiting," and set forth a program for doubling both PKP and HMB membership every four months, an arithmetical progression of growth that contemplated a party membership of 120,000 and a people's army of 160,000 by September 1951. A perspective was put forward that the coming two years would be decisive in the preparations for the seizure of power (a formulation that created a harmful general belief in the movement that victory would be won in two years).10

All plans, operations and raising of tempo were disastrously disrupted, however, on October 18, 1950, when agents of the Military Intelligence Service (MIS) under CIA direction simultaneously raided 22 houses in Manila, arresting the entire Secretariat of the PKP who were directing the overall struggle. They were: Jose Lava, general secretary, Federico Maclang, organizational secretary, and Ramon Espiritu, finance secretary. A large number of cadres of other organs were also caught in the raids.

Highly damaging was the capture of Secretariat's files, including plans, organizational documents, lists of members, inner-party correspondence, the disposition of PKP cadres and HMB forces around the country, and information on contacts. This windfall exposed the underground movement to its enemies. In general the mass arrests decapitated the movement at a crucial point in the development of the struggle, causing a loss of initiative and momentum precisely at the time when U.S. intervention and the reorganized government forces were launching their counterattack.

The wide dispersal of other Political Bureau and Central Committee members meant a considerable delay in rebuilding party organs and reinvigorating the struggle. An enlarged Central Committee meeting was finally held in February–March 1951 in the mountains on the Laguna–Quezon border. Its basic conclusions were that despite the imperialist-directed counteroffensive that was unfolding, nothing essentially had changed, the revolutionary situation remained, the crisis of the Filipino ruling groups would go on deepening and U.S. imperialism could not save them, and the call for the armed overthrow of the regime was still correct. A perspective was set for the boycott of the coming November 1951 senatorial and local elections, to hasten the collapse of the regime.

A new Political Bureau was elected, composed of: Jesus Lava (general secretary), Casto Alejandrino (military department secretary), Luis Taruc (organizational secretary), Mateo del Castillo (finance secretary), Peregrino Taruc (education secretary), Celia Mariano Pomeroy, Felicisimo Macapagal, Mariano Balgos, Domingo Castro, Jose de Leon and Bonifacio Lina. Alternate members were: Alejandro Briones, Ignacio Dabu, and Mario del Castillo.

This reorganized leadership tried hard to regain the initiative and to implement conference decisions. In 1951, however, the liberation struggle reached a peak that could not be heightened. All planned Recos, to one extent or another, were established, the expansion drive succeeding in extending the movement to 27 provinces. An HMB of 15,000 or more armed guerrilla fighters was built. Its revolutionary offensive, however, came up against the U.S.-directed counteroffensive which was able to take advantage of the exposure and dislocation caused by the arrest of the Secretariat.

The JUSMAG reorganized the Philippine Army, creating 28 Battalion Combat Teams, each of 1200 men, comprised of infantry, mortar, transport and communications sections, with exceptional fire-power and highly maneuverable. An army of 54,000 troops all told was put into the field, besides air and naval forces, equipped with extensive U.S. arms aid. The 8,000–10,000 strong Constabulary served as a support force, along with large numbers of civilian guards and local police, stationed in the towns and barrios while the BCTs penetrated mountains and forests. A greatly expanded intelligence network operated under CIA direction. Together these were able to conduct simultaneous operations in all Recos. The PKP-HMB bid to take the strategic offensive was thrown back upon the strategic defensive.

A string of military setbacks in 1951 marked the reversal of fortune. Recos 9 and 6 were decimated in that year, its leaders killed or captured. The entire City Committee was arrested and the HMB unit in Manila was destroyed. By 1954 the movement was crushed in virtually all expansion areas.

Other serious setbacks coincided with the military blows. In January 1951, as a follow-up to the Secretariat arrests, the leaders of the legal Congress of Labor Organizations were arrested, including Amado Hernandez, the CLO chairman, Juan Cruz, head of the printers' union, and a dozen others. The CLO secretary and PKP cadre, Alfredo Saulo, escaped arrest to join the party "outside." At the same time leaders of the Federacion Obrera de Filipinas (FOF) in the Visayas, which had provided mass base support for the HMB on Panay, were arrested in Iloilo, including its head, Jose Nava. These arrests were followed by the outlawing of both the CLO and the FOF, a repressive step that cleared the field for right-wing domination of the organized labor movement.

A political setback with graver implications came with the November 1951 election, which the PKP had determined to boycott. People were reminded of the fraud that had made a mockery of voting in 1947 and 1949. U.S. imperialism, aware that a repetition would produce a further swing of support to the HMB, exerted every influence to thwart preparations by Quirino to retain his control through another round of fraud. The JUSMAG and the CIA, holding control of the Philippine armed forces and of the Defense Department where their handpicked man, Ramon Magsaysay, had been installed, literally took the election process out of Quirino's hands, placing it under the army with the claim that the polls had to be defended against HMB attacks. As a result the opposition Nacionalista Party was able to score extensive successes. Drawn by the promise of a "clean election," the people even in HMB mass base areas chose to vote, ignoring the boycott call. The boycott was a complete failure.

It was admitted by the PKP leadership in December 1951 that the masses did not recognize "the immediate need of armed struggle" and that "the great majority of the masses greatly favor the existence of peace and order even though they suffer poor living conditions." If the people chose to vote rather than boycott it was because "the moment they sense any reason *not* to lose faith and confidence in elections, they adhere to it immediately. This illusion is hard to eliminate."[11]

Although mass supporters of the PKP-led movement did not turn against the party or HMB in the active sense, their unreadiness to follow the movement's calls to sharper struggle marked the beginning of a receding of the revolutionary flow in the country. That trend continued with the U.S. buildup of Magsaysay as a "reform" presidential candidate against Quirino and into Magsaysay's election as president in 1953. The realignment of political forces was featured by the switch of Magsaysay from the Liberal to the Nacionalista Party to run as its candidate, by the readiness of even the more nationalistic NP leaders to go along with this in order to get into power, and by Democratic Alliance remnants who had returned to the NP accepting it as well. In the process the PKP became increasingly isolated politically.

By the end of 1951 the PKP began to shift from a perspective of early victory to one of protracted struggle. An attempt was made to maintain the armed struggle as the main form of struggle up to 1954, but the decimation of the HMB and the loss by death or capture of most of the movement's political and military cadres forced an abandonment of that position. In 1954 the Recos were dissolved and the Field Commands abolished, armed units being formed of no more than 30 members and mostly of 5 or 6 to enable great mobility. After 1955 the further step was taken of merging armed units with the PKP's District Organizing Committees to form Organizers' Brigades. These were essentially armed organizing and propaganda units designed to help effect a shift from a defeated armed struggle to forms of legal struggle, or reconstituting banned mass organizations, or creating new ones. In 1958 the HMB itself as an army was disbanded, its members and PKP members mingling themselves with the people in barrios, towns and cities to build as best as possible an underground political movement. The capture of the head of the PKP's military department, Casto Alejandrino, in 1960 and of the PKP general secretary, Jesus Lava, in 1964, were climaxing losses.

All told, the losses suffered during the armed struggle by the forces of revolutionary nationalism were very great. Of the Central Committee of the PKP in 1948, when the decision to take the offensive was adopted, all members were either killed, arrested and imprisoned, or in a very few cases surrendered. Of the Central Committee members elected in 1951, all, too, were either killed, imprisoned or surrendered. Middle-ranking cadres of the PKP were decimated to a similar extent. (It is notable that only a tiny few of leading members surrendered, the principal renegadist example being Luis Taruc, whose careerist ambitions led him to the camp of collaboration after surrender in 1954.)

Of the HMB's armed forces, the Philippine Army claimed to have killed 6,000 and wounded 2,000 between 1950 and 1955 (in view of the usual case in warfare for wounded to exceed those killed by several times, these casualty figures indicate the ruthlessness of the suppression campaigns on the one hand and the determination of HMB soldiers to fight to the end on the other). If the entire period of armed struggle from 1946 to the end of the 1950s is considered, these casualty numbers could probably be doubled. The true cost of the imperialist-generated conflict needs to take account of the dead and wounded on the government side—army, Constabulary, police and civilian guards—and the unnumbered civilians who died chiefly in Constabulary-army punitive raids.

Hundreds of PKP and HMB members were sentenced to prison under an umbrella charge of "rebellion complexed with murder, arson, robbery and kidnapping," actually an illegal charge not contained in the Philippine penal codes, reportedly concocted by the JUSMAG. It kept political prisoners confined for an average of ten years, even after the Philippine Supreme Court ruled it illegal in 1956, making "simple rebellion" the applicable charge with a 12-year maximum penalty. Under "rebellion complexed," maximum sentences of death or life imprisonment had been given to those arrested in October 1950 and to others captured in battle. The October 1950 group were kept in prison for 20 years, being released only when a mass campaign demanded their freedom in 1970.

In its own subsequent objective and self-critical assessment of the postwar armed struggle, the PKP concluded that its defeat was due more to its own errors of strategy and tactics than to the strength of U.S. imperialism and the effectiveness of its policies. A basic error, it is believed, was the decision to make armed struggle the main form of struggle, which led inevitably to the mechanical discarding of all legal and peaceful forms of struggle that were existing and possible of development, to the attempt to advance the struggle too rapidly by arbitrary revolutionary stages, and to a premature contemplation of the winning of power. By placing reliance wholly on military struggle, which meant on a limited number of armed people, the involvement of the masses in the revolution was neglected. (A further factor not given attention was the isolation of the Philippine struggle from international support or fraternal assistance of a military or other nature, which most other liberation struggles in that period did enjoy; the islanded character of the Philippine contributed to this, but the failure to attempt to overcome the isolation lay with the movement's leadership.)

In particular the conclusion that a revolutionary situation existed at the beginning of 1950 has been considered a grave error. This created illusions about an early victory, about the supposed weakening of the enemy, and about the readinesx of the people to go over to the liberation forces. It was not true that the ruling groups could no longer rule in the old way or that the people were no longer ready to live in the old way.

Above all, the mistake was made of projecting an alleged hegemony of the PKP over the revolution and of abandoning the strategy of building a united front against imperialism and its collaborators, a united front of the working class, middle class and nationalist bourgeois elements. Besides leading to the isolation of the PKP, this was a failure to grasp the dialectics of what was developing and likely to develop at that time in regard to the class forces in the Philippines that could figure in a united front.

The fact was that precisely at that time U.S. neocolonial policies were producing a bourgeois nationalist trend that was ideally suited for building a broad movement of the Filipino people against imperialism.

MAGSAYSAY: HOW TO INSTALL A PUPPET

For U.S. imperialism the steps to contend with the neocolonial crisis in the Philippines did not end with the Bell Mission and with intervention via the Military Assistance Pact. There remained the Quirino Liberal Party regime, which had become irredeemably associated with corruption and abuses and therefore unstable. The political instrument that the U.S. had created to serve its interests had become, for the time being at least, a liability, needing replacement.

The severe criticism and blame heaped by inference upon the Quirino government by the Bell Report was a signal of U.S. inclination to abandon it. That the U.S. was looking for other alliances was evident, and the opposition Nacionalista Party was an obvious alternative. When Jose Laurel and other NP leaders backed away from unity with the revolutionary left during and after the 1949 election, it had the earmarks of an understanding for the future reached privately with U.S. interests. However, some nationalist tendencies within the NP made it distrusted by U.S. interests.

Not fully grasped at once were implications of the move to install Ramon Magsaysay in Quirino's cabinet as secretary of national defense.

It was a step forced upon Quirino. Magsaysay was not his man, and he was not happy about such an appointment involving control of the vital instrument of power, the army.

What made Magsaysay an important player in the political drama was not any outstanding ability or leadership qualities. He had an obscure, minor role as a USAFFE guerrilla during the war, and an undistinguished record as a congressman from Zambales province. He had been selected for the defense post more or less by chance due to a meeting with a CIA officer, Colonel Edward Lansdale, during a Philippine congressional junket to Washington early in 1950. It was his total readiness to serve as the front man for U.S. military and business interests, and to accept the counsel of Lansdale and his agents, that made him an ideal puppet. That CIA kingmakers began manufacturing him as a presidential commodity at such an early date indicated the orientation of removing Quirino.

The corruption, fraud and terror that discredited the Quirino regime were only part of U.S. reasons for wanting a change; moral considerations have never been at the heart of neocolonial policy. Quirino's streak of independent behavior that surfaced on occasion was more disturbing, particularly his employment of import controls to enable Filipinos to get an increased share of import allocations at the expense of U.S. commercial companies. Quirino was prone to disregard Bell Mission recommendations for "liberalizing" controls and for allowing U.S. companies to breach exchange controls by remitting their earnings. On July 1, 1951 his government adopted a further Import Control Law (RA 650) which provided that any importer not a producer had to reserve not less than 50 per cent of imports for Filipino merchants.

Electing Magsaysay the President

U.S. intrigues with Magsaysay mounted through 1951 and 1952, with Lansdale directing his every act and utterance. An alleged correction of army abuses against the civilian population was played up as his achievement. A Civil Affairs Unit set up in the Defense Department ostensibly to build the army's relations with the people was a Magsaysay propaganda vehicle, projecting him as the honest man fighting corruption. Increasingly he was contrasted with Quirino. The army's role in the 1951 election, preventing Liberal Party fraud, reinforced his image.

It also supplied him with the key instrument for election as president: a political machine. The Nacionalista Party had been enabled to win ín 1951 and had reason to be grateful to Magsaysay and the U.S. After the 1951 election Lansdale made secret contacts with NP leaders and began negotiations for Magsaysay to run as the NP presidential candidate in 1953. Finally on November 20, 1952 a secret agreement was reached between Magsaysay and his U.S. advisers and Nacionalista leaders Senators Jose Laurel, Claro Recto and Lorenzo Tañada, for the Magsaysay candidacy. This all took place while Magsaysay still sat in the Quirino cabinet as defense secretary. On March 9, 1953 he announced his break with the Liberal Party, his resignation as defense secretary, and his Nacionalista candidacy.

The readiness of Magsaysay to play his part, to be carefully marketed as honest, a reformer, a man of the people and all the other populist imagery, and to be known as "America's boy" as the U.S. press referred to him, marked the emergence of a more pitifully subservient collaboration in Philippine politics. The political leaders produced in the colonial period, who continued for some time to figure in the independence years, often had dignity, a certain pride, and a sensitivity to being too overtly known as U.S. allies. Quezon and Osmena could appear as nationalistic Filipinos while compromising the national interest. From Manuel Quezon onward the projection began of political leaders close to the Americans and therefore capable of getting "U.S. aid." The attitude of the U.S. officials engaged in manipulating such people had none of the respect accorded to allies as equals. Lansdale, in his own account of his Philippine assignment, boasted of having created Magsaysay, referring to him slightingly.[12]

Magsaysay's election campaign in 1953 had little of the usual character of Philippine politics but was loaded with Madison Avenue gimmicks. "Magsaysay is my guy," was the principal slogan, an American concoction alien to the Filipino vernacular but seen everywhere on leaflets, T-shirts, press and radio. The "man of the people" was coached by Lansdale to go about the rural areas in his bare feet, to eat with his hands peasant-style while sitting on the floor of *nipa* huts, and to dress like a peasant. He promised land reform and to bring government down to the people, "clean government."

Although U.S. interests had needed to make a deal with the NP to provide Magsaysay with a political machine and endorsement by Nacionalista leaders, they did not want him to be tied to such leaders, especially those taking nationalist positions like Recto and Tañada. Lansdale directed Magsaysay to reject a demand by Laurel and Recto that NP leaders be able to choose the members of the cabinet in a Magsaysay government. Choice was allowed only on his vice-presidential running mate, Carlos Garcia, an NP senator from the small island of Bohol.

Lansdale's tactic was to exploit the NP organization and name but to build also an electoral machine outside of the NP. A Magsaysay for President Movement (MPM) was set up, based on Magsaysay Clubs that sprang up immediately in all parts of the country, indicating preparations long underway. The MPM had an inner core of army officers, former USAFFE guerrillas, professionals and young businessmen of the Rotary Club type with links with U.S. business activities. Even more extensive was the National Movement for Free Elections (NAMFREL), originally created in 1951 as a nationwide watchdog and fraud-countering network acting in coordination with the Magsaysay-headed army to defeat Quirino's Liberal Party. The NAMFREL reportedly had 12,000 chapters in barrios and towns. In both NAMFREL and the MPM leading roles were played by a set of men who had belonged to a pro-U.S. wartime guerrilla unit, Hunter's ROTC, which operated in the provinces on the southern and eastern rim of Manila. Three Hunter's men spearheaded NAMFREL: Jaime Ferrer as director, Eleuterio (Terry) Adevoso and Frisco San Juan. Adevoso became national chairman of the MPM. Other Hunter's veterans were prominent in the CIA-directed Military Intelligence Service. MPM public relations were handled by Major Jose Crisol who had headed the Civil Affairs Office when Magsaysay was defense secretary.

Both NAMFREL and the MPM were recruited almost wholly from middle-class elements who had not previously been involved in traditional party machine politics, including lawyers, teachers, young members of the Junior Chambers of Commerce (JAYCEES) and the Lions Clubs (patterned after the U.S. like organizations to which they were affiliated), students, religious leaders. Around this kind of campaign were woven the new neocolonial threads of U.S. control.

Another important part of the Magsaysay machine was the hierarchy of the Catholic Church, which for decades after the Philippine Revolution at the turn of the century, had kept a relatively low political profile. The abusive friar religious orders were not forgotten by many Filipinos. In the post-independence period the Church, afraid of a growth of nationalism in an independent Philippines that would favor independent religious movements and alarmed by the rise of the PKP-led liberation movement that had revolutionary agrarian reform demands that could affect the estates still held by it, now moved into a more direct political role. One of its proteges, the attorney Raul Manglapus, became the MPM's campaign manager, and the Church lay organizations actively worked for Magsaysay.

Most of all, however, Magsaysay relied for advice and directives on his U.S. aides. Said a fulsome article in *Time* magazine on November 23, 1953:

> It was soon no secret that Ramon Magsaysay was America's boy. For a time, U.S. Colonel Edward Lansdale of the U.S. Air Force (sic) took a desk in Magsaysay's Defense Office, became virtually his mentor and publicity man. Polished, precise William Lacy, Councillor of the U.S. Embassy, became the man to whom Magsaysay turned daily for counsel.
>
> Lacy and other U.S. officials were worried by Magsaysay's open and unabashed exploitation of the friendship but not Magsaysay. "What do you know about Filipinos?" he would say. "I tell you, my people like Americans, and they like to see me with Americans."

For all the mustering of support for "America's boy," there were still trepidations among the U.S. manipulators about ousting Quirino and the Liberals. Quirino himself, following Magsaysay's defection and the undisguised U.S. backing for his candidacy, turned increasingly to attacking the U.S. for interference in Philippine affairs. He went to the extent of making overtures for electoral support to the imprisoned Communist leaders, releasing on bail before the election a large group of PKP and HMB members who were confined awaiting trial. (The official PKP position was one of not voting for either presidential candidate but of voting for congressional candidates who were friendly to the HMB or took a convincingly nationalist stand.)

With Magsaysay and his team no longer in the defense department, the possibility remained that Quirino might be able to use sufficient armed forces and fraud to stay in power. With U.S. assistance, therefore, large stockpiles of arms were secretly set up in Zambales province where a command headquarters for Magsaysay was established (it lay conveniently midway between the U.S. Clark and Subic military bases), with similar stockpiles in other areas. Army units loyal to Magsaysay were readied for seizure of key points, and JUSMAG officers, with the excuse of being on routine duties, were dispersed to such units to assure coordinated action. Finally, U.S. warships were moved down from Subic Bay to take up positions for all to see in Manila Bay.

Unsurprisingly, the 1953 election resulted in an overwhelmingly decisive victory for Ramon Magsaysay. In a campaign used subsequently as a model of interventionist tactics by U.S. covert agencies, a president of the Philippines had been installed who was an utter puppet. The political means were put in place for perfecting further U.S. neocolonial plans.

"AMERICA'S BOY" AS PRESIDENT

For U.S. imperialism there was no real difficulty in effecting a shift in alliance from Quirino to Magsaysay, and from the Liberal Party to the Nacionalista Party. Both parties were filled with politicians who had been raised in colonial politics and who had close and profitable links with the landlord-*comprador* groups that had grown rich from free trade and continued to do so. Reaching accomodation with an alternative group may have involved some financial cost—U.S. businessmen in Manila donated $250,000 to the Magsaysay campaign in one instance which was reportedly but a portion of their pay-out, while an unknown amount of CIA funds was channeled to Magsaysay's election through Lansdale[13]—but for U.S. interests it was a worthwhile investment. Magsaysay's switch from one party to another was not unusual: in postwar Philippine politics it became a common occurrence, from top to bottom, because the main bourgeois parties were not ideologically different but composed of rivals for the advantages of power for whom an opportunist change of party label meant no abandonment of belief.

From Magsaysay, U.S. imperialism had a number of objectives to realize. It was able to employ the Philippines for carrying out U.S. policy aims in South East Asia and Eastern Asia. Within a few months the Magsaysay government played host for the conference in Manila that created the South East Asia Treaty Organization, signed on September 8, 1954, a treaty designed for U.S. intervention against liberation or strongly nationalist movements anywhere in the region.

When the U.S. signed a military agreement with the Kuomintang exile government in Formosa in December 1954, giving the U.S. "the right to dispose of such United States land, air and sea forces in and about Taiwan and the Pescadores," Magsaysay responded to the U.S. demand with an abject statement on February 3, 1955 committing the Philippines to "stand squarely behind the United States" in defending Formosa against "communist aggression." This stirred nationalist protest in the Philippine Congress, which became stronger when Magsaysay declared Philippine recognition of the U.S.-backed puppet regime of Ngo Dinh Diem in South Vietnam on July 15, 1955. The Magsaysay government, in fact, played an important part in facilitating U.S. intervention in Vietnam, Laos and Cambodia, developing counterinsurgency operations from as early as June 1954 under the guise of "Operation Brotherhood" medical and welfare teams, and permitting the U.S. Clark Field base to be used for training right-wing Laotian armed forces.[14]

At home Magsaysay persisted with the anti-HMB campaigns of his defense secretaryship, saying in his inaugural address that he would not compromise with "armed dissidence" but would "welcome back the truly repentent" who had been "misled by the lies of the Kremlin." Guided by his U.S. advisers, he introduced a string of much-publicized agrarian reform gestures focused chiefly on Central Luzon, designed to win over or neutralize peasant support for the HMB. An Agricultural Tenancy Act (RA No. 1199) on August 30, 1954 and a Land Reform Act of 1955 (RA No. 1400) were proclaimed as improving relations between landlord and tenant and as opening the way for "as many as possible" family-size farms to be distributed to landless peasants. Both of these Acts were so riddled with loopholes by landlord representatives in the Congress as to be useless. They were surrounded by a host of cosmetic projects and rural committees, for drilling artesian wells in barrios and for promoting barrio "self-help" schemes to make poverty look neat and clean. None of these gestures or legislative acts went any distance toward solving the agrarian problem.

The main benefit that the U.S. expected to derive from Magsaysay was an enhancement of U.S. trade and investment privileges that had been hampered by the crisis created by the Bell Act. Magsaysay assumed office at a time when the eight years of free trade provided for in that Act were approaching termination. Quirino, indeed, had initiated steps to renegotiate the terms of the Bell Act to benefit the crisis-hit Philippines. The negotiations on its revision were conducted by the Magsaysay government.

Heading the Philippine panel in behalf of the Magsaysay regime was Senator Jose Laurel, who had had a nationalist image when he ran for president in 1949. Now he was negotiating the further life of the very Bell Act the Nationalista Party had opposed in 1946, revealing how far he and fellow Nacionalistas were prepared to go in readiness for accommodation with U.S. imperialism.

The Laurel-Langley Agreement as it is known (James M. Langley was the chief U.S. negotiator) altered the program for application of tariff duties, stretching out the applying of duties to Philippine quota exports to the U.S. and putting earlier dates on application of raised duties on U.S. goods entering the Philippines. Free trade itself was extended to the end of 1955, making it almost ten years instead of eight. These adjustments were made much of as concessions favoring the Philippines by the benevolent U.S., but buried in the Laurel-Langley Agreement was a frightful provision that was ruinous to the Philippines.

Article VII in the revised Act provided for "reciprocal non-discrimination" by either party with respect to citizens or enterprises of either engaged in "business activities" *of any kind.* In the original Bell Act, parity for U.S. corporations was guaranteed but it was limited to the exploitation of natural resources and the operation of public utilities. Now the U.S. had gained parity for its businessmen in every aspect of the economy. It was a bitter blow for Filipino industrialists or entre-preneurs striving to get off the ground. (Not less bitter was a U.S. pretense at "reciprocity," for Filipinos to have parity in the U.S. to match that enjoyed by the U.S. in the Philippines, as if capital-starved Filipinos could conceive of investing in the U.S.)

To this widened door for U.S. penetration, the Magsaysay adminis-tration early in 1955 introduced a companion piece, a Foreign Invest-ments Bill designed as a "special attraction" for U.S. investment, as if any were needed. It guaranteed such investors against losses, gave complete freedom for remitting profits abroad, and permitted for-eigners (especially Americans) to build industries relying on the impor-tation of raw materials rather than on those available locally.

The outcome of the latter provision was the distortion of what Filipino manufacturing industry had begun to emerge into little more than "packaging and assembly" plants based on the importation of U.S.-made parts and materials. The assembled product, as a rule, would be sold under the American brand name, for which the Filipino company had to enter a licensing agreement and pay royalties. Tech-nology and manufacturing processes also required licenses, the Philip-pine paint industry headed by the pioneering Henares & Sons being a prime example. In this way, fledgling Filipino industry was diverted into being adjuncts of U.S. export policies.

CLARO M. RECTO AND THE NATIONALIST UPSURGE

Of all the designs that U.S. policy-makers had for the Magsaysay presidency the most important for U.S. investment interests was to smother the nationalism that threatened to break through the neocolo-nial framework. Ruthless suppression had been employed to crush the PKP-led movement of revolutionary nationalism, but just as much a target, if the means were less violent, were the Filipino industrial interests that began to develop under the protective umbrella of import controls, laying the basis for a competing nationalist bourgeoisie.

The Filipino nationalism that came to flower in the 1950s was of a rather different character than that expressed at times in the U.S. colonial period, when it was used cynically by collaborator politicians to win votes. In the 1950s bourgeois nationalism acquired an economic base that was tangible and relatively dynamic. It was comprised of new Filipino manufacturing industries, set up to produce items formerly imported but now on the import control lists. In the first four years of controls, over 5,000 new Filipino manufacturing enterprises appeared, most of them on a very small scale, often unable to survive, but gradually growing in scope and variety. An industrial sector that had not previously existed was taking shape. A Philippine Chamber of Commerce had long been in being, mainly of import-export firms. In 1950, however, in the wake of controls, a Philippine Chamber of Industries (PCI) was set up, chiefly representing the new manufacturing industries and taking an increasingly nationalist position, becoming a growing economic rival of the U.S. Chamber of Commerce.

Despite controls, Filipino industries were emerging in restrictive and unfavorable circumstances. Economic departments in the Philippine government continued to be influenced by the U.S. advisers installed by the Quirino-Foster Agreement. Filipino firms were pushed into "packaging and assembly" category under Magsaysay. Capital accumulation was as yet relatively limited for the Filipino entrepreneur, and bank credit, the only other source of capital, was tightly restricted on U.S. insistence by both the Quirino and Magsaysay governments. U.S. technicians sat in the Central Bank, determining credit policy. While there was a surge of paid-in capital investment in newly-established industries from a total of P72.1 million in 1949 to P151.7 million in 1950, rising to P175 million in 1951, this could not be sustained, sinking to P110 million by 1955.[15] The small size of most enterprises made them fragile and vulnerable. Only 826 of those of all nationalties set up from 1948 to 1958 were significant enough to be classified as new and necessary and thereby permitted tax exemption for their first four years in operation. Of these only 431 were listed as Filipino (145 as Chinese, 22 as American, 62 as Filipino-Chinese, 47 as Chinese-Filipino, 24 as Filipino-American, 21 as American-Filipino). Of the total, 63 were capitalized at more than P1 million, and another 63 at more than P500,000; there were 49 at over P300,000 and 223 at over P100,000. The rest were capitalized at less, and 63 were merely between P5,000 and P10,000. Very few of the Filipino industries had the larger capitalization.[16]

However small and infirm the new Filipino industries were, they greatly disturbed U.S. investors on the scene, or potential and waiting for controls to be ended. Actually, U.S. companies did not do badly even with the controls. Although between 1950 and 1960 only $19.2 million of new foreign investment entered the Philippines as a result of this waiting game, there was an outflow in the same period of $215.7 million in earnings, profits and dividends.[17] This was not the whole profits picture during controls. These remitted funds were less than half of accumulated profits, the remainder kept on deposit in Philippine banks awaiting the lifting of exchange control. In spite of this profit-making, the U.S. Chamber of Commerce howled "discrimination" at any gesture or suggestion of support for Filipino businesses.

In March 1955 Magsaysay, at U.S. prodding, sent a directive to the Philippine National Economic Council to prepare a program centered on the abolition of economic controls. "It is vitally necessary," it said, "that we abolish economic controls as rapidly as possible." This would be for the benefit of "desirable private enterprises," implying U.S. and other foreign companies. When released, the directive drew such strong protest from Filipino businessmen, in both the Philippine Chamber of Industries and the conservative Philippine Chamber of Commerce, that it was pigeonholed.

For the emerging nationalist-inclined industry the key problem was the need for a political party to fight for its interests and demands, to the point of winning power. Lacking this, Filipino industrialists had to find accomodation in either of the two main parties, Liberal or Nacionalista, both essentially controlled by landlord-*comprador* groupings. The political need of nationalism began to be answered, however, with the coming forward of an extremely effective spokesman for the nationalist cause, the Nacionalista senator, Claro M. Recto.

In 1950 Recto was already 60 years old, with a long career in colonial politics dating from 1919, but chiefly as an oppositionist in the minority Democrata Party, not joining Quezon's Nacionalistas until the 1930s. An outstanding lawyer, he was chairman of the Constitutional Convention that wrote the 1935 independence constitution. A senator when the Japanese invasion occurred, Recto collaborated with the invaders but insisted that he did so to protect the people's interests. The postwar People's Court trying collaborators cleared him on those grounds. At that time Recto was the main author of the legal argument that collaboration with the Japanese was no different from Filipino collaboration with the U.S. conqueror.

Except for a strong independent tendency, Recto's career to this point did not make of him a nationalist leader. The U.S. neocolonial impositions and the collaboration and corruption of the Roxas and Quirino governments, however, produced from him a series of nationalistic and increasingly anti-imperialist speeches. The first, on April 9, 1949, entitled "Our Asian Policy," assailed the wholly U.S.-oriented Philippine foreign policy that assigned Filipino diplomatic representatives in Washington, London and Rome but none in New Delhi, Karachi, Rangoon, Hanoi, Bangkok, Singapore or Jakarta.[18] In April 1951, in a commencement address delivered at the University of the Philippines entitled "Our Mendicant Foreign Policy," he went further, condemning the fact that "our foreign policy was conducted from the very beginning, and is being pursued, on the erroneous assumption of an identity of American and Filipino interests, or more correctly, of the desirability, and even necessity, of subordinating our interests to those of America."[19]

When the PKP secretariat was arrested in October 1950 Recto agreed to be the defense counsel for the PKP general secretary, Jose Lava. He spoke in justification of the HMB's armed struggle because the notorious election of 1949

> had driven them to the conclusion that here in the Philippines democracy was a farce and the Constitution a myth, and nothing was left but a recourse to arms to do away with a fascistic, incompetent and corrupt government . . . We cannot permanently solve the problems of peace and order until we can dispel this conviction by eliminating or correcting the conditions which produced it.[20]

The process by which Recto in his latter years became a resolute and courageous nationalist had a catalytic acceleration from the Magsaysay presidency. Although he and Jose Laurel had been instrumental in agreeing to accept Magsaysay as the Nacionalista presidential candidate, it was an underestimation of U.S. intrigue and power manipulation that he did not make again. His conflict with Magsaysay began as soon as Magsaysay took office, condemning every step made in support of U.S. imperialist policy in Asia.

At the very outset, battle was joined over the issue of nationalism, arising from a speech by the new under-secretary of foreign affairs, Leon Ma. Guerrero, who had been an associate in the same law firm with Recto. Guerrero, obviously seeking to commit the Magsaysay government to a nationalist position, projected the slogan "Asia for the Asians," asserting:

> This administration is not only Nacionalista but nationalist. It believes in nationalism not only for itself but for others. It believes that Asia belongs to the Asians for the same reason that the Philippines belongs to the Filipinos.

Magsaysay, his coterie in the government and his U.S. advisers believed in nothing of the kind. Immediately Magsaysay repudiated Guerrero, declaring that he did not believe in slogans. Guerrero was removed from his post and replaced by the Magsaysay for President Movement campaign manager and Catholic Church protege, Raul Manglapus.

Recto promptly took issue with the attitude of the U.S. and of Magsaysay, calling on the U.S. to get rid of "the old and discredited 'white man's burden'" idea and to discard its "supercilious and patronizing attitude." Said Recto:

> Freedom-loving Asians correctly believe that it is not for any western people now to decide for any Asian nation what principles of foreign policy it may adopt or repudiate.[21]

The issue of nationalism which lay at the heart of the developing clash with Magsaysay was brought into the open by Recto in an uncompromising way. Magsaysay, for his part, squirmed to water down or nullify nationalism, to make it appear that it did not apply to relations with the U.S., that "the Philippines for the Filipinos" did not affect U.S. bases, U.S. investments or the multiple forms of U.S. influence in the lives of Filipinos. He sought to amend the principle of nationalism to death by introducing the adulterating term "positive nationalism," i.e., nationalism that was somehow not anti-imperialist or anti-American.

Opposition by Recto to a foreign policy of puppetry was soon extended to the neocolonial U.S. economic measures. The first major encounter was over the provisions of the Laurel-Langley Agreement that altered the original Bell Trade Act by stretching out imposing U.S. duties on Philippine products, and by accelerating Philippine duties on U.S. exports to the Philippines. Ostensibly this was a concession to Filipinos but the surrender of parity rights to U.S. businessmen in all areas of the economy negated any alleged gain. In a major speech on the floor of the Philippine Senate on April 27, 1955 Recto pointed to the earlier increase of duties on U.S. manufactured goods while opening wide the economy to U.S. business meant that U.S. direct investments would pour in to manufacture such goods in the Philippines itself.

"It is therefore easy to accept the view that the new revised Agreement will help accelerate the industrialization of the Philippines," said Recto. "Now whether it is the kind of industrialization that will be beneficial to us is another matter." What is really needed must be:

> ... industrialization of the country by Filipino capitalists, and not simply the prevention of industrialization by foreign capitalists; exploitation of our natural resources by Filipino capital; development and strengthening of Filipino capitalism, not foreign capitalism; increase of the national income, but not allowing it to go mostly for the benefit of non-Filipinos.[22]

Increasingly Recto became a thorn in the side of U.S. imperialism. It was plunged deeper by his attack on the wording of Magsaysay's Land Reform Act of 1955 as initially introduced in the Philippine Congress. Its Section 2 on Declaration of Policy had said: "It is the declared policy of the state *to establish and maintain* a peaceful, prosperous and democratic *agricultural* economy." Recto revealed that the draft of the Act had been written by the representatives of the U.S. Foreign Operations Administration in the U.S. Embassy. He said:

Under this bill . . . it is the declared policy of the state to perpetually chain itself to an agricultural economy, making us, Filipinos, mere suppliers and providers of raw materials and consumers of foreign manufactured goods. No more conclusive evidence is needed to prove the determined purpose of the foreign advisers of this administration to gear our economy to that of their own country. It was bad enough that they hatched this idea of making our economy subserve theirs but they wanted to add insult to injury, attempting to press us into legislating it as our declared national policy to make it appear that it was our own doing.[23]

The wording in the Land Reform Act was changed to: "It is the declared policy of the state to create and maintain an agrarian system which is peaceful . . . "

In January 1957 Claro Recto broke the Philippine political pattern by launching a new Nationalist Party (*Lapiang Makabansa*) with the perspective of running for president in the November election of that year. Subsequently the independent Senator Lorenzo Tañada joined his tiny Citizens Party to that of Recto, forming the Nationalist-Citizens Party (NCP).

The NCP had the most advanced bourgeois nationalist program of any Philippine political party to that time, standing for genuine independence, industrialization, land reform, greater democracy, and non-alignment in foreign policy. With this program Recto directly challenged Magsaysay for the presidency, promising to "hound Magsaysay from barrio to barrio." It was a confrontation that might have transformed Philippine politics with its forthright condemnation of collaboration.

Unfortunately, fate intervened. Magsaysay was killed in a plane crash on March 17, 1957.

His removal produced a confused four-way election in November 1957: Carlos Garcia, the vice-president who had replaced Magsaysay, as the Nacionalista candidate; Jose Yulo for the Liberals; Manuel Manahan for a newly-formed Progressive Party that claimed the mantle of Magsaysay; and Claro Recto for the NCP. U.S. support went chiefly to the Liberals again, not so much for Yulo as for his vice-presidential running mate, Diosdado Macapagal. The CIA alone gave $250,000 to the Yulo-Macapagal team.[24] Secondary U.S. support and funds went to Manahan. Garcia, who had never been an American choice, was frozen out as unreliable.

For U.S. interests in general the main target in the election was Recto. Above all, it was considered necessary to defeat Recto and his NCP decisively, to destroy the nationalist movement it was generating. This was not difficult. The NCP had but a skeleton leading group and no electoral organization. Liberals and Nacionalistas in Congress ganged up to deny it election inspectors, which left it vulnerable to fraud. The Catholic Church hierarchy, to which Recto was anathema for writing legislation making the anti-friar novels of Jose Rizal compulsory reading in colleges and universities, mobilized its Catholic Action movement against him. Most vicious, the CIA orchestrated a propaganda campaign attacking Recto as a "communist" and a "communist stooge." Manahan made this a central campaign issue.

Garcia won the presidency but Macapagal emerged as vice-president. Recto tailed the count with less than half a million votes and perhaps an equal number uncounted. If the CIA and U.S. corporations expected his defeat to halt a nationalist trend, they were much mistaken. Recto's first nationalist speeches may have had a vanguard character, but as time had gone on he was not speaking in a vacuum but as the spokesman for a growing social force. That force was an expanding Filipino industrial sector.

"FILIPINO FIRST"

Growth of a Filipino nationalist bourgeoisie was closely linked with the growth of manufacturing industry. In 1949 the share of manufacturing in the economy was but 3 per cent of the gross national product; it had reached 14 per cent by 1956 and kept increasing, attaining an 18 per cent share by 1960.[25] This was accounted for chiefly by Filipino domestic capital, which made up 55 per cent of investments in new enterprises in 1959 and jumped to 88 per cent in 1961. The total sum of such Filipino investments from 1949 to 1961 was P1.4 billion, while resident Chinese investments were but P425 million and U.S. investments entering the country were a tiny P34 million.[26]

Within the space of a decade the tentative industrializing steps made possible by economic controls had grown into a modest but promising base for an industrial economy. By 1960 that base included food, wood, pharmaceutical, cement, flour, textile, paint, pulp, paper, electronics, plastic, fuel refinery, intermediate steel, ship-building, motor vehicle, machine parts, engineering and other industries. Granted that many of these were of the packaging and assembly type fostered by U.S. agencies, and that most were relatively small scale, the trend was not only toward expansion but toward generating the capital for basic industry.

U.S. interests by the mid-1950s were increasingly chafing over economic controls. Magsaysay's move to abolish them in 1955 had been blocked by Filipino objections. U.S. agitation against controls mounted through the rest of the decade as it became evident that the emergency need for them had passed and that their maintenance had more to do with a protectionist policy of serving Filipino industry. With Magsaysay gone, the greatest alarm for U.S. investment interests that had been shying away from the Philippines while controls were in effect derived from an unanticipated source: the Garcia administration.

President Carlos P. Garcia, whose political home base was the relatively minor island of Bohol, had developed in the colonial period as a machine politician of the Nacionalista Party without particular association with U.S. colonial authorities. An anti-collaboration guerrilla on Bohol during the war, he had not been part of the USAFFE structure. He had opposed the Bell Act and the Military Bases Agreement although not outspokenly. His choice by Laurel, Recto and other Nacionalista leaders as vice-presidential candidate in 1953 was for party loyalty rather than ideology.

Owing nothing to the U.S. for his election in 1957 and unique among Philippine presidents in that respect, Garcia turned out to be independent-minded and his own man. Within a few months after his election as president he had made a number of moves that unsettled U.S. authorities, proposing the reexamination of the 1947 Military Assistance Pact and the establishment of a multiple foreign exchange reserve (i.e., not wholly reliant on the dollar), while coming out against involvement in the affairs of neighboring nations as Magsaysay had done in obedience to U.S. wishes.

Most important, however, was an economic development that rocked the U.S. Embassy and Chamber of Commerce. On August 21, 1958 the policy-making National Economic Council adopted a Resolution No. 204 which declared that "it is the policy of the Government to encourage Filipinos to engage in enterprises and industries vital to the economic growth, stability and security of the country" and that

this policy should be, as a national program, vigorously implemented so as to enable Filipinos eventually to attain a substantial share of the commerce and industry of this country, whether such enterprises are presently controlled by non-Filipinos or otherwise.

It resolved "that the National Economic Council adopts this program for the promotion of substantial Filipino participation in the aforementioned enterprises not only for those that are now in existence, but for such commercial and industrial enterprises as may be required in the future," and it laid down the following guidelines on the allocation of foreign exchange:

(a) That in instances where there are applications for foreign exchange allocations for the establishment of an enterprise whether it be commercial or industrial in nature, and there are among the applicants qualified Filipinos or enterprises owned at least 60 per cent by Filipinos, preference shall be given to the Filipino applicants.

(b) That in instances where Filipinos seek to enter a field now predominantly in the hands of non-Filipinos, such steps shall be taken as will enable the Filipino enterprises to participate in such field or activity at the earliest opportunity.

Finally, the Resolution recognized the need for foreign capital "in certain phases of the development of the country's economy" but suggested that this enter through joint ventures of foreign and Filipino capital in which "the Filipino participation is—or eventually will be—at least 60% of the capital stock ownership."[27]

This NEC resolution and its firm projection of a Filipino First policy, as it became known, were officially endorsed by President Garcia. Furthermore, the Philippine Chamber of Commerce, electing a set of nationalist-inclined officers, adopted Filipino First as a slogan and then proceeded to resign from the International Chamber of Commerce when that body opposed it on U.S. insistence.[28]

The *Journal* of the U.S. Chamber of Commerce fulminated against Filipino First, calling it "nothing less than insane, threatening not simple injury and damage, but measureless loss and waste, retrogression and demoralization." The *Journal*'s American editor could not restrain his rage against Filipino First:

It is inherently a fascist slogan, adopted here to further the game of a small group of local business buccaneers. It is the cry of the dispossessors who through government financial and other economic controls, pant after usurping the place and seizing the hard-earned wealth of others with no show of right other than that they are 'Filipinos.' The slogan is not inspired by an honest nationalism—let alone patriotism—but by greed and cupidity.[29]

Very soon afterward a stream of articles, news releases and letters to the press began to appear in U.S. and collaborator-owned papers attacking the Garcia government as allegedly friendly to communists and as "free spending," and playing up in contrast the virtues of General Jesus Vargas, the secretary of defense. Vargas, who had been armed forces chief of staff under Magsaysay, was a JUSMAG protege. Garcia was quick to heed what was taking place. On November 16, 1958 a congressman from the president's home province of Bohol, Bartolome Cabangbang, shook the political scene by exposing a plot among army officers to stage a coup to oust Garcia and install Vargas in his place. The episode was widely understood to show that the U.S. was out to get Garcia, but it also served notice on Vargas' U.S. backers that the president was ready to fight. Vargas resigned. U.S. interests turned to other means to regain full political control.

A propaganda campaign was begun by the Luce publications, *Time* and *Life*, both with sizeable circulations in the Philippines while quoted and reprinted in the Manila press, playing up opposition figures and depicting Garcia as a nonentity who had "stepped into the man-sized shoes of the Philippine National Hero Ramon Magsaysay." The *U.S. News and World Report* (February 27, 1959) attacked the Filipino First policy as "extreme nationalism" and said that it was not possible to distinguish the program of its advocates "from what the communists say and want."[30]

U.S. authorities were even more disturbed by two developments that signified the maturing of nationalist forces. The first of these was the coalition agreement reached at the beginning of 1959 between Garcia's Nacionalista Party and the Nationalist-Citizens Party of Recto. Appointed to the Council of State by Garcia, Recto was increasingly listened to by the president. The coalition was in preparation for the November 1959 senatorial election.

Second, the National Progress Movement was launched on February 26, 1959, intended as a mass organization to build broad support for a nationalist program, and for Garcia to stay in office to carry it out. It called itself "the first organized movement for Filipino Nationalism since the Philippine Revolution" (a bourgeois nationalist assertion that ignored the anti-imperialist movements of the left). "The Nationalist Manifesto" which the NPM issued on May 24, 1959 was the most forthright bourgeois nationalist declaration to appear:

Western writers claim that colonialism is dead, and that there is no more need for nationalism, but we way that colonialism is not dead . . . Filipinos today are still living under the shadow of a colonial past. They are still within the grip of alien domination. Foreign interests, secular and otherwise, still decisively influence our national life, politically, economically, culturally, morally—in brief, the entire fabric of society, a society which still manifests the shape and temper of a colonial order . . .

The real source of power in this country is the alien community; they control, directly or through dummies, the distribution of practically all commodities; they control, through financing, our transportation and public utilities; they have, in banks and in private hoards, a disproportionally large share of the currency not in the government treasury; they own or have a share in an overwhelming majority of manufacturing industries; their business associations are so tightly organized that they can 'tax' the people directly and immediately by manipulating prices through their control of supply; they can, through their control of wholesale and retail distribution, kill or stunt almost at will any Filipino industry, or decide arbitrarily the kind and price of goods that the Filipinos shall consume . . .

The economic plight of the aliens is, in turn, the root cause of graft corruption in the government and ultimately, in the entire society. Being an alien minority, they must employ all methods, particularly corruption, to protect themselves by maintaining at all costs their position of authority. They have unlimited funds with which to buy government employees and officials . . . They subsidize, finance to power, or simply purchase, the services of politicians. Their influence extends through all levels of politics and government . . .

Representing, protecting and advancing these foreign interests are Filipino renegades, flourishing at the expense of their own countrymen. Above all, there are those whose allegiance is determined by attachment to superior cultures and civilizations, parasites who feed without contributing to their own national community, its culture and the civilization it may yet attain. Among the majority are those who have been conditioned by five decades of American total conquest, accepting a benevolent slavery to noble, though challenging, independence.

The stated objectives of the NPM included: the abrogation of the parity amendment to the Constitution; the pursuance of an independent foreign policy; the adoption by the Administration of a nationalist program as a measure against "all forms of imperialism, ideological or otherwise"; the Filipinization of all major public utility industries; adoption and implementation of a vigorous program of social justice; and adoption and implementation of a nationalist industrialization program.[31]

With this program the NPM played an important part in the 1959 senatorial election, supporting the candidates of the Nacionalista-NCP coalition.

U.S. interests backed a grouping of former Magsaysay adherents calling themselves the Grand Alliance. Among them were Jesus Vargas,

Raul Manglapus, Manuel Manahan and Emmanuel Pelaez. All of them were defeated. One of the victors was the NCP candidate, Lorenzo Tañada. Garcia said that "through the ballot, the people have given their unmistakeable endorsement to the nationalistic policies of the administration."

Although the NPM announced that it "publicly acknowledges President Garcia and Senator Recto, the highest leaders of the NP-NCP coalition, as constituting the highest joint leadership of the National Movement in the Philippines today," its support for the Nacionalista Party as a whole was less wholehearted, saying "we find the nationalism of NP leaders still largely timid and half-hearted."[32]

In practical terms, under Garcia the Filipino First policy enabled Filipinos to obtain 51 per cent of foreign exchange allocations by the end of 1959. Furthermore, a liberalizing of credit to new Filipino enterprises by the Philippine National Bank and other government financial channels fostered the injection of Filipino capital into industry; whereas only 55 per cent of new investments were Filipino in December 1959, by 1961 the Filipino share had jumped to 88 per cent.

In 1959 the Filipino Oil Refining Co. (Filoil) was established, constituting a nationalist challenge to the big dominating U.S. and other foreign oil companies. The Iligan Integrated Steel Mill, Inc. (IISMI), a $1 billion venture, the first stage of a full-fledged Philippine steel industry, began loan negotiations with the World Bank, the U.S. Export-Import Bank and other banks. It was a joint venture of government and private Filipino capital and was a prime example of the Garcia's administration's policy of government aid to industrialization. In 1960 one of the major U.S.-owned companies in the Philippines, the Manila Electric Co. (Meralco), organized in 1903, was bought by a Filipino consortium headed by the Lopez family, for $66 million. In the ebullient climate created by these and related developments the belief that the Philippines was reaching the take-off stage for major industrialization was widespread.

One of the potent factors in these developments was the taking up of the nationalist cause by a sector of the Philippines press, in particular the daily newspaper, *Manila Chronicle.* A small postwar paper, it was acquired in 1947 by Eugenio Lopez of the Lopez sugar family, who financed it to build it into one of the three top large-circulation dailies in the 1950s. The Lopez family diversified its holdings into transportation and industry and saw the possibilities of growth under economic controls. It turned the *Chronicle* into a full-throated nationalist vehicle, boosting Recto, the Recto-Garcia alliance, and the NPM. Its weekly magazine, *This Week,* resurrected the history, the ideals and the national heroes of the Philippine Revolution and of the war against U.S. conquest. The answer of the members of the U.S. Chamber of Commerce to this was a damaging advertising boycott of the *Chronicle*.

President Garcia, encouraged by nationalist successes in the 1959 senatorial election, promptly staked out his position for the presidential contest in 1961, saying in a major speech on January 16, 1960:

> "The ugly, incontrovertible fact about our economy today is its dominance by aliens . . . Reduced to stark realities, such a condition makes a mockery of our independence and robs it of substance and meaning. As long as this condition persists, we shall remains in many way a colonial country . . . It is therefore the imperative of this epoch that the Filipinos acquire a major and dominant participation in the national economy of the Philippines. We propose to do this and we shall do this with malice toward none and with fairness to all."[33]

Fully aware of the U.S. aim to unseat him, Garcia moved to disarm that drive by offering opportunities to U.S. capital, stressing

> Philippine economic nationalism as a national policy is not anti-alien, much less anti-American. It is simply an honest-to-goodness effort of the Filipino people to be the masters in their own economic household for exactly the same natural reason that Americans would be masters of the United States national economy, the British in England, the Japanese in Japan, etc. In this country there is still room for foreign capital, especially in fields where Filipino capital is still deficient or timid. Such foreign friendly capital as is willing to help us realize our economic objective under the announced policy and is willing to collaborate with Philippine capital in joint venture to realize the vast natural resources of the country, is welcome to the Philippines under my Administration.[34]

U.S. interests were less impressed by this than they were by another trend: the solidifying of the NP-NCP coalition. The prospect was freely aired of a Garcia-Recto presidential-vice presidential ticket in 1961.

In reaction, U.S. money and propaganda were swung behind the Liberal who had been elected vice-president, Diosdado Macapagal. The CIA station chief in Manila, Joseph B. Smith, boasted of "the new coalition we started working on after November 1959," meaning Macapagal, the Liberal Party and the Magsaysay clones in the Grand Alliance.[35] While Macapagal was vice-president, the CIA paid him $50,000, while Smith had $250,000 to spread around in the 1961 election.[36] The program announced by Macapagal, running as the Liberal presidential candidate, came straight off the U.S. imperialist drawing board:

(1) Development of our economic resources under a system of free, private enterprise; (2) implementation of a social program for the masses under the direction of the government; (3) the complete withdrawal of the government from business ventures; and (4) the removal of the controls which have spawned so much corruption.[37]

It was the issue of corruption that was chosen by the CIA, the U.S. propaganda channels, and the Liberal opposition to bring down Garcia. It was charged that the Garcia administration was riddled with corruption that allegedly had its source chiefly in the operation of the foreign exchange allocation system in which Filipinos had won a majority share. Nationalism and Filipino First were thus linked with corruption. It was a particularly pernicious charge. Corruption, given such an enormous start as a factor in the U.S.-contrived first independence regime, had become established in Philippine politics, with each party in power resorting to a gigantic spoils system. For U.S. imperialism this was an ideal situation, enabling the undermining and ouster of any government by way of anti-corruption campaigns which had a ready response from an electorate grown cynical from politicans enriching themselves. President Garcia himself could not be implicated in the smears, but it was not difficult to discredit economic controls in the eyes of many people by claiming that under-the-table arrangements were made in some foreign exchange allocations.

Before the election campaign and issues could be clearly defined, the Filipino nationalist cause suffered a severely crippling blow with the loss of Claro Recto. This remarkable man who, late in life, had arrived at an utterly honest assessment of his country's condition and of what Filipinos themselves must do about it, died on October 2, 1960. He had spoken movingly of himself as one "who, in his declining years, still loves to plant trees knowing he will never sit in their shade, happy in the thought that some day, in a distant future, one may say of him and the nationalists of his generation: 'There were those who kept vigil in the night of our forefathers.'"

There was no one to replace Recto at the side of Garcia, or in the NCP. The Garcia administration, under heavy attack on the corruption theme, began a retreat from a firm nationalist position by defensively starting "gradual decontrol." A forthright nationalist vs. anti-nationalist contest did not materialize to the degree demanded by the circumstances. The corruption issue overwhelmed the nationalist issues. The team of Diosdado Macapagal and Emmanuel Pelaez won in November 1961 by a wide margin.

SMOTHERING ECONOMIC
NATIONALISM

The 1961 election restored to power a Liberal Party coalesced with the Magsaysay group, a collaborator combination wholly committed to the U.S. neocolonial design for the Philippines. Immediately after taking office, President Macapagal, declaring that free enterprise would be the keystone of his administration, announced on January 21, 1962 the lifting of exchange controls, the ending of import controls, and the devaluation of the Philippine peso (which was cut loose from its long-standing two-to-one ratio with the U.S. dollar and allowed to "float" to a 3.90 to one ratio). The Filipino First policy was formally abolished.

These steps constituted a sweeping victory for U.S. imperialism over Filipino nationalism's struggle to attain genuine independence and industrialization. The effects of the Macapagal policies were devastating to the nascent Filipino industries, which were stripped of their protection. Decontrol opened wide the door to unrestricted entry of U.S.-made consumer goods, with which Filipino manufacturers had difficulty competing: sales of Philippine-made goods markedly fell.

This occurred in spite of devaluation of the peso which theoretically tended to increase the price of imported goods. In actuality, devaluation had a far worse effect on the new Filipino industries than on the established U.S. commercial and investing groups. Most Filipino industries were in the process of equipping themselves with imported machineries and other capital goods including raw materials and had contracted debts in doing so. These now had to be paid off at P3.90 to the dollar instead of P2 to the dollar, which virtually doubled operating costs and debts. Even turning to local raw materials necessitated new processes and equipment at prohibitive cost.

The consequence of this was that innumerable new Filipino industries were driven to the wall. Within four years up to 1,500 such industries, many of them the cream of the industrialization surge, had collapsed due to bankruptcy, a large proportion disappearing and the rest absorbed or taken over by U.S. capital. Such a take-over process was facilitated by devaluation, which doubled overnight the value and investment power of the dollar in the Philippines.[38]

One of the saddest cases was that of Filoil, the independent Filipino refining and distribution corporation that had broken the monopoly of the big foreign oil companies. At its launching in 1959 Filoil had conceded a minority share to the U.S. Gulf Oil Co. in order to gain a supply of crude oil and access to technology. Decontrol shattered the

Filoil hopes. Within two years, by 1964, the company had been rendered bankrupt. It was swallowed by Gulf Oil, which acquired 67 per cent of the shares, only a minor Filipino stake, and the name, remaining in mockery. Filoil's managers, in a letter to stockholders explaining the disaster, pointed to "two very vital realities and conditions existing at the present time:

(1) The Philippines is now going through the tightest credit situation since the end of World War II.

(2) The petroleum industry is going through the most severe cutthroat competition ever experienced in the history of the country, brought about by decontrol and the consequent relentless competitive efforts of the international oil companies to get a larger share of the market.[39]

At this stage of the Philippine economy the most vital factor was credit. President Garcia's opening up of greater credit facilities to Filipino industry by both banks and government agencies was a prime stimulus in the latter 1950s. A severe squeeze on credit came, however, in 1962 from a disastrous step by the Macapagal government that was linked with, and worsened, the decontrol decrees.

That step was acceptance of U.S. policy advice for the Philippines to rely on stabilization loans from abroad instead of economic controls. The Macapagal regime negotiated a $300 million loan from the International Monetary Fund (IMF), the World Bank, and the U.S. Treasury. Actually, this was intended to finance or offset the immediate remittance of the blocked profits of U.S. companies that had been kept in the Philippines by the operation of exchange controls. Estimates of these profits ranged from $150 million to $300 million, which promptly flowed out of the country. Combined with the unlimited imports, the free remittance of profits drastically reduced foreign exchange reserves, compelling the government to go steadily further down the road of foreign debt and to seek continually additional stabilization loans.

President Garcia left office with a Philippine foreign debt of merely $200 million. In the decade from 1962 to 1972 the cumulative Philippine trade deficit amounted to $1 billion and the total profit remittances and other capital outflows came to another $1 billion, while over the same period the external debt rose to $2 billion, comprising a macabre balance with a negative effect on development.

In general, the IMF and World Bank have had four universal loan conditions: an open economy without import or exchange controls, an encouragement with incentives of foreign investment as the alleged key to economic development, strict monetary and fiscal policies including tight credit, and currency devaluation as a means of coping with depletion of international reserves. All of these conditions were accepted by the collaborating Macapagal government.

The consequence of these policies ended nationalist industrialization in the Philippines and strangled independent economic development. It must be stressed that the aim of the Filipino industrialists, of the fledgling nationalist bourgeoisie they constituted, was the growth of a Philippine capitalism, not of a socialist or non-capitalist economy. Nevertheless, this could not be abided by U.S. imperialism. Capitalism did develop in the Philippines from this point, but it was a stunted and dependent capitalism, a subsidiary of U.S. and other foreign capital, providing extremely meager benefits to an impoverished Filipino people.

A grim example of what took place was the Iligan Integrated Steel Mill, Inc. The Garcia administration initiated steps to build such a basic industry and to remove the need for steel imports that stood near the top of the import list. In 1955 it was launched by legislation that made it a wholly government project of the National Shipyards and Steel Corporation, a government body. However, the U.S. Export-Import Bank refused an implementing loan unless it was a joint venture with 49 per cent private capital. Garcia finally yielded on this in 1960 when Filipino private interests were allowed to subscribe as demanded. Under the Macapagal regime further U.S. pressure forced the project to be made entirely private, but even then the Export-Import loan of an initial $62.3 million was not agreed until 1964, and construction did not start until 1965. It was set up without a blast furnace. In 1970 IMF loan pressure compelled another devaluation of the peso, producing a floating rate that swelled the Iligan debt by 60 per cent, reducing the steel industry to bankruptcy and forcing its closure. U.S. loan tactics and conditions had blocked, then destroyed a Philippine steel industry.

In general, the aim of U.S. policies and terms was to eliminate the Filipino nationalist threat to win the predominant position in the Philippine economy, and to reduce it to a position subordinate to U.S. capital. Except for key basic industries like the Iligan steel mill, the intention was not so much to drive Filipino businesses into complete collapse as to convert them into joint ventures in which U.S. capital, made available as bankruptcies loomed, gained controlling shares. A Philippine capitalism was not to be killed off entirely but made a junior partner in the U.S. global system of trade, investment and lending.

THE LESSON
OF SUPPRESSION

For the majority of the Filipino people, in particular the class forces of genuine independence and nationalism, the decade of the 1950s—or more broadly the years from 1949 to 1962—was a time of disaster, of grave setbacks to national democratic goals. The causes of this could be traced more than anything else to the failure of those forces to achieve unity against the common enemy of foreign imperialism, and to the success of U.S. imperialism in dividing the Filipino people and pitting one class grouping against another.

During the 1950s two separate movements of a national liberation character arose, the revolutionary movement led by the PKP with a mainly peasant and worker base, and the bourgeois nationalist movement that drew support from sectors of the business and middle class groups. The NP-DA coalition that fought the 1946 election, for all its shortcomings, contained the embryo of broad unity, but it was shattered by the U.S. tactics of control and suppression, by the divisive politics of collaboration by the traditional landlord-*comprador* forces, and then by the leftist go-it-alone strategy of the revolutionary movement that discarded broad unity in an attempt to win power. In its national-democratic conceptions the PKP projected unity alliances with all anti-imperialist and democratic Filipinos, but after 1949 the drive for hegemony in the struggle and the related condemnation of all who did not support the armed struggle negated unity.

The nationalist movement that took shape around Recto's NCP and the Filipino First policy of President Garcia that had its program formulated in the manifesto of the National Progress Movement was the natural ally of the PKP-led movement, but it developed as the HMB was being crushed. Recto, at least, came to understand the link, agreeing to be the legal counsel of the PKP's general secretary and addressing sympathetically a gathering marking the 11th anniversary of the founding of the Hukbalahap. A national bourgeois unity with workers and peasants as a means of achieving nationalist control of the economy was neither projected nor, apparently, considered. If anything, the left bid for power frightened and antagonized Filipino business interests, and the massive anti-communist propaganda of U.S. imperialism had its effect as well.

Recto's bid for the presidency in the 1957 election clearly showed the weakness of the nationalist bourgeois movement. The NCP in that election campaigned virtually without a political machine, its organization limited to a scattering of individuals in some cities and towns, mostly intellectuals and middle class. In *illustrado* fashion, Recto relied on his personality and his speeches. Although the active remnants of the PKP and HMB supported Recto, they were in no position by then to organize a structure to deliver votes. Besides, the general demoralization after defeat of the armed struggle affected the population.

U.S. imperialism was able to deal with and to crush these two nationalist-inclined movements separately, one with armed force, the other with economic and political pressures. In essential respects, this amounted to a suppression of the Philippine nation for neocolonial ends as tragic as the suppression of that nation to create a U.S. colony early in the century.

VIII

Liberation is a Lengthening Road

The defeat of the PKP-led national liberatron struggle in the 1950s and the strangling of the Filipino bourgeois nationalist movement for independent industrialization by the early 1960s had given U.S. interests a clear path to shaping a neocolonial system in the Philippines closely fitted to the new features of imperialist control. That system, continually refined and expanded, has remained in being to the present time.

The new imperialist features of control, which became ascendent in the 1960s and all-pervasive in the 1970s and 1980s, have been: the internationally structured operations of transnational corporations (TNCs), and the interrelated, greatly expanded role and activities of finance capital as exemplified particularly in the World Bank and International Monetary Fund. Both wrapped the Philippines up in utter dependency, trussed up in the webs of their controls like an object to be devoured.

During the three decades after President Macapagal complied with U.S. demands for the abolition of economic controls that had aided the growth of nationalist industry, no further Filipino challenge of that nature was able to emerge with enough strength to win a position of power or of unshakeable influence on national policy. Nationalist movements and tendencies have persistently arisen but have been repressed with force or smothered by the overwhelming privileges yielded by ever more sophisticated collaboration with foreign, mainly U.S., investment and financial interests.

None of the three Filipino presidents in that period—Diosdado Macapagal, Ferdinand Marcos or Corazon Aquino—has been able or has had the inclination to break free of the neocolonial frame clamped upon Philippine economic, political and military affairs. Each has represented different, even conflicting, groupings and alignments among the Filipino elite, but U.S. imperialism has had no difficulty in obtaining everything it wanted from them, or in removing those whose usefulness declined.

In the colonial period and in the immediate post-independence years of the Bell Act, U.S. economic policy was operated in alliance with the traditional narrow semi-feudal Filipino landlord-*comprador* combination, which was adequate for the colonial relationship. The new imperialist features and their requirements, however, produced a neocolonialism in which more intensified and more ramified capitalist relations supplanted the semi-feudal. Between the 1960s and 1990s changes took place in Philippine society which altered to a considerable extent the class character of the neocolonial alliances on which U.S. imperialism relies. Although a Philippine capitalism of a kind took shape, it has been an inhibited, truncated capitalism, denied a basic industrial base, and made subsidiary to and dependent upon the massive presence of foreign corporations and banks. Throughout this process, a collaborating Filipino elite has remained essentially unaltered in its behavior; it is only the type of relations that has changed, not the essence of collaboration.

THE ECONOMIC WEB OF NEOCOLONIALISM

From President Roxas onward one of the cardinal tenets of collaborating Filipino leaders has been the contention that foreign investment and outside aid are the key to Philippine development. Every administration, with the relative exception of President Garcia's, extended further concessions and incentives to foreign investors who, it was claimed, would bring in dollars, technology and knowhow. It has been one of the great Philippine myths.

For the past half century the door has been wide open for U.S. direct investment in the independent Philippines. The total has become huge. In 1946 those investments, built up in the colonial period, were only $268 million. Despite the advantage of parity, these had climbed to but $375 million by 1962, or an average of less than $7 million a year over the intervening sixteen years.[1] Economic controls and their restriction of profit remittance had made U.S. investors cautious.

After the 1962 decontrol, which assured freedom of profit remittance and repatriation of capital, the U.S. investment total jumped. By 1968 it reached $650 million or about $46 million a year over the intervening six years. By 1982 a further $900 million had been added, bringing the book value of U.S. investments to about $1.5 billion, with a market value of $3 billion. At the beginning of the 1990s it was estimated that the book value stood at approximately $2 billion, the market value double that figure.[2]

In literal figures this sum is around eight times the 1946 investment. At that time the dollar had a 1 to 2 ration to the peso, giving U.S. holdings a local value of P536 million. In 1990, after repeated devaluations of the peso at U.S. insistence, the U.S. investments were equivalent to more than P50 billion. A survey of 76 selected U.S. companies in 1990, a fraction of those operating in the Philippines, showed their total assets standing at P154 billion, roughly $6 billion.[3]

This vast economic power in an underdeveloped country, however, has not been the engine of national development that its Filipino apologists have claimed. U.S. investment and aid have not been for Philippine development as such but for sheer profit-making. For one thing, it has not represented any significant transfer of investment or operating capital from the U.S. to the Philippines. The circumstances of parity worked out in ways not really contemplated by its colonialist architects, but even more advantageously.

A factor for which allowance had not fully been made at the time of Philippine independence was the tendency for Filipino capital to accumulate at a growing rate along with the rise of a Filipino entrepreneurial sector with a nationalist orientation on employing it. Under President Garcia this sector was aided by encouragement given to a strengthening and expansion of the Philippine banking system and of its capacity for lending. Although the Macapagal decontrol and devaluation policies had seriously crippled the new Filipino enterprises, it was obvious that these tendencies of independent capitalist development and the accumulation of capital to help finance them would continue to grow.

U.S. imperialism turned this situation to its own uses. The Philippines became viewed not merely as a source of raw materials but as a source of capital itself, for investment and for operating expenditures of foreign companies. It was a process that began soon after independence and became intensified as a reaction to economic controls. The growth of the U.S. investment total between 1946 and 1962 from $268 million to $375 million, previously mentioned, was accounted for to only a very minor extent by the entry of capital from outside. While investment grew by $107 million, the true inflow was far less, a mere $17 million in all from 1950 to 1961: some reinvestment occurred but the rest came from funds borrowed from banks in the Philippines.[4]

Between 1956 and 1965, a Filipino survey revealed, 108 of the U.S. firms in the Philippines had capital expenditures, chiefly operational, of $489.7 million, of which only $79.4 million (16 per cent) came from outside, while all the rest ($410.3 million or 84 per cent) was derived locally. One estimate is that up to 1968 the actual post-independence amount of U.S. investment capital entering the Philippines averaged no more than $3 million a year (i.e., about $68 million of the $382 million of increased investment in that 22 years); the rest was generated locally.[5] A study of the Philippine economy by a Hong Kong publication commented:

> An irony is that the foreign firms that control the economy are not really foreign investors, if foreign investment means the bringing in of capital from overseas. All they did to set up shop was incorporate with a few prominent Filipinos to grace the board of directors and some amount of equity participation from them, bring in elementary equipment with a minimal dollar value, and secure loans from Philippine banks, insurance companies, and even State credit institutions.[6]

This has not been a process confined to the control years or to the duration of parity. It has continued at an accelerated rate. One of the most notorious cases of this kind of operation was the Ford Corporation which in 1967 was registered in the Philippines with a paid-up capital of but P100,000 and then proceeded to borrow P30 million to P40 million from a Philippine syndicate of commercial banks.[7] When it set up its body-stamping plant later, its entire capital of $22 million (equivalent to P168 million) was derived from local sources.[8]

In 1979 a Filipino economist showed that from 1960 to 1977, for every 41 cents of U.S. investment coming from abroad, $1 was borrowed locally.[9] Another analyst has contended that this is an underestimation and that for every dollar brought in, $25 have been borrowed in the Philippines.[10] The practice continued throughout the Marcos years and tended to increase rather than diminish during the succeeding government of President Corazon Aquino which took over from Marcos early in 1986. In the three-year period from the beginning of the Aquino regime to the middle of 1989 the *major* foreign corporations alone borrowed P47.8 billion from the Philippine banking system.[11]

This absorption of Filipino capital resources has been facilitated by the presence of foreign banks, mainly U.S., which have been allowed to take local deposits and to channel them to foreign firms, while operating as parasites on the Philippine economy in the same way as foreign industrial or commercial corporations. As early as 1959, Senator Lorenzo Tañada, co-leader with Claro M. Recto of the Nationalist-Citizens Party, introduced a bill in the Philippine Congress to prohibit the acceptance of local deposits by the four foreign banks then in the country. In the hearings on the Tañada bill, testimony was given by the president of the Bankers' Association of the Philippines, Alfonso Calalang, who said:

> We can control the retail trade and the importing business and we can produce quality goods to induce consumption only if we control the banking business. We remain in a perennial state of economic vasselage unless we blaze new trails leading to economic security and maturity. It is in this stage of vasselage that the early American settler wanted to pin us so that the Philippines would always be a special preserve for him. In truth, if there is any economic activity which should be Filipinized, it is the banking business.[12]

Said Senator Tañada in recollection in 1967:

> Branches of foreign banks operate here without bringing in a centavo. They accept local deposits and lend these funds to foreign corporations. During the hearings [on his bill], of the four foreign banks, one admitted to having brought in no capital at all, two could not give any pertinent data, and the last admitted to having brought in only P2,200,000 ($1,100,000). The two banks that could not give any definite answer regarding how much capital they had actually brought in earned from 1945 to 1958 net profits of P30,402,667.08 ($15,201,333.54). The foreign bank that did not bring in any capital earned from 1947 to 1958 net profits of P11,321,996.79 ($5,660,998.39). The bank that brought in P2,200,000 earned net profits of P18,696,881.96 ($9,349,440.98). As of December 31, 1958 the total deposits of these alien banks amounted to P369,570,713.69 ($184,785,356.85). And the record showed that the loans granted by these banks, percentage-wise, went more to finance alien business activities than Filipino. What happened to the net profits earned by these banks? Records show that they have been remitting their profits to their home offices.[13]

The Tañada bill, needless to say, failed to pass in the Philippine Congress, dominated despite the nationalist tendency of the Garcia administration then in office by collaborationist landlord-*comprador* representatives.

A soaking up of Filipino capital by foreign corporations whose size and strength make them a favored financial risk has deprived Filipino businesses of loan capital, leaving many in a fragile and weakened condition leading to their continual collapse or to their take-over entirely or partially through having to accept foreign equity.

By the latter 1970s over 40 per cent of the top Philippine corporations had U.S. equity participation, i.e., over 400 of the top companies. This did not include the many other wholly-owned U.S. firms operating in the Philippines and also ranking high among the top 1,000, and it did not include the many other foreign corporations—Japanese, Chinese, West European and others—which also borrow locally and have equity participation at all levels of business activity.[14]

Overwhelmingly, Filipino industry acquired a joint venture, junior partner status. Although in a great many cases forced into this kind of status, Filipino industry and banking is today little more than the extension of the elite collaboration that prevailed in the colonial period.

To many Filipinos this prevalence of foreign investment and its encroachment into every corner of the economy would be acceptable and tolerated if it resulted in a national development raising the living standards of the whole population. On the contrary, however, a massive outflow of Philippine capital resources and generated wealth to the U.S. and other foreign countries has been caused precisely by such investment. It has been estimated that from 1946 to 1976 for every dollar of direct U.S. investment (the bulk of which, as indicated, has been drawn from local sources) a net profit of $3.68 was realized. Of this, about $2 was remitted to the U.S. and $1.68 was reinvested in the Philippines. In the early 1970s it was claimed that the rate of profit was as much as $7.08 for every invested dollar. Over the 30-year period (1946–1976), U.S. firms in effect through profit remittance de-capitalized the Philippines of $368 million.[15] This was stepped up in the latter 1970s, the net outflow of capital of this type to the U.S. hitting $443 million from 1972 to 1980.[16] In the 1980s the de-capitalization was more intensified, a study in 1989 of but 76 of the largest U.S. corporations showing that they had remitted abroad in that decade the equivalent of P8.7 billion or around $340 million.[17] The means of development were flowing out of the Philippines in far greater quantities than were coming in.

Direct foreign investment in the Philippines, wrote a Filipino analyst, is "a method of pumping surplus out of underdeveloped areas, not a channel through which surplus is directed into them."[18]

Nevertheless, despite the enshrining of parity for U.S. companies in the Bell Trade Act and its unlimited extension in the Laurel-Langley Agreement, every Filipino government agreed to further foreign investment laws giving ever more favorable "incentives" to foreign investors. Initially, areas of investment had been divided into pioneer and non-pioneer categories. Foreign investment had virtually limitless privileges in the pioneer sector, but a 60 per cent Filipino ownership had been required in the non-pioneer sector. In 1967 a Marcos Investment Incentives Act (RA 5186) allowed foreign companies without the required 60 per cent Filipino participation to operate in the non-pioneer fields.[19]

Long before the Bell Act's 28 years of parity expired (in 1974), the U.S. was pressing for a new agreement for indefinite "national treatment" (equal rights) for U.S. investors. A Philippine-American Joint Preparatory Committee for Discussion of Concepts Underlying a New Instrument to Replace the Laurel-Langley Agreement was set up at U.S. initiative and began talks in November of 1967. In the talks the U.S. team insisted that it was a general practice in most countries "on a basis of reciprocity, to accord foreign investment in most fields of activity treatment equal to that accorded local investment," a statement neglecting to mention that this invariably occurred between countries of relatively equal development. U.S. capital, it was said, had many alternative opportunities and wouldn't come to the Philippines if it wasn't "welcome."[20] The chairman of the Philippine panel, Cesar Virata, an arch-collaborator, compromised his own side by hastily assuring the U.S. panel that "national treatment" would indeed be included in a new agreement. As it happened, the Preparatory Committee never completed its work, which became unnecessary.

By the end of the 1960s, U.S. imperialism was recasting its neocolonial instruments under the pressure of changing international conditions. For one thing, an increase of nationalism in the formerly colonial developing countries was leading to the nationalization of foreign enterprises. Between 1960 and 1976 there were 1,369 such cases in 71 countries, with the tendency increasing from 47 a year in the 1960s to 140 a year in the 1970s.[21] For another thing, the growth of economic power of rival capitalist centers in Western Europe and Japan, which also had an interest in investment in the Philippines, made it unwise to insist on special rights for U.S. interests which might suffer retaliation wherever their rivals were dominant. Furthermore, such international bodies as the World Bank and the International Monetary Fund integrated operations of all imperialist countries and tended to negate "special relations." U.S. parity, in the form that it had, was allowed to terminate.

In 1973 President Ferdinand Marcos, through the decree-making authority he had assumed under martial law, proclaimed a new Philippine Constitution. One of its provisions formally ended parity and the national treatment for U.S. corporations provided for in the 1935 Constitution. Also, however, the Marcos Constitution included a clause permitting "service contracts," a clever device "which allowed Filipino citizens and qualified domestic corporations to enter into service contracts with foreign investors for financial, technical, management, or other forms of assistance. The terms of a service contract could involve the actual development of a given natural resource by foreign investors, thus legitimizing indirectly what was prohibited directly under the 1973 martial law Constitution. This anomaly was more pronounced when the active party in a service contract was a corporation wholly owned by foreign interests. In that case, the Filipinization requirement in the Constitution was virtually set aside completely, permitting foreign corporations to obtain actual possession, control, and direct exploitation of the country's natural resources."[22] The service contract was thus nothing more or less than an arrangement permitting an indefinite extension of the substance of national treatment or parity, enabling foreign control and exploitation of any area of the economy in a manner less likely to arouse nationalist protest.

Retention of parity had, in fact, become virtually irrelevant as new features of neocolonialism were developed from the 1950s. The most pervasive and dominant of these was the use of loan capital to pave the way for imperialist control. Since their establishment as postwar rehabilitation institutions, both the International Monetary Fund and the World Bank had become channels for all the leading capitalist countries to pursue their lending interests jointly, although in the proportionate subscription system the U.S. held the dominant share. Virtually all the large commercial banks also took part in the loan capital torrent that poured into the developing countries from the early 1960s onward.

In the 1970s this trend reached the significance of a major shift in the flow of financial resources from the U.S. and other powers to the developing countries, from direct private investment to international bank lending. The share of direct investment in that flow fell from 56 per cent in 1970 to 28 per cent in 1979, while international bank lending rose from 15.4 per cent of the total net financial flow in 1970 to 27.7 per cent in 1978.[23] An IMF study in 1984 explained the underlying reason for the shift:

> The decreased importance of private direct investment flows relative to external borrowing implies a reduction in the share of risk borne by foreign savers and an increase in risk borne internally, since payments on private direct investment are required only if the investment earns a return, whereas debt service payments must be made irrespective of the use made of the resources generated by borrowing.[24]

Such an advantage in profit from loans was but one aspect of the enormous benefits to be gained from this neocolonial area of operations.

The IMF and World Bank laid down a wide range of conditions to which debtor countries had to agree, committing themselves in Letters of Intent to lenders' demands. Loan conditions invariably included the following:

1. Commitment to an open economy, with no restrictions on imports or on remittance of profits and capital repatriation.
2. An encouragement of foreign investment, especially through legislation granting concessions and incentives.
3. Monetary or fiscal restraint, which means the cutting of budgets, subsidies and social services.
4. Devaluation of the local currency, a step that increases the strength of foreign investment funds in the local economy.

All of these conditions serve the interests of foreign corporations and their entry and operation in the borrowing country. The loan policies of the international banks have been designed not merely for financial profit through interest payments but for maximizing the takeover and control of whole sectors of the economies of developing countries.

The Philippine experience with IMF-World Bank lending policies began in 1958 when the finance minister under President Garcia, Miguel Cuaderno, journeyed to Washington to seek a loan from those agencies. They demanded one overriding condition: decontrol. Cuaderno proposed modified controls and a gradual decontrol but these were rejected: no absolute decontrol, no loan. Garcia's refusal added to his black marks in U.S. imperialist books. President Macapagal, elected three years later with commitments to his U.S. backers, at once abolished economic controls and was promptly awarded a $300 million loan from U.S. commercial banks which acted on the approval of the IMF and World Bank with which Macapagal had consulted.

This first major loan was refered to as a "stabilization loan" with the aim of offsetting the balance of payments deficit, but its chief purpose was to finance the remittance of the profits that had been accumulated in the Philippines by U.S. companies during the operation of exchange controls, a remittance that would otherwise have gravely affected the balance of payments position at the time. Stabilization loans henceforth have made up about one-fifth of the huge Philippine subsequent borrowing. It is a bizarre process in which the import duties that the Philippines cannot collect because of having to agree to the IMF's condition of import liberalization are made up by stabilization loans on which the Philippines has to pay interest as well as repaying the loans — and is thereby the overall loser.

The 1962 decontrol marked the disastrous watershed from which the Philippines descended with an ever greater rush into uncontrollable debt. An external debt of a mere $205 million in the 1950s had risen to $590.2 million by the end of 1965 when Macapagal left office.[25] President Marcos was elected in that year with U.S. backing largely because of his pledge to continue the decontrol process, and the rate at which dollars flowed out of the country through profit remittance, and an unrestrained import policy, led to accelerated borrowing. By 1969 the external debt had jumped to $1,911.7 million. In order to be re-elected in that year, President Marcos engaged in such a massive vote-buying spending spree that both the economy and the peso were undermined. This was the perfect setting for the IMF-World Bank to put further pressure on Marcos to subordinate his administration to imperialist plans for the Philippines. He was compelled, by an IMF-World Bank threat to withhold further loans, to devalue the peso in 1970 by nearly one-half, from an already devalued P3.90 to the dollar to P6.50 to the dollar. Further loans were then granted, boosting the external debt to $2,137.2 million.[26]

By the time the Marcos regime, extended by martial law to a 20-year rule, was overthrown early in 1986, the Philippine foreign debt had climbed to $28.6 billion. Of this, $21.52 billion was public sector or government-incrued debt, and $7.14 billion was from private sector borrowing. The borrowing had been done from 483 commercial banks in various countries, principally the U.S., as well as from the IMF and World Bank.[27] By the 1980s the interest paid out on foreign loans vastly exceeded the inflow of funds of all types: in 1989 the interest payments were $2.5 billion, or 40 per cent of export earnings.[28]

It needs to be pointed out that the increasing Philippine resort to borrowing was influenced by numerous factors that forced the Marcos regime unwillingly deeper into the debt hole. Prominent among these were the 1973-74 and 1979-80 increases in the world price of oil, which plunged the Philippine trade balance into steep deficit. (The first crisis sent the price of a barrel of oil from $2 to $10, the second saw the price soar to $20, then $30, then $40. It is estimated that the external debt of non-oil producing countries like the Philippines rose by an extra $260 billion from 1974 to 1982 as a consequence.) Another adverse factor was the precipitous drop in the world price of Philippine raw material exports during the 1970s and the shrinking of markets for them due to the economic recession in the developed capitalist countries. (The huge Philippine trade losses caused mounting trade deficits which reached $3.7 billion in 1982.) On top of these factors, an escalation of world interest rates from 1979-80 brought a further shock. (Developing countries in general had to pay out an additional total of $41 billion in 1981–82 alone. For the Philippine economy the doubling of interest rates between 1971 and 1984 while large scale borrowing occurred was highly damaging: each 1 per cent rise was adding $250 million to annual interest payments by the end of that period.) All of these factors were related to the total dependency of the Philippine economy on the outside dictates of foreign investments and loans.[29]

As the debt grew, stimulating further quest for loans, the Philippines became increasingly at the mercy of the Consultative Group of Creditors chaired by the World Bank, which laid down stricter terms with each round of borrowing. Demands for "structural adjustment" of the Philippine economy, for ever-greater concessions for foreign investors, for wage restraints and no-strike measures, and even for extending the agreement for U.S. military bases were conceded not only by President Marcos but by the succeeding Aquino regime. These demands were primarily pressed for by the U.S., which had dominated the international lending agencies and their policies, and were designed to impose new neocolonial structures desired by the U.S. TNCs. A Filipino analyst pointed to the reality of his country's situation:

> By all counts, the Philippine government has for some time now been broke. For, even by the standards set by the IMF before it allowed our country the use of the extended fund facility, the Philippine economy was shown to be suffering serious balance of payments problems and was in disarray. It cannot be argued that it is because the Philippines is considered a reliable debtor by its foreign creditors, that is why it could borrow so much from the latter. Although, according to the IMF's criteria, our economy is disoriented, the Fund and the Bank judge that the over-all advantage the U.S. economy would derive from the conditions accepted by the Philippines, before being granted loans, outweighs the risks involved in extending credits to the Marcos administration.[30]

A relentless chaining of the Filipino people into a helpless debt situation constituted part of a coldly planned process of reorganizing and reorienting the Philippine economy to suit the needs and global operations of U.S. big corporations. From the 1960s onward the structure was put in place stage by stage, starting with the acceptance by the Philippines of the principle of relying on loans instead of nationalistic economic controls. This enabled maximum U.S. pressure to be exerted for the expansion of rights and privileges for foreign investors.

The ease with which the Philippines could be molded to U.S. imperialist wishes reflected more the subservient character of the

Filipino elite than it did the irresistible power of U.S. interests. In the decade of the 1960s the U.S. began to come under severe strains and difficulties that weakened its once all-powerful position internationally. The Vietnam war in particular eroded U.S. strength, starting the decline into deficits and debt that became acute in the 1970s and 1980s. Growth of rival capitalist powers in Western Europe and Japan threatened the U.S. eminence in world trade and necessitated cost-cutting to maintain a competitive position. In every way, from the shift to loan capital as less risky than private investment, to the steps toward cheaper labor-intensive production wherever possible, the U.S. sought to maintain profit rates and power by intensifying the exploitation of developing countries.

The large-scale resort to the use of Filipino capital for investment and operation by U.S. corporations and banks was directly linked to this policy. In 1967 the U.S. Bankers Trust Co. was instrumental in setting up a major financial agency in the Philippines, the Bancom Development Corporation, the main purpose of which was to bring the Philippine banking system into line to serve the U.S. need. It disclosed in 1968 that "local affiliates of U.S. companies are being directed to increase their local borrowings to improve the American balance of payments position," i.e., by employing local capital and remitting the profits from such borrowing to the U.S.[31]

A great influx of foreign banks and their affiliates occurred in pursuit of this policy. Within a decade there were in the Philippines four branches of major foreign banks, 11 foreign banks operating as offshore units, 18 representative offices and 10 regional headquarters of transnational banks, 25 foreign investors in investment houses, and five in finance companies—all active in soaking up the accumulated resources of Filipinos.[32] This was but one aspect of the process of taking over the Philippine banking system for foreign use. By the mid-1970s 29 per cent of the net worth of all private domestic commercial banks in the country was owned by foreign banks. In March 1982, 21 foreign banks had equity investments amounting to $283.72 million (P1.8 billion) in 21 Filipino commercial banks, investment houses and finance companies, the equity reaching 40 per cent in a number of cases. The top ten U.S. banks (Citibank, Bank of America, Chase Manhattan, Manufacturers Hanover Trust, J.P. Morgan, Continental Illinois, Chemical Bank, First National Bank of Chicago, Security Pacific Bank, and Bankers Trust) were involved in this drive.[33] The offshore banking units were particularly active, boosting their total assets from $1.19 billion in 1978 to $4.8 billion in 1982.[34]

Coincident with this, a key step in the evolvement of the new order was the creation of a body of Filipino technocrats for staffing the top-level economic departments and agencies of the Philippine government. These were economists and financial advisers trained in the U.S. or U.S.-controlled institutions, recipients of special scholarships, grants and study programs, completely committed to U.S. policy aims. Above all, this special group of collaborators have been the chief implementing agents of the World Bank and its terms. The Department of Finance, the National Economic Council, the Board of Investments, the Central Bank and its Monetary Board, the Philippine National Bank and virtually all departments having to do with trade, industry, investment, natural resources and education (particularly economic and business training) came under the direction of the technocrats.

The technocrats comprise a special form of elite collaboration with imperialism. Among them have been: Cesar Virata, a former chairman of the Development Committee of the World Bank, who served as Finance Minister and eventually Prime Minister in the Marcos regime; Gerardo Sikat, chairman of the National Economic Council, who obtained his study grants from the Rockefeller Foundation; Vicente Paterno, head of the Board of Investments; Placido Mapa, Jr., former World Bank Director for Latin America, who became director general of the National Economic and Development Authority and then president of the Philippine National Bank; Jaime C. Laya, Central Bank governor and Minister of Education, and Ruben Ancheta, Bureau of Internal Revenue commissioner, both of whom held office in the World Bank. These are but a few of the array of such technocrats who have been regularly added to by the U.S.-World Bank training channels.[35]

It became only gradually apparent that a major design was being perfected and implemented to harness the Philippine economy more fully to new U.S. imperialist interests (and to merely a lesser degree to the interests of the other capitalist powers) than it had ever been during the colonial period. Above all, the aim was to make the Philippines a subordinate part of the global division of labor, devised to minimize production costs and maximize profits for the TNCs.

Whereas in the former colonial relationship, and in the "aid" programs of the 1950s, the U.S. had discouraged and prevented industrialization in the Philippines, the neocolonial policies now implemented were for intensive industrialization. It was, however, of a distorted kind, serving not the social, consumption, employment and other needs of the Filipino people but the sourcing and trading needs of the giant TNCs. The Philippines was turned into a subcontracting branch of the internationalized transnational production chain, where the manufacture of parts, components and process materials for the transnationals was carried on with cheap labor. For such an economy no basic industry was required and no foreign loans or investment were permitted for it.

To bring about the full mobilization of Philippine capital and material resources, as desired by the TNCs, a transformation of many features of the economy was considered essential. In the jargon of the international lending agencies, "structural adjustments" were necessary. U.S. policy-makers were in the forefront of this but it was carried out with remarkable thrust and efficiency by the World Bank, employing coercive loan tactics, threats, demands and the all-pervading opportunity for corruption wherever large sums of money are involved.

A prime feature of the adjustment was the breaking-up of the still strong feudal remnants that had impeded the free mobility of Philippine capital as well as the extension of capitalist production to agriculture. However, the main demand of the World Bank was for a shift in manufacturing from import substitution (which had prevailed in the economic control years and had helped to produce a Filipino nationalist industrial sector) to export industries. The industrialization under World Bank direction has been heavily export-oriented, to suit the requirements of the transnational companies. It has gone hand in hand with import liberalization, which also benefits the transnationals. In the process many Filipino businesses producing for internal consumption have been swamped by imports and either bankrupted or forced into the joint venture control of large foreign firms oriented to exporting.

In the course of the transformation it was asserted that economic development long claimed as the aim of successive Philippine governments was being achieved. It was possible to point to the growth of the gross national product and of per capita income, of higher figures in trade and other areas. However, the salient aspect of the export orientation that became the dominant feature of the Philippine economy was that it was *not* designed for the consumption, use or improvement of life for the Filipino people, nor did the profits from it which contributed to the national income flow *to* them. It was one more giant scheme to drain the wealth out of the country.

During the 1970s and 1980s the Philippines certainly was the recipient of a massive injection of investment and loan capital. The structural adjustments contemplated required great capital resources. From the World Bank alone came $205 million in 1974–78 for an Industrial Investment Credit Program, $55 million in 1975–79 for a Medium Industries Investment Program, $60 million in 1975–78 for a

Corporate Development Program. These were apart from very large infrastructure loans.[36]

Virtually all of the industrial loans went for small and medium industries designed for subcontracting work to serve the TNCs, for the manufacture, processing or sub-assembly of parts, components or intermediate products for machineries, appliances, electrical or electronic equipment. All of this was intended for foreign sales of local procurement by foreign transnationals.

General Motors subcontracted production of parts for its diesel engines, and nearly 1,000 parts and sub-assemblies for home appliances and electrical goods. Kodak set up a subsidiary for components and accessories for cameras. The Philippine textile industry, food industry, iron and steel, pulp and paper, wood, ceramics and glass, electric and electronics, leather products and others were all oriented to export production, Japanese firms proliferated in these fields, and the West German Siemans established numerous sub-contract projects.[37]

Benefit to the Philippine economy from export orientation may have been generated if Philippine materials and inputs for such production had been used, but this was very limited. The lending agencies and the transnationals demanded, and got, the reduction of tariff rates on the importation of materials needed for export industries. Of the items on the tariff reduction lists adopted under the Marcos regime, 75 to 78 per cent were of this type. They came mostly from the U.S. and U.S.-controlled sources and thus constituted an additional form of profit in the scheme of things. The World Bank had promoted the shift to an export economy as supposedly designed to help solve the Philippines' perpetual balance of payments deficits. Instead the import bill for raw materials and intermediate goods needed in the export program constantly grew, soaring from $1.3 billion in 1976 to $2.3 billion in 1979.[38]

One of the best examples of the transnational division of labor has been the Progressive Car Manufacturing Program set up during the Marcos period for the big Japanese and U.S. car companies. Called a complementation program, it was devised as a regional operation, spread around South East Asia. The Philippines produced body panels, transmissions and rear axles; Malaysia made spokes, nipples, timing chains, seat belts, crown wheels, pinions; Singapore turned out universal joints, V-belts and oil seals; Indonesia did diesel engines; Thailand produced body panels and shock absorbers. Numerous subcontracts were farmed out in each country for these components.[39] In the Philippines the Ford "Fiesta" program alone had 33 small subcontracting firms. A consolidated Parts Producers Association Inc. that was formed out of these and others complained that the arrangement "has always been a one-way street where part manufacturers are under the thumbs of car and truck makers who buy their products."[40]

A salient program of the Marcos government set up under IMF-World Bank direction in the 1980s has been the establishment of Export Processing Zones, actually free-trade zones, which have been the chief centers of the export economy. Twelve such zones were projected, the first three set up with World Bank financing in the early 1980s, in Bataan, Mactan and Baguio. The World Bank surveyed and approved further sites in Davao, Iloilo, Zamboanga, Bohol, Tacloban, Legaspi, Angeles and Cavite.[41]

EPZs are huge industrial estates specially constructed with the necessary physical plant and facilities. The manufacturing plants located there are solely for export. They are free of taxes and duties, enjoy special financial incentives, and are labor-intensive with cheap labor. A brochure put out by the Bataan EPZ to attract further foreign industries had this description: "Asia's most modern maximum efficiency industrial estate which charges the lowest utility rate in the world. Strategically located, the zone has an abundant supply of trained and English-speaking manpower at a minimum wage of US$.15 an hour, the cheapest in Asia."[42] Importing the bulk of their raw materials and sub-assembly items and exporting the product, the EPZs contributed virtually nothing to the growth of the national economy; they are a part of the international economic system of the transnational companies.

World Bank programs for redirecting the Philippines to an export economy were not confined to the financing of export industries and their subcontracting network. The greater loans in the 1970s went to infrastructure building—roads, bridges, ports, airfields, dams, hydroelectric projects and electrification systems. Such construction is of course a necessary part of the development of any national economy, but the planning, locating and concentration of infrastructure programs in the Philippines, mapped out under World Bank supervision, have been to suit the requirements of the export orientation: transport systems are along the export routes to improved ports; electric power is fed into the EPZs and other transnational industry sites.[43]

While the main thrust of the neocolonial development has been to make the Philippines a subsidiary supplier of the world capitalist economy dominated by the TNCs, at the same time the TNCs rule the internal market. Virtually everything manufactured that is purchased by the Filipino consumer is produced in local industries that are subsidiaries—owned either 100 per cent or through controlling equity —of U.S., Japanese or European TNCs.

Soaps, toothpaste, shampoos, margarine, cooking oils, tissues, toilet paper, milk, coffee, chocolate, soft drinks, beer, almost all drugs, transport vehicles, rubber tires, rubber products in general, electrical appliances, most oil and gasoline, processed foods like soup, mayonnaise, peanut butter, jellies, condiments, corn oil, processed meat, electric lamps, bathroom fixtures—the list is endless—and the manufacturers read like a rollcall of the everyday brand names known to Americans.[44]

A number of these companies had subsidiaries in the Philippines pre-dating the intensification of neocolonial policy from the 1960s, but the major influx of the TNCs came after the organization of the local banking system to service borrowing by foreign corporations, after investment laws were in place to enable equity participation and control of Filipino firms, and after the IMF-World Bank lending net had well-entrapped the Philippines and could impose virtually any conditions. Much of the groundwork for this had been laid by the Marcos government in the latter 1960s, when the TNCs began to arrive in quantity, but the real influx came in the 1970s under the highly favorable climate of martial law.

Shortly after the September 21, 1972 declaration of martial law by Marcos, he made a pledge to foreign investors: "We're interested in all forms of foreign capital and . . . we will offer as much incentive as possible. Foreign capital will be protected. There will be no confiscation while I am President. Such things as amortization of investment, retirement of capital, and transmittal of profits are guaranteed."[45] Banning of strikes, compulsory labor dispute arbitration, streamlining of government machinery to aid foreign business, removal of nationality limitations in most areas of investment, unimpeded profit remittal and capital repatriation were among the martial law policies. TNCs were encouraged to set up their regional headquarters in the Philippines along with regional warehouses.

The maximum wide-open exploitation of the economy was most evident in the Marcos steps to deliver the Philippine finance system to the TNCs, which was one of the principal structural adjustments advocated by the IMF-World Bank. A host of small Filipino banks, rural banks, savings banks and private development banks had been established since the 1950s—there were over 1500 small rural banks alone—and a series of Marcos decrees forced these into merger. Local banks were required to raise their capital to P100 million, which could only be done by merging with one or several others, or, more often, by accepting equity participation from large banks, which inevitably meant foreign banks. Presidential decrees did away with existing limitations on foreign bank operations. PD 113 allowed foreign investment in savings banks, PD 114 extended foreign participation not only to other small banks but even to pawnshops. PD 129 permitted foreign equity in investment houses. The most serious decree, most damaging to the Philippine financial system, was PD 1034 in 1976, which permitted foreign offshore banking units (OBUs) to operate in the country; it gave extremely generous concessions to the OBUs, requiring a mere 5 per cent payment on both offshore and onshore earnings, and even that was abolished by PD 1773 in 1981.[46]

In the concentration of the Philippine financial system for the benefit of U.S. and other foreign interests, the crowning step was Philippine Central Bank Circular 739 that provided for the establishment of "unibanks," very large banking units created out of the merger of commercial bank and investment operations. The unibank requirement was for a minimum capital of P500 million, which was possible for very few Filipino banks. A 1985 Filipino study made this assessment:

> Another focus of the structural adjustment program is the promotion of unibanking in the domestic financial system, which envisions the eventual phasing out of small banks such as rural banks, thrift banks, savings banks and small development banks in favor of a few, big commercial banks which can engage in practically all areas of banking, industry and agriculture. The debt crisis and the general climate of economic uncertainty it engendered intensified the crisis of the small banks. According to official figures, less than five per cent of the more than 1,100 rural banks are still viable. On the other hand, the big unibanks, including the Philippine branches of foreign banks, are beneficiaries of the massive transfer of funds by nervous Filipino depositors. Thus, indirectly, the debt crisis is hastening the full realization of the unibanking system, which will see only ten or so unibanks, with the predictable foreign tie-ups, lording it over the entire financial system.[47]

Such concentration of banking and of bank capital and deposits, together with the very wide lattitude of activity permitted to foreign banks, had the obvious purpose, under IMF-World Bank direction, of enabling the placing of large local funds at the disposal of big foreign corporations, for borrowing. As early as 1976, before the unibanking system was introduced, U.S. corporations were scooping huge sums of borrowed capital from the local sources: Caltex, P702.6 million; General Motors, P200 million; International Harvester McLeod, P200 million; Philippine Packing Corporation, P100 million. Heaviest of the borrowers were the U.S. banks and finance companies: First National City Bank of New York, P2.5 billion of short-term capital; FNCB

Finance, P800 million; Bank of America Finance Corporation, P500 million.[48]

Transnational companies have flocked to this highly favorable climate of abundant credit and ever-expanding investment incentives. In 1972, prior to the Marcos martial law declaration, there were 66 TNCs operating in the Philippines. Within two years, in 1974, there were 93, all of them standing at the upper level of the country's top 1,000 corporations. At that time they had total sales of P11.5 billion a year, which exceeded the total income from taxation of the Philippine government in the same year (P10 billion).[49]

By 1990 the number of TNCs in the Philippines stood at 215. Of these, 147 were U.S. corporations with a global structure. A survey of slightly over half of them revealed combined assets of P154 billion, and employment of 74,394 Filipinos.[50] Although the TNCs of other countries had moved in during the Marcos years, particularly the Japanese, U.S. economic control was greatest by far.[51]

That control is well illustrated in the case of the drug industry. In 1980 an array of 23 big foreign companies including 14 TNCs controlled 70 per cent of the local market for drugs and 82 per cent of the combined net income of the industry, or P171.7 million.[52] In truth, it could hardly be called a Philippine drug industry: very few local materials are used in the production process, and 95 per cent of the raw materials are imported. Furthermore, the drug TNCs hold 90 per cent of the patents on drugs and prevent Filipinos from manufacturing and selling them.[53]

In 1978 the Marcos administration, in one of its few confrontations with the TNCs, introduced amendments to the Philippine Patent Law (Presidential Decree 1263), to guarantee the transfer of technology on drug manufacture, to prevent transfer pricing done through importing raw materials from the parent firm at excessive prices and passing them on to the Filipino consumer, and to sell drugs under their generic names instead of the brand names which enable the enormously inflated pricing of drugs. The TNCs applied great pressure against the Patent Law amendments by getting their governments to protest against them. The U.S. State Department expressed "indignation," the Japanese and West German governments dispatched notes of "concern." Marcos withdrew the amendments, and the drug industry remained TNC-controlled as before.[54]

The inordinate extent of importation of raw materials and other inputs that occurs in the drug industry is a part of the pattern affecting almost all industry in the Philippines, and most perniciously in the dominant export-oriented sector. Imported materials account for over 75 per cent of the export value of semiconductor devices, one of the principal exports, and for more than 50 per cent of garments, which is another.

It is for TNC global operation, farming out or subcontracting of components to be produced by cheap labor and exported along the international assembly-line to world markets, that the IMF-World Bank policies have shaped the Philippine economy. "Export oriented industrialization," has said a Filipino analyst, "has meant the transformation of the Philippines into the sweatshop of the global assembly-line of the TNCs."[55] That orientation is not merely found in the numerous small industrial plants in and around Manila and other major cities, in the Export Processing Zones, and in rural cottage industries. It has also penetrated and changed considerably the character of agriculture.

By the early years of Philippine independence U.S. policy-makers had begun a change of attitude toward the agrarian situation. Land reform, which had never been seriously undertaken by the U.S. colonial regime because the Filipino landowning class was a bulwark of U.S. rule, was seen in a different light when the mainly poor peasant-based HMB became a major threat and when new forms of investment by U.S. interests were contemplated. The Bell Mission Report in 1950 had acknowledged the depressing effect of a semi-feudal agrarian system on agricultural production and had recommended "a larger share of the crop to those who till the soil, to open to them the hope of owning their own land."[56]

In 1952 the U.S. Mutual Security Agency, in charge of implementing the Bell Mission recommendations, subsidized publication of two significant studies: *The Rural Philippines,* a sharp criticism of worsening tenancy conditions by a Filipino-American team, Generoso F. Rivera and Robert T. McMillan, and *Philippine Land Tenure Reform: Analysis and Recommendations,* by Robert S. Hardie, a wholesale condemnation of the tenancy system and an argument for its abolition.

The Hardie report was of particular importance. It had the pronounced aim of a capitalist agriculture in the Philippines and of shaking capital loose from the land to be available for investment in industry. Written at the height of the HMB's armed struggle, it said:

> The bulk of Philippine wealth is concentrated in the hands of a few and invested in land. This group enjoys an adequate and stable income (excepting only the possibility of political upheaval). So long as rentier wealth is invested in land, it is thus denied to needs attending the development of Philippine industry. In this regard, existing potentials for investible funds of industry diminish as rentier wealth, apprehensive of the political chaos which derives from the tenure system itself, is moved out of the Philippines [57]

A storm of opposition struck the Hardie report when it was released. President Quirino called it an "MSA attack" on his administration, a part of the build-up for Magsaysay in the 1953 election. The main resistance, however, came from the landlord groups (whose congressional representatives had even held up approval of the emergency Bell Mission Report for six months because of its recommendations on land redistribution). As a perceptive writer on U.S. policy in the Philippines later commented: "In the Philippines, the officials of the United States were recommending that the Filipino elite, holding political and economic power based on land ownership, should undermine its own economic, social and political position."[58]

In the Philippine Congress, the U.S.-aping House Committee on Un-Filipino Activities, chaired by Rep. Tito V. Tizon, produced in January 1953 a lengthy assault on the Hardie Report, calling it "Marxist" and asserting that "the continued existence of the land tenure system in the Philippines—with all its defects which nevertheless can be corrected or whose deleterious effects can be assuaged by constitutional means—will weaken the growth and will frustrate the program of Communism here and thus strengthen the position of the United States as an ally of the Philippines."[59]

What Tizon was really saying was that Filipino semi-feudal landlords and U.S. imperialism were allies and that the U.S. should stand with its allies against the Communist threat. U.S. policy-makers took heed and withdrew the Hardie report. The land reform measures of the Magsaysay administration that followed also changed nothing; they were allowed to be riddled with amendments and loopholes by landlord interests. Succeeding administrations to the present time did not go further than scratching at the surface of the land question.

However, for U.S. imperialism the development of capitalist relations in and around agriculture in the Philippines became an increasing concern. It was achieved not through a frontal assault on the feudalist system or through any comprehensive redistribution of land ownership. Capitalism, in effect, infiltrated the countryside in a variety of ways, through development of the market, rural banking, the modernization of farming methods, promotion of leasehold in place of sharecropping tenancy, and the development of agro-industry.

It was the administration of President Ferdinand Marcos, using martial law as the means for hastening capitalist development, that made the greatest strides in that process. His suspension of Congress and resort to decrees to implement policy removed the factor of landlord sabotage of law-making. An actual transformation of tenancy, however, proved illusory. Marcos' Presidential Decree No. 2 proclaimed the entire country a land reform area, the reform itself supposedly encompassing 1,422,988 hectares and affecting 914,914 tenants, of whom 393,778 could conceivably gain land transfer on 759,015 hectares while 521,136 could get lease-hold on 663,973 hectares. However, only a tiny percentage of tenants ever finally obtained land titles of ownership or leasehold status from the Marcos reform; land values were set high for purchasers, the amortization period was too short, the procedures complicated; in a high proportion of the cases initiated the land reverted by default to the original owner or to another, the new corporate landowners. This phase of reform of agriculture under Marcos left the landowning class still largely intact, but its character was changed by other aspects of reform.

Capitalism in Philippine agriculture developed in this period not so much from serious reform in land ownership or agrarian relations but from penetration of the rural aras by the TNCs. During the 1970s and 1980s large agribusinesses made their appearance. The way had been prepared for them by a series of careful steps from the early 1960s, when the International Rice Research Institute (IRRI) was established in the Philippines, at Los Banos, Laguna. It was financed by the Rockefeller and Ford Foundations and concentrated on developing high-yielding varieties of rice, the yield achieved through the massive use of chemical fertilizers, together with pesticides, irrigation (both pumping systems and reservoirs requiring dams), and farm machinery. A propagandist of the project wrote:

> Fertilizer is only one item in the package of new inputs which farmers need in order to realize the full potential of the new seeds. Once it becomes profitable to use modern technology, the demand for all kinds of farm inputs increases rapidly. And only agribusinesses can supply these inputs efficiently. This means that the multinational corporation has a vested interest in the agricultural revolution along with the poor countries themselves.[60]

The IRRI was the spearhead of the Green Revolution that was hailed as bringing an agricultural or food revolution to Third World countries. In actuality, the Green Revolution was designed to serve the international market drive of big TNCs. Among the financial backers of IRRI, besides the Ford and Rockefeller Foundations, were: American Cyanimid Company, Monsanto, Chevron Chemicals, Stauffer Chemical Company, Cyanimid Far East Limited, Potash Institute of North America, International Potash Institute, World Phosphate Rock Institute, Shell Chemicals Company, Hoechst Company, Montedison, FMC International SA, International Minerals and Chemicals Corporation,

CIBA-Geigy, and Boots Company. These are all manufacturers of fertilizers.

Pesticides are a major complementary item of the Green Revolution. A large number of Philippine TNC subsidiaries sprang up to import, blend, package and distribute for: Agchem Manufacturing Corporation, BASF (Phil.) Inc., Bayer Philippines Inc., Chevron Chemicals International Inc., CIBA-Geigy Agrochemicals, Cyanimid Philippines Inc., Dow Chemicals Pacific Ltd., Du Pont Far East Inc., Eli Lilly Philippines Inc., Hoechst Philippines Inc., Interchem Philippines Corp., Marsman & Co. Inc., Monsanto Philippines, Pesticides Producers Industrial Co. Inc., Planters Products Inc., Rhone-Poulenc Philippines Inc., Rohm and Haas Philippines Inc., Shell Chemicals Co. (Phil.) Inc., Transworld Trading Co. Inc., Union Carbide Philippines Inc., Velsicol Chemical Corporation, Warner Barnes & Co. Inc., Zuellig Agrochemicals.[61]

A Filipino inventor of a pesticide, Gonzalo Catan, Jr. and his Manila Pest Control Co. tried to enter the agricultural pesticide market only to discover that the governmental Fertilizer and Pesticide Authority was completely under the thumbs of the TNCs and barred Filipino manufacturers from the market. The Catan bid was rejected.[62]

Along with fertilizers and pesticides, an expanding market for TNC farm machinery was developed, essential for cultivating the new high-yielding grains. Previously farm machinery was limited to export crops like sugar or pineapples. Although the average rice farmer—smallholder or tenant—had an improved income initially from the higher yield of the new rice, the ascending cost of the "farm inputs" that accompanied its production soon swallowed incomes and led to debts, with the larger landowners the chief beneficiaries.

In fact, the landlords in a great many cases became the agents or partners of the TNCs. By the early 1970s up to 2,700 dealers in fertilizers, other chemicals, and farm machinery had appeared in the rural areas, with innumerable landlords acting simultaneously as capitalist entrepreneurs.

The development in the Philippines of a capitalist agriculture was intensified by a series of decrees by President Marcos. His General Order No. 47, issued on May 27, 1974 provided that big corporations employing 500 or more people should supply the rice and other cereal needs of their workers by engaging in cereal production. They were encouraged to acquire land for the purpose and to set up corporate farms.[63] By December 1978 a total of 242 companies were engaged in the subsidiary production of rice, corn and other grains on an area of 36,000 hectares, employing modern mechanized methods, including aerial seeding.[64]

More far-reaching was the Marcos 1977 Presidential Decree 1159, the Agribusiness Incentives Act, which gave broad incentives to foreign firms to enter export-oriented food-growing and industrial crop-growing. The biggest U.S. TNC agribusinesses moved in: United Fruit (now United Brands), Del Monte, Dole, Castle & Cook, Hershey Foods (cocoa), Firestone, Goodyear and Goodrich (rubber). The British-Dutch Unilever (coconut products) and the Japanese Sumitomo and Fuji (bananas for export to Japan) were among others. Dole and Del Monte, which today dominate the Philippine pineapple industry from planting to canning to marketing, shifted to the Philippines from Hawaii. A document published in the U.S. Congressional Record (Senate) of November 9, 1973 gave the reason:

> The main concern that Del Monte and other corporations are abandoning their Hawaii production is the cheap cost of labor elsewhere. While Hawaiian plantation workers earn $2.64 per hour, Del Monte pays its Philippine workers 15 cents an hour. Hawaiian cannery workers get paid $2.69 an hour compared to the 20 cents Del Monte pays Philippine workers for the same job. Even if all other costs of production remain the same in the Philippines, Del Monte saves 47 per cent in canning pineapple there rather than in the United States.[65]

These sectors of agribusiness account for a large proportion of Philippine exports but they are not the most ambitious of the TNC schemes. The Agribusiness Incentives Act was aimed particularly at developing an export-oriented meat-processing industry. The dimensions of this were indicated by the acquisition in 1975 by the big U.S. King Ranch of a 40,000 hectare [100,000 acres] ranch on Palawan Island. Intended for cattle raising, this is only the largest of around 100 modern ranches with areas of 10,000 to 15,000 hectares and 500 to 10,000 head of cattle that have been set up since the 1970s. Most of these have a Filipino front but are controlled by the U.S. meat-processing companies. Swift, Armour and Hunts Wesson Foods, Purefoods, Hormel and others are among them. Armour, for example, is behind the Philippine Integrated Meat Corporation (PIMECO) which set up the largest and most modern meat canning and processing firm in South East Asia in 1975; it exports corned beef, luncheon meat, chopped ham, Vienna sausage, liver spread, potted meat, hotdogs, ham and numerous other items to Japan, Hong Kong and as far as Europe.[66]

Large ranches are not the only cattle-raising enterprises. The World Bank, considering meat production a significant profitable sector of the TNC export operations, financed a government program channeled through rural banks and the Development Bank of the Philippines for "backyard cattle-fattening" in which small farmers are enabled to obtain loans for the purchase and fattening of a few head of cattle which are sold to the meat-processing companies. They produce low-quality meat suitable for the proliferated hamburger trade spread by the big U.S. food monopolies into the Third World countries, while the high-quality meat from the well-capitalized ranches goes to the tables of the better-off in the U.S. and other developed countries.

Part of the Green Revolution has been devoted to the production of feedgrains to service the cattle/meat industry. According to President Marcos' minister of agriculture, Arturo Tanco, the greater production of rice per hectare due to the higher yielding IRRI varieties would enable hectarage of rice to be cut to two million hectares from the existing three million by the year 2000, with the one million freed hectares to be devoted mainly to feedgrains for raising meat: sorghum, yellow corn and soybeans. Tanco grandiosely forecast that the Philippines would become "the food bowl of Asia" by that time. What this means is that the giant U.S. agribusiness food corporations would be exporting fresh or processed foods from the Philippines for their international markets. The food is not produced for consumption by the Filipino people, the vast majority of whom cannot afford to sup from "the food bowl."[67]

How the Filipino peasant producer relates to this process of capitalism in agriculture has been described by a leading Filipino social scientist:

> Through various forms of mediations, including feudal personal relations, a Filipino farmer who fattens a head of cattle in his backyard or raises beef cattle on the coconut plantation of his landlord, or cultivates sorghum for feedgrain export on cash-rent basis, becomes merely an incident of a larger decision initiated by big corporations. The changes in the material basis of his life are determined by the operations of capital even as he continues to see his immediate exploiter in the image of a feudal landlord; "the subordination of his labor to capital is covered up by thousands of the remnants of medieval relations, which prevent the producer from seeing the essence of the matter." The reality is that the character of a major part of the peasant's earnings is now controlled by forces brought into motion by the investment of capital, and he is compelled to work for the market. It is the nature of capital, acting on outmoded relations to take hold of production on the old basis, "creating a dependence that, however differently it expresses itself (whether in the forms of usury capital or of the capital of the buyer-up, who monopolizes marketing), always leads to an enormous part of the product of labor falling into the hands of the owner of money and not of the producer. Hence, it is purely capitalist in essence."[68]

THE NATIONAL DEVELOPMENT OF POVERTY

To the Philippine nation in general, the wholesale reorganization of the economy that was carried out from the 1960s to the 1990s, and the huge amount of investment and borrowing indulged in in that period, were presented as evidence of national development. For a time the Philippines was categorized in international surveys as having reached the ranks of the medium capitalist countries and the take-off stage for a more advanced status.

This was illusory. The weight of debt, the absence of fundamental basic industry in the neocolonial form of growth, and the tremendous drain of foreign-taken profits, dividends and loan interest brought economic and political crisis by the early 1980s, striking the Philippines from the list of allegedly promising developing countries. Nevertheless it has still been claimed that national development has been impressive, measured, that is, in figures of gross national product.

Such figures conceal an appalling record of exploitation and misery. The World Bank itself published a report in May 1988, *The Philippine Poor: What Is To Be Done?*, showing a grave worsening of the conditions of the Filipino people precisely in the years when the Bank's programs were mobilizing the economy for the benefit of foreign corporations. Said the report, surveying the previous three decades, the Philippines "is the only ASEAN country where the average living standard is declining and the number of people living in poverty is increasing." In the decade from 1975 to 1985 the incidence of poverty had risen from 46 per cent of the population to 52 per cent, and in that time 12 million additional people had become "absolutely poor."[69]

Filipino economists and researchers, basing themselves on Philippine statistical surveys, have indicated a grimmer picture than this, tracing an accelerating deterioration in living standards: 40 per cent of Filipino families in a state of impoverishment in 1965, 50 per cent in 1975 and 60 per cent in 1980.[70] In May 1984 the Manila newspaper *Business Day* published a survey showing that 70 per cent of families, roughly 40 million people, were living "below the total poverty threshhold" with their income insufficient to meet their needs for clothing and shelter. Among these, 51 per cent of families, or around 29 million people, were eating "below the food threshhold," that is, below "the minimum needed for nutrition or the barest minimum budget a family of six would need to maintain life and to maintain an individual for productive work." This was considered "the lowest level of absolute poverty."[71]

The World Bank declared that the minimum monthly subsistence income needed by an average family of six living on the poverty threshhold was P4,903.80 in 1985. At that time the average monthly salary of an urban worker family was P1,206 (25 per cent of the World Bank's minimum) and the average monthly rural family's income was P842 (22 per cent of the World Bank's minimum).[72] These figures do not show the actual worsening of conditions that was occurring because a steep fall in real wages had been taking place. Using 1978 as a base year, P1 could purchase the equivalent of only 28 centavos by 1985. The nominal average daily urban wage stood at P29.84 in 1980 but the real wage was P20.24; in 1984, although the nominal wage had been boosted to P57.08, the real wage had fallen to P16.88.[73]

As incomes of the working people declined, unemployment grew. In 1969, as export-oriented industrialization was being developed, unemployment was 1,067,000.[74] In 1985, with the TNC export economy in full career, the Philippine Ministry of Labor and Employment put the figure at around two million, while the National Census and Statistical Office arrived at three million. The "visibly underemployed" were counted at 3.4 million, in addition. Poverty and unemployment caused hundreds of thousands of Filipinos to flock abroad, particularly to contract labor in the Middle Eastern oil states or to menial jobs in Western Europe. By the 1980s between one and two million Filipinos had found it necessary out of desperation to leave home to seek work overseas; this included the brain drain that sent over half of Filipino doctors and 88 per cent of trained nurses to obtain decently paying jobs in other countries.[75] In the export-oriented Philippine economy the export of labor had become one of the major items. Overseas workers, in fact, were the biggest dollar earners, remitting home between $1 billion and $2 billion a year, although the bulk of this became channeled into the black market to no economic effect except the swelling of corruption.

The increasing mass poverty lay on one side of a gap that widened enormously in the society in the neocolonial decades. A 1965 report revealed that the top 20 per cent of the population was receiving 42 per cent of the national income, up from 30 per cent in 1948.[76] By 1987 the top 20 per cent had 53 per cent of the income, and the bottom 20 per cent only 5.7 per cent. The top 10 per cent were receiving 15 times more than the bottom 10 per cent.[77] The gross inequality that had steadily worsened during U.S. colonial rule became maximized under an independence still dominated by a U.S. imperialism that had an even more pervasive grip on the lives of Filipinos. That grip was maintained in collaboration with substantially the same elite few that had upheld the colonial system. In 1969 a mere 2.6 per cent of families, about 12,000, had incomes of P10,000 ($2,560) a year, and a tiny handful, an elite 400 families, had each P1 million or more.[78]

In 1988 the Asian Development Bank commissioned a study, conducted by Jardine Fleming Holdings Ltd. of Hong Kong and Russel & Co. of New York, on the feasibility of a capital market in the Philippines. It came to the conclusion that this would be extremely difficult because up to 80 per cent of the national wealth was controlled by a mere 2 per cent of the population, the rest having virtually no savings and unable to save.[79] The accumulation of capital that did occur came chiefly from the ruthless exploitation of the propertyless. Among the controlling 2 per cent, the 400 dominant families, most of whom had maintained their elite position uninterruptedly from the time of Spanish rule, with only a few additions as new entrepreneurs emerged, remained in top-level ties with U.S. and other foreign companies. In the interwoven equity and joint venture arrangements of the independence period was a present-day *comprador* system that was more entrenched than ever in Philippine society.

PICKING AND DISCARDING:
THE U.S. AND PHILIPPINE PRESIDENTS

During the imperialist process of shaping the Philippine economy into a subsidiary and subservient component of the global system of the transnational corporations a succession of Filipino presidents were elected and changed. Each has played a collaborating part in carrying out the programs of U.S. and other foreign interests, but the administrations of each have been affected by and have reflected the increasing tensions and conflicts in a Philippine society of warped and abnormal development. Included in each has been the growth of contradictions with U.S. policies that has made the question of collaboration more complex.

Although there have been changes in Philippine society in the nearly half century that has elapsed since independence was proclaimed, none have been decisive enough to alter its basic features. Many of the old landlord-*comprador* allies of the U.S. were absorbed into the agribusiness and new export activities of the TNCs, continuing in the new relationship to be a strong sector of collaboration among the Filipino people. Feudal landlordism, however, formerly one of the bulwarks of the colonial system, has been a diminishing social force under the impact of capitalist development thrusting into the Philippine countryside. The biggest landowners today are the agribusiness corporations and the corporate farmers. Former feudal landlords themselves pay wages to agricultural laborers instead of shares to tenants. Increasingly they are capitalist farmers, rural bankers, tractor renters, farm input dealers tied to foreign fertilizer and pesticide companies, handicraft manufacturers on a cottage industry basis, and exporters. As a collaborating force they remain strongly pro-imperialist.

One of the biggest Filipino agribusinesses is Planters Products Inc., which is a principal distributor of imported farm input on a national scale. It is headed, significantly, by Alfredo Montelibano, of the Negros sugar bloc, and typifies the shift of the agrarian elite into the capitalist mainstream.

The new wealth-creating industrial features of the economy have been woven into the collaborationist neocolonial structure. A multiplying of Filipino capitalist enterprises has gone on. In the Manila area alone, at the beginning of the 1990s, there were 56,000 registered businesses, ranging from the small shopkeeper to the large industrial plant employing over 1,000 workers. Big Filipino monopoly or conglomerate groups, among them the Ayala, Zobel, Elizalde, Lopez, Yulo and other interests, all part of the 400 family strata, particularly those of Spanish and Chinese origin, which had branched out from land and real estate ownership and expanded into many sectors of the economy. Invariably, these monopolies had a maze of interlocking connections with TNC and other foreign capitalists, in joint ventures, licensing of technological processes, or subcontracting arrangements. Many medium or small industrial enterprises had proliferated which all too frequently had a struggle to survive, against the import liberalization forced by the World Bank or against the constricting conditions of relying on TNCs for technology. Subject to foreign takeover, and to joint venture/equity control, Filipino industrialists have frequently had a precarious existence.

Even as a minority equity holder in a Filipino corporation, a transnational company invariably exerts a dominant influence, because its management skills are superior, it can bring in technical assistants that run the business to suit TNC wishes, it has the access to sources of raw materials, equipment, finances, or to markets.

The independent Filipino business that tries to avoid foreign control has a competitive disadvantage even in labor relations. Unable to match the marginally higher wages and somewhat better working conditions that the better-financed TNC subsidiaries may concede, it is more likely as a consequence to be involved in labor disputes and in strikes that can force a shoestring firm into bankruptcy.

About one-third of the Philippine foreign debt that was nearing $30 billion by the early 1990s is accounted for by the private sector, chiefly the larger Filipino manufacturing, mining and public utility companies. This has added a further major pressure on Filipino business interests to yield to foreign demands.

In general, the controls and influences that U.S. financial and manufacturing interests have been able to exert on Philippine industrial sectors have constituted a form of forced collaboration. Whether given willingly by the larger Filipino monopoly groups that have a traditional colonial background or given unwillingly by the more recent capitalist enterprises under a kind of economic duress, U.S. imperialism obtains today the collaboration of the Filipino elite it needs to extract the super-profits of neocolonialism.

However, the constraints and distortions imposed on Philippine society continually tended to produce nationalist protests and outbursts, acquiring sufficient strength to compel the political parties and leaders to give voice to them. Since the experience of Recto and the smothered Nationalist-Citizens Party, nationalist politicians and businessmen sought accommodation in the main political parties, so that movements developing outside the parties frequently found support from individual congressmen or government officials. The total puppet figure of a Ramon Magsaysay was never again attained by U.S. kingmakers as Philippine politics reflected the pressures building up under the frustrations and abnormal circumstances of a nation made to conform to foreign interests.

President Diosaldo Macapagal and his administration encountered the problem of contending with a renewed upsurge of nationalism in the 1960s while yielding to U.S. demands. Although Macapagal had given U.S. corporations and banks the decontrol they wanted and had adopted "liberalized" foreign investment measures that gave them fresh concessions, he then lost the trust of U.S. authorities by trying to present a Filipinist balance to his administration. He made nationalist-sounding speeches about "the uncompleted Philippine Revolution." He shifted Philippine Independence Day from the U.S.-bestowed July 4 to June 12, the date of the initial independence proclamation declared by the revolutionists in 1898, and ignored by the U.S. He unceremoniously cancelled a state visit to the U.S. in reaction to a U.S. Congress rejection of a Philippine war claims bill. He launched in 1962 together with President Sukarno of Indonesia and Prime Minister Tungku Abdul Rahman of Malaya a regional organization called Maphilindo which the Sukarno-hating U.S. opposed.

As a result, in the 1965 presidential election U.S. support was withdrawn from Macapagal and shifted to his opponent, Ferdinand Marcos, who in the classical opportunist pattern of neocolonial politics had shifted from Macapagal's Liberal Party to become the candidate of the opposition Nacionalista Party.

Macapagal, who had been a CIA informant earlier in his career and a recipient of $50,000 from the CIA station chief, Joseph B. Smith, in 1961 to aid his election as president,[80] was extremely bitter about his abandonment by the U.S. in 1965, telling a Manila editor on the eve of that election: *"If I should get re-elected, I would abrogate parity and even scuttle the [Military] Bases Agreement. I will give the Americans a dose of their own medicine!"*[81] He never had that chance. The U.S.-supported Marcos won.

U.S. interventionist tactics were somewhat more subtle in 1965 than in previous elections. Although Macapagal tried to win back the U.S. support that was obviously shifting away from him—by agreeing to send a Philippine Civic Action Group (an engineer battalion with security troops) to Vietnam to aid the U.S. invasion and by withholding implementation of a Retail Trade Nationalization Law recently passed by the Philippine Congress and objected to by U.S. companies,—U.S. disfavor was reflected in attacks on the Macapagal administration in the U.S.-controlled press and news services and in the drying-up of funds for the Macapagal election campaign from U.S. businesses and from Filipino sources with U.S. links. Marcos on the other hand was not a U.S. propaganda target, and his campaign organization had plenty of money, dispensing P400,000 a day to buy votes as polling day neared.[82] His connections with the Americans were blurred by his bid to win nationalist votes by pledging to withdraw Filipino troops from Vietnam but that mask was dropped as soon as the votes were in: within 24 hours he reversed that pledge, announcing his intention to keep the troops in Vietnam. As a U.S. analyst subsequently wrote: "This raised the possibility that American interests might have reached some kind of understanding with Marcos prior to the elections."[83]

Macapagal's bitterness over the intrigues that removed him was still deep in 1968, when he said in a speech:

> This mutual practice of Filipino presidents and presidential candidates on the one hand and American government authorities on the other must be reappraised. Indeed it must be stopped. American officials should lay off the Philippine presidential elections. They should maintain authentic neutrality in our presidential contests. Their acts, which tend to affect the campaign and its result, are not only improper in international relations but cause an injury to the welfare of the Filipino people who alone must make the choice of their president.[84]

During the initial U.S. honeymoon with President Marcos (whom U.S. President Lyndon Johnson in 1966 called "my right arm in Asia" because of the pro-U.S. Philippine policy on the Vietnam question) the new neocolonial prescriptions for the Philippines were set well under way, especially the IMF-World Bank loan policy and the process of foreign control and milking of the Philippine banking system. However, Marcos soon lost his luster for U.S. policy-makers when he began to show signs of wanting to strike a better bargain for collaboration, and to make independent arrangements for the Filipino bourgeois interests he represented. He began to object to the rapacity with which U.S. interests were literally decapitalizing the country, and he started to move away from the past subservience to U.S. foreign policy, taking preparatory steps toward trade and diplomatic relations with socialist countries and exhibiting an interest in ties with the non-aligned bloc of countries. By 1967 the tell-tale indications of U.S. dissatisfaction appeared in smear stories in U.S. press channels about corruption in the Marcos government and about its inability to maintain law and order (the latter charge related to the resurgence of left-wing movements in the latter 1960s.)

On January 29, 1969, in a speech to the Manila Rotary Club, Marcos made a sharp attack on the practice of U.S. companies of borrowing virtually all their investment and operating funds from local sources and of then making huge outward profit remittances to the U.S. Said Marcos, "their outward remittances should not be financed by domestic borrowings."[85] This pleased Filipino businessmen whose own borrowing was made difficult by the large-scale TNC use of Philippine banks but they were also disappointed by the Marcos failure to follow through with concrete implementing measures. The logical way of stopping the U.S. profit drain was to re-apply exchange controls but nothing like that was done. At the same time U.S. groupings which wanted total compliance from Filipino allies made it plain that they did not like the Marcos deviation.

U.S. annoyance was heightened later in the same year when the Philippine Congress adopted a Joint Resolution No. 2 (given the title "Magna Carta of Social Justice and Economic Freedom") which was a comprehensive policy document for genuine national development. It was maneuvered through the Congress by Speaker of the House of Representatives Jose B. Laurel, Jr. (son of the wartime president) and Senator Jose W. Diokno (earlier with the Democratic Alliance) who were both concerned with preventing a worsening economic condition and a threatened devaluation of the peso. The Resolution was a sweeping repudiation of the IMF-World Bank ideology and of freedoms granted to foreign investment. It called for restrictions on transnational company operations, for Filipinizing the economy including domestic credit, and for import and exchange controls. It went further, demanding the end of parity and pursuit of an independent foreign policy. On August 4, 1969 President Marcos signed the Resolution, giving it the status of a law.

In the election of November 1969, in another cynical shift, U.S. support went heavily to the opposition Liberal Party candidate, Sergio Osmena, Jr., who campaigned blatantly for even closer relations with the U.S. and for unrestricted entry and concessions to foreign investment. Marcos, pledging resistance to devaluation of the peso and to foreign dictates in general, won re-election. It was the first time a Philippine president had succeeded in doing so. By all appearances, the nature of his victory should have put him in a strong position to carry out the independent policies of Joint Resolution No. 2.

Marcos did not. He did completely the opposite, bowing to an IMF-World Bank call in February 1970 for the devaluation of the peso by allowing it to "float." The peso promptly sank from the existing rate of P3.90 to the dollar to P5.50 and subsequently to P7.50. As in the Macapagal 1962 devaluation, the result was a prostrating of Filipino industry and a huge benefit to foreign investment and imports. Utterly negated, Joint Resolution No. 2 vanished from the scene.

The 1969 election reached new depths of corruption. As the U.S. choice of candidate, Sergio Osmena, Jr. exemplified the type of leader U.S. policy-makers wanted in the Philippines. He had the reputation of being one of the most corrupt and unprincipled of Filipino politicians. His black-market dealings with the occupying Japanese, which made him a millionaire, would have made him liable to a treason-collaboration charge if he had not been the son of President Osmena. As the opponent of Marcos, he had the financial backing particularly of Filipino businessmen who had joint venture ties with U.S. firms. He would have been ideal for facilitating the neocolonial program on the transnational drawing-boards.

In a Philippines increasingly shaped to fit imperialist designs, nothing demonstrated the economic benefits of political power more than the means used to attain it. Fraud, violence and the indiscriminate dispensing of funds for vote-buying, resorted to by the main parties and their regional satrapies, were an indication of the profits to be gained from winning. As Filipino industry and other enterprises did grow, rival business groupings lined up behind the parties, expecting concessions in government contracts, lines of credit and state financing. There were any number of channels for U.S.-controlled funds to be employed.

President Marcos proved to be the more ruthless player of the game. He defeated the Osmena bid through a gigantic expenditure of campaign funds, estimated to have exceeded P300 million, far beyond anything previously seen in Philippine elections. The vote-buying splurge was so massive that it seriously undermined the peso and the stability of the economy, causing Marcos to lose control of whatever economic policy he had in mind. It was the principal reason why, immediately after the election, he was forced to yield to a World Bank demand for devaluation, a step that strengthened the hand of U.S. corporations.

From the standpoint of U.S. imperialism, there were growing reasons for desiring to replace Marcos. More than any other Philippine president he undertook to develop what amounted to an economic empire, acquiring holdings in a host of companies spread across every area of industry and trade: oil exploration, mining, auto assembly, sugar refining, airlines; the media ranging from newspapers to television and radio; tobacco, land, the export trade and many others. American investors at times had to concede Marcos a share in order to win approval for new ventures.

In Marcos a relatively new Filipino phenomenon was emerging, featured by the mingling of political and economic power. Political rivalry now had the greater aim of economic advantage, and capitalist growth brought a far greater sharpening of rivalry between elite ruling groups than had occurred among the old landlord-*comprador* sectors. It was highlighted by a battle between Marcos and the Lopez family, who were building a conglomerate in sugar and its export, regional transport, newspapers and radio, besides the prize acquisition of the country's biggest public utility, the Manila Electric Co. (Meralco). Fernando Lopez, who had contributed large sums to Marcos' 1969 campaign in exchange for running and winning as vice-president, broke with Marcos over who was to be the joint venture partner with the U.S. Caltex oil company. Caltex had major plans for oil exploration and for distribution in the Philippines and Marcos wanted the companies in which he was involved to be in on the very profitable projects. The Lopezes, however, were already in on the ground floor because Caltex was the fuel supplier of Meralco. It was a classic case of collaborators falling out over neocolonial alliances.

What mattered in the U.S. view was that Marcos was acquiring the means to behave independently. This was added to by his ties and profitable arrangements with other foreign interests. In 1967 Marcos opened the door for 18 large Japanese trading groups to enter the Philippine market, and then did the same for Japanese loan capital; he built shares in Japanese companies. His preparation of the ground for relations with socialist countries was also a break with the U.S.-dictated foreign policy.

Constitutionally, Marcos was limited to two terms as president, but his ambition for a continuation in power was unconcealed. In 1972 a Constitutional Convention was called, to write a new constitution, in which the Marcos forces pressed for a change from a presidential to a parliamentary system: it would enable Marcos to be a prime minister almost indefinitely.

In these circumstances, U.S. support was transparently developed behind opposition figures. The options were clear in the bell-weather U.S. media. Most prominently favored to contest the presidency with Marcos in 1973 was Senator Benigno Aquino, leader of the Liberal Party (the son of Benigno Aquino, the collaborator with Japan). A buildup was also given to Raul Manglapus, head of the Catholic Church-backed Christian Social Movement (whose election as senator had been financed by the CIA)[86] and to Jaime Ferrer, who had headed the National Movement for Free Elections that helped elect Magsaysay and who was also in the Christian Social Movement. All three of these U.S. choices had ties with the CIA, and were promoted as anti-corruption reformists, the standard U.S. tactic.

It was important for U.S. interests that a compliant government be elected in 1973 because in 1974 the Bell Trade Act/Laurel-Langley Agreement and the parity rights provision would terminate and extension or replacement were considered essential. Furthermore, the plans of transnational corporations and finance capital for making the Philippines an appendage of their new global system of production and marketing were just being unfolded and needed full collaboration.

On September 21, 1972 President Marcos upset the imperialist applecart. He proclaimed martial law and instituted rule by his own decree over the entire Philippines.

MARTIAL LAW

The assumption of authoritarian rule by President Marcos came at a time when political turbulence, resurgent nationalist forces, and left-wing movements were growing in the Philippines. To U.S. policymakers that situation was not particularly worrying because it provided an appropriate background for managing and justifying the replacement of Marcos. The martial law proclamation was received with varying reactions in U.S. quarters.

In Manila the American Chamber of Commerce sent Marcos a telegram on September 27, a few days after the proclamation, which said:

> The American Chamber of Commerce wishes you every success in your endeavors to restore peace and order, business confidence, economic growth and the well-being of the Filipino people and nation. We assure you of our confidence and cooperation in achieving those objectives. We are communicating these feelings to our associates and affiliates in the United States.[87]

However, the *New York Times* viewed martial law as "dubious medicine" and thought that the Marcos promise to institute reforms "invites skepticism." Said the paper, usually considered a reflector of the more sober U.S. policy-makers:

> The crucial question for the Philippines—and for the United States, which has important sentimental, military and economic interests in its one-time colony—is whether President Marcos will indeed temper tyranny with genuine reform and move speedily to restore democratic procedures. The suggestion by a high Marcos aide in Washington that martial law might be maintained for as long as two years is not reassuring.[88]

An investigative team sent to the Philippines in November 1972 by the U.S. Senate Foreign Relations Committee made a report that reassured the skeptics:

> We found few, if any, Americans [i.e., in the business community in Manila] who took the position that the demise of individual rights and democratic institutions would adversely affect U.S. interests. In the first place, these democratic institutions were considered to be severely deficient. In the second place, whatever U.S. interests were—or are—they apparently are not thought to be related to the preservation of democratic processes. Even in the Philippines, our own colonial step-child and "showcase of democracy" in Asia, the United States appears to have adopted a new pragmatism, perhaps because there was no other choice, turning away from the evangelical hopes and assumptions with which it has tended to look at political evolution. Thus, U.S. officials appear prepared to accept that the strengthening of presidential authority will . . . enable President Marcos to introduce needed stability; that these objectives are in our interest; and that . . . military bases and a familiar government in the Philippines are more important than the preservation of democratic institutions which were imperfect at best.[89]

The new U.S. ambassador in the Philippines (1973), William H. Sullivan, told the Senate Committee at his confirmation hearings: "It would be arrogant for representatives of countries with one form of democratic experience to dictate the exact form the democratic processes should take in other countries."[90]

This rather uneasy and "pragmatical" acceptance of martial law by the U.S. persisted throughout its duration. The U.S. attitude toward Marcos was markedly ambivalent. During martial law every aspect of the U.S. neocolonial design was achieved, either with or without the desire of Marcos, but at the same time the Marcos policies came increasingly into conflict with U.S. interests, which maneuvered and eventually succeeded in ousting him.

The Marcos martial law Proclamation 1081 based the drastic step wholly on the alleged need to contend with a Communist threat to "overthrow the Republic of the Philippines by armed violence." Supposedly, the threat that required the suspension of democratic processes was an armed struggle that had been launched by a Maoist group in 1969. The Proclamation directed the armed forces "to maintain law and order throughout the Philippines, prevent or suppress all forms of lawless violence as well as any act of insurrection or rebellion and to enforce obedience to all the laws and decrees, orders and regulations promulgated by me personally or upon my direction."

This initial Proclamation was then immediately followed by a host of presidential decrees and orders that had nothing to do with suppressing rebellion but which radically altered or reordered the economic and political life of the country. The aim of martial law, it was soon announced, was to fashion "the New Society" in the Philippines.

Martial law as such was maintained for nearly a decade, until lifted early in 1981, but Marcos retained his powers to rule by decree until the beginning of 1986. In that space of a dozen or more years considerable change was effected in the Philippines, but when Ferdinand Marcos was finally removed it was not a new society that he left behind but a more thoroughgoing neocolonialism that made it more difficult for the Filipino people to free themselves from poverty and foreign control.

It has been simplistic, as various opponents of Marcos have done, to depict this period of his presidency as a "fascist dictatorship" or an "imperialist-puppet regime." In truth, it was a complex period in which diverse and conflicting forces were in sharp struggle. The corrupt and repressive features of the regime, with which it became wholly identified, have obscured certain positive and progressive aspects of many of the Marcos acts.

The martial law step was, in essence, a decisive strategic move by a sector of the Filipino national bourgeoisie aimed at transforming the backward semi-feudal features of the economy and at advancing capitalist industrialization. President Marcos was the spokesman, leader and an active participant of this sector, and his "new society" was a bourgeois state form that acted to curtail the political and economic power of the semi-feudal landlords and to bring them more fully into the capitalist system of relations.

Seizure of full state power by this grouping, which was not of a national-democratic character, did not represent a full-fledged nationalist change or any throwing off of foreign imperialist control of a national liberation kind. It was, in fact, a refined form of collaboration with imperialism, of advancing this elite sector's ambitions within the neocolonial system being perfected chiefly by the U.S. The processes it set in motion, however, led inevitably to heightened capitalist ambitions by Marcos and his group and to contradictions and conflicts with the transnational corporations.

At the outset a rapid succession of decrees suspended all political parties and their activities, dissolved the Philippine Congress, banned all demonstrations and public meetings, prohibited strikes and picketing, closed major opposition newspapers and imposed military censorship on the media in general, ordered the expulsion or suspension from schools and universities of all students suspected of "subversive" activity, and in other ways banned channels of opposition.

In this way economic and political steps that otherwise may have been blocked, amended to pieces or sabotaged were quickly implemented. The banning of opposition was welcomed by U.S. and other foreign interests: during martial law, foreign corporations and banks gained virtually unlimited concessions, IMF-World Bank conditions and policies were imposed, and the wholesale subordination of the Philippine economy to their global programs was achieved, unhindered by opposition.

One Marcos martial law objective was the crushing of rival sectors of the Filipino elite. Leading bourgeois opponents were arrested and detained, including Senators Benigno Aquino and Jose Diokno and members of the Osmena and Lopez families. Eventually only Benigno Aquino, the U.S. choice to replace Marcos, was kept in detention (a lenient form of house arrest), charged with conspiring with and supplying arms and funds to those waging armed struggle against Marcos. Some wealthy owners of big business enterprises were detained for a time, especially those associated with the political opposition. Marcos termed these "the oligarchs" or reactionary supporters of the "old society." Such detentions were followed by the outright seizure or expropriation of the Lopez-owned Manila Electric Co., the Jacinto Iligan steel complex, and other enterprises. More than anything else the expropriations had to do with which Filipino grouping was to be the ally of foreign capital, as joint venture partners and as recipients of World Bank and other foreign financial loans.

While the elite rivals of Marcos received one edge of martial law, the other sharp edge was directed at thousands of trade unionists, organized peasants and progressive people in every field who were arrested and detained, including many PKP members engaged in legal organizational work. A number of the most active organizations were banned, ceased to exist, or went underground. Intensified military operations were mounted against those conducting armed struggle.

Virtually all of those detained in the early days of martial law were released relatively soon. Intimidation to forestall a growth of resistance was the obvious intention. Such steps reflected the continuing basic attitude of the Filipino ruling elite toward the people and their mass organizations. Even the Recto-led nationalist movement had failed to give attention to a mass base and to reliance on organizations of the people. The Marcos-led sector of the national bourgeoisie which, for all its collaborationist and ambitiously capitalist features, had objectively positive policies such as land reform and industrialization and tendencies toward independence which could have gone further and faster with the active involvement of the people. However, Marcos was more concerned with reassuring foreign investors and banks against trade unions, strikes and the nationalist demands of militant movements. To the end, ever more entangled in the neocolonial nets, he failed to recognize that a Philippine capitalist development has to have a national-democratic character and to involve and to energize the whole people if it is to escape restricting imperialist controls.

Even in the case of land reform, propagandized as a great progressive step, the peasants turned out to be the least benefited. Presidential Decree 27 provided for share tenants to acquire land on farms above 7 hectares, which enabled 393,778 tenants who were cultivating 758,015 hectares theoretically to purchase the land they were tilling. Share tenants on land below 7 hectares could transfer to leasehold or lessee status, which affected 521,136 tenants tilling 663,973 hectares. The former group acquiring land had to abide by an amortization period of 15 years and to pay a purchase price of $2\frac{1}{2}$ times the average harvest of three normal crop years immediately preceding the Decree.[91]

This may in effect have ended the outdated semi-feudal share tenancy system but it did not end inequalities of land ownership.

Amortization was extremely difficult for most tenants (land prices ranged from ₱6,000 to ₱14,000 per hectare) and only 77,494 potential beneficiaries had entered amortizing agreements by 1979. The majority of these, encumbered by the enormous cost of fertilizers and other inputs, were unable to keep up payments and many relinquished the land.[92]

An independent Philippine capitalism with popular support, based on giving the people a role and a share in its building, was realistically possible at this stage. Instead, beginning with Presidential Decree 151, which put into effect the service contract device that replaced parity, one obstacle or limitation after another was removed from the operations of foreign corporations and banks. By the early 1980s the Philippine economy was fully adjusted to suit the aims and needs of foreign capital. A Philippine sub-contracting economy had been put into place with the least opposition.

It is inaccurate, however, to term the Marcos regime an "imperialist-puppet administration." For all its readiness to accept a state of neocolonial dependence, the "new society" program of Marcos had the elements of a Filipino national bourgeoisie endeavoring to grow and strengthen itself through foreign investment and loans. Its steps for expansion of the infrastructure, dispersal of industry throughout the country instead of chiefly in the Manila area, capitalist permeation of agriculture, growth of non-traditional industry and exports, all may have benefited foreign interests but even in its subordinate joint venture position the Filipino capitalist industrial and manufacturing sector had increased significantly. In particular the role of the national government in economic planning had been greatly enhanced, and the succession of development plans projected under Marcos put their faith in the beginning largely in the accumulation of Filipino financial means and in rising government and Filipino private expenditure.

A significant growth of national bourgeois capital took place, particularly in the 1970s. In the year before martial law (1971) the total of corporate equity investment in domestic corporations was ₱787 million; by 1976 it had hit an annual rate of ₱2,602 million. Whereas foreign equity investments from the beginning of the special incentive decrees issued by Marcos from March 1973 to the end of 1978 totalled ₱4,545 million ($606 million), Filipino equity investments in the same period were ₱8,738 million ($1,165 million). Filipino capital, in other words, was growing at double the rate of the entry of foreign capital.[93]

Much of the new Filipino capital admittedly was tied up in joint venture arrangements with foreign firms, but a growing proportion was independent Filipino capital that objectively represented a strengthening of the national bourgeoisie. Unfortunately virtually no heavy industry was in existence as a base of support. The Marcos government, envisioning an expanding capitalism, undertook to overcome this, putting out development plans in the latter half of the 1970s which looked to the rise of the share of industry in Gross National Product from 26 per cent in 1975 to 43 per cent by the year 2000. It called for a decisive shift from light manufacturing to heavy industry. The stage of the Marcos plan that ran up to 1985 included eleven major industrial projects.

Above all, that was not what the World Bank and the transnational policy-makers desired. Five of the big Marcos projects, of a key heavy industry nature, had to be abandoned by 1983 under World Bank pressure of withholding loans for their establishment. In June 1984 the most important of the projects, for an integrated steel mill, had to be cancelled. The Marcos industrialization program was never able to be carried beyond labor-intensive light manufacturing, two-thirds of it in joint ventures geared to export in accordance with the designs of the TNCs, which determined what was to be produced.

The Marcos program had other features that were a departure from the policies of previous Philippine governments. Most important of these was the development of a more independent foreign policy, especially in regard to relations with socialist countries. In September 1966, in a speech to the United Nations, the Philippines president singled out the Soviet Union for praise for successfully mediating the India-Pakistan conflict. His foreign affairs secretary, Narciso Ramos, said in January 1967 that the "possible relaxation of the Philippine ban against trading with the Communists is very much in our minds." Exchanges of cultural groups, journalists and trade exploratory missions were initiated. In 1968 Marcos announced that "the Philippines is prepared to open trade relations with Eastern Europe."[94]

Diversification and expansion of markets for Philippine exports were the prime considerations in this move, especially the raw items like sugar and copra or coconut oil. Diplomatic and trade relations were first established, in 1973, with Yugoslavia and Romania, usually depicted as "independent of Moscow." Significantly, this was after the martial law proclamation, when opposition to the step was stifled. Ties were then quickly reached in the same year with Czechoslovakia, the German Democratic Republic, Hungary and Poland, with Bulgaria following by 1974. Diplomatic Relations with China came in June 1975 and with the Soviet Union in June 1976, President Marcos himself visiting both countries to sign the agreements. At the signing ceremony in Moscow Marcos said: "Philippine foreign policy has come

of age from colonialism and 'special relations,' to complete independence and self-reliance."

In the most marked separation from U.S. foreign policy, relations
were established with Vietnam and Cambodia, which only a few years
before had been attacked by U.S. planes from bases in the Philippines.
Marcos spoke of a "fundamental re-orientation" in foreign policy and
elaborated this in a major policy speech on May 23, 1975:

"First, to intensify, along a broader field, our relations with members of
the Association of South East Asian Nations;

"Second, to pursue more vigorously the establishment of diplomatic
relations with Socialist states, in particular with the People's Republic of
China and the Soviet Union;

"Third, to seek closer identification with the Third World with whom
we share problems;

"Fourth, to continue our beneficial relationship with Japan;

"Fifth, to support Arab countries in their struggle for a just and
enduring peace in the Middle East;

"Finally, to find a new basis, compatible with the emerging realities in
Asia, for a continuing healthy relationship with the United States."[95]

Action was taken along all of these guidelines. The Philippines
joined with the other ASEAN members in declaring their region "a zone
of peace, freedom and neutrality," which conflicted with the presence
of U.S. military bases. Marcos was demonstrably desirous of membership in the Non-Aligned Group of Third World states and chafed
at being rejected on the logical grounds that the Philippines could
not be considered non-aligned as long as U.S. bases remained on
Philippine soil. He did, however, establish membership in what
was initially launched in 1967 as the Group of 77, the Third
World bloc that pressed for a New International Economic Order
that would restructure the economic relations of the developed
and developing countries. In February 1976 the Philippines hosted
the third ministerial meeting of the Group at which a 17-point
Manila Declaration was adopted for joint action to achieve equitable
relations.

In regard to the Middle East, the Marcos administration took a
position of support for the Palestinian struggle for a homeland, which
was in opposition to the basic U.S. pro-Israeli policy. Philippine alignment with the Arab countries was a case of the national interest
overriding the relationship with the U.S.: Saudi Arabia, Libya and the
Islamic Conference were playing a mediating role in a rebellion of
autonomy-seeking Moslem Filipinos in Mindanao and Sulu, and Fili-

pino migrant workers in huge numbers were being employed in the Arab Gulf states.

For the U.S., the pronounced signs of a Marcos tendency to shift the Philippines toward a more independent foreign policy became increasingly disturbing. This was aggravated when repeated Marcos speeches in 1975 and 1976 called for the revision of all military and security agreements with the U.S. The assertion that "a new basis" had to be found for a "healthy relationship" was carried into the initiation of talks on a new bases agreement that opened on June 15, 1976. The Philippines raised eight major demands, including Philippine control over use of the bases, jurisdiction over U.S. servicemen committing criminal offenses while in the country, reduction of the lease period, an increase in rent, application of customs duties on goods imported for use of base personnel, income tax on earnings by U.S. base personnel from Philippine sources, and others. While the talks occurred, the government-controlled press, and organizations of the people tacitly aided and encouraged by the government, conducted a virulent anti-bases campaign, condemning them as a continuation of colonialism and of imperialist intervention.

U.S. stalling on the talks caused them to drag on for nearly three years, until a revised agreement was signed on December 31, 1978. By that time the Marcos posture was being weakened by the growing Philippine debt situation and by the narrowing options of reliance on loans from U.S.-dominated sources. The Philippines was rebuffed on key demands like operational control of the bases, but did gain the renegotiating of the agreement every five years, a condition that introduced some uncertainty of tenure in the U.S. presence. In the latter stage of the talks bitter Filipino anti-imperialist feeling was voiced. President Marcos's daughter, Imee, as titular head of the national association of Philippine youth councils which had left-wing participation, led a campaign denouncing the bases as an imperialist presence detrimental to Philippine interests. The Minister of Justice in the Marcos cabinet, Vicente Abad Santos, in a speech on November 24, 1978, called for the abolition of the bases which he said infringed on Philippine sovereignty and acted as "lighthouses of American domination in the country." They "perpetuate this country's colonial economy by protecting American transnational corporations and strengthening their monolithic grip on the Philippine business community," and they "signify a neo-colonial imperialism which can only embarrass our relations with other Asian countries in the Third World."[96]

It is quite evident that a decisive point was reached in this period in the U.S. attitude toward President Marcos. Martial law had now extended beyond the anticipated limits. The suppression of bourgeois opposition groups made it difficult for U.S. interests to build an alternative to Marcos. His relatively independent foreign policy and military bases tendencies were, furthermore, not the whole picture. Threatening to grow into a bigger problem was an increasing concentration of economic power in the hands of the Marcos-led sector of the Filipino national bourgeoisie.

Much of this was centered around the Marcos family, its close relatives and friends who were relatively recent entrants in the top elite, although the grouping also included certain old wealthy families like the Elizaldes, Ayalas, Zobels, Yulos and a section of the Cojuangco family of Tarlac. According to an anti-Marcos study in 1979, the immediate Marcos family controlled 47 companies while the family of Mrs. Imelda Marcos, the Romualdezes of Leyte, and its business partners had control of 72 companies. A close associate of Marcos, Roberto Benedicto, had acquired 10 companies, and another, Rodolfo Cuenca, 17. Benedicto built monopoly holdings in the sugar industry, from sugar-growing to milling to trading, becoming head of the governmental National Sugar Trading Corporation. Cuenca's interests developed from a small construction company in 1966 to the biggest Filipino construction firm, the Construction and Development Corporation of the Philippines. Eduardo Cojuangco gained control of the huge coconut industry, of COCOFED, the government's Philippine Coconut Authority and the United Coconut Planters Bank. A close Marcos friend, Herminio Disini, starting with a small company manufacturing tobacco filters, rose to conglomerate size with 37 corporations under his Herdis Management and Investment Corporation.[97] The Ayalas were enabled to move from real estate, banking and manufacturing into agribusiness and food processing.[98]

Most of these emerging Filipino monopolies were boosted to their meteoric growth through government contracts funneled to them by Marcos, who issued repeated presidential decrees awarding them tax and credit concessions and advantages over competitors, including over foreign companies. Anti-Marcos forces called this bourgeois sector "crony capitalism." It was, however, a phenomenon not unrelated to the primitive accumulation of capital and to the "robber baron" type of capitalist development in the U.S. in the latter half of the 19th century. It was a Filipino form of capitalism developing within the context of a neocolonialism in which the main areas of enterprise, from banking to manufacturing, were increasingly dominated by foreign TNCs.

A salient way through which the Marcos regime sought to advance this sector was the building of an extensive range of government corporations, partially through the expansion of existing government-owned entities, partially through the takeover of the properties of opposition "oligarchs" like the Meralco of the Lopezes, and partially through the setting up of new government firms and agencies. Contracts, funds and preferences were channeled to Marcos associates by way of these bodies, which were frequently headed by the monopolists themselves. Inevitably, vast corruption and tapping of government funds occurred, including by the Marcos family, which not only helped shape an image of the president as an unparalleled looter of the national wealth but also sapped his capabilities as a leader.

In part, the process was fed by bribes obtained from U.S. companies bidding for infrastructure contracts or for major installations. The most notorious case was the construction of the Bataan Nuclear Power Project, for which Westinghouse won out over General Electric although the former's bid was twice as high as that of General Electric. The Westinghouse deal was made through the Disini Herdis Management and Investment Corporation which was reportedly paid a "fee" of up to $35 million, with Disini supposedly acting as the middleman in a transaction that channeled the money to Marcos.[99] (An inquiry into the case in the post-Marcos period that exonerated those involved was more likely designed to whitewash Westinghouse than Marcos.)

The growth of wealthy and widely ranging Filipino monopoly groups under the umbrella of government corporations with the direct hand of Marcos assisting them by way of presidential decrees and special orders was an accumulating of independent power that U.S. interests did not like. It became more of a threat when these groups began to take over U.S. firms.

Most active in this was the business group under the Coconut Federation (COCOFED) headed by Eduardo Cojuangco. Many U.S. and other foreign-owned companies had been established since the colonial period in the multifaceted coconut industry, in oil mills, dessicated coconut plants, soap, detergent, margarine and other foods, and in marketing of coconut oil and copra. Cojuangco's group took over Granexport (a subsidiary of the U.S. TNC Cargill), PVC International (also a U.S. subsidiary), the Japanese Mitsubishi and other coconut oil mills. The U.S. San Pablo Manufacturing Corporation, the Franklin Baker dessicated coconut firm (a subsidiary of U.S. General Foods) and others found themselves in the process of being taken over.[100]

For these U.S. companies the Marcos regime had become a growing menace and they protested. The main pressure in their behalf was applied at first through the World Bank. When the World Bank Consultative Group on the Philippines met in Washington in 1979 to decide on a Philippine request for a $1 billion loan, it laid down stiff conditions. There were the usual demands for further "incentives" for foreign investment, and for import and tariff relaxations (despite the grave Philippine balance of payments deficit), but along with those was a condition that the Marcos government withdraw from economic and industrial undertakings; in other words, to curtail the expanding role of the government corporations. By now Marcos had an increasingly desperate reliance on foreign loans and had little alternative but to pledge compliance. The conflict of interest, however, continued to grow. Increasingly, in U.S. imperialist eyes, Marcos was a liability and had to go.

One of the main factors in the ambivalent U.S. attitude toward martial law was the Marcos destruction of the political system of two or more parties created during the colonial period and especially fostered during independence. This was ideal for U.S. imperialism: to shift support to other parties when the one in power became too nationalistic or too unstable. The U.S. could be satisfied with two or three years of martial law but when it threatened to continue indefinitely, while Marcos displayed a dual character of collaborator and independent capitalist, the steps began to get rid of him.

The pressure grew for the release of the detained Benigno Aquino, the pre-martial law U.S. choice to replace Marcos. Finally, in 1980, he was released from detention and allowed to go to the United States. There Aquino was installed with a fellowship in the Center for International Affairs at Harvard University. He promptly broke a release vow made to Marcos, to keep public silence about Philippine affairs, by delivering speeches assailing Marcos and including a call for his armed overthrow. Aquino, who had close association with the State Department and with his old CIA contacts, actively prepared for a return to the Philippines to lead an anti-Marcos political movement.

A large number of opponents of Marcos, right and left, had fled to the U.S., to use it as a base for anti-Marcos movements. Among them was Raul Manglapus, reported to have slipped out of the Philippines through Clark Air Base in 1972 to escape arrest. Basing himself in Washington, he set up a Movement for a Free Philippines. It had Catholic Church support and recruited a following from conservatives in Filipino communities in U.S. cities.

Members of Filipino organizations of the Maoist left also fled abroad, chiefly to the U.S., where they set up subsidiary organizations, published newspapers and issued anti-Marcos pamphlets and leaflets. Among U.S. liberals a Friends of the Filipino People organization campaigned with echoes of the old Anti-Imperialist League for the "restoration of democracy" in the Philippines.

The Filipino-U.S. anti-Marcos groups were active throughout the martial law period in lobbying the U.S. Congress to deny military or economic aid to the Marcos government and in calling on the IMF-World Bank to withhold loans. During Senate and House foreign affairs committee hearings, they put on record a lengthy list of Marcos violations of human rights.

Detention, torture and the frequent killing ("salvaging") of opponents were the inevitable accompaniment of martial law and of resistance to it. These, however, were but the extension of measures used to deal with the Maoist-led guerrilla armed struggle launched in 1969, long before martial law. They were little different from the suppressive policies of the Roxas-Quirino-Magsaysay regimes against the PKP-led Huk Movement. The principal difference between these two uses of suppressive violence was the type of people on whom it was applied. Resistance to Marcos came not just from peasants and workers but from opponents in the middle class and elite and from religious groups, especially in the Catholic Church. The arrest and maltreatment of priests, nuns, seminary students and foreign missionaries attracted more attention than the arrest and brutal treatment of ordinary working people. The detention of the elite politician Benigno Aquino drew protests that were never aroused over the jailing in the 1950s of PKP trade union leaders.

In particular, the Catholic Church became an active center of anti-Marcos activities. Much of this was due to Marcos policies that sought to bring the Church's semi-feudal and privileged status into line with the capitalist orientation of the regime. Land reform affected some large landed estates of the Church. Marcos proposed to tax the extensive Church properties which extended increasingly to banking and business, and in particular the numerous private schools in the Church's nationwide education system. A Marcos policy of population control that involved the dissemination of family planning birth control methods, advanced to contend with the effect of a high 3.6 per cent population growth rate on worsening poverty, ran counter to Catholic doctrine. The more conservative sectors of the Church opposed Marcos because of these policies, but they did so indirectly, on human rights grounds.

The Catholic Church, however, was no longer the monolithic body of reaction that it had been in the past. Three distinct tendencies had appeared, in the hierarchy, in the ranks of the bishops, and among the priesthood. At least a third of the hierarchy supported martial law and the leadership of Marcos, chiefly for its suppressive measures Next, the broadest, "moderate," middle section of the Church took a stance of "constructive criticism" of martial law which became, in fact, growing opposition. The third sector, the most vocal and the most direct in action against the Marcos regime were radical priests and nuns influenced by the "liberation theology" ideas and the social reform movement within the Church internationally; a number of them joined in the armed struggle to overthrow Marcos. All three tendencies had support from parallel groups in the Church in the U.S. and Europe.

From Protestant sects in the Philippines also came increasing anti-Marcos sentiment, as well as from their parent church bodies in the U.S. The chief theme was the human rights issue. In general, the moral condemnation of Marcos, establishing his image as a ruthless, brutal and corrupt dictator, came from the religious organizations.

From the mid-1970s to the end of the Marcos rule a half-seen tussle went on between U.S. imperialism and the Filipino leader. In this, the U.S. and the U.S.-dominated lending agencies held the whip hand and Marcos, in increasingly desperate need for more loans, had gradually to submit.

At first, in 1978, Marcos went through a semblance of restoring democratic processes by holding an election to a revived national assembly. It was a rigged ballot, set up to display alleged popular support. Opposition political parties were allowed to reorganize. In January 1981, at U.S. insistence, martial law as such was lifted, but Marcos retained virtually all of his authoritarian powers and his apparatus of control.

A return to some form of representative government that would enable imperialist interests to have a range of alternative leaders or groupings to support was the U.S. aim. The rebuilding of alternative political parties of the elite was viewed as essential, too, to forestall the assumption of an anti-Marcos leadership by the forces of the left. A Maoist-led armed struggle had persisted and spread during martial law, while the semi-legal left, resurgent trade unions and progressive nationalist middle class elements were developing against Marcos. The question of how to replace Marcos without overt U.S. intervention, without a prepared replacement in position, and without an uncontrollable popular upheaval, was severely taxing State Department-Pentagon strategists.

The dilemma worsened when Benigno Aquino, the leading U.S. choice for the succession, returning to the Philippines to establish his leadership on the spot before others edged him out, was assassinated as he stepped off his plane at Manila airport on August 21, 1983. It set off a wave of political turmoil that aggravated the instability in the country.

Persisting expressions of support for Marcos by President Ronald Reagan and by Vice-President George Bush (who met and toasted Marcos on a visit to Hawaii in July 1981 with the adulatory words "We love your adherence to democratic principles and democratic processes") seem designed to soothe the Philippine president and to prevent a drastic anti-U.S. reaction to moves against him. Truer attitudes in the U.S. government were indicated by a poll conducted by the U.S. columnist Jack Anderson on "The World's Worst Leaders," the results of which were published in January 1983. He submitted the question "Of all the rascals, despots and buffoons who have made themselves the leaders of nations, who are the world's worst?" to 50 "international experts" who were mostly "foreign affairs specialists in the State Department, Pentagon, Central Intelligence Agency and Congress." They voted Marcos No. 8 in a list of ten.[101]

There is reason to believe that the ill-fated return of Benigno Aquino was in coordination with the growing policy in U.S. foreign affairs quarters of disassociation from the Marcos regime and of promoting opposition leaders. Shortly before the Aquino move, U.S. Secretary of State George Shultz said in a July 1983 interview:

> The Marcos regime is entering its twilight, and we don't want to find ourselves in the same position as we did in Iran when the shah was overthrown.[102]

A U.S. sense of urgency in resolving the deteriorating Philippine situation was especially displayed in the aftermath of the Aquino assassination. The former U.S. ambassador to the Philippines, William H. Sullivan, wrote that "we must not miss the opportunity in the Philippines, as we did in Iran, to assist in the emergence of a new democratic government." Wrote Sullivan:

> The Reagan Administration must face the fact that Mr. Marcos has run out his political string. Our national interests and our obligation to the Filipino people require us to protect them from civil war, and the Administration must take action, however messy, to assist a peaceful and democratic transition in Philippine politics. Only we can lead such a transition but we will have the overwhelming majority of Filipinos as our allies if we act quickly, wisely and decisively.

Sullivan strongly stressed that he did not recommend "a violent revolution, one that Mr. Marcos would fight tooth and nail," but a "constructive intervention," that is, "a formula for political transition . . . a compromise that would be acceptable to the Marcos government and the leaders of the democratic opposition."[103]

1983 was a critical year in the developing crisis situation in the Philippines. Political turmoil, marked by large anti-Marcos demonstrations in Manila in the wake of the Aquino assassination, was interwoven with economic crisis brought on by the cumulative effects of World Bank-IMF-TNC policies. By December 1983 the Philippine foreign debt had risen to $25.6 billion and debt servicing in that year drained the economy to the amount of $2.5 billion. The 1983 balance of payments deficit was over $2 billion. Twice in that year Marcos had to bow to IMF austerity demands and to devalue the peso, by 7.3 per cent in June and by another, huge 22.5 per cent in October; a further 27 per cent devaluation came in June 1984.

Forced to seek debt-rescheduling and further loans in September 1983, Marcos was left dangling for a year until he agreed to an onerous set of IMF conditions: peso devaluation, the removal of the already riddled protection for Filipino industry by the wholesale reduction of tariffs on imported products, the elimination of Filipino "monopolies," a raising of taxes and fees on public services (aimed at reduction of the public sector in utilities), removal of subsidies to domestic producers, budget cuts, credit curbs, greater privileges to foreign investment, increase of unibanking, and wage controls. In particular, the "structural reform" was demanded: curtailing government-owned industrial and financial corporations and breaking up the coconut and sugar industry monopolies. In general, Marcos was made to submit humiliatingly to a far-reaching opening up of the economy to foreign penetration and to a further shrinking of the Filipino capitalist development he had sought.

It was in the course of negotiations on this agreement that the public statements of U.S. officials on the need for "a new, democratic government" were made. One of the clearest statements of the U.S. demands was made by Business International, a big international consulting firm for the TNCs, in a report entitled "Outlook for the Philippines" issued on October 22, 1983. It set out possible scenarios ranging from a Marcos submission to transitional steps to a coup d'etat by U.S.-trained Philippine army officers. Among the "requisites" demanded of Marcos were the removal of key individuals from government posts having to do with political and economic decisions, and "dismantling of major economic fiefdoms like the sugar and coconut monopolies of Benedicto and Cojuangco."[104]

By the Marcos constitution, a presidential election was scheduled for the latter part of 1987, and the U.S. perspective was for building up a contender to meet Marcos by that time. On November 3, 1985, however, he made the bold move of calling a snap presidential election for February 7, 1986, hoping to get himself installed for another six years.

This move quickly brought to a head the issue of who and how to replace Marcos. Numerous rivals came forward, as the president's days seemed numbered. The choice finally fell upon the widow of Benigno Aquino, Corazon Cojuangco Aquino (a cousin of Eduardo). A U.S. decision to support her was influenced by the strong backing she had from the majority sections of the Roman Catholic Church which, at a time when opposition political parties had not yet been able to build local organizations, had the nationwide machinery to deliver votes. "Cory" Aquino had utterly no experience as a politician but she could win public sympathy as "Ninoy" Aquino's widow and from the image created for her as a kind of Joan d'Arc confronting the dictator.

U.S. support for Mrs. Aquino avoided the blatant, open Lansdale manipulation of Magsaysay. Her election campaign and image-building, however, were handled by the New York public relations firm, D.H. Sawyer and Associates. Fund raising for her was managed by a U.S. banker based in Hong Kong, William Overholt, who was married to a daughter of a retired Filipino general; his assistant in the Philippines was the president of the big U.S.-built Benguet Mining Corporation, Jaime Ongpin. The $6 million reportedly raised for her came largely from the "oligarchs" dispossessed by Marcos. A U.S. Jesuit priest, James Reuter, ran the 19-station Catholic Church radio network, Radio Veritas, as the main propaganda channel for Mrs. Aquino. Radio Veritas operated with a grant from the U.S. Agency for International Development funneled through the Asia Foundation office in Manila. The aid agency of the U.S. Embassy in Manilla funded and revived the National Committee for Free Elections (NAMFREL) which had helped elect Magsaysay, with the old CIA-linked Jaime Ferrer again at its head. In the U.S., the press in general boosted Cory Aquino and blasted Marcos, the *New York Times* exposing the Marcos war record as fraudulent; as in the past, these stories were featured in opposition newspapers in Manila. Finally, a group of 20 U.S. congressmen with other top officials, headed by Indiana Senator Richard Lugar, arrived to act as election observers.[105] The February 7, 1986 election precipitated the turbulent period that ended the lengthy rule of Ferdinand Marcos. Accurate voting results could not be ascertained, both contestants announcing their own figures, both claiming victory, both charging the other with fraud. Proclaiming that he had won, Marcos refused to concede to Mrs. Aquino.

U.S. official and covert moves were employed in the chaotic post-election situation to force Marcos to step down. A total withholding of U.S. aid was threatened if he did not. A succession of U.S. representatives—Senator Lugar, Nevada Senator Paul Laxalt, Ambassador Stephen Bosworth, State Department troubleshooter Philip Habib, former ambassador Michael Armacost, and eventually State Secretary George Shultz—visited or communicated directly with Marcos, advising his departure and offering him residence in the U.S. Marcos resisted.

This was the more open picture of the transfer of power. There were less visible and more effective steps. On February 22, suddenly, Defense Secretary Juan Ponce Enrile and General Fidel Ramos, chief of the Philippine Constabulary, abandoned Marcos and set up a pro-Aquino command center in Camp Aguinaldo Philippine army headquarters on the eastern rim of Manila. Both men had close U.S. connections and would not conceivably have acted in that way without U.S. encouragement and promises of support. Sections of the armed forces began to shift to them, including from the air force, whose helicopter gunships were allowed to refuel and rearm at Clark Air Base. When Marcos ventured to talk of putting down the revolt with loyal troops, the U.S. officials in contact with him warned him of a shutting off of military assistance.

As Enrile and Ramos made their move, the Catholic Church took its decisive step. Using Radio Veritas, Cardinal Jaime Sin made an emergency call for the Catholic faithful to turn out at Camp Aguinaldo in support of Enrile and Ramos and Corazon Aquino. Thousands of people, especially from Catholic schools, nunneries and lay organizations, swarmed to the army camp on Epifanio de los Santos Avenue (or EDSA, as the avenue was commonly known). Between February 23 and 25 the crowd swelled, forming a barrier that could not have been dispersed without much bloodshed.

This incident was hailed as the "People Power" revolution by the Aquino propagandists, an unarmed demonstration given credit for ousting Marcos. It is noteworthy, however, that only the Catholic organizations were present at EDSA. No sector of the left took part, no trade unions or other organizations of the people. This was because virtually none of these forces had supported Mrs. Aquino in the election and because they did not find it politically possible to come to the aid of Enrile and Ramos who had headed the suppressive instruments of the Marcos regime. Significantly, no similar anti-Marcos demonstrations or sympathy actions in support of the EDSA events took place anywhere else in the country, except for units of the armed forces declaring for Enrile and Ramos. Kept relatively obscure was

U.S. intrigue with Enrile and the army and the rug-pulling pressure exerted on Marcos by the U.S. government, which was content to let the "People Power" myth occupy the foreground. Not mentioned, for example, was the fact that when Marcos troops attacked and destroyed the Radio Veritas transmitter at the beginning of the showdown, the CIA quickly moved to install alternative facilities.[106]

On February 25, 1986 President Marcos and his family were airlifted out of their Malacanang Palace residence in Manila by a U.S. helicopter, flown to Clark Air Base and from there transported in a U.S. plane to Hawaii and exile. Sworn in as the new Philippine president was Corazon Cojuangco Aquino, who owed her victory to the pervasive hand of the U.S., the strong arm of the military, and the sword and shield of the Church.

IX

The Philippine Left and Resistance

From the 1960s onward the Philippines had become a more complex country, featured by changing relations and contradictions between imperialism and a more varigated Filipino elite and among rival groupings of the elite. The forces of the left were also affected by the changing circumstances, including the rise of new forms of struggle and the development of serious divisions.

Defeated in armed struggle and suffering severe decimation, the *Partido Komunista ng Pilipinas* from the latter 1950s faced grave problems of survival and of maintaining a national liberation struggle. Recovery from a period of such setback and of ruthless suppression is always a major test for a revolutionary movement. It requires a resolute confronting of reality and a readiness to make changes in strategy and tactics. It necessitates the adoption of skillful security measures during the time when the party is in a weakened condition, and the creation of new forms of organization for moving forward. It requires the replacement at all levels of seasoned cadres who have been killed, imprisoned or demoralized into surrender or betrayal, as well as educating and training fresh recruits who are drawn into the movement.

In the case of the PKP and HMB, suppression never meant annihilation. Although members who remained alive and free, able to be active, were reduced to a small percentage of peak 1950 membership, they kept the movement in being. Hundreds of others who had been captured and imprisoned were only temporarily removed from the struggle and resumed work when released. While the PKP and HMB were decimated, their prestige among many sections of the people remained very high; the cause for which they fought and the ideas they stood for were not really suppressed, becoming enhanced in perspective.

For a time the PKP leadership, headed by Jesus Lava as general secretary, still felt that armed struggle had to be the main form of struggle and could be revived. However, it was not inflexible. The PKP even agreed to talks with Magsaysay in November 1953 soon after his election. This was at Magsaysay's initiative, his only known independent move, apparently made in the naive belief that he had reduced the PKP-HMB to a state of capitulation and could exhibit such an achievement before his U.S. mentors. His envoy, Colonel Osmundo Mondonedo, met first with the chosen PKP negotiator, Casto Alejandrino, near Lukban, Quezon, and Alejandrino was helicoptered to meet Magsaysay in Fort McKinley (now Fort Bonifacio) on the outskirts of Manila. A democratic settlement of the armed struggle was discussed, with initial broad agreements on a widening of democracy and on genuine Philippine independence. Expanded talks were agreed upon but before these could be held the U.S. Embassy and JUSMAG intervened to stop them. General Jesus Vargas, Philippine army chief of staff and a JUSMAG instrument, was directed to make an abrupt public demand for the surrender of the PKP and HMB or else an all-out army offensive would be launched. Vargas's intervention was made without the prior knowledge of Magsaysay, who displayed his "independence" by quickly bowing to U.S. demands. The armed struggle continued.

The decision was finally made in 1956 to make the shift from armed to legal, parliamentary struggle as the main form. This was decided largely in recognition of the growth of nationalism headed by Claro Recto and of the positive features of the Garcia presidency. It was felt that the PKP should support and reach unity with such forces to help make possible a pro-Filipino government which, however bourgeois in nature, would weaken control of U.S. imperialism, the main enemy.

Implementing the shift was not easy, due to the outlawing for many years of mass organizations that had been led by the PKP and to the saturation activity of government intelligence agencies. In the provinces party organization was maintained as usual, although underground, but in Manila a "single file" system was resorted to in which a member would know only the comrade who recruited him and the one whom he recruited. Nevertheless membership and activity grew.

A legal struggle policy was strengthened by the gradual emergence from prison of PKP members sentenced for rebellion. In 1956 the Philippine Supreme Court, in the appealed case of Congress of Labor Organization leaders headed by Amado Hernandez, declared the JUSMAG-manufactured charge of "rebellion complexed with murder, arson, robbery and kidnapping" used to impose death sentences and life imprisonment to be illegal and that only "simple rebellion" with sentences of 12 years maximum or less was applicable. Trade union cadres like Juan Cruz of the printers' union and others were released and began restoring PKP influence in the trade union movement. Former political bureau members, on release, like Felicissimo Macapagal (Ramirez), Domingo Castro (Alembre) and Alejandro Briones (Florante) in the late 1950s and early 1960s undertook the contacting and reactivating of passive or disconnected members, rebuilding the party organization in provinces and towns.

By the early 1960s it was possible to project new democratic and patriotic organizations with a clear anti-imperialist and national-democratic position. The first of these was the *Lapiang Manggagawa* (Labor Party), set up by left trade unionists close to the PKP. Its program declared:

> We believe in the inviolability of the national will and in the primacy of the Filipino in his own country.
>
> We shall oppose any infringement of our national sovereignty and independence.
>
> Up to this day, our economy is colonial in structure and orientation. This is the basic cause of the prevailing alien domination of our economic life and of the widespread poverty and the other evils it inevitably breeds. We shall, therefore, work for the adoption and enforcement of policies and measures designed to decolonize the economy by shifting the control and direction of our economic life from them to Filipino hands.
>
> Filipino businessmen and industrialists shall be guaranteed protection against foreign domination. But nationalism shall not be allowed to become a convenient tool for the advancement of the interests of a few. We shall institute a program which shall make the benefits of nationalism permeate down to the masses.[1]

The *Lapiang Manggagawa* was set up as the decontrol measures of President Macapagal were having their destructive effect on the nationalist movement. As a workers' party projecting unity with the nationalist-inclined sections of the bourgeoisie, it sought to broaden the forces set in motion by Recto and Garcia. A Socialist Party was also set up, early in 1964, to put forward the more basic alternative of socialism, but it proved impracticable to maintain two parties with a working class base, especially when the problem remained of reconstructing a militant trade union movement that had still not recovered from the outlawing of the PKP-led Congress of Labor Organizations in 1951. The labor parties contributed, however, to the formation of a new Congress of Trade Unions of the Philippines (CTUP) in 1964 which began the revival of left-wing trade unionism.

Coinciding with this step was the creation in the countryside, with

PKP guidance, of the *Malayang Samahan Magsasaka* (MASAKA) or Free Union of Agricultural Workers. Also set up in 1964, it was essentially a revival and continuation of the PKM that had been outlawed in 1948. The MASAKA grew rapidly in Central Luzon where the peasant movement had been strong for decades, and expanded to Northern and Southern Luzon. The long-standing peasant base of the PKP, in which the barrios of many towns had been solidly organized, was rejuvenated by MASAKA.

A key part of the left revival was the launching by the youth section of the PKP in March 1964 of a particularly active and vocal organization, the *Kabataang Makabayan* (Nationalist Youth). It was headed by leading students in Manila universities who had been recruited by the PKP and it drew many students as members, although it eventually set up chapters of young workers and peasants as well.

The nationalist movement among the youth that burst out in the Philippines from the mid-1960s had its most vociferous expression among middle-class students from families that felt the limited opportunities for advancement in the neocolonial society and whose own post-graduate hopes were not bright. Claro Recto's speeches were having a posthumous impact and the struggle of the HMB had already acquired the historical glow of a just national liberation cause. The articulate students, in demonstrations and literature, had a greater propaganda effect than the larger and basically more important worker and peasant movements.

Proclaiming itself as "inspired and guided by the patriotism of the Filipino youth who first formulated the terms of our nationhood in the [19th century] Propaganda Movement," the KM program said:

> *Kabataang Makabayan* pledges itself as the vanguard of the Filipino youth in seeking full national freedom and democratic reforms and in combatting imperialism and feudalism. In order to achieve its national-democratic mission, *Kabataang Makabayan* is determined to integrate into the anti-imperialist and anti-feudal fight the vigor of students, young workers, young peasants, young teachers, young professionals, young soldiers and all other young men and women who compose the vast majority of our young nation.[2]

On January 25, 1965 the first large mass demonstration of an anti-imperialist character since suppression of the people's movement in the early 1950s occurred in Manila. Over 15,000 workers, students and peasants assembled outside the U.S. Embassy and the Congress building—"awakened sectors of organized labor, the peasantry, youth and students, the intellectuals and the emerging entrepreurial class," as speakers proclaimed — and presented a manifesto demanding: abrogation of parity, immediate abrogation of the U.S.-Philippine military bases agreement, the Filipinizing of retail and wholesale trade, decisive implementation of genuine land reform, abrogation of the U.S.-Philippine military assistance pact, full respect for civil liberties, adoption of a full employment program, a law to raise the minimum wage from P4 to P6 a day, relief of Filipino businessmen from a foreign-inspired credit squeeze, and extension of diplomatic and commercial relations with all countries in order to correct the neo-colonial "special relations" with the U.S. The manifesto was signed by the LM, MASAKA, KM, the National Anti-Parity Council, AKSIUN (*Ang Kapatiran sa Ikauunlad Natin,* or Brotherhood For Our Development, an unemployed organization), and several other organizations with PKP participation.

A Philippine peace movement was also created in this period, campaigning mainly against the U.S. military bases and against involvement in the U.S. war in Vietnam. It was set up as a Philippine council of the British-based Bertrand Russell Peace Foundation, but unlike the committee nature of that body was a mass organization with chapters in many cities and provinces.

Through the mid-1960s, as the Macapagal government was replaced by that of Ferdinand Marcos, the rebuilt people's movement developed without alignment with any of the political parties of the elite, supporting only individual political figures who took a nationalist position, the most prominent of whom was Senator Lorenzo Tañada.

The important need was for a national-democratic political party that would take a position independent of the parties of collaboration. For this, an organized mass base was essential. A major step in that direction was taken with the setting up of a broad movement embracing all progressive organizations and linking them with nationalist bourgeois representatives. Called the Movement For The Advancement of Nationalism (MAN), it was launched at a founding congress held in the auditorium of the National Library in Manila on February 7–8, 1967.

Among the charter members of MAN were 22 prominent businessmen, 61 trade union leaders, 86 peasant leaders, 91 youth and students, 21 leading women, 29 outstanding academics, 24 lawyers and other professionals, 6 scientists, 13 editors and top journalists, 17 writers and artists, 7 political leaders including 3 members of Congress, and 13 civic leaders. In the General Declaration adopted, MAN set out its general principles:

> All nations aspire and fight for full, unimpeded, and unencumbered control over their destiny, their internal security, and foreign relations

because it is only through and by means of such control that they may develop and advance to their fullest capabilities and potentials their national resources, commerce and trade, industrialization, and their most important assets of all—their human, especially spiritual, resources. The Filipinos have not yet fully achieved such an aspiration, and they have yet to struggle unitedly and mightily to attain it for themselves and their posterity. MAN is a national crusade for the attainment of those legitimate and rightful objectives.[3]

Publishing and distributing numerous pamphlets, bulletins and periodicals, MAN made a major impact on many sectors of Philippine society, with regional bodies in Northern, Central and Southern Luzon, the Visayas and Mindanao. It was the most significant national-democratic development since the Democratic Alliance in the latter 1940s. Although forced to work underground—with a large number of members able to function legally and prominently—the PKP was an influential factor in that development. The prospect of a broad, united anti-imperialist struggle was bright.

At the same time another occurrence contributed to the strengthening of the Philippine left. This was the reestablishment by the PKP of its ties with the International Communist movement, from which it had been cut off from the time of the Japanese invasion in 1941. That isolation had extended throughout the liberation struggles of the Hukbalahap and of the HMB. As the PKP rebuilt itself in the 1960s, the international links were also regained. The most important fraternal tie, with the Communist Party of the Soviet Union, was reestablished in 1965. The process was completed with the attendance of a PKP delegation at the world conference of Communist Parties held in Moscow in 1969. It may be noted that this development coincided with steps by the Marcos government to separate from U.S. foreign policy and to open relations with socialist countries, reflecting a common need, for differing purposes, of differing Filipino class forces.

The decade of the 1960s was a time when international factors combined to make a deep impression on Philippine affairs. U.S. imperialism and the IMF-World Bank agencies injected their readjustment policies to shape the Philippine economy to TNC needs. Both the PKP and the Marcos government formed their varying links with Communist governments or movements abroad. Another international aspect also arose that profoundly affected the course of the Philippine liberation process: the intervention of a Chinese Maoist influence in the Filipino people's movement.

It was inevitable that the Philippines, with its proximity to China and its large Chinese and Chinese mestizo population, should be affected by the growth of China as a world power, with ideas of Mao Tse-tung in command. From the mid-1960s a drive by the Mao-directed Chinese Communist Party to assert leadership over the international Communist movement was a facet of that emerging world role. That drive, amounting to an imposition of the Chinese strategy and tactics of winning power upon the struggles of other parties, including a call for guerrilla-style armed struggle in the Chinese model, was especially directed at the countries of South East Asia.

In the Philippines the Maoist ideas infiltrated the PKP and gained a foothold in its leading body. It derived from the recruitment in 1962 of a young student-instructor in the University of the Philippines, Jose Maria Sison. Whether through connections with Maoists in the Chinese community in the Philippines or during a period of study in Indonesia where the Communist Party was strongly influenced by Maoism, Sison developed a dogmatic and crusading commitment to that ideology. Within the PKP he hid his Maoist connections. Possessing organizational and propaganda skills, in a time of cadre depletion, he was rapidly advanced to a PKP political bureau post and put in charge of youth work, becoming the head of the *Kabataang Makabayan* when it was set up. He volunteered for other leading posts, as editor of *Progressive Review,* an influential left/nationalist magazine started with PKP approval in 1965, as secretary of MAN, and other activities. Secretly, he developed a factional Maoist group in the PKP under his leadership.

By 1966 it became obvious from polemics conducted by Sison and his group that he had greater ambitions, for leadership and a commitment to the Maoist ideology for the PKP as a whole. Sison's following, however, was limited to a small number of newly recruited student members. Nevertheless he made a move for a Maoist take over of the PKP.

This occurred at a time when the PKP was engaged in a reorganization process, to normalize the structure of the party after the tight, very centralized organization maintained for security in underground conditions. Leading organs needed adjustment. Former general secretary Jesus Lava had been arrested in 1964, Casto Alejandrino of the secretariat earlier in 1960; new members had come to the fore, experienced veteran leaders had come out of prison. By 1967 a plenum of leading cadres was held to elect a full central committee, political bureau and general secretary.

Sison chose this time to make his bid for control. His tactic was to call for delegates to the plenum to be chosen only from new PKP members recruited from 1962 (the year of his own entry), on grounds that there was a new situation which should be dealt with by the new generation. He prepared a thesis which assailed "the Lava Dynasty" for having allegedly led the PKP into defeat in the armed struggle and called the existing PKP leadership in general "bankrupt." (Sison has bizarrely persisted with the "Lava Dynasty" claim, although a new leadership came to the fore in the PKP from the 1960s.) The Sison thesis posed a false issue of the "young and dynamic" versus the "old and moribund" in the PKP. This was but a stepping stone, however, for the main Sison argument: that the PKP strategy and tactics developed from the latter 1950s to make the full transition to legal, parliamentary struggle, including the attainment of legality for the party, were wrong and embodied betrayal and surrender of the struggle for national liberation. Sison contended that the PKP should swing totally to the Maoist line of employing armed struggle as the main form, to be waged as a protracted struggle for the overthrow of the "imperialist-puppet regime," with legal organizations to serve the armed struggle by being led into sharp confrontation with imperialism and the neocolonial state.

When Sison, knowing his position and group would be overwhelmingly defeated, refused to attend the PKP plenum and began attacking the party leadership publicly, he was at first suspended and then expelled from the party. The 1967 plenum elected a central committee which chose a new political bureau. In 1970 it chose a new general secretary, Felicissimo Macapagal,[4] a party member since the 1930s, a central committee member through the armed struggles of both the Hukbalahap and the HMB, then a political prisoner. "Feling" Macapagal came from Cabiao, Nueva Ecija, from a peasant background, had extensive organizational experience, and was particularly effective as a unifying figure in the rebuilt PKP. He was general secretary until 1990.

The 1967 plenum rejected the Maoist position. It opposed a return to armed struggle as not appropriate for the existing conditions in the Philippines and upheld the strategy and tactics of legal, parliamentary struggle as correct. (The PKP did maintain an armed HMB force as a defensive, security means for the underground organization, especially in the rural areas.) Emphasis continued to be placed on the building of mass organizations of the people as the main basis of a united front policy including alliance with nationalist bourgeois strata.

RESISTANCE DIVIDED

Having lost out within the PKP, Sison and his small group resorted to bitter attacks on the party in the conservative press and in particular in student periodicals and intellectual circles where a ferment of discussion of Marxist ideas was occurring, using an undiluted Maoist style, insulting and provocative, depicting the PKP as "moribund" and "dying," as "revisionist." Sison went to the extent of publishing and posting up in public places a list of the names of central committee members and other cadres of the underground PKP.

The factional campaign was carried to all the mass organizations of the left, in an effort to swing them over to the movement Sison sought to create. This was done in MAN where the Sison group lost out resoundingly in a bid to capture leading posts, and left the organization. Similarly, in MASAKA, the Bertrand Russell Peace Foundation, the trade unions, the HMB units, the rebuff to the Maoists was overwhelming. Only in the *Kabataang Makabayan* did the Sison group retain a hold, but only in the student section, and not all of that; the large peasant and worker sections under PKP leadership scrapped the KM label to which Sison laid claim and established themselves as the *Malayang Pagkakaisa ng Kabataang Pilipino* (MPKP) or Free Union of Filipino Youth.

Nevertheless Sison and his group went ahead with plans to set up a party of their own. On January 3, 1969 he and eleven student followers met secretly in a farmhouse near Mangatarem, Pangasinan and proclaimed the launching of the Communist Party of the Philippines, Marxist-Leninist/Mao Tse-tung Thought. The small gathering, which was without a worker or a peasant representative, was referred to as the Congress for the Re-establishment of the Communist Party of the Philippines.

Declaring that "the conditions for revolution are excellent," the program document approved by the 12 youth called for an armed struggle of a protracted character to achieve a people's democratic revolution, which was on the order of the day because "U.S. imperialism, modern revisionism and all reactionary forces are receiving crushing blows from the oppressed peoples of the world and are in a state of disintegration."

Having put forward this perspective, the 12 then had the problem of finding an armed force to carry it out. That problem was not solved through the mass organizations of the people and their struggles but through an arrangement with none other than Senator Benigno Aquino of the Tarlac landowning elite. Aquino had an intimate, feudalist relationship with a former HMB local commander, Bernabe Buscayno, known as Commander Dante, who, after the dissolving of the HMB as a national army, had maintained his own unit in Southern Tarlac in the barrios around Hacienda Luisita, the vast sugar plantation owned by the Cojuangco family with which Aquino had merged through marriage to Corazon Cojuangco. For an ambitious politician aiming for the Philippine presidency like Benigno Aquino, Dante and his armed followers were an electoral asset in the country's violent politics. For Aquino, too, it was convenient to have allies on the left as one of the segments of his machinery for winning power. Aquino himself brought Sison and Dante together, personally driving Sison to a barrio meeting with Dante in January 1969.[5]

On March 29, 1969 (the anniversary date of the 1942 founding of the Hukbalahap which Sison emulated despite his condemnation of the PKP) Sison and some of his student central committee members met with Dante and several of his armed peasants in Tarlac and agreed on the establishment of a New People's Army (NPA), of which Dante's group would be the nucleus. A document, "The New People's Army," written by Sison, which was read to and approved by those present, declared that the NPA was "under the supreme guidance of Mao Tse-tung's Thought" and projected the concept of a protracted people's war conducted from bases in the countryside from which the NPA would finally "march in on the cities to seize power."[6] With the majority of his student group, Sison moved from Manila to Tarlac to stay in a barrio on Aquino-Cojuangco land where Dante's unit operated.

At the outset the CPP-led NPA had great difficulty in establishing itself. It was soon exposed in Tarlac by a Philippine Army patrol that discovered a clumsily built dugout filled with documents, followed by a military sweep that scattered the freshly born movement. The CPP sought to shift the base of the armed struggle to the north, to the Sierra Madre mountains of Isabela province where Sison, always viewing the Philippine situation in terms of China's liberation war, hoped to create an "NPA Yenan." It may be noted that the HMB in the early 1950s in its expansion drive had built a mass base along the route through Isabela and Cagayan provinces, and that NPA made contacts there by creating the impression that they were a continuation of the HMB. However, the NPA base was not secure. During 1971 and 1972 large-scale government army operations drove the NPA out of the region and nearly wiped it out.

The armed struggle thus launched by the small Maoist group did not spring from mass organizations of the people or follow logically from their struggles. It was artificially imposed on a situation that was not revolutionary. It was not a case of turning to armed struggle because the channels of legal peaceful struggle had been barred or denied. Legal organizations, in fact, and their activity were unimpeded at the time. The PKP had made considerable headway in helping to build a broadening national democratic movement. Sison's strategy and tactics sought to impose, from outside, concepts based on China's conditions and on Chinese experience. Mao's military doctrine of "surround the cities from the countryside" was mechanically and rigidly pursued.

That this should have come about was mainly due to the international differences that had developed between China and the Soviet Union and other socialist countries from the early 1960s, in which Mao Tse-tung and his associates had proclaimed the feasibility of a "great leap forward" to socialism in China, had called for revolutionary armed struggle against imperialism and reactionaries everywhere, and had condemned the Soviet Union and the international Communist movement for right-wing "revisionism" for seeking detente and peaceful co-existence with the capitalist powers. It became an international policy of the Chinese Maoists to win over other Communist parties to their position and, failing in this, to support the setting up of separate, rival Communist Parties wherever possible.

Without this outside factor it is unlikely that Jose M. Sison and his small group would have come on the scene and have taken the course they did. Their claims that conditions for revolution in the Philippines were excellent, was a mere echoing of Mao Tse-tung's sloganizing: no revolutionary situation existed in the Philippines then nor was any ever created by the New People's Army. This was one more historical instance of the Filipino people having their fate influenced by an outside force.

As the dominant ideologue of the CPP, Jose Sison (employing the pseudonym "Amado Guerrero") wrote several tracts which lay down the doctrine of his movement. His book *Philippine Society and Revolution* was the movement's basic text. It imbued a generation of young Filipino radicals with a distorted conception of the social forces at work in the Philippines. It is threaded with a grossly false account of the history and struggles of the PKP. Geared wholly toward armed struggle, it declares that "political power grows out of the barrel of a gun," and that "the New Peoples Army shall advance wave upon wave over a protracted period of time to destroy the enemy in the whole country."[7]

One of the main Sison precepts has been that feudalism is the main base of imperialism in the Philippines. "The preservation of feudalism in the Philippines is a matter of prime necessity for U.S. imperialism. If landlord power were to be overthrown in the countryside, U.S. imperialism would have nothing to stand on." This assumption underlay the whole military strategy of the NPA of basing the armed struggle in the rural areas, of "surround the cities from the countryside."[8]

Sison made this conclusion and projection precisely at the time when U.S. imperialism and its World Bank-IMF instruments were engaged in transforming feudal relations into capitalist relations in Philippine agriculture and in fitting the economy in general into the global capitalist system of TNC production, trade and marketing. Such concepts by Sison were eventually, inevitably, to create contradictions and a crisis of strategy in the CPP.

For the struggles of the Filipino people the gravest consequence of the CPP/NPA emergence was the division of the Filipino left and the disruption of the promising broad national democratic movement. Large anti-imperialist, anti-neo-colonial demonstrations, particularly by students and other youth, that had been developing since the mid-1960s either degenerated into clashes between the rival organizations (especially between the KM students and the MPKP) or were diverted toward violent confrontations with police by CPP-led factions that broke away from larger demonstrations to fight with the police or to cause destruction of property. This antagonized middle class and nationalist entrepreneurial elements that had been tending toward a national democratic position.

Between 1969 and 1972, a period of great turbulence in the Philippines, when U.S.-World Bank-IMF programs of neocolonial adjustment were being initiated and when U.S. intrigues to replace Marcos were in progress, the forces of the left were unable to mount a unified resistance to imperialist and local capitalist plans. It was significant that Sison's CPP in those years directed its struggle wholly against Marcos and considered the opposition Liberal Party its ally, maintaining close relations with the Liberal leader, Benigno Aquino. The PKP, on the other hand, denounced both the Nacionalista Party of Marcos and the Liberal Party as "two political parties both of whom stand for the same conviction—the preservation of our exploitative and oppressive status quo." PKP-led mass organizations set up a People's Movement to Boycott the Elections in the 1969 Marcos-Osmena contest, and called for a "Total Boycott" of the mid-term senatorial and local elections in 1971. It was the PKP's position at the time that imperialism and the neocolonial system should be the targets of the people's struggle and that the party should not identify itself with rival personalities who were a part of the system and out to benefit from it, not to change it.[9]

In this period the PKP regarded the CPP/NPA with the utmost suspicion. The splitting of the left and of the mass movement, accompanied by virulent, slanderous propaganda attacks on the PKP with the aim of discrediting it, was reason enough for this but was only part of it. Benigno Aquino, Sison's close ally, who provided funds and arms to launch the CPP/NPA—this was the basis for the Marcos case against Aquino used to detain him under martial law—was an admitted trainee of the CIA and was the U.S. choice to replace Marcos. His financial support for the NPA, however, could have been only a fraction of the funds that suddenly appeared to be at the disposal of the CPP. While the PKP, like all other Communist Parties in the third world, survived on a meager shoestring of funds, the CPP/NPA within a year or two of launching blossomed as the most well-financed revolutionary movement in the world, able to issue large amounts of printed material and to pay its leading activists P200 to P400 allowance a month. Within a year of its creation the CPP was publicized as having expanded its mass organizations from the Ilocos region of northern Luzon to Davao in Mindanao in the south.

The CPP/NPA from the beginning received enormous publicity in the Philippine press and internationally through the U.S. news services and China's Hsinhua News agency. Together with this was an echoing of the Sison attacks on the PKP as "moribund" and as no longer a revolutionary party or with any influence. This depiction of the situation in the Philippines, which has been persistent since that time, was clearly aimed at dividing the left and at playing up the extremist section of it to serve right-wing purposes. For a time the PKP made the mistake of being drawn into bitter polemics with the CPP, answering slanderous attacks, but this was stopped to prevent further division of the left, the PKP since then calling for unity of all patriotic and anti-imperialist forces.

Marcos propaganda channels in particular played up the CPP/NPA. The purpose was revealed on September 21, 1972 in Marcos's Proclamation 1081, declaring martial law. Its sole stated pretext, to which the Proclamation was totally devoted, was the "armed insurrection and rebellion" of the CPP/NPA which were depicted in extravagant language as having "assumed the magnitude of an actual state of war against our people" and as having "a well-trained, well-armed and highly indoctrinated and greatly expanded revolutionary force" which had "produced a state of political, social, psychological and economic instability in our land." Yet the NPA that had supposedly achieved all this was said to have as of January 1, 1972 no more than 1,028 regular fighters.[10] Marcos, in other words, had magnified an alleged CPP/NPA threat as an excuse for proclaiming martial law ostensibly to repel an imminent armed overthrow of the government, but actually for wholly other reasons of being able to decree the economic and political measures of the Marcos neocolonial capitalist program.

The prolonged martial law period was marked by the further divergence of the two main sections of the Philippine left. While the CPP continued with its Maoist blueprint of armed struggle, building an underground party mainly devoted to providing an armed struggle support base, the PKP persisted with its strategy and tactics of adhering to and giving increased emphasis to legal struggle and mass organization regardless of the suppressive nature of martial law, which had initially banned or dissolved existing organizations of the people.

On February 11, 1973, less than five months after the Marcos Proclamation, the PKP held its Sixth Congress in underground conditions and adopted a new and updated program, designed to advance the movement for a national democratic revolution. It declared, first of all, that

> the struggle of all anti-imperialist and patriotic forces must be directed against the main enemies of the people. These are the forces of imperialism, the members of the big bourgeoisie who collaborate with foreign monopoly capital, and the strong remnants of the feudal oligarchy. But the principal enemy is still U.S. imperialism.

Calling for "a united front of all exploited classes, of all patriotic and democratic forces, under the leadership of the working class," it said that this

> with the PKP, will wage every form of open and legal struggle, including electoral struggle, that will lead to a change in the balance of forces and the setting up of a national democratic government.

The PKP program defined the party's attitude toward violence and armed struggle, saying that it

> rejects putchism, coup d'etat, foco guerrillaism or anarchoterrorist revolutionism that stands apart from the sentiment of the masses . . . It is in the interests of the masses that the road to revolution is without bloodshed, and they desire that the transfer of power from the forces of imperialism, feudalism and monopoly capital to the political parties of all exploited classes be peaceful. The conditions for violence are necessarily determined by those who possess the instruments of violence, namely, the ruling circles of imperialism, feudalism and monopoly capital. The PKP and all revolutionary forces must be vigilant and must always be in a state of preparedness in every way to prevent the enemies of the people

from obstructing the people's way to peaceful revolutionary transformation of our society. The PKP upholds the right of the people to use force against those who use force against the people.

On the question of unity the PKP program said:

No party or organization can carry out the demands of the national democratic revolution single-handedly. The decisive pre-condition for the national democratic revolution is the formidable alliance of all anti-imperialist forces, based on a broad mobilization of the masses under the leadership of the working class.[11]

The PKP decision to pursue rigorously the strategy and tactics of open legal struggle came under test in the latter part of 1973 when the Marcos government, conceivably in reaction to a study of the party's program, initiated contacts with the underground PKP, proposing talks aimed at a "national unity" agreement. For months the PKP's leading organ debated such a step and eventually decided to accept the Marcos proposal. Negotiations took place through the spring and summer of 1974 and a "national unity" agreement was finally announced by both sides on October 11, 1974.

In essence, the PKP agreed to support certain reforms being undertaken by the Marcos regime, in exchange for which Marcos, for his part, would give amnesty to all PKP leaders and members, including the release of political prisoners who were PKP members, and, most pertinent, would enable the PKP to conduct legal activity without hindrance.

A PKP policy document set out the features of the Marcos program which the PKP was ready to endorse. These included: the anti-feudal land reform (as far as it went, the PKP calling for its extension to all agriculture), the emphasis on intensified nationally-distributed industrialization, the reconstruction of trade unions along the line of industrial unionism which the regime had proposed in place of their extremely fragmented and dispute-ridden state, and the pursuance of a more independent foreign policy with diplomatic and trade relations with socialist countries.

However, the PKP refused to endorse martial law and stood firm in opposing it:

The central point in the struggle of the PKP and that of the working class movement in the Philippines is the establishment of a truly democratic political, economic and social order in the country. Thus, the PKP vehemently objects to the proclamation of martial law throughout the country and its continuance. The PKP calls for the immediate termination of the martial law "emergency" situation; the restoration of the liberties of the people suspended or abolished by the imposition of martial law, particularly freedom of speech, of assembly and of the press, and of the right to strike; and the release of all political prisoners.[12]

President Marcos, for his part, held back from conceding full legality to the PKP, which was now able to operate legally and above-board as a political *organization* in building mass organizations, in recruitment of members, and in issuing statements, leaflets and published materials, but was not recognized as a political *party* with the right to run candidates in elections.

In reaching such an agreement with Marcos, the PKP was adhering to the political decision it had reached in the latter 1950s to make the full transition to legal struggle. No distinction had been made regarding the political parties and leaders of the ruling elite as far as negotiating agreements or policy positions was concerned. In dealing with Marcos, condemned widely as a dictator, the PKP took a calculated risk that was debated long and hard but was considered worth taking because it enabled the party to attain a position of realizing far broader ties with the people, and to mobilize, politically educate and influence greater numbers of working people, intellectuals and nationalist bourgeois sectors. To reach such a point, and to prove its sincerity, the PKP publicly disarmed and disbanded its armed force.

Part of the risk involved in this overall step materialized soon afterward when President Marcos violated the spirit of the agreement by announcing that the PKP had "surrendered" to him. Marcos may have been trying to protect himself from U.S. charges of being "soft on Communism" for dealing with the PKP but it began the agreement on a sour note and gave ammunition to the CPP to propagandize the PKP as "renegade." The PKP in a press statement strongly denied the Marcos allegation but had to prove itself in subsequent activity and in mounting and eventual total opposition to a degenerating Marcos regime.

Despite the restrictions of martial law, the PKP was able to help rebuild banned organizations and to create new ones. Trade unions had not been dissolved by Marcos, who was mainly concerned with satisfying the TNCs by banning the right to strike; a new PKP-guided labor federation, the *Pambansang Katipunan ng mga Manggagawa* (National Congress of Workers) was set up to unify left-led unions. The peasant union MASAKA had been suspended and in its place a new organization, the *Aniban ng mga Manggagawang Agrikultura* (AMA, or Association of Agricultural Workers) was created which was more suited to the changing agrarian relations under the Marcos land reform. A new youth organization, SIKAP, was established as the successor of the MPKP. The new women's organization, *Katipunan ng Bagong Pilipina* (KBP, or Association of the New Filipina), grew rapidly especially among peasant and worker women as the biggest women's organization that the Philippines had known. Replacing the former Bertrand Russell Peace Foundation was a new Philippine Peace and Solidarity Council. All told, at least 16 legal organizations identified with the positions of the PKP arose in the 1970s and were able to carry on anti-imperialist, national-democratic activity without hindrance.

The joint demonstrations and organized protests of these organizations forced the cancellation in 1975 of an official visit to the Philippines of the fascistic ruler of Chile, General Pinochet. One of the most effective campaigns was against U.S. military bases, carried on especially during the prolonged negotiations of 1975–1978 for a new bases agreement. The freedom with which the PKP was able to publish and disseminate anti-bases and anti-imperialist propaganda and hold related demonstrations was an indication that Marcos (whose own daughter took a prominent part) was not averse to having the PKP and the organizations it influenced generate anti-imperialist sentiment to strengthen his negotiating position.

However, the semblance of a national unity agreement with Marcos was short-lived, soon negated by the increasing foreign debt servitude of the Marcos regime, which cancelled out any prospect of independent national development, worsened mass poverty, and led to more brutal martial law repression as popular disaffection grew. By 1977, the 7th Congress of the PKP, again held underground, distanced itself from the program of the Marcos regime, declaring that

> Due to the lack of meaningful participation of the people, this program has only succeeded in transforming the landscape from a largely feudal to a predominantly capitalist one dominated by the giant American, Japanese and Western European transnational corporations, [with industrialization occurring but] under the aegis of foreign monopoly capital and imperialist-dominated lending agencies such as the IMF and World Bank [while] the Philippine countryside will be taken over by foreign-dominated agribusiness corporations.[13]

From that point, PKP opposition to Marcos martial law policies grew and became total. The party's 8th Congress in December 1980 adopted a program that contained a wholesale denunciation of the regime:

> From a historical and national standpoint, martial law has strengthened the imperialist hold on the country . . . Politically, the country's economic

independence has reduced to mere rhetoric the administration's claims of political independence ... The neo-colonial program inspired by the World Bank and the transnational corporations have tended to even magnify social inequalities as the fruits of expanded production do not seep down to the masses ... The entire bureaucracy is still full of undesirables and corruption reaches the highest levels of administration ... With the obvious failures of the administration to deliver the reforms and instil national discipline, efforts to prolong martial law rule or pave the way for its lifting by keeping the authoritarian powers of the president intact appear to be selfish moves on the part of the Marcoses to simply perpetuate themselves in power.[14]

From the outset of martial law the PKP had consistently called for the unity of all anti-imperialist and democratic forces, as the only way of building the mass movement essential to achieve national democratic aims. This was reiterated with increasing emphasis in the 6th, 7th and 8th Congresses of the PKP, the Political Resolution of the latter declaring:

Today, the PKP is ready to work with any and all groups in all aspects of the struggle against imperialism and for the removal of all barriers to the realization of a democratic political life which is essential to national independence and social progress.

To the imperialist policy of divide and rule, the people must counter with the forces of mass unity. It is therefore necessary that all the artificial barriers of misunderstanding and hostility engineered by imperialism between and among the democratic sectors of society be exposed and removed. The need of the hour is mass anti-imperialist unity to counter the onslaughts of foreign monopoly capital.[15]

For the other section of the Philippine left, led by the CPP of Sison, martial law provided both justification and opportunity for the strategy of armed struggle. CPP leaders theorized that an authoritarian regime left no alternative to the people but to resort to arms. As Proclamation 1081 made plain, an intensified military response to the CPP/NPA challenge would be made. The CPP in effect welcomed this, expecting its ruthless measures to bring support and recruits to the guerrilla forces.

Major government operations were mounted wherever the NPA sought to establish itself. For the NPA, most of the decade of the 1970s was a fight for survival. Rash CPP attempts to establish and defend liberated base areas, in Isabela, Sorsogon, Samar and other regions met with easy encirclement, isolation, air attack and near annihilation. The casualties were great. Almost all of the original founding leaders of the both the CPP and NPA were killed, captured and imprisoned, or surrendered to cooperate with the government, by the latter 1970s. Sison himself was arrested in 1977, Bernabe Buscayno (Commander Dante in 1976), Victor Corpuz in 1976.[16]

However faulty the overall armed struggle line, the young revolutionaries drawn to the movement displayed the same dedication and heroism shown by the HMB before them. A large number of the recruits for the CPP/NPA came from the universities of Manila and other cities, from a generation of youth growing up in the climate of an incomplete and corrupted independence, imbued with nationalist ideals and readily stirred by revolutionary slogans for liberation. They joined both the PKP and the CPP/NPA, but their motivations were the same in both cases, and the basis for unity of the two left movements was strong for that reason. Although divided, the forces of the left during the Marcos period represented in sum a considerable growth of the anti-imperialist, national-democratic sector in the country, of which both movements were legitimate parts.

By persisting with its initial dogmatic Maoist line of aping the Chinese liberation war, the CPP/NPA were facing disaster by the mid-1970s. The saving grace for the CPP at this time was an alliance with the left wing that had developed in the Catholic Church. A theological left had begun to take shape in the 1960s among students for the priesthood in the Catholic seminaries. During the spread of student action movements in the latter 1960s, students from Catholic universities in Manila—La Salle, Letran, Ateneo—had taken part. A group of young priests, including Father Edicio de la Torre of the Society of the Divine Word (SVD), Father Jose Nacu of the La Sallette Order, and Father Luis Jalandoni of the Jesuits, after embracing the "theology of liberation" formulated by Gustavo Gutierez, had made the transformation to features of the Marxist theory. Although inspired also by the national liberation struggle of the PKP-led HMB, the left connections they made were with the ultra-left CPP.

In 1972, several months before martial law, a conference of 72 radical priests headed by Father de la Torre met in Manila and established Christians for National Liberation (CNL), which eventually, by the 1980s, drew several hundred priests and nuns as members besides Catholic lay workers. Contacts with the underground CPP existed from the CNL's launching and in 1973 a Preparatory Commission for a National United Front was created with CNL and CPP representatives. Finally, in 1975, a National Democratic Front (NDF) was formally established by the Commission (which was made up of the CPP/NPA and *Kabataang Makabayan* on one side and the CNL and the *Katipunan ng mga Gurong Makabayan* — Association of National-

1st Teachers made up of some teachers in Catholic schools—on the other). The NDF, actually a committee, eventually became the spokesman and negotiating arm of the CPP-led movement.

Although the NDF described itself as "a framework or channel for the unity, cooperation and coordination of all national democratic forces in the country" and its 10-point program proposed to "unite all anti-imperialist forces," it was never more than a narrow committee of tightly-controlled CPP-headed organizations: the CPP, NPA, CNL (de la Torre, Jalandoni, Nacu and others all admittedly became CPP members in the early 1970s), KM, and some organizations with a transparently paper character to pad out the "united front" (the Revolutionary Movement of Peasants, the Revolutionary Movement of Workers and the Nationalist Association for Health—none of which was ever seen in material form—along with the Catholic Association of Nationalist Teachers). All calls for unity by the PKP and organizations associated with it were persistently spurned by the NDF and its CPP members, as was a relation with other left groups.

However, the CNL provided the important link for the CPP to the powerful Catholic Church and its vast network of social, political and economic institutions and activities. By the latter 1970s the predominant sections of the Philippine Church had turned increasingly against Marcos, particularly the majority in the Catholic Bishops' Conference who had been identified as moderates. In the interest of opposing and removing Marcos (it is interesting that this occurred at the same time that the U.S. pressures against Marcos developed), the moderate and left Catholic groupings tended to join forces. In practice, a major aspect of this was Church support for the NPA. The growth of NPA support structure and combat strength and its expansion into many provinces parallels this trend.

In this period, from the setting up of the NDF onward, CNL and other left Catholic elements moved into the top echelons of the CPP. The severe attrition of CPP leaders and of NPA commanders left gaps in leadership that were readily filled by the Christian militants, including in the CPP's central committee. Some Catholic radicals at the time boasted of having "taken over the revolutionary left—it's ours."[17] A number of the most publicized NPA commanders were priests from this point, especially Father Conrado Balweg in Mountain Province and Father Zacharias Agatep in the Ilocos region. The Basic Christian Community, the grassroots organization of the Church, became a key part of the NPA support structure all over the country. Church school buildings and the homes of priests were used as hiding places for arms, literature and supplies, as well as safe houses for guerrillas. In the view of some observers, the CPP was converted from a Maoist party to a Christian party. This was an exaggeration; the change was not that extensive, but it was noticeable that much of Maoist phraseology disappeared from CPP literature. The fact that a discrediting of Mao Tse-tung himself had occurred in China contributed to the process. This combination of factors caused two different outlooks to become established and increasingly in contradiction within the CPP and CPP-led movement.

The CPP/NPA were able to become established in key regions chiefly due to the link with the Church. On the island of Negros, the major sugar-producing area, the Church-led Federation of Free Farmers had spearheaded the organization in the latter 1960s of a National Federation of Sugarcane Workers among the extremely exploited sugar workers. This was done in implementation of the Vatican encyclical on the rights of labor. Bishop Antonio Fortich of Negros denounced the injustices of the sugar baron landlords in 1969. He appointed a young Jesuit priest, Luis Jalandoni, born into one of the wealthiest plantation families of Negros, as director of the diocese's social action center. Jalandoni, who helped organize sugar workers, priests and nuns, joined the CPP and served as the principal agent for building a CPP/NPA force on the island, backed by a Christian-Marxist alliance.

Jalandoni, who was defrocked by the Jesuit order, subsequently became the chief NDF international representative based in Utrecht, Netherlands. From there, he was active in creating Support Groups for the CPP/NPA/NDF, set up in 15 countries by the mid-1980s.

A principal aim of the CNL and CPP was to infiltrate and control the social action programs of the Church throughout the Philippines. Many of the priests who were to play leading roles in the NDF, NPA and CPP served as social action directors (SADS) in various dioceses, including Jalandoni, Edgar Kangleon (largely responsible for creating the substantial NPA base on Samar island), Santiago Salas, Frank Navarro, Zacharias Agatep, Nicholas Ruiz.

One of the chief functions of the SADS was channeling aid funds to social action projects. The main aid agency in the Philippine Catholic Church, however, was the National Secretariat of Social Action, Justice and Peace (NASSA), the social action arm of the Catholic Bishops' Conference of the Philippines. This was set up in 1966 in pursuance of the Vatican II social action policy. The two members of the CBCP who successively headed NASSA, Bishop Julio X. Libayen and Bishop Antonio Y. Fortich, were both from Negros, where a strong link between the CPP/NPA network and the Church organizations existed. NASSA received the bulk of its funds for program projects from international agencies.

These have included: Swiss Lenten Fund, Dutch Lenten Fund, Misereor, the Dutch Cebemo, Assistance Program for Human Development, Trocaire, CAFOD, ICCO, and Caritas. Situated in Western Europe, these agencies have been a principal concentration for the NDF group based there.

The funds involved have been very large. A NASSA report showed that from January 1980 to December 1981 alone it processed 247 projects costing ₱48,488,925 of which 78 per cent went to "community-building programs" of the social action centers through which money easily flowed to CPP-led bodies. It was subsequently concluded by Church authorities that scores of millions of pesos went to the CPP/NPA/NDF through this channel.[18]

Funds have also been gathered to the CPP-led movement from other sources. The overseas support groups have money-raising drives in Filipino communities abroad, especially for "aid to political detainees," and appeals are made to progressive organizations for contributions to the struggle against dictatorship. In the Philippines the NPA has operated a "taxation" system for landowners, large and small, executing those who refuse to pay up. All told, the CPP/NPA have never lacked the financial means of conducting a struggle. When a CPP finance secretary was arrested in 1989, bank deposit books for Philippine and foreign banks found in her possession showed accounts totalling millions of dollars.

However, the CPP, although projecting itself as the "re-established Communist Party of the Philippines," never attained real status in the international Communist movement. In its early Maoist period and until the latter 1970s it called only China and Albania its allies, condemning the Soviet Union and the rest of the world's Communist movements as "revisionist" and "running dogs of imperialists." Following the discrediting of Maoism plus the establishment by Marcos of relations with China (marked by a pledge by then-Foreign Minister Chou En-lai not to interfere internally in the Philippines or to aid the CPP), the CPP/NDF gradually shifted its position and sought to form links with the international Communist movement including the Soviet Union. Fraternal exchanges were made with a few parties, but the main goal of ties with the Soviet Union in hopes of material support never materialized.

U.S. news agencies, however, and the conservative Philippine press gave massive publicity to the NPA, printing uncritically the extravagant claims to strength by the CPP. A 1981 report of the CPP claimed for the NPA 10,000 full-time guerrilla soldiers in 26 guerrilla fronts in 40 provinces, plus five times that number in armed people's militia. In those fronts, it was said, five million peasants and others gave *active support* to the armed struggle and ten million were counted on in mass base areas. It was claimed that there were 800,000 *active members* in revolutionary organizations allegedly led by 40,000 mass leaders. Subsequent claims in the following decade greatly magnified these numbers.[19]

During 1984 and 1985 when the U.S. was developing moves for the removal of Marcos and helping to build the bourgeois opposition to replace him, the publicity given to the NPA reached a peak. It was alleged that mass unrest caused by the Marcos regime was driving people to the NPA and that "the communists" (the CPP) were in line to win power in five years. In other words, the same threat that Marcos himself had used as reason for martial law in 1972 was being used in 1985 for getting rid of him.

NEOCOLONIALISM, NEO-COLLABORATION
AND NEW FORMS OF RESISTANCE

The transfer of power from President Marcos to President Aquino was not a sudden act of revolutionary change. It was carefully pre-pared by U.S. imperialism and the rest of the international consortium of imperialist interests, using the subtle pressures of the lending agencies and military aid programs, forcing Marcos to lift martial law in 1981. This meant a removal of the ban on political party activity, the enlargement of press freedom, and greater freedom to demonstrate. Organization of the elite political alternative could begin, built around the politicians and the businessmen (the "oligarchs") whom Marcos had dispossessed.

Above all, U.S. interests were desirous that the power shift should be a controlled one, kept in the hands of collaborators, with the left frozen out of the process as much as possible. It was useful to boost the CPP/NPA with aid and propaganda during martial law, chiefly through the Catholic Church, as a means of undermining the Marcos position, but that was not wanted in the change itself. Whereas the CPP and radical Catholics had been a focal point of anti-Marcos sentiment in the 1970s, in the early 1980s Church moderates and opposition elite political leaders became active in organizing anti-Marcos demonstrations.

A turning point for this trend was the assassination of Benigno Aquino in 1983. As his intended return to the Philippines became known, the CPP offered him security in an NPA "liberated zone" on his arrival, a gesture that indicated the continuing relations of the CPP/NPA with Aquino. He did not respond to the offer. The popular reaction to his assassination showed the mass base on which he was actually relying in risking a return. The huge protest demonstrations and funeral processions of up to a million or more people that took place were largely organized by the Church.

In this period the nature of the new order to replace Marcos took shape. By this time the CPP, aware of the mass organizational activity of the PKP, had given attention to building legal movements as well as the NPA, in particular aided by its church links in setting up a Manila-based trade union "center", the *Kilusang Mayo Uno* (May First Movement) or KMU. These joined with the anti-Marcos demonstrations mourning Aquino, along with new committees and movements of Church, middle-class and wealthy elite inspiration. For the CPP/NDF this was an ideal opportunity to advance a broad united front policy but it was dissipated through persisting with the standard Maoist attempt to insist on hegemony or domination in organizations that arose. One of these was the *Bagong Alyansang Makabayan* (BAYAN, or New Patriotic Alliance) which was set up in 1985. From its founding congress, BAYAN was wracked with divisions when representatives of CPP/NDF-led groups tried to pack the leading posts with their people. National democrats invited to attend, like Jose Diokno, Lorenzo Tañada, Agapito Aquino and others, walked out of the congress in protest. BAYAN remained a narrow movement. The anti-Marcos movement that came into the streets at this time and up to the ouster of Marcos moved not to the left but to the fold of the bourgeois opposition.

The presidential election on February 7, 1986 between Marcos and the final U.S.-approved choice, Mrs. Corazon Aquino, showed the extent to which the left had been marginalized. The PKP and the mass organizations it influenced had taken no part in the mourning for Aquino or in the Church-elite anti-Marcos demonstrations. In the presidential election the PKP considered that neither candidate deserved the support of the people. Its election statement said that "the present struggle is essentially a contest between or among prospective caretakers of American interests in this country," and pointed out that

> The opposition, which enjoys considerable moral and material support from Washington, has failed to raise the issue of sovereignty on the campaign trail. Worse, the economic blueprint bared by Cory Aquino sounds too close to the IMF prescription for the country, e.g., less government in business, against local monopolies without mwntioning transnational monopolies, etc. To Marcos' stand amenable to extending the RP-U.S. Bases Agreement beyond 1991, the lady standard bearer refuses

to make a categorical statement on abrogation or extension. The opposition is simply against the continued rule of the Marcoses.

However, the PKP declared that

it would be very simplistic indeed if elections of this kind were summarily dismissed as mere exercises in futility. For the masses could learn vital lessons from such elections, especially when the meaning of the political exercise is laid bare to them and connected with the reality of economic conditions and social injustice.

Therefore the PKP called for "Active Participation to Expose Imperialist Deception" through taking at least a propaganda part in the campaign, and urged "On election day, let us go to the polls and register our protest on our ballots." People were called on to write anti-imperialist slogans on ballots or the names of anti-imperialist left leaders.[20]

This position was in recognition of the widespread popular desire to exercise a democratic right that had been denied for a decade and a half. Only the loyal PKP supporters may have heeded the call, but even limited participation was in accord with the overwhelming sentiment of the people and at least did not isolate the party from the masses.

For the CPP, however, the election precipitated crisis. Mrs. Aquino had strong Catholic Church backing (its Cardinal Jaime Sin had a key part in the intrigues that made her the candidate) and the Catholics in the CPP leadership and structure fought for electoral support for Aquino. In the bitter debate that occurred, the Maoist extremists prevailed, and the CPP called for a total boycott of the election. The CPP-dominated BAYAN echoed the boycott call.

It was a disaster. The Filipino people flocked to the polls, especially to vote for Mrs. Aquino, including in the areas of supposed CPP/NPA control. Leading BAYAN figures defied the party and swung to Mrs. Aquino, and even some regional CPP committees called for an Aquino vote. Response to the boycott was so miniscule that election analysts could not detect it. It was such a rebuff for the CPP and showed such disarray in its own ranks that the party was plunged into a damaging internal dispute.

The left thus played no part in the vote for Mrs. Aquino that precipitated the end of Marcos rule. It was absent as well from the EDSA demonstrations of February 23-26 that figured in the actual removal of Marcos. In the whole transfer of power neither sector of the left took sides, abstaining from what was seen as a struggle between rival imperialist-linked collaborator groups.

Having isolated itself politically and organizationally with its boycott, the CPP was immersed for months in internal debate and assessment.

In May 1986 a public self-criticism had to be made to restore the party's image. It admitted that the CPP leadership had "failed to grasp the essence of the whole situation that was in flux at the time," which was that "the snap election became the main channel of large-scale mobilization and deployment of the masses for the decisive battle to overthrow the dictatorship."

Said the self-critical CPP statement:

> The boycott policy not only failed to give enough value to the question of reaching and mobilizing the majority of the people. It directly and openly went against the desire of the broad masses to pursue the anti-fascist struggle by means of critically participating in the snap election . . . This showed an insufficient understanding of the tasks of political leadership during such a time, as well as a lack of appreciation of the current level of mass participation in revolutionary struggles.

In essence this statement was an apology for not having supported Aquino in the election, as well as an admission that the millions of followers the CPP claimed did not pay heed to its political leadership.[21]

CPP failure went further than the adoption of incorrect tactics. It lay, too, in not grasping the full role of U.S. imperialism, seen always in alliance with Marcos and not as the manipulator of the removal of Marcos, and not seen as the eminence behind Juan Ponce Enrile, Fidel Ramos, Corazon Aquino, Cardinal Sin, and "People Power."

The government of Cory Aquino that took office in February 1986 had, on the surface, a reformist, populist appeal exceeding that of the well-gilded Ramon Magsaysay. "People Power" had toppled Marcos the dictator, was the report flashed to the world. It was made to appear like an achievement by the Filipino people, with the foreign hand minimized.

Behind the Aquino government, however, was a familiar combination of forces. The World Bank-IMF and the Consultative Group of international bankers that had "structurally adjusted" the Philippines to their loan terms and had a powerful creditors' whip hand over its economy and people, had set the stage for the Marcos exit and had command over virtually every move that Cory Aquino could make. Within the country, the alliance that had elevated Aquino and her opposition grouping to power was made up of U.S. financial, transnational and military interests, the conservative sectors of the Catholic Church, the Filipino "oligarchs" whom Marcos had expropriated, the joint-venture bourgeoisie that swung the way its senior foreign partners wished, and the reactionary Filipino armed forces that were steeped in decades of counter-insurgency warfare against their own people. This was a deadly combination that held no promise of genuine change for the better for Filipinos.

There had been changes. The out-of-power politicians were now the rulers, and the economic rivals whom Marcos had expropriated were now the expropriators. A feature that was unchanging, however, was the dominant position of the TNCs, whose privileges and operations continued as usual and were even enhanced under the new regime.

A forecast of what to expect from the new government could be read in the election campaign position on the economy voiced by Mrs. Aquino. She echoed the World Bank-IMF prescription to the letter, calling for "less government in business" and opposing "local monopolies" in the public sector. She said nothing about TNC monopolies, or about the onerous terms of foreign lending agencies.

Equally ominous was the electoral stand she took on U.S. military bases, which had become an increasingly sensitive issue, the one most capable of arousing nationalist feeling. At the time when Mrs. Aquino was trying to unify oppositionists including the nationalist-inclined around her, she had spoken in favor of getting rid of the bases. However, once her candidacy was assured she backtracked, amending her position to one of "leaving my options open," i.e., refusing to state categorically if she favored either abrogation or extension of a bases agreement. To all discerning Filipinos this modification, coupled with the U.S. support for her election, was a clear sign that she had privately promised the U.S. that as president she would retain the military bases.

From the beginning of the Aquino government its commitment to a collaborationist neocolonial pattern became obvious. Its economic policies were virtually identical to those that had been squeezed out of Marcos: an open door for foreign investment, an export-oriented agriculture and industry, import liberalization that enabled foreign products to flood in and drown domestic business, and a continued reliance on foreign loans despite the enormous foreign debt burden inherited.

There was one grave difference. Whereas Marcos had built up the public sector as a national bourgeois base, President Aquino acceded wholly to the demands of foreign capital and promptly began the dismantling and privatizing of the public sector, in the name of "de-cronification." Nearly 200 government-owned corporations and agencies with a value of P150 billion were put up for sale to both foreign and Filipino investors.

The controlling economic posts in and outside of the Aquino cabinet went to the same type of technocrats that had been installed at the behest of foreign finance capital in the same posts in the Marcos period: Harvard graduates and products of the Jesuit-run Ateneo de Manila who were associated with the most conservative wing of the Catholic Church, "oligarch" members of the anti-Marcos sections of the bourgeoisie, and representatives of the powerful Sycip, Gorres and Velayo accounting firm that was a major business intelligence and economic penetration instrument linked with the World Bank, Asian Development Bank and big transnational commercial banks.

For the first year and a quarter of the Aquino presidency she governed by special powers that approximated the decree-making rule of Marcos, pending the writing and adoption of a new constitution and the election of a new Congress. Mrs. Aquino had the power to decree economic policies that could at least amend and curtail the all-pervasive operations of the TNCs, that would protect Filipino businesses, and that would cut down the severe drain on the economy caused by foreign debt servicing and repayment. Instead the Aquino government went to even further extremes of collaboration.

In 1987 it adopted an Omnibus Investment Code which handed far more benefits and guarantees to foreign capital than given by the Marcos regime. The Code was drawn up by Secretary of Trade and Industry Jose Concepcion, Jr., a businessman with strong joint venture ties with transnational corporations. He said the Code would attract foreign investments that were tending to flow to other countries in South East Asia. That was believable. The Code guaranteed freedom from expropriation and ensured virtually unlimited repatriation of investments, remittance of earnings, and the local availability of loans and contracts by foreign interests. It gave unprecedented incentives to pioneer enterprises, in particular income tax holidays for eight years, exemption from the 40 per cent ceiling on foreign ownership of capital, 100 per cent tax and duty exemption on imported machinery and equipment, 100 per cent tax credit on purchased domestic capital equipment, exemption from export tax and duties, employment of foreign nationals in supervisory, technical and advisory positions, and simplified customs procedures.[22]

Foreign investors felt so free under the Aquino regime that they ignored the limitations put on their activities in the Marcos foreign investment laws, invading areas reserved for Filipino enterprise. In July 1990 the chairman of the Senate committee on economic affairs, Senator Vicente Paterno, proposed a new Foreign Investment Act. Paterno, wholly amenable to encouraging even more foreign investment, nevertheless felt it necessary to complain about its behavior:

Lately foreign businessmen have been investing in economic activities adequately explored by local investors. This violates the spirit of allowing foreign investments in the country. They are now in real estate, banking, retail business and other enterprises where they unnecessarily compete with Filipino businessmen.

Paterno said that foreign investments should complement or supplement local investors, not drive them out of business.[23]

The Paterno bill and several other Senate bills of a similar character brought an immediate charge by transnational companies that "the Philippines is unfriendly to new investments." Two powerful blocs of TNCs, the Philippine Association of Multinational Companies' Regional Headquarters, Inc. and the American Chamber of Commerce in the Philippines each issued statements condemning "policies of disincentive to multinational corporations that are scaring off foreign investors." Of the 131 TNCs with regional headquarters in the Philippines, 11 transferred to Malaysia, Indonesia or Thailand in the first half of 1990. Others threatened to do so, and the Aquino government obediently put a clamp on foreign investment bills with a nationalist tinge.[24] Another Senate bill, the Filipinization of Domestic Credit Act, filed by Senator Wigberto Tañada, sought to limit borrowing by foreign firms from local sources—which was depriving Filipino investors of needed credit—but it also met with furious opposition from TNCs and suffered a similar fate.[25]

Submission to the TNCs on investment policy extended to agriculture as well, determining the character of agrarian reform legislation adopted by the Aquino government. In the first year of Cory Aquino's presidency she was strongly pressed by peasant, trade union and other organizations to make use of her special decreemaking powers to proclaim a new land reform law more comprehensive and more easily implemented than that of Marcos. Mrs. Aquino refused to do this, with the excuse that it should be left to "democratic enactment" by a new Congress whenever it would be elected. The new Congress elected in 1987 had, as in its past forms, a large percentage of landowner representatives, and the Comprehensive Agrarian Reform Program (CARP) that was passed by it in 1988 was so amended and stripped of reform that might benefit the peasant and farm worker that liberal congressmen who were among its initiators disowned the final law.

That land reform should be one of the main demands upon the Aquino government, after decades of land reform acts by each succeeding president, was a commentary upon the failure of those acts to end the injustices in the countryside. U.S. agencies and World

Bank-IMF programs had been instrumental in promoting the capitalist-oriented agrarian reform that had largely phased out semi-feudal relations, establishing corporate farms and agribusinesses in agriculture. Benefiting least were the peasants who were supposed to be able to receive land. Of the 400,000 peasants who were said to be potential beneficiaries of the 1973 Marcos Presidential Decree 27, only one-third had had their applications processed up to 1987 by the Land Bank through which transfer of land by purchase was handled, and of these less than 10 per cent were able to make their amortization payments regularly.

Far from ameliorating this situation, the Aquino CARP worsened it by reformulating the way land value and purchase price were set: the Marcos law had declared these to be based on $2\frac{1}{2}$ times the average harvest of three normal years prior to purchase, but CARP upset this by basing "just compensation" on a vague "fair market value" without any indication of how that was to be determined. It was a formula for excessive landlord purchase price demands and for endless disputes in clogged Agrarian Courts where the poor peasant had scant means for contesting his case with the more affluent landlord.

This aspect of land reform concerning the transfer of privately owned land was, however, not the main concern of CARP, which focused on public lands where the big agribusiness TNCs have been able to lease very extensive areas and where capitalist corporate farming has been developed. The Philippine Constitutions have limited single corporate leases to 1000 hectares, echoing the old U.S. colonial Organic Act of 1902. According to a 1980 agricultural census there were 722 corporate farms with an average of 216 hectares each, but the U.S. Dole and Del Monte corporations alone controlled 50,000 hectares each, chiefly in Mindanao. CARP tried to deflect nationalist protest at this by specifying that these huge areas should be distributed to agricultural worker beneficiaries within three years, but it said at the same time that the beneficiaries or the cooperatives or associations they may form must enter into grower service contracts with the self-same big U.S. corporations. Under this arrangement land ownership becomes relatively meaningless. As a Filipino authority on capitalist relations in agriculture commented:

> This is exactly the position of the commercial export-oriented banana growers. The transnationals in the rubber, palm oil, banana, pineapple and other export crop production lines have long known that profits need not come out of direct land ownership. What is important is control over

production, marketing, processing and technology. Contract growing is the alternative to the colonial-type plantation arrangement.[26]

The collaborating readiness of the Aquino government to accede to every wish of the foreign TNCs was conditioned in particular by the massive foreign debt that had been inherited from the Marcos regime. That debt, to foreign governmental agencies, the World Bank and IMF, and commercial banks, totalling 438 foreign creditors, stood at $27 billion in 1986.

That this was inherited did not mean that Aquino and her elite grouping were not in agreement with reliance on foreign loans. They favored it, if anything, even more than Marcos had. Considering the crisis conditions in the country at the time of her taking office, President Aquino would have had every justification to halt the drain on the economy by suspending debt servicing and repayment and by at least taking steps to repudiate a few of the major debts that were tainted with corruption, such as the multi-billion dollar Westinghouse nuclear reactor project. However, no such moves were made. Mrs. Aquino, instead, soon after her installation, promised to honor the country's entire external debt. Her compliant attitude was displayed in the appointment of top officials most closely associated with foreign capital, Central Bank Governor Jobo Fernandez and Finance Secretary Jaime Ongpin, to handle negotiations with creditors.

Submission to foreign finance capital was clung to despite a worsening of the debt problem in subsequent years. By 1988 over half of Philippine export earnings and 40 per cent of the budget were being expended for debt servicing and repayment. By the government's own estimates, up to $21.4 billion would be flowing out of the country for this purpose from 1987 to 1992, while only $4.2 billion would be coming in. Arrangements to adjust the debt, to which the Aquino government agreed, were not for the Philippines' benefit but that of foreign capital, in particular the debt-for-equity scheme by which foreign interests would acquire large slices of the Philippine economy. Seeking ever further loans rather than decisively reducing the debt obligation, Mrs. Aquino led the country to a foreign debt topping $30 billion by 1990.

The collaborationist character of the Aquino government, in acceding to every demand of foreign investors and creditors, exceeded that of the Marcos regime. The clearest example of this was the so-called "Marshall Plan for the Philippines" which was originally brewed in U.S. financial and strategic policy circles in the early 1980s as a reaction to the troublesome Marcos call for a comprehensive review of military and security agreements with the U.S. as well as to the growing economic and political instability of his regime. At that time an Inter-Agency Task Force in the Reagan administration, composed of members drawn from the CIA and the Defense, State and Treasury Departments, buttressed by the Congressional Research Services, produced a document late in 1984, "U.S. Policy Toward the Philippines," which stressed the "prime importance" of the Subic and Clark bases to "our security and defense goals" and contended that "political and economic developments in the Philippines threaten those interests." Marcos was seen as the main liability and the document spoke of the need to "try to influence him through a well-orchestrated policy of incentives and disincentives to set the stage for peaceful and eventual transition to a successor government." The major inducement was to be a program of "greatly increased economic assistance," referred to as a "Marshall Plan approach."

As it happened, the events leading to the Marcos downfall intervened before this program could be implemented, or was felt necessary. An Aquino government ushered in with U.S. backing was viewed as less difficult than that of Marcos. The main problems that had produced the U.S. policy document, however, persisted. A surge of sentiment among Filipinos against the U.S. bases arose after Marcos, complicating the pending renegotiation of the bases agreement, and the general situation in the Philippines remained relatively unstable. Consequently U.S. policy-making sectors re-generated the idea of a "Marshall Plan for the Philippines" which was proposed in a letter to President Reagan on November 25, 1987, signed by Alan Cranston, chairman of the U.S. Senate Subcommittee on East Asian and Pacific Affairs; Richard G. Lugar, member of the Senate Foreign Relations Committee; Stephen J. Solarz, chairman of the House Subcommittee on Asian and Pacific Affairs; and Jack Kemp, member of the House Subcommittee on Foreign Operations.

Two central factors emerged from the resurfaced proposal. One factor was a report of the Subcommittee on Asian and Pacific Affairs of the U.S. House of Representatives, dated April 18, 1989, which declared that

> the successful implementation of the Plan would certainly be extremely helpful in terms of creating a favorable climate in the Philippines for renewal of the bases agreement.

The interlocking of economic aid and extension of the military bases was very clear.[27]

The other factor had more profound implications. This was implied in the U.S. Congressional report which called for aid amounting to $1 billion a year over five years but which referred to this as "worldwide foreign assistance" and urged the encouragement of "international investment" in the Philippines. It was not solely a U.S. program that was being projected but one embracing other sectors of foreign capital as well. The term "Marshall Plan," in fact, was discarded, for its U.S. connotation, and replaced by Multilateral Aid Initiative (MAI) which in turn was altered to Philippine Assistance Plan (PAP). Underlying this policy approach was the increasingly glaring fact that U.S. economic supremacy had declined in the world and that the U.S. could not, with its global array of commitments, undertake the financing of its conceived plan for its own neo-colony. The limit of its contribution to the Plan was put at only $200 million for the first year, subject to Congressional appropriation.

Put together under the slogan of "burden sharing," a PAP donor consortium of the U.S., Japan, Britain, Germany, France, Belgium, Italy, Canada, Denmark, Netherlands, Norway and Australia met for a pledging session, significantly in Tokyo, in January 1990. An initial $1 billion was pledged in loans and grants, with Japan assuming the largest share, an indication of the changing power relations internationally. It was clearly understood that the funds provided were linked with the Philippine retention of U.S. military bases, which seemed to be assuming the evolving function of serving overall imperialist interests. President Aquino, attending the Tokyo gathering, was reported to have agreed confidentially to support a new, extended bases agreement.

The Philippine Assistance Plan, however, had a much greater list of conditions attached to it. A "Philippine Agenda for Sustained Growth and Development" had to be accepted. It included import liberalization (i.e., further reduction of tariffs on foreign goods), privatization of public sector corporations, deregulation, emphasis on the private sector in development programs, additional foreign investment incentives, and "cost recovery" for investors in water, power and irrigation services.[28]

Although the Philippines had to assure the PAP donors that it would abide by these terms, the assurance of aid itself was far from definite. Each country was to contribute its share through a parliamentary appropriation, with no guarantee that all or any of the sum would be approved. The U.S. share, for example, was $200 million for the first year, but the U.S. Congress whittled it down to $150 million. By 1990 the capitalist countries in general that were involved in aid programs for developing countries were retrenching on their international pledges, and no PAP promise could be considered ironclad. Whatever trickles of aid the Philippines might receive, it had to conform to its side of the agreement or receive even less.

Readiness of the Aquino government to submit itself to this beggar's position was reiterated in negotiations with the IMF that coincided with the finalizing of the PAP arrangement. In return for another round of IMF stabilization funds (to offset the worsening balance of payments deficit caused chiefly by the import liberalization demanded by foreign creditors and TNCs), the Philippines had to submit a Letter of Intent to the IMF pledging to adhere to its loan terms.

It was the 20th Letter of Intent demanded of the Philippines by the IMF and World Bank. Submitted in the latter part of 1989, it was accompanied by a required document, "Memorandum of the Philippine Economic Stabilization Plan for 1991-1992," which made specific promises of compliance to the terms. These were virtually identical to the PAP conditions.

They included: maintenance of import liberalization, budget priority for repayment and servicing of the foreign debt, unrestricted repatriation of capital and profits by foreign investors, cutting the budget for social services, new taxes and increased existing taxes to augment budget capability for debt repayment, an increase in rate charges for such services as water and power, further devaluation of the peso from P22.40 to the dollar in December 1989 to P28 to the dollar by October 1990, and stepping-up the sale of public sector corporations to private buyers. On the last particularly vital point, which meant stripping the Philippine government of whatever control it had over essential areas of the economy, the Memorandum pledged to reduce its corporations from 298 to only 78; those not sold would be liquidated or merged. Furthermore, those remaining would have their subsidies severely cut and government guarantees for covering their debts eliminated; they would be thrown into competing with the private sector for credit, a disadvantageous position threatening their survival.[29]

In the long succession of collaborationist acts by neocolonial governments in the Philippines, few have embodied such sweeping surrender as those by President Corazon Aquino.

The surrender has been not merely to U.S. interests but to the corporations and banks of all the other capitalist powers as well, jointly making their demands through the IMF, the World Bank and the Consultative Group of Creditors. The U.S. may still have the major slice of the Philippine pie but other foreign hands are taking shares and leaving less to Filipinos.

Transnational companies in general see the Philippines as wide open for exploitation and anticipate that future Philippine governments will open the door even wider. This was reflected in a gathering of big international mining companies that met in London on February 18, 1992. A principal agenda point was the global hunt for profitable mineral resources, and the Philippines received particular attention, seen as almost virgin territory with deposits of iron, nickel, zinc, lead, platinum, cobalt, manganese, aluminum, molybdenum and mercury that have been little explored because of the Philippine constitutional provision making mandatory a 60 per cent Filipino ownership of companies that exploit natural resources.

The mining companies saw this "disadvantage" as unlikely to last. According to the representative of the big Australian-based Western Mining Corporation, the Philippines presents "a window of opportunity which no longer exists in many parts of the world," because "a strong body of responsible opinion in the country" indicated to him that the Filipino ownership provision is "detrimental." He predicted that the next Philippine government would change the constitution and literally turn the country's mineral resources over to the transnational mining companies, which had complained about "only receiving 40 per cent of the prize."[30]

After 46 years of independence, the Philippine economy was still regarded as a prize to be shared out among foreign corporations. The prize was larger, the economy had grown, the statistics on production were greater, but proportionately the share of the Filipino people was less and foreign investors and creditors constantly demanded that they surrender more. The change from Marcos to Aquino worsened the neocolonial economic conditions.

If that was the state of the economy, the state of democracy in the Philippines was equally distorted in the post-Marcos years. The removal of Marcos had within it a democratic impulse as far as most Filipinos were concerned, a desire for what was called a restoration of democracy after authoritarian rule (although democracy had never been more than elite-deep in the Philippines). It meant different things to different sectors of the population. To the majority of the people, living in the barrios, it meant almost nothing; life was virtually the same under any government of the elite, amounting to little more than a communal sharing of poverty. To those with an experience of organization, it meant the hope of greater freedom for trade unions, peasant associations and other mass organizations, as well as for a right to form political parties and movements. Most of all, the changeover had been desired and worked for by the out-of-power elite and middle class sectors, for whom it meant a regaining of opportunities to enjoy the fruits of politics that had been reserved for the Marcos adherents, as well as the opportunity to get their hands on the sections of the economy that had been parcelled out to the "crony capitalist" associates of the deposed president.

One of the first acts of President Aquino was her Proclamation No. 3 which abolished the single-chamber parliament of Marcos (the Batasan), set aside the 1973 Marcos Constitution to be replaced by a new charter, and provided for a recomposition of the bureaucracy. Provincial governors and town mayors who had been elected in the latter Marcos years were arbitrarily thrown out and replaced with appointed persons belonging to anti-Marcos parties. In the administrative recomposition steps about 200,000 employees or officials including those in nonpolitical career civil service posts responsible for efficient administration of government were abruptly dismissed in a sweep reminiscent of the spoils system at its worst.

In place of the Batasan the previous two-chamber Congress of U.S. origin was restored. In its election, in 1987, the old patterns of regional warlordism, vote-buying, fraud and intimidation returned. Attempts by the left to contest congressional seats were met with by violence from the army and from hired thugs of elite contestants, and by floods of money to buy votes. The new House of Representatives was little different in composition from pre-martial law days, with numerous landowners and landowner-chosen members, and with various kinds of collaborators. In spite of the furor of opposition protest against Marcos for being undemocratic, those who succeeded him brought no real enhancement of democracy to the Philippine political or social system.[31]

The politics of the "restored democracy" did not settle down into a system of well-defined parties, such as the Liberal, Nacionalista and one or two minor parties of the past. Instead a fragmentation of politics occurred, with many continually changing, combining or splitting parties built around individual politicians whose power depended on wealth. By the presidential election of 1992 no fewer than eight such figures launched their candidacies, with little difference in vaguely-stated programs to be discerned, especially in readiness to conform to World Bank-IMF-TNC prescriptions for the Philippines. The opportunist nature of such politics was ideal for imperialist intervention and imposition.

A feature of the unstable political and economic period that followed the deposing of Marcos was a succession of mutinies and coup attempts by sections of the Philippine Army, six of which occurred between July 1986 and December 1989. In the last and most serious of these planes of the U.S. air force from the Clark Air Base intervened against the rebels, the first time open U.S. military intervention had been resorted to under the military agreements. This act of propping up President Aquino put a stop to rebellion in the army, serving notice that a "democratic" civilian rule was preferable for the neocolonial Philippines, while making President Aquino further obligated to her U.S. allies. It may be noted that the complete acquiescense of President Aquino to the terms of the multinational Philippine Assistance Plan in Tokyo occurred in the month after her rescue by the U.S. air force from the December 1989 army revolt.

As in every stage of Philippine history since the turn of the century, the meaningful substance of democratic development during the Aquino regime was in the mass organizational activity among the people and in the resistance to the neocolonial impositions on the country. The so-called "People Power" incident that contributed to the Marcos removal was not related to the popular movements; it did not spring from an organized movement nor did it continue in any organized form after the incident. As usual, the most significant democratic struggles and movements for change came from the forces of the left.

In the months that immediately followed the inauguration of the Aquino government there was a widespread euphoria about democracy being restored. It was called the "democratic space." The electoral team of Mrs. Aquino had included a number of national democrats, human rights defenders and liberals, to whom government posts had been promised. A few were rewarded initially with cabinet positions: Augusto "Bobbit" Sanchez as secretary of labor, Joker Arroyo as President Aquino's executive secretary, and Aquilino Pimentel as secretary of local government. Sanchez, who undertook to support trade union rights and to criticize openly the operations of transnational companies, soon drew the ire of U.S. businessmen, and Mrs. Aquino, under strong pressure from the American Chamber of Commerce and the U.S. Embassy, was forced to replace him. U.S. pressure also drove Arroyo and Pimentel from the cabinet. Within two years nationalist or liberal-inclined figures had been weeded out of the Aquino administration.

A steady move to the right by the Aquino government was in direct contrast to a strong democratic trend that was occurring outside the government, the formation of innumerable cause-related organizations among the people. The propaganda about a restoration of democracy that was employed to create a popular image for Mrs. Aquino was taken seriously by many people. The "democratic space" was filled by a wave of activism.

New left organizations—BISIG (*Bukluran sa Ikaunlad ng Sosyalistang*

Isip or Movement for the Advancement of Socialist Ideas and Action), the PDSP (*Partido Demokratiko Sosyalista ng Pilipinas* or Philippine Democratic Socialist Party), and the VPD (Volunteers for Popular Democracy)—each of which had begun to take shape in the closing days of the Marcos regime, spread out in organizing drives from 1986, each, as in the cases of the PKP and CPP, creating a periphery of mass organizations. BISIG, mainly an academic movement headed by an expelled former PKP political bureau member, Francisco Nemenzo, and a fellow University of the Philippines professor, Randolf David, called for a Philippine socialism with mixed public and cooperatively owned enterprises run by workers' councils. The PDSP, a variant of Christian socialism (a priest, Father Romeo Intengan, was one of its principal leaders), condemned "imperialism, dependent capitalism and feudalism" as the "three structural evils of Philippine society" but also took an anti-communist position. The VPD, set up by former priest Edicio de la Torre of Christians for National Liberation and fellow-Catholic and NDF member Horacio Morales, was termed "a conscious effort to overcome sectarianism and hostility among different left tendencies and to promote dialogue and mutual respect, while recognizing that differences will not be resolved quickly." De la Torre's position, one of the most positive-sounding coming from the post-Marcos groups, grew out of the heated debate within the CPP over strategy and tactics that was precipitated by the disastrous 1986 CPP boycott stand.[32]

The popular movements that arose in the latter 1980s were stimulated by the increasing failure of the Aquino government to respond with national democratic answers to the grave problems inherited from the Marcos period: the deep foreign debt-ridden economic crisis, the transnational stranglehold on the economy and the Aquino readiness to surrender to all of its demands, the still-incompletely solved agrarian situation, the question of U.S. military bases, the resolving of the armed conflict within the country.

In regard to the latter issue, the CPP, after admitting the error of its election boycott, swung to an opposite tactic, maneuvering for negotiating a settlement with the new Aquino government. Talks opened in July 1986 and ran until January 1987, featured by a ceasefire in the NPA armed struggle in November 1986. During the talks CPP spokesmen/NDF officers Antonio Zumel and Saturnino Ocampo went to the extent of proposing a form of power-sharing coalition government with Aquino in which the CPP/NDF would hold key cabinet posts while the NPA would retain its arms.[33] It was reported that some government members, including Mrs. Aquino, were at least inclined to grant legality to the

CPP. (It may be noted that one of the first acts of President Aquino was to release from prison Jose Sison and Bernabe Buscayno, whom she visited in prison and obtained their endorsement, at variance with the CPP boycott position.) The negotiations were eventually undermined and disrupted by U.S. intervention, the CIA and the Pentagon pressing the Philippine Army to arrest CPP officials and finally to have its death squads murder the chairman of the KMU trade union center, Rolando Olalia, in December 1986. When these occurred, the CPP broke off the talks.

At this time the PKP, noting the inclination of the Aquino government to concede legality to the CPP if its armed struggle ceased, wrote an open letter to Mrs. Aquino notifying her of its own continuation of "legal and open activities among the people" and expressing a hope for "an opportunity for a meeting with your Excellency" to discuss the extension of such democratic rights. The PKP letter was ignored while President Aquino proceeded to open talks with the CPP.[34]

Following the breakdown of its negotiations, the CPP resumed the armed struggle of its NPA, beginning a policy of confrontation with President Aquino that was virtually identical to its confrontation with President Marcos. When, in May 1987, a national referendum was held on the adoption of a new Philippine constitution, the CPP again called for a total boycott.

There were many aspects of the Aquino constitution that were opposed by the popular movements. It was written in 1986 by a 47-member Constitutional Commission that was not elected but was hand-picked by Aquino and her advisers and heavily-weighted with pro-U.S. and very conservative business, landlord and Church figures, but it had a minority of vocal national democrats who had the support of strong nationalist sentiment voiced outside the Commission. In its final draft the Constitution had grave neocolonial features, particularly in regard to economic concessions to foreign capital, but the Commission was also compelled by expressed popular feeling to include a provision stating that "The Philippines, consistent with the national interest, adopts and pursues a policy of freedom from nuclear weapons in its territory," which struck at U.S. military policy that had violated Philippine sovereignty. More important was the inclusion, in Section 25, Article 18 of the following:

> After the expiration in 1991 of the Agreement between the Republic of the Philippines and the United States of America concerning Military Bases, foreign military bases, troops or facilities shall not be allowed in the Philippines except under a treaty duly concurred in by the Senate and,

when the Congress so requires, ratified by a majority of the votes cast by the people in a national referendum held for that purpose, and recognized as a treaty by the other contracting state.

This provision, which automatically terminated U.S. bases in 1991, was welcomed by the PKP "as it will work for cause of national sovereignty and independence."

The new Constitution also had clearer definitions than in the past on the rights and freedoms of the people, including workers' rights to form unions, and severely restricted the freedom of a president to declare martial law. In its assessment the PKP saw "serious deficiencies" in the Constitution but also considered that "much of what is new in the democratic features has been distilled from the people's struggle against the Marcos dictatorship" and that it amounted to "significant ground on which to build the further expansion of the democratic forces." Consequently it was declared that "the Partido Komunista ng Pilipinas will vote for the proposed Constitution with full knowledge of its limitations." The party used the referendum period for an intensive educational campaign, on both its neocolonial and democratic features.[35]

In the referendum, the Constitution was approved by a "yes" vote by over 80 per cent of the Filipino people, the "no" votes being generated by opposition bourgeois political parties. The boycott call by the CPP was a total failure; there was no discernable evidence that any more than a handful had responded to it.

That fact arouses speculation about the actual strength and influence of the contemporary popular movements in the Philippines. There was an appearance of organization proliferation, but frequently the same people set up different groups, termed "democratic" or for "human rights," under various names, or each regional or local branch of a single nationally constituted organization adopted a name of its own. This was a tactic particularly favored by the CPP, an imprint left on CPP methods by the propaganda devices of Jose Sison, who resorted to unlimited exaggeration to project his movement. The NPA thus by 1990 was claimed to have up to 26,000 regular fighters with "guerrilla fronts" allegedly in 57 provinces. The CPP/NDF was said to have the support of one-fifth of the Filipino people, i.e., of over 12 million people. The strength of the related *Kilusang Mayo Uno* (KMU) trade union body was asserted to be from 500,000 to 750,000. A peasant organization with CPP guidance, the *Kilusang Magbubukid ng Pilipinas* (KMP) or Philippine Peasant Movement, was said, within four months of its creation, to have 500,000 members, which would have made it the most phenominal peasant organization in history. Every CPP-influenced organization was made to appear with an enormous mass following. This picture was disseminated abroad, creating a misimpression internationally of this sector of the Philippine left.

Not surprisingly, the response by Filipinos to the CPP/NDF calls for support did not match the claims of strength. Neither of its boycotts, of the 1986 election or of the 1987 constitutional referendum, drew any measurable support. In 1988 the CPP abandoned its boycott policy to participate in the first post-Marcos election, for a restored two-chamber Congress, acting through a legal front party, the *Partido ng Bayan* (People's Party), which ran or supported candidates for all senatorial and house of representatives seats. The PnB confidently boasted that, on the basis of the movement's own estimates of its strength, it would win from one-fifth to one-third of all seats. However, it won only two seats in the House of Representatives, from remote and little-populated districts of Mindanao and Samar. (Both of these people, after taking their seats, eventually transferred their allegiance to bourgeois parties in the Congress.)

A major debilitating effect on the CPP/NPA/NDF was caused by the crippling withdrawal of support for them by the main sections of the Catholic Church. The Church was aligned strongly with Mrs. Aquino and advocated an end to the NPA's armed struggle, now that Marcos was out of the way. The gravest blow to the CPP-led movement was cutting off funds that had been channeled through Church social action bodies: NASSA, the principal channel, was dissolved by the Church hierarchy. Among the consequences of this loss of funds was a drastic diminishing of the activity of the movement's Support Groups and Resource Centers abroad. Another blow was the withdrawal of priests and nuns and other activists who figured prominently in the NPA armed struggle. Among them was the much-publicized NPA commander in Northern Luzon, Father Conrado Balweg, who went through a ceremony of surrendering his command to President Aquino after which he and his armed force were allowed to keep their arms. Balweg then led an anti-NPA campaign in the same region.

Catholic Church links with the CPP/NPA/NDF were not entirely severed. The small left sector in the Church, of radicalized priests, liberation theology advocates, social action groups, and a few pro-Marxists, have remained either in or around the CPP-led movement. The Church influence in the KMU and KMP was continued, besides the more direct connection with the Federation of Free Workers and Federation of Free Farmers.

In general a crisis of strategy and tactics had developed for the CPP in the wake of the Marcos ouster. During the Marcos period the CPP, to all intents and purposes, had allied itself with the bourgeois opposition to overthrow "the imperialist-Marcos dictatorship" and to "restore democracy." When the actual ouster had occurred, the CPP had literally sidelined itself with boycott and inaction. Its attempts to establish itself in the new order—in the failed negotiations with the Aquino government and in its failure to win significant representation in the new Congress—had shown the CPP's relative weakness in political struggle and in the relation of forces in the country. Instead of putting major effort into building the political struggle, which it was in a position to do with existing mass organizations, a renewed emphasis was put on armed struggle, extended from an anti-Marcos war to a war against the Aquino government. The Maoist tendencies of Sison were placed to the fore, in particular the Sison military prescription of moving by stages from the strategic defensive to the strategic stalemate and to the strategic offensive, conducted within the overall strategy of surrounding the cities from the countryside.

A crucial factor was that to attain a strategic stalemate and go beyond the NPA needed to acquire and master the use of heavy weapons—artillery, rockets and rocket-firing means, anti-tank and anti-aircraft weapons, effective mines, and others. To capture these from the Philippine Army with light weapons was unlikely. The NPA even found it difficult to mount attacks with forces of more than 50 fighters due to the helicopter gunships of the government armed forces. The alternative was to obtain weapons from abroad but, with the diminishing of financial support, it was difficult to procure them on the international arms market. An apparent source was socialist countries that had given support to liberation struggles elsewhere. In its regurgitation or modifying of Maoist ideology, the CPP had abandoned its former sweeping condemnation of the Soviet Union and other socialist countries and CPP emissaries now went all out in an international relations drive to establish contacts with such countries and their Communist parties that might lead to arms arrangements. At the same time the CPP sought to displace the PKP from its position in the international Communist movement. CPP contacts were established with a few Communist parties but not to the detriment of the PKP. At this point it could be said that history had passed the CPP by. The Soviet Union at that time had begun its "perestroika–new thinking" foreign policy that was in the direction of reducing confrontation with imperialism and of ending regional conflicts. No arms for the NPA were forthcoming from such quarters. Frustrated CPP/NDF arms-shopping expeditions wound up with a delegation to Iraq, in a masterpiece of bad timing, as the Gulf War climax was being reached. Subsequently the downfall of socialist governments in Eastern Europe and the Soviet Union and its negative impact on socialist-oriented countries and movements meant the closing off of avenues and hopes of armed struggle aid.

A further objective of the CPP's international relations campaign was to gain what Sison and other leaders called "belligerent status." This meant recognition of the NPA's struggle in the Philippines as a civil war in which the CPP/NPA/NDF could be recognized as an oppressed entity, as a legitimate contender for power, and as having the right to assistance from the United Nations, international bodies, or individual countries, including international intervention for a settlement. The belligerent status hope foundered on the changing international realities.

In the face of the adverse developments domestically and internationally the dominant section of the CPP leadership continued to project victory through armed struggle. Opposition grew within the CPP, however, to the militarist frame of the struggle and to Sison's formulations for conducting it. Demands were made for an emphasis on political struggle in urban areas or at least a combination of legal and armed struggle. The problems of such a combination were displayed in the 1988 congressional election, when the identification of the *Partido ng Bayan* with the NPA resulted in the killing of a number of *PnB* candidates and campaigners by army and vigilante death squads. It caused Bernabe Buscayno, the former Commander Dante of the NPA and now a *PnB* leader and senatorial candidate, to make a public criticism of the NPA's conduct of armed activities during the election.

Advocates of greater emphasis on urban legal struggles were conceded to but this was accompanied by the extension of armed actions in the form of "partisan warfare" to the cities. Small armed "sparrow" units engaged in the indiscriminate assassination of ordinary policemen, including traffic police, and of minor government employees. This essentially terrorist activity antagonized and alienated many people, particularly middle class elements who made appeals for its cessation.

The resort to terror tactics was part of an overall policy of intensifying the armed struggle. It had other features, one of which was to make targets of U.S. servicemen and businessmen (as well as Japanese and other foreign businessmen). A CPP spokesman, perhaps irresponsibly, was quoted as saying that the intention was to provoke U.S. military intervention, which was expected to bring about greater anti-imperialist understanding than existed among the masses and to lead to a real people's war of liberation. Another military feature was a concentration on economic targets, launched by blowing up bridges and railway lines in southern Luzon. However, aroused angry peasants protested against such thoughtless acts which prevented them from transporting their produce to markets. The tactic was abandoned.

Gravest of the armed struggle consequences was the reaction of the Aquino government and of the Army, which retaliated by the activating of death squads that kidnapped and murdered leaders and active members of CPP-linked legal organizations. In vain the CPP issued a guiding document insisting on the strict separation of armed and legal organizations; it was a distinction not observed by the death squads. As in all counter-insurgency campaigns, progressive organizations in general suffered. Mrs. Aquino herself endorsed setting-up civilian vigilante death squads, that most often took the form of "born again" religious fanaticism in their "anti-communist" killings of ordinary peasant and trade union members. Death squad organization was particularly stimulated by the visits of retired U.S. General John Singlaub who toured the counter-insurgency areas as a representative of the World Anti-Communist League, promoting the "low-level intensity conflict" tactics of the Pentagon. The ruthless suppressive measures against the NPA and the CPP-led movement in general brought as much condemnation of President Aquino for violating human rights as was directed against Marcos, rapidly eroding Mrs. Aquino's initial democratic image.

A bizarre aspect of the NPA's armed struggle was that Jose Sison himself found the claimed mass base of 12 million people insecure to live amid: he left the Philippines by the latter part of 1986 and established himself in the Netherlands, from whence he issued directives on "the revolution" scarcely altered from those that launched his movement in 1969. For a time he wrote of victory being won in from two to five years, but in 1990 he spoke of his "strategic stalemate" being achieved in ten years, i.e., past the turn of the century.

However, within the CPP and NDF the debate over strategy and tactics had become intense. In 1991 a quarterly magazine, *Debate: Philippine Left Review,* began publication in the Netherlands among other exiles of the movement. One of its editors was Edicio de la Torre. It proposed to be a forum for the theoretical views of all left groups in the Philippines, with a unity perspective. The main contributions to this were from people in and around the CPP, but there were severe criticisms of the movement's primary emphasis on armed struggle, especially a refutation of the Maoist doctrines of protracted warfare and of surrounding the cities from the countryside. The need to give attention to forms of struggle more suitable to the Philippines was projected, although a tendency to think of insurrection as the end of mass political struggle was favored.

The CPP and its associated organizations were the only left grouping in the Philippines which viewed the struggle against U.S. imperialism and neocolonialism and for a people's national democratic government in military terms. All of the other left groupings, around the PKP, BISIG, PDSP and VPD, saw legal political struggle and the mass organization and political education linked with it as primary; armed struggle was not rejected as a conceivable possibility for the people's movement but, as an alternative, it was considered feasible only when all open or other means of political struggle were denied to the people. The PKP had proved that such organization and activity were possible under the conditions of martial law and authoritarian Marcos rule. Although grave violations of democratic rights occurred under the Aquino government, particularly as a reaction to the CPP's armed struggle that gave free rein to the most reactionary forces, nevertheless the freedom to organize, demonstrate, strike, express opinion, vote, publish and conduct judicial procedures was much greater than under Marcos and could be exercised by the left.

To one degree or another, all of these left groupings put anti-imperialism in the forefront of their programs and activity. One of the first issues on which steps toward unity began to be taken was the continued presence of U.S. military bases. Although the new Constitution had anti-bases provisions written into it, the U.S. moved toward negotiating a new bases agreement, expecting President Aquino to maneuver it past the constitutional barriers.

In December 1987 the PKP called for a united campaign for removal of the bases:

> The struggle on the bases question should be the focus of all the forces for national independence and popular democracy, given the impending renegotiation and the function of the U.S. military installations here in the maintenance of imperialist domination and aggression in the region. The bases not only endanger the survival of the Filipino people in case of nuclear attack or accident; they also make a mockery of our national sovereignty, subject third countries to U.S. military threats emanating from our territory, degrade our women and children through military prostitution, provide a breeding ground for deadly diseases such as AIDS and dangerous habits like drug addiction. No amount of rent, aid, employment and other "benefits" can compensate for the degradation and indignity of our people, violation of national freedom, usurpation of sovereignty, and the denial of the right to self-determination of the Filipino nation.[36]

Considerable unity was attained around the bases question. An anti-Bases Coalition was formed with broad participation from across the spectrum of popular organizations. Conferences, marches, demonstrations outside the U.S. Embassy and Clark Air Base, and lobbying of Congress against ratification of any new agreement were maintained throughout the negotiating period that was spread over nearly four years from 1987. A petition drive to collect two million signatures against the bases was carried out.

This broad campaign proved to have laid the ground for a major U.S. defeat when the issue of a new agreement came to a head in 1991. Although the Aquino government negotiated a new agreement extending the U.S. military bases for another ten years, the agreement was rejected on September 16, 1991 by a majority of the Philippine Senate. The surge of national feeling in the Senate that produced this act of independence, the first such Philippine rebuff to an imperialist demand, was most unlikely without the mobilization of popular sentiment by the left and national-democratic groups.

However, the issue of the U.S. bases was not wholly settled by the Senate vote. Within a few days, on September 26, a member of the U.S. congressional committee on Asian affairs, Rep. Stephen Solarz, told a congressional hearing,

> it is entirely possible that someone could be elected as the next president of the Philippines, and a two-thirds majority could win seats in the Senate, committed to the ratification of the bases agreement.[37]

Significantly, despite the manufacture of a democratic image for President Aquino, a greater growth of nationalist and anti-imperialist sentiment occurred during the Aquino administration than during the Marcos regime. The foreign debt issue and the refusal of Mrs. Aquino to stand up to the demands of the World Bank, the IMF and the Consultative Group of foreign creditors, for debt servicing and repayment, added to nationalist feeling. Early in 1987 a Freedom from Debt Coalition came into being, with the initial affiliation of 40 organizations from across the political spectrum.

A national movement with regional chapters, the FDC conducted an extensive information and pressure campaign for a debt policy that would serve the national interest and would be based on the capacity of the country to pay without adversely affecting economic growth. It was insisted that there be a moratorium on debt service payments until an agreement embodying that principle be reached, and that the agreement must put a ceiling on annual service payments of no more than 10 to 15 per cent of annual export earnings. The FDC, in other words, demanded that development needs be safeguarded before the profits of the foreign banks.

A major part was played by the PKP in the activity of the FDC, providing the main analytical and informational material for its campaign. This inevitably was an education in imperialism and its methods of exploitation. Simultaneously the role of the transnational corporations in coordination with World Bank-IMF programs was publicized, making the Philippines during the period of the Aquino administration a virtual school of nationalist political education. The Coalition, which by 1991 had gained the affiliation of nearly 80 organizations, was the major influence that led the Philippine Senate to pass a "debt capping" measure that put a ceiling on annual servicing payments. President Aquino vetoed the measure, which widened the gap between her and broad sections of the people.

The Freedom From Debt Coalition was a unity body, bringing together organizations from all left and other progressive tendencies. It was not an isolated unity step; in the same year of 1987 unity action was taken in virtually all mass organizational areas.

Among the organizations that helped to generate these efforts was the PKP which, at its 9th Congress at the end of December 1986, issued a widely distributed "Appeal to All Democratic and Left Forces for Unity Against Imperialism." It said:

> We are now faced with a challenge which will test our readiness and sincerity in seeking a real solution to the crisis which afflicts our countrymen. The expulsion of Marcos is only a first step in the long and complicated process of expanding democracy towards complete freedom and liberation of the country. Imperialism is still here; it continues to exploit our economy and dictate our politics. The rightist and pro-fascist forces still aim to restore the dictatorship and drown the aspirations of the organized masses in blood. Danger still lurks and any time threatens to erase whatever benefits have been achieved in our struggle for greater democracy, real independence and social justice.
>
> It is clear that one of the main tactics of our enemies is to divide us so that they can continue to prevail. They sow intrigue so that we will not trust each other. They use anti-Communism to isolate the Marxist groups from possible allies in the struggle against imperialism. They themselves create incidents like murders and quarrels to make us annihilate each other and spend all our energies in fighting each other.
>
> In the face of this reality, it is only proper that we conduct a thorough assessment so that we will not be swayed by the tactics of the enemy. Let us hold dialogues and establish lines of communication in order to clarify our differences quickly and concretize points and issues of possible unity. It is only natural for us to have differences in ideology, strategy and tactics,

but these can be discussed and approached in ways which are non-antagonistic and should not be a hindrance to any form of unity, however limited this may be in the beginning.

The main contradiction in our society today is between imperialism and the Filipino people. A broad anti-imperialist front of all patriotic forces is a necessity. The PKP, as a party of the working people, is ready to cooperate towards the success of this endeavor.[38]

Forms of unity against U.S. military bases and the foreign debt were matched by similar steps for trade unions and peasant organizations. The first minister of labor in the Aquino cabinet, the relatively progressive Augusto Sanchez, took the initiative to set up a Labor Advisory and Consultative Council (LACC), with representation from the main trade union federations, to facilitate the formulation and implementation of a labor policy. His friendly dealings with organized workers was the principal reason why the transnational corporations and other employers forced him out of the cabinet.

The LACC, however, remained in being and was preserved as a unity body. It had the participation of the main union federations, left, moderate and right-wing, including the World Federation of Trade Unions affiliates in which the PKP had influence, especially the KATIPUNAN, NATU and TUPAS federations; the CPP/NDF-linked *Kilusang Mayo Uno* (KMU); the government-related Trade Union Congress of the Philippines (TUCP); the Catholic-led Federation of Free Workers (FFW); and the independent *Lakas ng Manggagawa* (Workers' Strength) Labor Center.

These were the main trade union federations in the Philippines but they did not embrace all organized workers. At the time of the LACC's formation in 1986 there were 1,829 plant-level trade unions and 120 federations registered in the Ministry of Labor, with a total membership of about 1.8 million out of a labor force of 8.8 million wage and salary workers. Rivalry with political undertones among LACC affiliates led to the making of highly exaggerated claims of strength, particularly by the far left KMU which claimed up to 750,000 members and by the conservative TUCP claiming a million members. Considering the size of the other federations which were several hundred thousand strong, these boasts were absurd. The true strength and effectiveness of the trade unions could be measured by their achievement of collective bargaining agreements for their members: at the end of 1985 only 266,537 workers were covered by collective bargaining agreements, a figure that rose by no more than half in the latter 1980s, and was more or less equally distributed among the various federations.

The problems of trade union unity, which is indispensable for the independent development of the people's movement in the Philippines, are associated with the problems of the divided left, and in particular with the confrontational policies of the Sison group in the CPP/NDF and its attempt to dominate movements. In the LACC this tendency was checked by a majority agreement to rotate the LACC chairmanship, as well as to cease or minimize the KMU practice of "raiding" other federations to get control of their unions. The KMU has insisted on disregarding the opinions of other LACC members in launching extremist strike action, making "general strike" calls that gain little support, the most harmful example being a transport *"welgang bayan"* (national strike) in 1991 in which the NPA participated by ambushing and burning many buses and by killing some leaders and non-strikers of other unions. The only successful general strike with popular support was conducted in 1989 by the LACC as a whole.

A more successful unity step occurred in the peasant movement, with the launching on May 31, 1987 of the Congress for a People's Agrarian Reform (CPAR). More than 70 organizations of farmers, fishermen, government and non-government agrarian bodies, cause-oriented and Church groups affiliated. Included and playing an initiating part were the long-existing organizations like the *Aniban ng mga Manggagawang Agrikultura* (AMA, which is ideologically the successor of the KPMP and PKM) and the Catholic-led Federation of Free Farmers (FFF), and the new CPP/Catholic-generated *Kilusang Magbubukid ng Pilipinas* (KMP). CPAR was initially formed to lobby and demonstrate for the passage of a genuine agrarian reform law during the Aquino government. The emasculating of Aquino's Comprehensive Agrarian Reform Program (CARP) by the pressures of foreign agribusiness and Filipino landed interests kept CPAR in active existence. Like the LACC, it has had a rotating chairmanship.

In September 1987 unity along another line occurred, setting up the National Movement for Civil Liberties (NMCL). A Civil Liberties Union had been in existence since the 1930s and remains in being; it is an organization of progressive lawyers of a relatively select character. The NMCL, however, is organized on a national level, with an affiliated mass organization base. It has the active affiliation of the various legal left groupings: CONFREDEM (Congress for Freedom and Democracy, which embraces nearly a score of PKP-influenced organizations), BAYAN, BISIG, VPD and others. This movement has had an effective information and education program, particularly around the U.S. military bases issue, the nature of TNC exploitation, the roots of political corruption, and the defense of democratic rights.

As the final decade of the twentieth century unfolded, the need for a decisive resolution of the issue that has divided the left for many years—of whether to give the prime emphasis to legal and peaceful or armed struggle—has moved to the top of the agenda for the anti-imperialist, national-democratic forces in the Philippines. The potential for left unity and for its attraction of other nationalist, patriotic and democratic groups to broad programs of action was never greater than in the early years of the 1990s. Although the left is but one sector of the contemporary Philippines, it has been and is the core of resistance to foreign domination and to collaboration with it, and is the most important factor in building the mass base of support for a fully independent democratic country. It was not surprising that a bourgeois nationalist movement, like that of Claro Recto, failed to develop while the left was under severe suppression.

One of the most important tendencies on the left has been the growth of serious debate within the CPP/NDF/NPA over the course of the movement that by 1992 had conducted an armed struggle for 23 years without achieving strategically significant aims. In that period the greatest gains for the people's movement had been in the development of legal struggles, in the cities that the NPA was supposed to be surrounding from the countryside. Indeed, the armed struggle was serving as less of a stimulation and more of a disrupting and retarding factor for the even greater possibilities of the legal movement. It was, in fact, provoking anti-democratic policies of militarization and repression by the government. Within the CPP a questioning of the Sison concepts developed into a formulation of alternative strategy and tactics. From 1990 overtures began to be made by CPP/NDF leaders for negotiations with the government for a democratic settlement of the armed struggle.

From the outset of organized political life in the Philippines, parties of the left have either been forced underground or to the margins of electoral politics. The gaining by the left of full legal, equal rights of political parties, able to put programs to the people without hindrance, requires a change of attitude by much of the Filipino elite, which needs to be made aware that real national development and its fruits, in a country as rich in natural resources as the Philippines, will come from involving the whole people in democratic effort. Above all these must be Filipino solutions, without intervention from outside.

AN AFTERWORD

For the Filipino people, the 1990s constitute a decade of acutely significant anniversaries: July 7, 1992—the centenary of the founding of the *Katipunan* by Andres Bonifacio; August 26, 1996—the centenary of the start of the revolution against Spanish colonial rule, led by the *Katipunan;* June 12, 1998—the centenary of the Filipino declaration of independence; January 23, 1999—the centenary of the inauguration of the First Philippine Republic; February 4, 1999—the centenary of the launching of U.S. imperialist military conquest, destroying Philippine independence and the Republic. These are heroic centenaries of a freedom-loving people that culminate in a tragic centenary of a repressed nation.

Historically conscious Filipinos and Americans both need to understand why the past hundred years may be marked as a century of shame. The hundred-year role of the United States in the Philippines has been a shameful one, and it has been paralleled by the shameful role of those Filipinos who have collaborated, at the expense of their own people, with the foreign businessman, banker, military chief and imperialist policy-maker.

As a result, one hundred years from the time the Filipino people began their national struggle for independence from foreign domination, that goal has still not been fully achieved. It would be erroneous, however, to conclude that nothing has been changed, and that the Filipino people have nothing to celebrate in observing their patriotic anniversaries. Against the shameful behavior of a minority must be inscribed the magnificent record of the many who have resisted the colonialism and the neocolonialism, who have given their lives, been imprisoned, or suffered great hardship and sacrifice to gain genuine freedom. Philippine history has gone on at two levels, interpreted differently by the social forces of each. Nevertheless it has moved forward. The political independence attained in 1946, for example, may have been nominal in basic respects, freedom in form rather than substance, but it was an important forward step. It was a point from which the next stride, to economic independence, could be made. All the main movements and struggles of the people in the second half of the 20th century have revolved around making that vital step, without which a national democratic Philippines is impossible.

If any central lesson stands out from the course of events over the past century, however, it is that there is no simple, direct shift from the colonial condition to a completely liberated society. The power and ruthlessness of imperialism and the unprincipled depths of the acts of collaboration with it have blocked the road to real liberation, making its attainment complex and the shape it might take unpredictable.

At the close of the 20th century, that complexity seems to have grown. The great allies of national liberation, the socialist countries and the anti-imperialist forces of the third world, have suffered a grim historical setback. U.S. imperialism ventures to proclaim itself the triumphant head of a "new world order" in which the Philippines, among other countries, is presumably to remain a subservient transnational component.

U.S. imperialism today, however, is not the cocky conqueror of 1898 nor the arrogant victor in Asia over its Japanese rival in 1945. At the very time when it was converting the Philippines into a debt-enslaved TNC subsidiary in the 1970s and 1980s, and was claiming to be the world's sole superpower after triumph in the "cold war" against the socialist countries, the U.S. was becoming a debtor nation itself, undermined by the reckless cost of setting back socialism, its supremacy challenged by Japan, and by Germany at the head of a European Community. The World Bank and the International Monetary Fund which essentially manage the Philippines as a TNC adjunct are not solely agencies of the U.S., which may be for the time being the largest partner but must increasingly rely upon the strength and decisions of its partner-rivals. It is a changing situation that is reflected in Philippine foreign trade and investment, overwhelmingly dominated by the U.S. at independence but now diversified. Despite its subserviency, the range for maneuver by the Philippines, given a leadership prone to take advantage of international contradictions, is greater now than previously.

The formal withdrawal of U.S. military bases, pressed for by Filipino nationalist movements and a Philippine Senate decision in 1991, is a feature of changing relations with the U.S. It has not signified a U.S. withdrawal from Asia and the Pacific, projected by the geo-theorists as the coming region of market growth and economic development, where U.S. military power remains widely distributed, but for the Filipino people the effect on their sense of sovereignty and independence can be great. That continues to be illusory as long as collaboration persists in the Philippine economy and politics.

In May 1992 the first full-scale Philippine election occurred since 1969. It might well have been a point for turning to new directions, for choosing leaders capable of responding to the message of the impending centenaries. Popular discontent was in the air. It was apparent in the decision of President Corazon Aquino not to seek re-election, her government discredited for failing to fulfill the hopes of a new life that had risen with the alleged restoration of democracy after the ouster of Marcos. The hopes had withered as the grip of the TNCs and of the Consultative Group of Creditors had tightened on the lives of Filipinos. Under Mrs. Aquino, "honoring the debt" had resulted in the foreign debt growing between 1986 to 1992 from $26 billion to $30 billion, with over half the annual national budget used to repay it, at a rate of $6 million a day. In that time the number of Filipinos living in absolute poverty increased by 10 per cent, putting over 70 per cent of the population below the poverty line.

However, it was not an election that gave the people any real choice of leader for the future. Although there were seven presidential candidates, all of them represented the interests of the elite. None of them put forward a genuine alternative program for nationalist economic development that would place the interests of the country above those of foreign creditors and TNCs. Fidel Ramos, the victor and new president, is the first military figure to head a government of the Philippines, with a background of heading military suppression under both Marcos and Mrs. Aquino. His switch to Aquino at the vital point to topple Marcos in February 1986 was in coordination with U.S. moves for a change of rule. He assumed office as the epitome of conservative collaboration, standing for removal of all impediments to foreign investment, for a full honoring of the foreign debt, for a treaty allowing renewal of U.S. military bases and their "gradual withdrawal," and for a tough "peace and order" policy regarding the NPA. As for human rights, Ramos said in an interview: "Our laws oftentimes tilted toward the protection of civil liberties which tend to be exploited as a cover for subversives."

Collaboration, however, is not immutable in the present-day Philippine situation. The extension of capitalist relations throughout the economy as a consequence of imperialist need, and the encouragement and financing by imperialist agencies of manufacturing and agribusiness, albeit subsidiary to the TNCs, contain the seeds of problems for U.S. and other foreign interests. An inevitable rise of Filipino capitalists, monopolists and conglomerate groups has occurred. There is more possibility of contradiction in U.S. association with Filipino capitalists and monopolists than with feudal landlords.

It is not inconceivable that a loosening of ties with the U.S. could come from the right as well as from the left. In the Marcos regime there was an element of such a tendency, but it was unable to transcend the fatal dependence on foreign loans and investment. The idea that Philippine economic development has to depend on foreign capital should have been negated long ago by the fact that foreign, especially U.S., corporations have drawn heavily upon Filipino savings and capital accumulation to finance their own massive operations and acquisitions in the Philippines. It is astonishing that the realization and significance of that has not sunken in and taken hold of the Filipino capitalist outlook. The development from collaboration to contradiction in major areas of the economy is not a long step to take and is not to be ruled out in such a process.

The Filipino left, for its part, remains as the main factor of uncom promising resistance to imperialism and the neocolonial order. Its mass base is in the still unchanging conditions of a population in which over 70 per cent barely exist, far below the poverty line. From their inception both the PKP and the CPP based themselves on the conviction that only a systemic change to socialism could liberate the vast majority of the Filipino people from poverty and inequality. They were encouraged and emboldened to militant action by the victorious growth of socialism and by the social emancipation where socialist-oriented national liberation movements had won power. That the Filipino left was part of a universal historical process that was changing the world made their own victory in the Philippines seem inevitable. There was the reasonable prospect that if their struggles were won, they could rely on the support of the major socialist countries to protect a liberated Philippines and to assist its independent, national democratic development.

That prospect, and the major moral and material factors of international left unity, has receded with the collapse of socialist countries (for whatever reason) in the early 1990s. It has not altered the conviction, shared by popular movements elsewhere in the world, that a form of socialism is still the answer to the problems of poverty, underdevelopment and lack of democracy in the Philippines. However, the Filipino left is faced with the need to adjust to the realities of the changing relations of forces both nationally and internationally. Above all, there is the necessity for greater than ever reliance on the forces and circumstances in the Philippines itself.

It seems likely that the programs of the left, as a new century opens, will focus on contending with imperialism and collaboration in the political and economic fields, and not in the military arena. Armed struggles, unless there is truly an unmistakeable revolutionary situation which no responsible revolutionary movement could evade, often have the unintended consequence of augmenting imperialist interventionism, of frightening ruling groups into greater extremes of collaboration, and of enabling the most reactionary elements in the society to gain power or dictate policy.

Up to now, the Filipino left has scarcely realized the possibilities of organizing and mobilizing effective mass movements around political and economic issues. A legal political party of the left, or even a broad party of progressive nationalism, so glaringly absent from the 1992 election, requires such a mass base. It could come about if there were forms of unity of the divided left, perhaps of the coalition type, with inclusion of the diverse democratic organizations that have arisen in recent years. No single organization or movement in the Philippines today has the capability of achieving complete independence and national democracy or can justifiably claim hegemony over the forces that might do so. The process, at any rate, could probably be long and complex. It has taken a century to reach the present inconclusive point in Philippine history.

As the Filipino people in the 1990s observe the centenaries that set them on the long and much-interrupted road toward freedom and a democratic progress, they will be better prepared to complete that historical journey if they fully understand the nature of the friends and enemies, foreign and domestic, of their national freedom.

NOTES

Notes—I, pp. 1-15.

1. Prescott F. Jernegan, *A Short History of the Philippines,* For use in Philippine schools. D. Appleton & Co., N.Y., 1905, pp. 258-64. (Jernegan was an American teacher in Philippine history in the Philippine Normal School, Manila)

2. *Reports of the Philippine Commission: 1900-1903.* Government Printing Office, Washington, 1904, p. 370.

3. *Letters of Theodore Roosevelt.* Vol. IV. Harvard University Press, 1951-1954, p. 839.

4. W. Cameron Forbes, *The Philippine Islands.* Vol. II. Houghton Mifflin, 1928, p. 354.

5. Rafael Palma, *Our Campaign for Independence from Taft to Harrison.* Bureau of Printing, Manila, 1923, p. 30.

6. Forbes, op. cit., p. 355.

7. Major William H. Anderson, *The Philippines.* Putnams, N.Y., 1939, pp. 116-118.

8. Moorfield Storey & Marcial P. Lichauco, *The Conquest of the Philippines by the U.S..* G.P. Putnams Sons, 1926, p. 214.

9. *Official Gazette.* (Philippine Commission). Vol. 5, No. 5, Manila, 1907, p. 570.

10. *Official Gazette.* Vol. 8, No. 39, Manila, 1910, p. 1709.

11. Ibid., p. 1710.

12. F. Arsenio Manuel, ed., *Dictionary of Philippine Biography.* Filipiniana Publications, Quezon City, Philippines, 1955, p. 257.

13. Ibid. p. 289.

14. Ibid., p. 2.

15. *Official Gazette.* Vol. 3, 1905, pp. 705-706.

16. W.H. Taft (Secretary of War), *Address Delivered Before the Harvard Alumni Association,* June 28, 1904, p. 23.

17. Garel A. Grunder & William E. Livesey, *The Philippines and the United States.* University of Oklahoma Press, 1951, p. 166.

18. Forbes, op. cit., pp. 543-544.

19. Dean C. Worcester, *The Philippines: Past and Present.* MacMillan, 1930, Appendix, pp. 821-822.

Notes—II, pp. 16-44.

1. Charles Robequain, *Malaya, Indonesia, Borneo and the Philippines.* Longman, Green & Co., London, 1934, p. 279.

2. *Census of the Philippine Islands, 1903.* Vol. IV. 1903, Government Printing Office, Washington, 1903, p. 32

3. *Public Hearings in the Philippines upon Proposed Reduction of the Tariff,* August 1905. Bureau of Printing, Manila, 1905, p. 158

4. *Eighth Annual Report of the Philippine Commission,* 1907. Government Printing Office, Washington, 1908, Part I, p. 172

5. *Senate Document No. 169, 55th Congress, 3rd Session,* "Report on the Financial and Industrial Condition of the Philippine Islands," R.W. Harden, p. 6

6. Cesar Adib Majul, *Mabini and the Philippine Revolution.* University of the Philippines, 1960, p. 52

7. Gerald Brennan, *The Spanish Labyrinth.* Cambridge University Press, 1943, 1960, p. 7

8. Teodoro A. Agoncillo & Oscar M. Alfonso, *A Short History of the Filipino People,* University of the Philippines, 1960, 1961, pp. 148-153

9. Victor S. Clark, *Labor Conditions*

in the Philippines. Bureau of Labor Bulletin No. 58, Government Printing Office, Washington, 1905, p. 724

10. Teodoro A. Agoncillo, *The Revolt of the Masses.* University of the Philippines, 1956, p. 28

11. Ibid., Appendix A, *"Constitution of La Liga Filipina, "* p. 376

12. *Census of the Philippine Islands,* op. cit., p. 25

13. Ibid., p. 15

14. Ibid., p. 54

15. *Revolt of the Masses,* op. cit., pp. 107–108

16. John Foreman, *The Philippine Islands.* Scribners, 1906, p. 643

17. Emilio Aguinaldo & Vicente Albano Pacis, *A Second Look at America.* Robert Speller, 1957, p. 34

18. *Senate Document No. 62, 55th Congress, 3rd Session,* Part I, "A Treaty of Peace Between the U.S. and Spain," p. 334

19. Ibid., p. 339

20. John R.M. Taylor, ed., *The Philippine Insurrection Against the United States,* Vol. I, Eugenio Lopez Foundation, Pasay City, Philippines, 1971, p. 523. (This collection of the records of the Philippine Revolution and Philippine Republic, part of thousands of documents captured by the U.S. forces, were compiled with notes and introduction by Taylor, a U.S. army captain, and deposited in government archives in Washington. They were finally turned over to the Philippines in 1957 by a legislative act, and published there in a private edition.)

21. *Senate Document No. 331, 57th Congress, 1st Session.* "Hearings in Relation to Affairs in the Philippine Island," p. 2927

22. Ibid., p. 772

23. *Report of the Philippine Commission to the President. The Schurman Report. Vol. II.* Government Printing Office, Washington, 1900, pp. 22, 26, 51-52, 256, 190, 383

24. Ibid., Vol. I, p. 121

25. Jose Batangbahal, *The Life of Cayetano Arellano.* University Publishing Co., Manila, 1923, 1947, p. 18

26. Dapen Liang, *The Development of Philippine Political Parties.* South China Morning Post, Hong Kong, 1939, p. 57

27. *Senate Document No. 331,* op. cit., pp. 310–311

28. Ibid., p. 312.

29. Daniel R. Williams, *Odyssey of the Philippine Commission.* A.C. McClurg, Chicago, 1913, p. 286

30. *Correspondence Relating to the War with Spain.* Vol. II. Government Printing Office, Washington, 1902, p. 1009

31. Ibid., p. 1011

32. *Senate Document No. 331,* op. cit., pp. 1945, 1946

33. *Public Laws and Resolutions Passed by the Philippine Commission.* Government Printing Office, Washington, 1901, p. 130

34. Dean.C. Worcester, *The Philippines Past and Present.* MacMillan, 1914, 1930, p. 220

35. Dapen Liang, op. cit., p. 63

36. *Reports of the Philippine Commission, 1900-1903.* Government Printing Office, Washington, 1904, p. 371

37. Agoncillo & Alfonso, op. cit., p. 307

38. James A. Leroy, *Philippine Life in Town and Country.* Putnams, 1905, p. 201

39. Joseph Ralston Hayden, *The Philippines: A Study in National Development.* MacMillan, 1945, 1948, p. 278

40. William Cameron Forbes, *The Philippine Islands.* Vol. II. Houghton Mifflin, 1928, p. 467; *Public Laws and Resolutions,* op. cit., pp. 133, 168

41. *Census of the Philippine Islands, 1903,* Op. cit., Vol. II

42. Charles Burke Elliott, *The Philippines to the End of Commission Government.* Bobbs Merrill, 1917, p. 398

43. Ibid., p. 124

44. *Eighth Annual Report of the Philippine Commission, 1907.* Government

Printing Office, Washington, 1908, pp. 46-47

45. Forbes, op. cit. Vol. I, p. 155; *Eighth Annual Report*, op. cit., p. 47

46. Manuel Quezon, *The Good Fight.* Appleton Century, 1946, pp. 88-94, 101-102

47. *Eighth Annual Report*, op. cit. Part II, p. 270

48. M.M. Norton, *Builders of a Nation.* Manila, 1914, p. 142; Forbes, op. cit. p. 163

49. "The Anti-Imperialist League," Maria C. Lanzar. *Philippine Social Science Review,* October 1933, pp. 258-259. (This full-length study of the Anti-Imperialist League appeared in the PSSR in August and November 1930 and July and October 1933.)

Notes—III, pp. 45-75.

1. John R.M. Taylor, ed., *The Philippine Insurrection Against the United States.* Eugenio Lopez Foundation, Pasay City, Philippines, 1971. Vol. I, p. 62.

2. Teodoro Kalaw, *The Philippine Revolution.* Manila Book Co., 1925, p. 188.

3. Taylor, op. cit., Vol. IV, p. 144.

4. *Report of the War Department,* Government Printing Office, Washington, 1900, Vol. I, p. 61-62.

5. Antonio K. Abad, *General Macario Y. Sakay: Was He a Bandit or a Patriot?* J.B. Feliciano & Sons, Manila, 1955, p. 8.

6. Teodoro A. Agoncillo & Oscar M. Alfonso, *A Short History of the Filipino People.* University of the Philippines, 1960, p. 304.

7. John Foreman, *The Philippine Islands.* Scribners, 1906, p. 550.

8. James H. Blount, *The American Occupation of the Philippines, 1898-1912.* G.P. Putnams Sons, 1912, p. 429.

9. Abad, op. cit., pp. 11-12.

10. Ibid., p. 53.

11. Ibid., p. 101.

12. Ildefonso K. Runes, *History of Philippine Labor.* Unpublished typescript, 1959, pp. 17-19.

13. Jose L. Llanes, "The Life and Labors of Isabelo de los Reyes," *Comment,* Manila, 2nd Quarter, 1960, pp. 71-72.

14. Runes, op. cit., p. 32.

15. Ibid., pp. 34-35.

16. *Official Gazette.* Manila, 1907, Vol. 5, No. 43, pp. 705-707. (Gazette of the U.S. Philippine Commission.)

17. Victor S. Clark, *Labor Conditions in the Philippines.* Bureau of Labor Bulletin No. 58, GPO, Washington, May 1905, pp. 846-847.

18. Ibid., pp. 849-850.

19. Kenneth K. Kurihara, *Labor in the Philippine Economy.* Stanford University Press, 1945, pp. 62-63.

20. Ibid., p. 38.

21. Ibid.

22. James A. Richardson, "The Genesis of the Communist Party of the Philippines". Doctoral Thesis, School of Oriental Studies, University of London, 1984.

23. Alfred Wagenknecht papers, in possession of author.

24. Ibid.

25. Ibid.

26. *Labor Party Manifesto,* Manila, December 30, 1925. (In English and Tagalog.)

27. *Pan-Pacific Worker.* Vol. II, No. 5, April 1, 1929.

28. *Bulletin of Proceedings of the Hankow Conference.* No. 3, May 22, 1927.

29. *Pan-Pacific Worker.* Vol. I, No. 2, July 15, 1927.

30. Ibid., Vol. II, No. 5, April 1, 1929.

31. *International Press Correspondence (Inprecor).* Vol. 8, No. 50, August 16, 1928, pp. 875-876.

32. *Pan-Pacific Worker,* op. cit.

33. Crisanto Evangelista, "The Split in the Philippine Labor Movement," *Red International of Labor Unions Magazine,* August 1929.

34. "For Immediate and Unconditional Independence of the Philippines," *Pan-Pacific Monthly,* No. 30-31, September–October 1929.

35. *Archives of the Communist Inter-*

national. Philippine section. Formerly housed in Institute of Marxism-Leninism, Moscow.

36. Ibid.

37. "The Communist Party of the Philippines and the Comintern, 1919-1930." Doctoral thesis of Antonio S. Araneta, University of Oxford, 1966, p. 186.

38. *G.R. No. 36276.* Philippine Supreme Court. "The People of the Philippine Islands vs Guillermo Capadocia, et al.," October 26, 1932.

39. *Philippine History and Class Struggle,* (Official history of the Partido Komunista ng Pilipinas, prepared by History Commission of the PKP), Chapter 6. *PKP Courier,* Vol. II, No. 3, July–October 1986.

40. *G.R. No. 36278.* Philippine Supreme Court. "The People of the Philippine Islands vs Crisanto Evangelista, et al.," October 26, 1932.

Notes—IV, pp. 76–100.

1. William Cameron Forbes, *The Philippine Islands.* Houghton Mifflin, 1928. Volume II, appendix, p. 564.

2. G. Aquila, "Philippines and American Imperialism," *The Pan-Pacific Worker.* Vol. I, No. 4, May 15, 1928.

3. Forbes, op. cit., pp. 566-570. (Has Philippine planks in Democrat and Republican election platforms, 1900-1928.)

4. Garel A. Grunder and William E. Livezey, *The Philippines and the United States.* University of Oklahoma Press, 1951, p. 200.

5. A.V.H. Hartendorp, *History of Industry and Trade of the Philippines.* American Chamber of Commerce of the Philippines, Manila, 1958, p. 54.

6. *Independence for the Philippine Islands: Hearings U.S. Senate 71st Congress 2nd Session.* Government Printing Office, Washington, 1930, p. 71

7. Hartendorp, op. cit., pp. 29-30.

8. Ibid., p. 54.

9. Ibid., p. 55.

10. Dapen Liang, *The Development of Philippine Political Parties.* South China Morning Post, Hong Kong, 1939, p. 250

11. Joseph Ralston Hayden, *The Philippines: A Study in National Development.* MacMillan, 1945, p. 294.

12. PKP Leaflet, "Fight Against the Coalition and Struggle for Immediate Independence." May 10, 1935. (In author's possession.)

13. James S. Allen, *The Radical Left on the Eve of War..* Foundation for Nationalist Studies, Quezon City, Philippines, 1985, p. 30-31.

14. *Philippines Herald,* Manila, November 1, 1937.

15. PKP Memorandum, August 30, 1938. (In author's possession.)

16. *Resolutions of the 3rd Congress, PKP.* Kalayaan Press, Manila, 1938.

Notes—V, pp. 101–146.

1. Renato Constantino and Letizia R. Constantino, *The Philippines: The Continuing Past,* Foundation for Nationalist Studies, 1978, pp. 18-19.

2. Ibid., p. 26.

3. Teodoro Agoncillo, *The Fateful Years: Japan's Adventure in the Philippines,* Vol. I R.P. Garcia Publishing Co., Philippines, 1965, p. 64.

4. Manuel L. Quezon, *The Good Fight,* D. Appleton Century Co., 1946, pp. 177-178.

5. Carlos Quirino, "Dr. Sun Yat-sen and the Philippine Revolution," *Fookien Times Yearbook,* Manila, 1963, p. 267.

6. Quezon, op. cit., pp. 270-275.

7. Agoncillo, op. cit., pp. 272-274.

8. Ibid., Vol. II, p. 659.

9. Ibid., p. 722.

10. Constantino, op. cit., p. 159.

11. William Manchester, *American Caesar: Douglas MacArthur 1880-1964,* Hutchinson of London, 1979, pp. 368-370.

12. Agoncillo, op. cit., Vol. I, p. 248

13. David Bernstein, *The Philippine Story,* Farrar Strauss & Co., 1947, pp 189-90, 197

14. Agoncillo, op. cit., p. 302.

15. Constantino, op. cit , p. 54

16. Agoncillo, op. cit., p. 502; Bernstein, op. cit., pp. 162-163.

17. Bernstein, op. cit., pp. 169-170.

18. Agoncillo, op. cit., Vol. II, pp. 829-831.

19. Ibid., Vol. I., pp. 342-344.

20. Bernstein, op. cit., p. 165.

21. Luis Taruc, *Born of the People,* International Publishers, 1953, pp. 52-53. (Although published as the autobiography of Taruc, this book was written wholly by William Pomeroy and was based on PKP-Hukbalahap documents and on interviews with all PKP and Huk top leaders. The account of the guerrilla movement here was drawn from these sources including the author's wife, Celia Mariano Pomeroy, who played a leading role in the Hukbalahap.)

22. PKP document.

23. PKP document in author's possession.

24. Bernstein, op. cit., p. 217.

25. A.V.H. Hartendorp, *History of Industry and Trade of the Philippines.* American Chamber of Commerce of the Philippines, 1958, pp. 154-156; Shirley Jenkins, *American Economic Policy Toward the Philippines,* Stanford University Press, 1954, p. 47.

26. Hartendorp, op. cit., p. 209.

27. These intelligence reports were seen by the author while serving as a member of the Fifth Historical Writing Team during the Philippine campaign.

28. Hernando Abaya, *The Untold Philippine Story,* Malaya Books, Philippines, 1967, pp. 16-17.

29. Hernando Abaya, *Betrayal in the Philippines,* A.A. Wyn Inc., 1947, p. 251.

30. Ibid., p. 252.

31. PKP document in possession of author.

32. Abaya, op. cit., p. 244.

33. Ibid., p. 244.

34. Ibid., p. 272.

Notes—VI, pp. 147–182.

1. The author saw a proclamation containing this statement distributed among officers of the Fifth Air Force on Okinawa in August 1945.

2. A.V.H. Hartendorp, *History of Industry and Trade of the Philippines,* American Chamber of Commerce of the Philippines, 1958, p. 225.

3. Alejandro M. Fernandez, *The Philippines and the United States,* University of the Philippines, 1977, p. 215.

4. Renato and Letizia Constantino, *The Continuing Past,* Foundation for Nationalist Studies, Quezon City, Philippines, 1978, pp. 203-204.

5. Hartendorp, op. cit., p. 252.

6. Ibid.

7. Renato Constantino, *Neo-Colonial Identity and Counter-Consciousness,* Merlin Press, London, 1978, p. 112.

8. Hartendorp, op. cit., pp. 154-156, 726.

9. Hernando Abaya, *The Untold Philippine Story,* Malaya Books, Quezon City, Philippines, 1967, p. 23.

10. Shirley Jenkins, *American Economic Policy Toward the Philippines,* Stanford University Press, 1954, p. 56.

11. Ibid., p. 59.

12. Ibid., pp. 62-63.

13. Abaya, op. cit., p. 16.

14. Ibid., p. 14.

15. Stanley Karnow, *In Our Image; America's Empire in the Philippines,* Random House, 1989, p. 335.

16. *Journal of the American Chamber of Commerce,* Manila, July 1946.

17. Constantino, *The Continuing Past,* op. cit., p. 200.

18. Abaya, op. cit., p. 23.

19. A.V.H. Hartendorp, *The Magsaysay Administration,* Philippine Education Co., Manila, 1961, pp. 170-171.

20. *United States Military Bases in the Philippines,* International Studies Institute of the Philippines, 1986, pp. 91-92.

21. Ibid., p. 90.

22. *The Pentagon Papers,* Bantam Books, 1971, p. 62.

23. Teodoro A. Agoncillo, *The Fateful Years,* Volume I, R.P. Garcia Publishing Co., Quezon City, Philippines, 1965, pp. 426, 458–459.

24. Hartendorp, *History of Industry and Trade,* op. cit., p. 176–180.

25. Ibid., pp. 176–177.

26. Rosalinda Pineda-Ofreneo, *The Manipulated Press,* Cacho Hermanos Inc., Manila, 1984, pp. 193–199.

27. Hartendorp, op. cit., pp. 177–178.

28. Ibid., p. 178.

29. *PKM-Democratic Alliance Memorandum to President Roxas,* August 17, 1946. Copy in possession of author.

Notes—VII, pp. 183–228.

1. Thomas Hibben, *Philippine Economic Development: A Technical Memorandum.* Prepared for the Joint Philippine-American Finance Commission, Manila, 1947, p. 2.

2. Shirley Jenkins, *American Economic Policy Toward the Philippines,* Stanford University Press, 1954, p. 142 footnote.

3. A.V.H. Hartendorp, *History of Industry and Trade of the Philippines,* American Chamber of Commerce of the Philippines, 1958, pp. 657–658.

4. Ibid., pp. 657, 664.

5. Ibid., p. 662.

6. A.V.H. Hartendorp, *The Magsaysay Administration.* Philippine Education Co., Manila, 1961, p. 321.

7. Ibid., p. 369.

8. This section is derived from the personal knowledge of the author who was a participant in the events related.

9. "Aggressively Project the Party Leadership Over the Struggle for National Liberation!" PKP document issued in April 1950.

10. "Overall Plan of Expansion and Development of the Party, HMB and Mass Organizations." PKP document issued in May 1950.

11. "Political Transmission No. 2." PKP document issued in December 1951. The numbering of this dates from the time

Jesus Lava became general secretary. Political Transmissions previously issued while Jose Lava was general secretary were numbered separately.

12. Edward Lansdale, *In the Midst of Wars.* Harper and Row, 1972.

13. Claro M. Recto, *My Crusade.* Calica & Carag Publishers, Manila, 1955, pp. 145–146.

14. *The Pentagon Papers.* New York Times. Bantam Books, 1971, p. 62.

15. Hartendorp, op. cit., p. 415.

16. Ibid., p. 313.

17. *Progressive Review,* No. 5. Quezon City, Philippines, January–February 1965, p. 81.

18. Renato Constantino, *The Making of a Filipino.* Malaya Books, Quezon City, Philippines, 1969, pp. 140–141.

19. Ibid., p. 153.

20. Ibid., pp. 155–156.

21. Recto, op. cit., p. 11.

22. Ibid., pp. 82, 86.

23. Ibid., pp. 23–24.

24. Renato & Letizia Constantino, *The Continuing Past.* Foundation for Nationalist Studies, Quezon City, Philippines, 1978, p. 308.

25. Rosalinda Pineda-Ofreneo, *The Manipulated Press.* Cacho Hermanos, Inc., Manila, 1984, pp. 5–6.

26. Constantino, op. cit., p. 312.

27. Hartendorp, op. cit., pp. 356–357.

28. Constantino, op. cit., p. 304.

29. Hartendorp, op. cit., pp. 366–367.

30. Pineda-Ofreneo, op. cit., pp. 66–67.

31. *Manila Chronicle.* May 24, 1959.

32. *Sunday Chronicle.* October 25, 1959.

33. Hartendorp, op. cit., p. 369.

34. Ibid., pp. 369–370.

35. Pineda-Ofreneo, op. cit., p. 96.

36. Stanley Karnow, *In Our Image.* Random House, 1989, pp. 362–363.

37. Pineda-Ofreneo, op. cit., p. 77.

38. Alejandro Lichauco, *The Lichauco Paper; Imperialism in the Philippines.* Monthly Review Press, 1973, p. 35.

39. Ibid., pp. 36–37.

Notes—VIII, pp. 229–281.

1. A. James Gregor, *Crisis in the Philippines: A Threat to U.S. Interests,* Ethics and Public Policy Center, Washington, D.C., 1984, p. 23.

2. Ibid., pp. 23–24.

3. *Daily Globe,* Manila, January 30, 1990.

4. *Progressive Review,* Philippines, May–June 1963.

5. Alejandro Lichauco, *The Lichauco Paper,* Monthly Review Press, 1973, p. 28.

6. Ibid.

7. Ibid.

8. Renato Constantino, *The Nationalist Alternative,* Foundation for Nationalist Studies, Quezon City, Philippines, 1979, 1984, p. 44.

9. Vivencio Jose, ed., *Mortgaging the Future: The World Bank and the IMF in the Philippines,* Foundation for Nationalist Studies, 1982, p. 53.

10. *International Debt Crisis: Focus on the Philippines,* International Studies Institute of the Philippines, 1984, IV-4.

11. *Philippine Daily Inquirer,* March 11, 1990.

12. *Movement for the Advancement of Nationalism,* Documents of Founding Congress, 1967, p. 14.

13. Ibid.

14. Alejandro M. Fernandez, *The Philippines and the United States,* NSDB Integrated Research Program, University of the Philippines, 1977, p. 410.

15. *Mortgaging the Future,* op. cit.

16. *The Nationalist Alternative,* op. cit., p. 48.

17. *Daily Globe,* Manila, January 30, 1990.

18. Merlin M. Magallona, ed., *Imperialism and Transnational Corporations,* Philippine Peace Council, Quezon City, 1980, p. 21.

19. *The Philippines and the United States,* op. cit., p. 452.

20. Ibid., pp. 447–457.

21. *World Bulletin,* Vol. IV, No. 1, Quezon City, 1988, pp. 15–16.

22. Ibid., p. 14.

23. *International Debt Crisis,* op. cit., pp. 53–54.

24. Ibid., p. 54.

25. *Mortgaging the Future,* op. cit., p. 54.

26. Ibid., p. 73.

27. *The Debt Trap: How to Get Out of It,* Papers of Symposium held by International Studies Institute of the Philippines, 1987, p. 6.

28. *Daily Globe,* Manila, February 18, 1990.

29. Rosalinda Pineda-Ofreneo, ed., *Foreign Capital and the Philippine Crisis,* International Studies Institute of the Philippines, 1985, pp. 23–26.

30. *Mortgaging the Future,* op. cit., p. 62.

31. Ibid., p. 40.

32. *The Nationalist Alternative,* op. cit., p. 44.

33. *Foreign Capital and the Philippine Crisis,* op. cit., p. 2.

34. Ibid.

35. *The Lichauco Paper,* op. cit., pp. 60–63; *The Nationalist Alternative,* op. cit., p. 7.

36. *World Bulletin,* September-December 1987, Quezon City, Philippines.

37. Ibid.

38. Ibid.

39. *The Nationalist Alternative,* op cit., p. 42.

40. Ibid., p. 48.

41. *Mortgaging the Future,* op. cit., p. 83.

42. *World Bulletin,* op. cit., pp. 7–8.

43. *Foreign Capital and the Philippine Crisis,* op. cit., p. 11.

44. *The Nationalist Alternative,* op. cit., pp. 12–13; *World Bulletin,* op. cit., p. 19.

45. *The Philippines and the United States,* op. cit., p. 414.

46. *Foreign Capital and the Philippine Crisis,* op. cit., p. 28.

47. Ibid., pp. 53–54.

48. *The Nationalist Alternative,* op cit., pp. 44–45.

49. *Imperialism and Transnational Corporations,* op. cit., p. 20.

50. *Philippine Daily Inquirer,* March 11, 1990.

51. *Daily Globe,* Manila, January 30, 1990.

52. *The Nationalist Alternative,* op. cit., p. 36.

53. *Imperialism and Transnational Corporations,* op. cit., p. 86, 87.

54. *The Nationalist Alternative,* op. cit., p. 29.

55. *Foreign Capital and the Philippine Crisis,* op. cit., p. 21.

56. *Report of the Bell Mission,* Manila, 1950, p. 48.

57. Rene Ofreneo, *Capitalism in Philippine Agriculture,* Foundation for Nationalist Studies, Quezon City, 1980, p. 35.

58. Hernando Abaya, *The Untold Philippine Story,* Malaya Books, Manila, 1967, p. 75.

59. Ibid., p. 76.

60. *Mortgaging the Future,* op. cit., p. 100.

61. Ibid., p. 108–109.

62. Ibid., p. 109.

63. *Capitalism in Philippine Agriculture,* op. cit., p. 78.

64. *Feudalism and Capitalism in the Philippines,* Symposium, Foundation for Nationalist Studies, Quezon City, 1982, p. 28.

65. Ibid., p. 27.

66. *Capitalism in Philippine Agriculture,* op. cit., pp. 127–128.

67. *Mortgaging the Future,* op. cit., pp. 110, 111.

68. *Feudalism and Capitalism in the Philippines,* op. cit., pp. 29–30. (Quotation from "The Economic Content of Narodism," by V.I. Lenin, *Collected Works,* Vol I, Moscow, 1963.)

69. *PKP Information,* September 12, 1988.

70. *PKP Courier,* No. 1-2, 1987.

71. *The Times,* London, May 29, 1984.

72. *PKP Information,* op. cit.

73. *PKP Courier,* No. 1, 1986.

74. Mark Selden, ed., *Remaking Asia,* Pantheon Books, 1974, p. 196.

75. *PKP Courier,* No. 1-2, 1987.

76. *Remaking Asia,* op. cit., pp. 195–196.

77. *PKP Information,* No. 8, 1988.

78. *Remaking Asia,* op. cit.

79. *PKP Information,* op. cit.

80. Stanley Karnow, *In Our Image,* Random House, 1989, p. 363.

81. *The Untold Philippine Story,* op. cit., p. 230.

82. Ibid.

83. Rosalina Pineda-Ofreneo, *The Manipulated Press,* Cacho Hermanos Inc., Manila, 1984, p. 91.

84. *The Lichauco Paper,* op. cit., p. 14.

85. *Mortgaging the Future,* op. cit., p. 39.

86. *In Our Image,* op. cit., pp. 353, 363; *The Continuing Past,* op. cit., p. 311.

87. Daniel B. Schirmer and Stephen R. Shalom, eds., *The Philippines Reader,* South End Press, Boston, 1987, p. 230.

88. *New York Times,* September 27, 1972.

89. *The Philippines Reader,* op. cit., p. 168.

90. *The Philippines and the United States,* op. cit., p. 258.

91. *Capitalism in Philippine Agriculture,* op. cit., pp. 63–64.

92. Ibid., p. 66.

93. *Political Affairs,* New York, September 1978.

94. *The Philippines and the United States,* op. cit., p. 279.

95. Ibid., p. A-255.

96. *Daily World,* New York, January, 1979.

97. *The Philippines Reader,* op. cit., pp. 169–174.

98. *Financial Times,* London, January 25, 1983.

99. *The Philippines Reader,* op. cit., p. 172.

100. *The Nationalist Alternative,* op. cit., p. 54.

101. *Parade Magazine,* January 9, 1983.

102. *Far Eastern Economic Review,* July 21, 1983.

103. *WHO,* Manila, April 15, 1984.

104. Ibid.

105. *In Our Image,* op. cit., pp. 412-413.

106. Ibid., p. 417.

Notes—IX, pp. 282-331.

1. *Progressive Review,* May-June 1963, Quezon City, p. 60. ("The Lapiang Manggagawa Platform")

2. *Progressive Review,* No. 6, 1965, p. 68 ("Program of the Kabataang Makabayan").

3. *Movement for the Advancement of Nationalism,* op. cit., pp. 20-21.

4. No relation to the Philippine president of the same surname.

5. Gregg R. Jones, *Red Revolution.· Inside the Philippine Guerrilla Movement,* Westview Press, 1989, p. 29.

6. Eduardo Lachica, *HUK: Philippine Agrarian Society in Revolt,* Solidaridad Publishing House, Manila, p. 315 (Founding document "The New People's Army").

7. Amado Guerrero (Jose M. Sison), *Philippine Society and Revolution,* Pulang Tala Publications, Manila, 1971, p. 288-289.

8. Ibid., pp. 202, 282.

9. PKP leaflets: "On With the People's Movement to Boycott the Elections," "Boycott the 1971 Election."

10. Proclamation 1081 (*The Philippines and the United States,* op. cit., p. A-214).

11. *Information Bulletin,* Prague, No. 3, 1975. "Attitude of the PKP Toward New Policy Orientation of the Martial Law Government."

12. Ibid.

13. *Documents of the PKP 7th Congress, 1977.*

14. *Documents of the PKP 8th Congress, 1980.*

15. Ibid.

16. Victor Corpus was an army lieutenant when he defected to the NPA from the Philippine Military Academy in December 1970. During a ten-year imprisonment after capture in 1976 he turned against the CPP and after release by President Aquino early in 1986 he was accepted back in the army with the rank of lieutenant-colonel! He then wrote a manual on counter-insurgency, on how to deal with the NPA. A similar case is that of Nilo Tayag, who was general-secretary of the CPP for a time in its early years. Imprisoned in the early 1970s, Tayag also switched to the government side during confinement and after release became an anti-CPP, counter-insurgency lecturer for the army.

17. This was asserted to the author by an anti-Marcos Catholic leader in 1980.

18. A lengthy, detailed series of articles on how Catholic funds were channeled to the CPP/NPA and on the steps to stop it appeared in the overseas Filipino newspaper *Pahayagan* (London), June-December 1987 reprinted from the Manila paper *Business Day.*

19. *Philippines: Repression and Resistance.* Papers submitted to the a Permanent Peoples Tribunal, Antwerp, Belgium, 1981, pp. 203-204.

20. PKP leaflet: "Participate in the Election to Expose Imperialist Deception," January 1986.

21. *Ang Bayan* (CPP organ), May 1986.

22. *PKP Courier,* Vol. III, No. 3-4, 1987.

23. *Daily Globe,* Manila, July 11, 1990.

24. *Daily Globe,* Manila, July 7 and July 28, 1990.

25. *Philippine Daily Inquirer,* March 3, 1990.

26. *Philippine Currents,* Manila, June 1988.

27. *Philippine Currents,* July 1988.

28. *Philippine Currents,* March 1990.

29. *Philippine Currents,* March 1991.

30. *Financial Times,* London, February 19, 1992.

31. *PKP Courier,* op. cit.

32. James B. Goodno, *The Philippines: Land of Broken Promises,* Zed Books, 1991, pp. 178-179.

33. *Business Day,* Manila, December 15, 1986 ("Reds Propose Power Sharing").

34. *PKP Courier,* Vol. II, No. 2, 1986 ("Open Letter to President Corazon Aquino").

35. *PKP Courier,* Vol. II, No. 4, 1986 ("The PKP Stand on the Proposed Constitution")

36. *PKP Courier,* Vol. III, No. 3-4, 1987.

37. *Daily Globe,* Manila, October 2, 1991.

38. *Documents of PKP 9th Congress, December 1986. PKP Courier,* Vol. II, No. 4, 1986, Vol. III, No. 1, 1987.

KEY TO MOST OF THE ACRONYMS LISTED IN INDEX

AKSIUN, *Ang Kapatiran sa Ikauunlad, Natin* (Brotherhood for our Development, the unemployed movement)

AMA, *Aniban ng mga Manggagawang Agrikultura* (Assn. of Agricultural Workers)

AMT, *Aguman ding Maldang Talapagobra* (General Workers' Union)

BAYAN, *Bagong Alyansang Makabayan* (New Patriotic Alliance)

BISIG, *Bukluran sa Ikaunlad ng Sosyalistang Isip* (Movement for the Advancement of Socialist Ideas and Action)

BUDC, Barrio United Defense Corp

CARP, Comprehensive Agrarian Reform Program

CLO, Congress of Labor Organizations

CNL, Christians for National Liberation

COF, *Congreso Obrero de Filipinas*

CONFREDOM, Congress for Freedom and Democracy

CPP, Communist Party of the Philippines

CTUP, Congress of Trade Unions of the Philippines

EDSA, Epifanio de los Santos Avenue

FFF, Federation of Free Farmers

FFW, Federation of Free Workers

FOF, *Federation Obrere de Filipinas*

FTF, Federation del Trabajo del Filipinas

HMB, *Hukbong Mapagpalaya ng Bayan* (Army of National Liberation)

JUSMAG, Joint U.S. Military Advisory Group

KAP, *Katipunan ng mga Anak Pawis sa Pilipinas*

KBP, *Katipunan ng Bagong Pilipina* (Association of the New Filipina)

KM, *Kabataang Makabayan* (Nationalist Youth)

KMP, *Kilusang Magbubukid ng Pilipina* (Peasant Movement)

KMU, *Kilusang Mayo Uno* (May First Movement)

KPMP, *Kalipunang Pambansa sa mga Magbubukid sa Pilipinas*

LACC, Labor Advisory and Consultative Council

MAN, Movement for the Advancement of Nationalism

MASAKA, *Malayang Samahan Magsasaka* (Free Union of Agricultural Workers)

MIS, Military Intelligence Service

MPKP, *Malayang Pagkakaisa ng Kabataang Pilipino* (Free Union of Filipino Youth)

Namfrel, National Movement for Free Elections

NASSA, National Secretariat of Social Action, Justice and Peace

NATU, National Assn. of Trade Unions

NMCL, National Movement for Civil Liberties

PDSP, *Partido Demokratiko Sosyalista ng Pilipinas* (Democratic Socialist Party)

Philcusa, Philippine Council for U.S. Aid

PKM, *Pambansang Kaisahan ng mga Magbubukid* (Peasants' Union)

PKP, *Partido Komunista ng Pilipinas*

PQOG, Pres. Quezon's Own Guerrillas

TUCP, Trade Union Congress of the Philippines

TUPAS, Trade Unions of the Philippines and Allied Services

UOD, *Union Obrera Democratica*

UODF, *Union Obrera Democratica de Filipinas*

USAFFE, U.S. Armed Forces in the Far East

INDEX

AKSIUN, 286
AMA, 297-98, 330
AMT, 96, 126, 142
Abad, Juan, 11
Abad Santos, Jose, 114, 121
Abad Santos, Pedro, 96-7, 125
Abad Santos, Vicente, 271
Ablan, Roque, 133
Act No. 78 (1901), 31-33, 36
Adevoso, Eleuterio, 206
Agatep, Zacharias, 301-02
Aglipay, Gregorio, 50, 91
Agoncillo, Felipe, 40
Agribusiness Incentives Act (PD 1159), 252
Agricultural Tenancy Act (1954), 209
Aguinaldo, Emilio, 10, 21-26, 30, 32-3, 38,
   46, 92, 117, 118, 148
Alejandrino, Casto, 131, 139-40, 181, 199,
   201, 283, 288
Allen, James S., 93-4
Amer. Chamber of Commerce (Manila), 159,
   186, 264, 310, 318
American Chamber of Commerce Journal,
   153, 171, 187
Amer. Farm Bureau Fed., 82
AFL, 54, 61, 82
Anderson, Bernard, 132
Anderson, Jack, 277
Anti-Bases Coalition, 327
Anti-Imperialist League, 2-3, 43-44, 60, 82
Aquino, Agapito, 305
Aquino, Benigno, 117-18
Aquino, Benigno, Jr., 263, 266, 274-76, 291,
   293-94
Aquino, Corazon, 229, 232, 279, 281, 291,
   305-13, 315, 317-18, 320, 325, 330,
   334
Aquino, Eusebio, 131
Araneta, Gregorio, 25
Araneta, Salvador, 88
Arellano, Cayetano, 25-6, 28, 32
Arroyo, Joker, 318
Asedillo, Teodoro, 90
Asian Development Bank, 256
Assn. of S.E. Asian Nations, 254, 270
Atkins, Kroll & Co., 186
Auerbach, Isabelle, 93
Ault & Wiborg Co., 186
Avenceña, Ramon, 117
Ayala family, 257, 272

BAYAN, 305-06, 330
BISIG, 318-19, 325, 326, 330
BUDC, 128, 139
Bagong Buhay, 172
Balgos, Mariano, 73, 181, 197, 199
Baluyot, Sotero, 117, 134
Balweg, Conrado, 301, 322
Bandholtz, H. H., 40, 50
"Bandolerismo Statute" (1902), 49
Bancom Development Corp., 240
Bankers Trust Co., 240
Bank of America, 240
Bank of America Finance, 247
Barrera, Jesus, 175
Basa, Jose Maria, 24
Basic Christian Community, 301
Bataan Nuclear Power Project, 273

Bell, Daniel W. (Mission and Report), 189-90,
   194, 248
Bell, Jasper, 156; Bell Trade Act, 150, 156-59,
   161, 182, 184, 188, 209, 230, 234-35, 263
Benedicto, Roberto, 272
Bertrand Russell Peace Foundation, 290, 298
Bewley, Luther B., 174
Beyster Corp., H.E., 185, 193
Bigasang Bayan, 123
Blue Eagles Guerrillas, 132, 141
Bocobo, Jorge, 117
Boguslav, Dave, 171
Bonifacio, Andres, 8, 20, 22, 30, 45, 64, 71, 73,
   332
Boun Oum (Lagos), 165
Bournes, Frank, 23-4, 28
Briones, Alejandro, 199, 284
Browder, Earl, 65
Buencamino, Felipe, 29-30
Burgos, Jose, 19
Buscayno, Bernabe, 291, 300, 320
Bush, George, 277

CARP, 310-11, 330; CPAR, 330
CLO, 142, 179-80, 200, 283-84
CNL, 300-02, 319
COF, 55-6, 65-69
CONFREDOM, 330
CTUP, 284
Cabangbang, Bartolome, 219
Cabili, Tomas, 133, 137
Cailles, Juan, 32
Calderon, Felipe, 26, 27
Caltex, 246, 262
Cando, Jose, 145
Canton Conference (1924), 61-2
Capadocia, Guillermo, 197
Carreon, Francisco, 48
Castle & Cook, 252
Castro, Domingo, 199, 284
Castro, Pedro, 180
Catan, Gonzalo, 251
Catholic Bishops Conference, 301-02
Catholic Church, 68, 96-7, 206, 216, 219-20,
   275, 280, 300-07, 309, 322, 330
Cawal ning Kapayapaan, 99
CIA, 200, 216, 222-23, 259, 263, 274, 294
Chase-Manhattan Bank, 240
Chemical Bank, 240
Chinese Communist Party, 127, 288, 292
Chinese Revolution, 148, 171, 189, 288
Chou En-lai, 303
Christian Social Movement, 263
Chuidian family, 17
Citibank, 240
Civil Affairs Unit, 204
Civil Liberties Union, 141
Clark Air Base, 140, 164-65, 180, 208, 274,
   313, 317, 327
COCOFED, 272-73
Cojuangco, Eduardo, 273
Cojuangco family, 17, 272-73, 279
Commonwealth, 83, 89-92, 98-100, 115, 119,
   169
Communist Int'l, 57, 61, 67, 70, 93
CPP (1969), 291-95, 299, 300-04, 306-7, 319,
   320, 322, 324-26, 330
Communist Party, USA, 61, 82, 93-4, 96

Other books by the author

Born of the People
Beyond Barriers: Sonnets to Celia (prison poems)
The Forest. A personal record of the Huk guerrilla struggle.
Guerrilla and Counter-Guerrilla Warfare
Guerrilla Warfare and Marxism
Half a Century of Socialism
Apartheid Axis
Trail of Blame (short stories)
Chelobek na Daroga (Man on a Road, short stories)
American Neo-Colonialism: Its Emergence in the Philippines and Asia
An American-Made Tragedy: Neo-Colonialism and Dictatorship in the Philippines
Soviet Reality in the Seventies
Apartheid, Imperialism and African Freedom (1986)